WIND AND STRATEGY

By the same author

WIND

AND

STRATEGY

By

STUART H. WALKER, M.D.

Illustrations by JACK KARABASZ

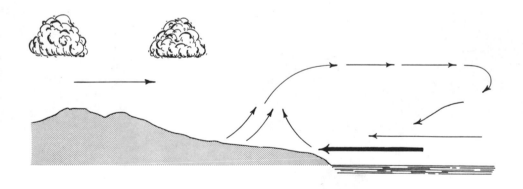

W · W · NORTON & COMPANY · INC · New York

FIRST EDITION

Library of Congress Cataloging in Publication Data
Walker, Stuart H.
    Wind and strategy.
    Bibliography: p.
    1. Sailboat racing. 2. Winds. I. Title.
GV811.5.W3   797.1'4   72-6453
ISBN 0-393-03136-5

1 2 3 4 5 6 7 8 9

*To my competitors—who have taught me
most of what I know about sailboat racing
and who continue to teach me how much there
is to be learned.*

Contents

V. *Strategic Implications*

Preface

I have been led to a study of the phenomena of surface wind variation through necessity. It has been clearly evident that races are lost because of a lack of understanding of changes in the wind, and equally evident that dramatic victories follow successful prediction of the wind to come. There is little that is useful in the literature of meteorology or sailing that provides insight into the determinants of variations in surface wind, so I have had to do my own research. Recurrent phenomena are evident and their recognition leads to understanding. When "local knowledge" is associated with an understanding of basic determinants, the proliferation of knowledge is dramatic. It is the detection of the common factor in a set of racing experiences that provides predictive ability.

This book is intended to provide a shortcut to this understanding. It demonstrates how the surface wind is affected by such fundamental phenomena as season, time of day, temperature disparity, cloud cover, stability, and geography. The racing sailor needs to know the manner in which these factors will affect the race. Recognition of the probable changes in the surface wind permits the exploitation of variations in wind direction and velocity both upwind and down. The "need to know" takes one to a study of basic meteorology. It soon becomes evident that variations in the surface wind are dependent upon vertical as well as horizontal features of the weather over a given racing area. The aspects of meteorology essential to an understanding of surface wind are presented in the second section of the book, entitled "The Origins of Wind Flow." In the third section a classification of wind shifts is provided to indicate the possible explanations for a given event. Each of these explanations is explored in the major portion of the book, the section entitled "The Winds of the World." Here a vast range of circumstances are presented to illustrate the possible variations in surface wind. Each of the areas included has been selected because it is illustrative of a general determinant of surface wind flow. Selection was also based upon the likelihood that a large number of readers would have personal experience in these areas and thus be able to observe the illustrated features in practice and profit directly from the reading. In many cases where specific patterns are common compass headings, location, and time of day have been included which will be of immediate use to local sailors. It is hoped, however, that the illustrations used will provide an insight into the cause of wind variations that will be valuable in racing anywhere and that each reader will profit from the example of the particular to acquire an understanding of the general.

Examples of the application (or the failure of non-application) of the principles discussed are provided with each chapter. The practical use of the principles learned is presented in the final section. A scheme for planning a race and for interpreting the meteorological data and the weather clues available on a given day is presented. Navigation in the light of such a plan requires alertness to evidence that an expected change in the surface wind *is* or *is not* occurring. Finally when, as so often happens, the data is insufficient to certain prediction, a conservative "formula for success" is included so that disasters resulting from major unexpected variations in surface wind flow can be avoided.

The book is further designed to provide an understanding of the surface wind along the shore and thus is particularly useful to those who sail around triangles on coasts, lakes, and rivers. It is, however, of equal value to those who engage in long-distance sailing where that sailing is wholly or in part along the shore. The ability to predict that at 8:00 A.M. on a given day the wind will be strongest close along the north shore of Long Island will, in fact, be of more value to the sailor in an overnight race than to the round-the-buoys sailor whose race will not commence until 11:00 A.M. Both, however, need to know why the wind behaves as it does at 8:00 A.M. in order to predict its behavior at 11:00 A.M. or 12:00 noon.

I have only discussed areas of the world in which I have had personal experience. I have in all instances profited by the experience of sailors who were particularly familiar with the specific areas presented and checked repeatedly to determine that my observations were consistent with theirs. The emphasis, of course, has been upon conditions present when I have raced in particular waters, but these occasions generally coincide with the season of greatest use of the waters. No effort has been made to discuss every possible surface wind condition at a given site, but the dominant factors that determine the wind in each area are included. The intention of selection was to illustrate a specific surface wind determinant. This may in some instances have required the selection of an unusual, rather than typical, aspect of local conditions. I would like to express my particular appreciation to Tom Rosmond, who provided an evaluation of the major winds effecting Puget Sound, to Jim Linville, who corroborated my analysis of the anabatic and katabatic winds of Lake Garda, and to Roger Welsh, whose long experience in racing off Los Angeles supported my construction of wind determinants in southern California.

A language new to many readers is used of necessity. A complete glossary, which should be referred to when the slightest doubt as to meaning exists, is included. Many of the expressions used I have had to coin, as I did with the terms oscillating and persistent shifts many years ago. Similarly created expressions such as divergent or convergent wind flow, are used to provide an exact meaning, otherwise unexpressible. The reader must utilize the glossary and understand precisely what is meant when such expressions are used. Otherwise he may be misled and will certainly be confused.

I hope that the book will be used—not just read and filed away. Ideally the racing sailor will discover a puzzling wind variation on a particular day and return to the book to seek an explanation. If he keeps a written plan for each race and records the compass headings and other data accumulated referable to a particular time of day and location during the race, he should be able to compare his experience with the experiences recorded in the book. Only by testing the information presented in the light of need and personal experience will understanding be acquired. One or more of the surface wind determining factors which are discussed will undoubtedly account for the phenomena observed. In order to insure that the explanation will be recoverable an extensive cross-index has been included. Thus the experience can be researched in terms of the circumstances surrounding it. In addition to the Contents, which organizes the material chiefly by geographical area, the index will permit recovery of information according to season, time of day, origin of wind, weather system condition, cloud cover, wind velocity, origin of wind shift, and so forth. The basis for a persistent shift occurring in late morning in midsummer in a light southeasterly under stratocumulus cloud cover will be discoverable as each of the given circumstances is investigated. Perhaps a waterproof copy of the book should be carried aboard when racing!

Mrs. Edwin Lowe deserves much of the credit for this publication. Without her transcription into type of my "prescription scrawl," the book would never have reached print.

WIND AND STRATEGY

I. *Significance*

How variations in wind velocity and direction determine the outcome of races.

The principles underlying the utilization of wind shifts.

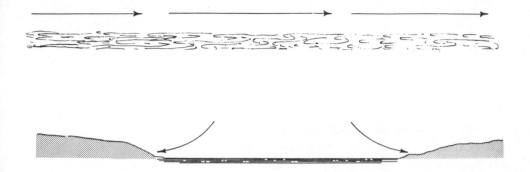

A. What the Racing Sailor Needs
to Know about the Wind

"Mackerel sky and mare's tails
Make tall ships set low sails."

Most sailors leave the starting line without a clear conception of how they will sail the race and without a firm understanding of how the wind will change to determine its outcome. Not knowing, most do poorly. Some with fast boats are able to overcome the disadvantages that result from a lack of understanding. Some are lucky. Many good sailors are able to apply the general principles of conservative racing and do well despite a lack of understanding. After the race, however, most will agree that had they known what the wind would do during the race, they could have significantly improved their finishing positions. The really good sailor can predict what the wind will do and thereby gains a constant advantage over his less knowledgeable competitors. This book is designed to provide that advantage.

An understanding of the wind is beneficial at all times and on all courses, but there are three situations in which such an understanding determines the outcome of the race: (1) In light air it is essential to sail to where the wind is strongest or to where it is when others are where it isn't. (2) To windward it is essential to recognize and to place oneself in an appropriate position relative to the appearance of a persistent shift. (3) In an unstable airflow, when oscillating shifts appear, the weather leg must be managed by a series of tacks timed appropriately to each oscillation. The racing sailor needs to know from where the wind will develop and where it will be strongest in light air. He needs to know whether and from what direction a persistent shift will appear. He needs to know whether the airstream will be vertically unstable.

The racing sailor must ask himself a series of questions concerning the expected wind conditions and (as presented in a later chapter) he should record the answers and plan his race accordingly. It will not always be possible to answer all questions completely, but asking them is an excellent means of stimulating an awareness of the possible changes that may lie ahead. It is as important to recognize that a persistent shift may not occur as it is to recognize that it will occur. Great gains are possible from the correct prediction of a wind change, but great losses can be avoided and a better average in a series insured if unpredictable shifts are conservatively managed. Six major questions need answering. These provide a convenient checklist of all the significant variables:

1. *What are the origins of the present or expected wind?*
   What weather system is present in the area?
   Is the observed wind consistent with the wind expected?

2. *Will the weather system change position or will its pressure gradient change resulting in a change in wind velocity or direction during the race?*

3. *Will a local persistent wind develop during the race? A sea breeze?*
   Will exposure of the land to the sun create a sufficient temperature disparity to generate a sea breeze?
   Will thermal lift-off be sufficient to maintain a continuous circulation between low pressure over land and high pressure over water?
   Will an inversion facilitate or block the development of a sea breeze?
   A land breeze?
   Will the land be sufficiently colder than the water to generate a land breeze?

A *thunderstorm?*
> Will condensation occur in lifted air, and if so, will it be sufficient to cause thunderstorm development?

A *mountain or valley wind?*
> Are mountains or valleys present which will generate upslope (anabatic) or downslope (katabatic) winds?

A *transmountain wind (Santa Ana)?*
> Will a dry, hot transmountain wind outflow in the area?

A *drainage wind (Bora)?*
> Will a cold, dense drainage wind from an upland plateau outflow in the area?
>
> Will the addition of a local persistent wind result in replacement of the weather system wind, reinforcement of the weather system wind, the variable presence of two winds with oscillating shifts between the two, or an area of calm?

4. *Will the wind be stable or unstable?*
> Will the rate of change in temperature with height (the lapse rate) result in buoyancy and instability?
>
> Will the airflow be unstable and associated with frequent oscillating shifts?
>
> To what level will instability persist and how strong will be the associated downdraft gusting?
>
> Will an inversion be present which will limit convection?
>
> Will the airflow be stable and the water surface so cold that the wind will be separated from the surface?

5. *Will the wind increase (or decrease) in velocity or veer (or back) during the period of the race?*
> Will diurnal variations in surface heating affect the strength of the existing wind or modify the contribution of a local thermal wind?
>
> Will the airflow veer significantly with time as its velocity increases or greater portions of the upper airflow reach the surface (or back as velocity and admixture of upper airflow decrease)?

6. *Will geographic factors result in a change in wind velocity or direction in some portion of the racing area?*
> Will the surface wind be stronger near the weather or the leeward shore?

At what distance from the windward and leeward
shores will wind interference be least?

Will an offshore wind be refracted as it leaves the shoreline?

Will the wind be channeled as it flows over a water
surface with an irregular shoreline?

In summary, six simple questions should be asked before each
race:

1. What is the origin of the expected wind?
2. Will there be a weather system change?
3. Will a local wind appear?
4. How stable will the wind be?
5. Will there be a general alteration in velocity or direction?
6. Will there be a local alteration in velocity or direction?

The chapters ahead provide the means of answering these questions. Section II describes the basic determinants of wind flow. Section III provides the understanding that will permit the questions to
be answered on a typical day in racing areas in many parts of the
world. Section IV presents the application of this understanding, the
techniques by which it is applied, the strategy that wins races.

The discussion of current is not limited because of its lesser significance but because it is more certainly predictable. Current in the
racing area can be accurately observed and predicted. Its significance can thus be accurately determined and provides a background
against which the relative significance of wind changes may be as-
sessed. It is useful to try to assign a proportionate significance to the
simultaneous presence of conflicting strategic factors. Wind is almost
always more significant than current, but current is a known factor,
wind often an unknown one. Consequently, it may be more appropriate to take advantage or to avoid the disadvantage of the known
current rather than to seek the less certain advantage of the less
predictable wind.

A third factor has strategic significance but its manipulation is so
straightforward that it requires little discussion. If waves are large,
they are detrimental to a boat sailing to windward but beneficial to a
boat sailing off the wind. If their size varies within the racing area,
portions of the course with smaller waves should be sought when
beating and portions of the course with larger waves when reaching
and running. On most racing courses no such disparity exists, and
even when it does, other factors—current and particularly variations

in wind direction and velocity—are of such greater importance that waves must be disregarded. Technique in overcoming or utilizing waves is always essential, strategy in seeking or avoiding them is usually of little consequence. Either current or waves may cause one tack to be favored relative to the other. But, as each boat must spend the same time on each tack as her competitors, no strategic advantage results unless the current or the waves vary in direction or velocity within the racing area.

Above all, the racing sailor must be aware of the timing of changes in the wind. On most closed-course races the appearance of a new or stronger wind, a persistent shift or an oscillating shift within the wind flow is extremely significant during the windward leg but less so on the downwind legs. The correct prediction of a persistent shift of the weather system wind from northwest to northeast is of no value if the shift does not occur until after half the fleet rounds the weather mark. At the 1971 Spring Soling Bowl in Annapolis I took an early port tack, in expectation of such a shift, only to watch the majority of the fleet race by in a transient recrudescence of the northwesterly, while I sat becalmed just beyond the starboard end of the starting line. As I approached the weather mark, a poor eighteenth, the northeasterly filled in. One must become sensitive to the nuances of shifts, their ebb and flow, their moment by moment variations. The shorter the course, the more accurate must be the prediction of shift timing and the more likely the prediction will be in error. A persistent shift is usually associated with a premonitory period of oscillation. Which will occur next, a recrudescence of the old wind or the establishment of the new, is often "anybody's guess." Because of these difficulties in timing, many short-course racers ignore shift strategy and play the percentages. The shorter the course the more this approach is justified and the more the sailor must take the conservative course. With understanding and experience, however, predictions become more and more accurate and the sailor more and more successful.

Changes in wind velocity are usually of less strategic significance than changes in wind direction. Light air races, however, are won by the helmsman who positions his boat where the wind is strongest (or where the wind is present in the midst of general calm). Light air also requires positioning to obtain the best possible sailing angle on reaches and runs as two-fold differences in boat speed may result between boats on close or broad reaches. Geographical factors may cause major variations in wind velocity within the racing area requiring the helmsman to consider the interfering effects of blanketing and the reinforcing effects of channeling. When a wind is dying or developing, the boat must be positioned to obtain the benefit of the dying wind as long as possible and/or to obtain the benefit of the developing wind as soon as possible. The velocity of the surface wind will vary with distance from shore, dependent upon the direction of flow relative to that shore and the vertical stability of the airflow.

Finally, changes in wind velocity require changes in sail trim to achieve maximum performance. No boat is ever properly trimmed; sail trim must be constantly adjusted for every change in wind velocity and/or boat speed and, except when beating, for every change in wind direction. A simple anemometer may be the most useful instrument (after the compass) to the racing sailor. In small boats, however, the helmsman must usually rely instead upon the appearance and feel of changes in wind velocity. He must learn to distinguish modest changes and to be aware of their presence as slight changes in velocity result in major changes (velocity squared) in the force applied to the sails. I have a crew member call out changes in wind velocity (along with compass readings) periodically so that I am reminded to make appropriate alterations in trim. The racing sailor must learn to recognize changes to at least the accuracy of the Beaufort Scale. Preferably he should recognize variations of 2 knots and maintain a record of trim changes appropriate to wind strengths at 2-knot increments.

B. The Utilization of Wind Shifts

"When the southeast trades run free and fast,
Then shorten sail for Hatteras;
If safely ye get by Cape May,
Ye'll catch it, sure, in Boston Bay."

If the racing sailor can answer the six questions listed in the previous chapter and, in addition, accurately predict the time that changes in the airflow will occur, he can expect success on almost every windward leg. It is obvious that in light air major increases in boat speed can be obtained by the boat that positions herself to receive the wind sooner, stronger, and longer than her competitors. Clearly in these circumstances the development of a new wind must be predicted and the boat sailed to the side of the course from which it is expected. The major determinants of success to windward, however, are the correct utilization of wind shifts to shorten the distance sailed. The management of wind shifts is not as simple as the management of velocity variations, as two different types of wind shifts must be handled in different and essentially opposite manners.

A complete discussion of the tactical determinants of sailing to windward is not within the scope of this book. The intention here is simply to provide the understanding that will permit the prediction of persistent and oscillating shifts. The basic principles involved in the utilization of the shifts, once predicted, however, must be included. The essential need is to distinguish between persistent and oscillating (or recurrent) shifts and to recognize that a persistent shift is of paramount importance. A persistent shift is one in which the wind changes in direction and during the period of the windward leg does not shift back to its initial direction. It may shift abruptly

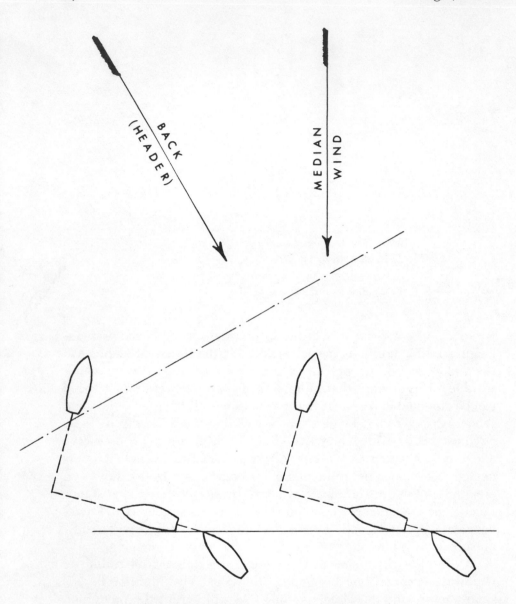

to a new direction and never vary thereafter, or it may progressively
or erratically shift (veer or back) further and further from its initial
direction. Either is a persistent shift. An oscillating shift, on the other
hand, is one in which the wind shifts from its initial direction and
then shifts back to (or beyond) its initial direction. The cycle may
be repeated many times depending upon the duration of the windward leg. Note that classification is dependent upon the duration of

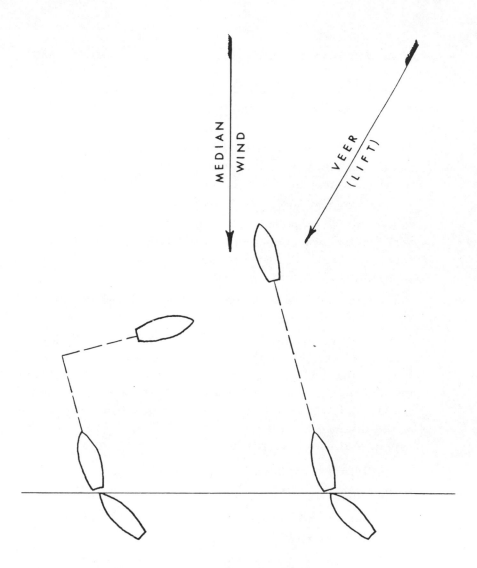

the weather leg. A wind flow that oscillates between two extremes every five minutes will result in a persistent shift during a four-minute beat. The appearance and disappearance of a sea breeze during an afternoon will create two persistent shifts for one-design sailors racing on beats of twenty-minute duration but will constitute a set of oscillating shifts for a cruising boat sailor in a long-distance race. The duration of the beat is as much the determinant of the management of the shift as is the origin of the change in the wind flow.

A persistent shift is of paramount importance. If a persistent shift is expected:

1. *Tack toward the direction of the shift and continue on that tack until nearer to the new layline (the layline in the new, shifted wind) than any competitor.*

> The boat that makes her final approach (to the mark) tack nearest to the new layline will be farthest "inside and to weather" of her competitors on that final tack and will sail the shortest course to the weather mark.
>
> If the shift is progressive (continues to veer or back), the boat that tacks precisely on the new layline (a curved line on which the boat will lift to round the mark) "inside" of her competitors will sail the shortest course.
>
> The optimum course is therefore the headed tack toward the shift and the lifted tack toward the mark.
>
> The length of the initial tack toward the shift will be inversely proportional to the degree of the shift and the time spent on that tack prior to the shift. The layline is reached at the starting line when a 45° shift occurs at the start, whereas if a 20° shift occurs after the boat has sailed a major portion of the distance toward the original layline, the new layline may have already been reached.

2. *Avoid the lifted tack initially.*

> If the initial tack is lifted, it is directed away from the shift.
>
> Tack from the lift (into a header) back toward the shift as soon as it is recognized.
>
> The farther one sails away from a progressive persistent shift the more one loses.
>
> Beware of a lift significantly beyond the range of lifts observed before the start or during preceding beats.

3. *Keep inside and to windward of competitors for the final approach tack to the mark.*

> The last tack to the mark in an oscillating wind occurs in a

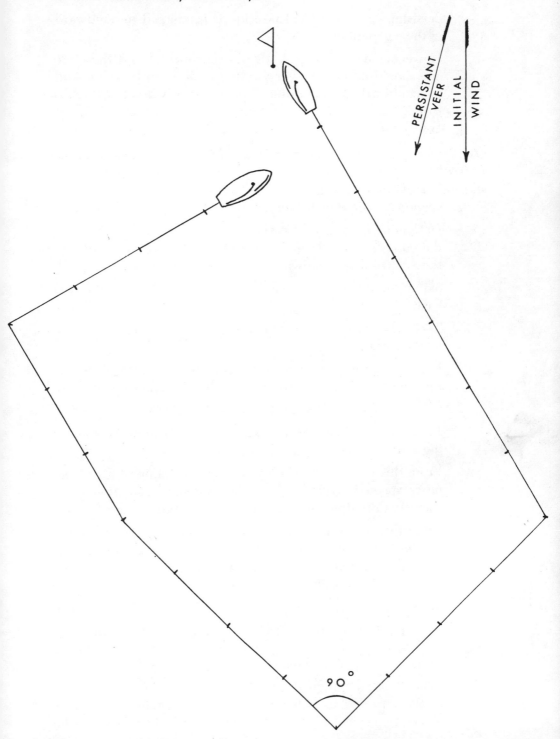

persistent shift; the ideal position is inside and to windward of the competition.

However, overstanding is always detrimental and therefore one should never risk overstanding in order to be inside and to windward. When in doubt, particularly when the mark is still distant, tack ahead and to leeward of the competition, so as to avoid overstanding.

Oscillating shifts should be utilized in addition to persistent shifts. If oscillating shifts are detected (by compass observation prior to the start or direct observation):

1. *Keep to the lifted tack—sailing toward an expected header.*

   Determine the range of variations in the wind direction (by the compass) and keep to the tack that is lifted relative to the median wind (midway between the extremes).

   Sailing the lifted tack in each shift shortens the course to the weather mark.

   Tack when headed, when the course is headed relative to the median wind.

   Usually a significant header is presumed and tacking is justified when the compass shows a heading 5° below the median.

2. *Keep ahead and to leeward of competitors.*

   From this position maximum gains will be made when a heading shift appears.

   From this position, in a lift, one is always sailing toward the next expected header, since in a randomly oscillating wind the next shift after a lift will (eventually) be a header.

   From this position, when a header appears, the boat will be farther to the side of the course than her competitors, a position that results in the greatest gain from a single shift (as in a single persistent shift).

   When ahead, cover competitors from ahead and to leeward.

   Covering from dead to windward results in a loss with every shift (whether a lift or a header) and therefore should not be utilized except in the final stages of a beat.

   When boats are aligned laterally across the wind, as they are at the start, a shift will cause the greatest gain or loss. It is therefore particularly important to be on the lifted tack at the

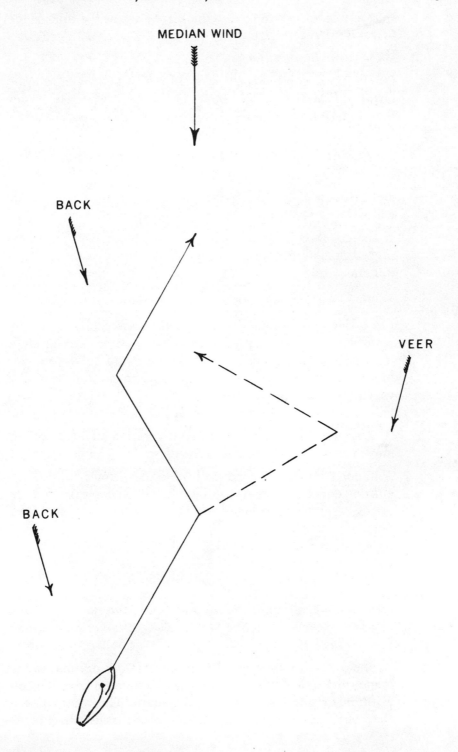

MEDIAN WIND

BACK

VEER

BACK

start and to be able to tack to the lifted tack at the time of the first shift after the start.

3. *When in doubt, don't tack.*

It is better to continue on a tack through a header so as to be farther to the side of the course in the next expected header than to tack inadvertently away from the next expected heading shift.

4. *Sail toward a persistent shift in addition to tacking in oscillating headers.*

Sail through minor headers so as to move to the side of the course from which a persistent shift is expected.

If the compass indicates a lift beyond the range of the expected oscillations, suspect a persistent shift and tack toward it immediately.

RULES FOR DOWNWIND STRATEGY

(In order to determine wind direction while tacking downwind it is essential to predetermine an optimal sailing angle for varying wind speeds, to fix the sails and spinnaker pole in a trim appropriate to that angle, and to sail the boat on a varying course appropriate to that trim. Thereafter compass headings will reveal wind direction.)

Assume the jibe which at the pre-determined ideal sailing angle is closest to the rhumb line unless:

A major advantage in reduced adverse current, a more up-current course, stronger wind or larger waves exists on the opposite side of the course.
(or)
A persistent shift is expected.

A persistent shift is of paramount importance. If a persistent shift is expected:

1. *Assume the jibe away from the shift and continue on that jibe until just short of the new layline (the layline at the optimal sailing angle in the new, shifted wind).*

A jibe away from the persistent shift at the optimal sailing angle carries the boat into a progressively more advantageous position for the return jibe to the mark. The return jibe to the mark, initiated from a position which is just short of the

(c) Sail the course to the next mark (check
don't be misled by the change in sailing angl

2. *Oscillating shifts affect the strategy of windw
wind legs particularly but may be detected on all le
advantageous tack or jibe for the initiation of a subs
run by determining the direction of the last oscillation
ing reach.*

3. *Rules for reaching:*
   (a) When the wind is moderate and steady,
   line.
   (b) When the wind is strong and gusty, sail
   down in the gusts.
   (c) When the wind is light and dying, sail to
   rhumb line initially, saving the better sailin
   in the leg when the wind will be lighter.
   (d) When the wind is light and increasing, sa
   of the rhumb line initially, saving the slow
   for late in the leg when the wind will be stro
   (e) When a new wind is developing, sail to (
   mum sailing angle after its arrival (usually
   the rhumb line).

4. *Rules when two winds are present simultaneou:*
   (a) Sail so as to obtain maximum benefit from
   or old) which will be present at the next
   arrives there.
   (b) If the new wind will be present at the ti
   the next mark, and its presence will cause
   come a beat, sail directly toward the new w
   to windward of the fleet upon its arrival.
   (c) If the new wind will be present at the ti
   the next mark, and its presence will cause the
   a reach, run, or "one-leg beat," sail away from
   so as to be to leeward of the fleet (at th
   sailing angle) upon its arrival.

What the racing sailor needs to know about the wi
will vary significantly in velocity in different parts of
whether it will be associated with persistent or oscil
both, and when the latter will occur. If he can pre
wind will be strongest in light air, he can position h

new layline, will provide a progressively more advantageous course, higher and higher on the wind if the persistent shift is progressive.

2. *Avoid the jibe that is progressively headed early in the leg if the heading appears to be consequent to a persistent shift.*

3. *Keep outside and to leeward of competitors on the final approach jibe if a persistent shift is occurring.*

Oscillating shifts should be utilized in addition to persistent shifts.

1. *If oscillating shifts are detected (by compass observation prior to the leg or direct observation), keep to the headed jibe—sailing away from an expected lift.*

Keep the sails trimmed for the optimal sailing angle and continue on the jibe until the boat is lifted beyond the optimal angle to the rhumb line. Thereafter jibe and continue on the opposite jibe until once again the boat is lifted beyond the optimal angle to the rhumb line.

When in doubt as to whether a persistent shift will occur, sail so as to avoid major losses.

1. *Hold the lifted jibe til outside of competitors or the headed jibe inside of competitors, jibing back before they do.*

2. *Jibe back toward the rhumb line early so as to be in the middle of the course about one-quarter the way to the leeward mark.*

3. *Keep alert to the possibility of a persistent shift.*

Observe the other boats to detect persistent shifts affecting the extremities of the course.

When boats on the opposite jibe are being lifted (sailing at greater than the optimal jibing angle to one's course), jibe to their jibe. When boats on the same jibe are being headed (sailing lower than one's own course), jibe. (They may be experiencing a persistent shift and you are sailing toward it.)

GENERAL RULES FOR SAILING THE COURSE

1. *A persistent shift affects the sailing angles for all legs:*
   (a) Windward legs may become "one-leg beats". Keep to leeward on the major tack.
   (b) Plan the sails (jib, large spinnaker, small spinnaker, reacher) which will be appropriate to the changed sailing angles of each reach.

(c) Sail the course to the next mark (check the compass);
don't be misled by the change in sailing angle.

2. *Oscillating shifts affect the strategy of windward and downwind legs particularly but may be detected on all legs. Decide the
advantageous tack or jibe for the initiation of a subsequent beat or
run by determining the direction of the last oscillation on the preceding reach.*

3. *Rules for reaching:*
(a) When the wind is moderate and steady, said the rhumb
line.
(b) When the wind is strong and gusty, sail up in the lulls,
down in the gusts.
(c) When the wind is light and dying, sail to leeward of the
rhumb line initially, saving the better sailing angle for late
in the leg when the wind will be lighter.
(d) When the wind is light and increasing, sail to windward
of the rhumb line initially, saving the slower sailing angle
for late in the leg when the wind will be stronger.
(e) When a new wind is developing, sail to obtain the optimum sailing angle after its arrival (usually to leeward of
the rhumb line).

4. *Rules when two winds are present simultaneously:*
(a) Sail so as to obtain maximum benefit from the wind (new
or old) which will be present at the next mark when one
arrives there.
(b) If the new wind will be present at the time of arrival at
the next mark, and its presence will cause the leg to become a beat, sail directly toward the new wind so as to be
to windward of the fleet upon its arrival.
(c) If the new wind will be present at the time of arrival at
the next mark, and its presence will cause the leg to become
a reach, run, or "one-leg beat," sail away from the new wind
so as to be to leeward of the fleet (at the best possible
sailing angle) upon its arrival.

What the racing sailor needs to know about the wind is whether it
will vary significantly in velocity in different parts of the racing area,
whether it will be associated with persistent or oscillating shifts, or
both, and when the latter will occur. If he can predict where the
wind will be strongest in light air, he can position himself between

that location and his competitors. If he can predict the direction from which a persistent shift will occur, he can sail toward that shift and markedly shorten his course to the weather mark. If he recognizes that oscillating shifts are occurring, he can utilize them in addition to sailing toward the persistent shift. He must distinguish whether the shift is in fact persistent or oscillating and/or whether both are occurring, as he must handle each differently. The ability to make this distinction on the course is the essence of tactical success to windward. Failure to make the distinction is the essence of disaster. Even more useful, the determinant of the big win, is the understanding that permits the prediction of the time and the direction of persistent and oscillating shifts. The following chapters provide this understanding.

II. *The Origins of Wind Flow*

Solar energy and airflow.
Upper-level wind flows.
Vertical airflow-convection.
Surface airflow-pressure gradients.
Sequential weather systems.

A. The Atmospheric Engine

*"If the barometer and thermometer rise together,
It's a very sure sign of fine weather."*

The ultimate source of the energy required for air movement is the sun. The sun's energy heats the atmosphere in a variety of ways; the common result of its heating is a change in the density of the atmosphere. Changes in density result in changes in atmospheric pressure because density determines the weight of a given segment of the atmosphere and pressure is the sum total of the weight of the atmosphere above a given level. Changes in pressure resulting from vertical changes in density produce horizontal movement of the atmosphere—wind. Wind is the consequence of variation (1) in the receipt of energy from the sun, (2) in the density of the atmosphere, or (3) in the atmospheric pressure that results. A fourth factor which determines the receipt of energy from the sun and continually modifies the resultant changes in density and pressure is (4) the water content of the atmosphere. On each racing day the racing sailor must consider the temperature, the pressure, and the water (moisture) content of the atmosphere—information obtainable from local weather sources—in order to predict the nature of the wind flow to come.

The sun is a huge furnace that turns hydrogen to helium, releasing vast amounts of energy in the form of ultraviolet, infrared, and visible light radiation. Only about one two-billionth of this energy is received by the earth but this amount is sufficient to operate the gigantic atmospheric engine. The radiation received by the earth is converted into heat—the energy of molecules in motion—by the process called insolation. About 48 percent of the radiant energy reaching the earth's atmosphere is intercepted by clouds which reflect more than half this energy back into space. Nineteen percent of the total reaches the earth's surface directly and about 23 percent after diffusion through the clouds. Another 19 percent is absorbed by the atmosphere, almost entirely by its water vapor. The earth reradiates the energy it receives as infrared radiation but 15 percent of this energy is absorbed by moisture in the air and retained in the atmosphere as heat.

The earth itself modifies the receipt of solar energy because its spherical shape, its elliptical orbit about the sun, and its tilt referable to its orbital plane limit the intensity and location of its exposure. The equatorial regions are heated to a far greater extent than the remainder of the earth and retain a greater amount of energy in the form of heat than they reradiate back into the atmosphere. The polar regions, on the other hand, receive little heat from the sun as they are exposed to its radiation tangentially, and they dissipate a greater amount of heat than they retain. The result, of course, is the heat balance of the total earth, with total energy gain equalling total energy loss. Distribution of the heat received, from the equator toward the poles, is the function of the atmospheric engine (aided by global water circulation).

The atmosphere which stores and distributes the sun's energy is not only essential to oxygen-breathing life on the earth's surface but essential to the retention of the heat provided in the daytime by exposure to the sun. Without the atmosphere, the heat gain each day would be lost each night, searing heat would be replaced by intolerable cold. The atmosphere is a massive substance whose weight is 14.7 pounds over each square inch of the earth's surface. All but 1 percent of the weight of the atmosphere is in its lower 19 miles and half of its weight is in its lower 18,000 feet. Thus the pressure that this weight exerts rapidly decreases with height and is half as great, or 7.8 pounds per square inch, at 18,000 feet.

Wherever the sun's energy is absorbed by water, evaporation takes place. Evaporation increases the energy of each water molecule so that the molecules repel each other sufficiently to convert the liquid into a gas/water vapor. Water vapor thus stores energy, energy that can be returned to the atmosphere as heat when the water vapor condenses back into a liquid. In addition to the cycle of direct heat absorption by the earth's surface and by water vapor, which is stored until reradiated back into space, a second cycle of energy storage is available in the evaporation of water. The major site of action of the atmospheric engine is in the equatorial regions where water is constantly evaporated and then condensed. The northeast trades pick up vast quantities of water vapor as the sun evaporates the oceans over which they blow. Localized convection systems carry this moist air aloft into towering thunderheads which condense the vapor and return its stored energy to the atmosphere. Tremendous quantities of heat are released back into the atmosphere from thousands of giant cumulonimbus heat towers each day and this heat is distributed over the globe by the global wind circulation.

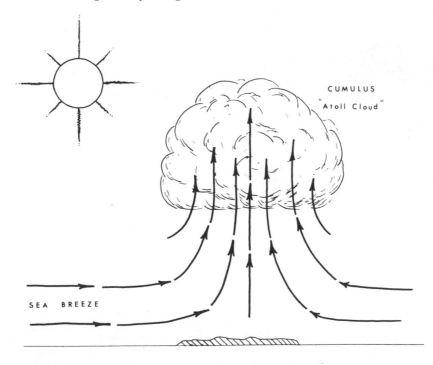

CUMULUS
"Atoll Cloud"

SEA BREEZE

Three-quarters of the earth's surface is covered by water, and the air over this water is loaded with water vapor. The heat absorbed by the earth and reradiated as long-wave (infrared) radiation is partially absorbed by the moisture in the overlying air. This heated water vapor reradiates infrared radiation back to earth. The process is known as the "Greenhouse Effect" and decreases the heat loss of the earth to one-seventh of the loss that would occur in the absence of moisture in the overlying air. Marked temperature variations at the earth's surface occur where the air is dry, as it is over the deserts, whereas diurnal temperature variations are minimal in moist climates where marked cloud formation occurs.

Water vapor is almost entirely restricted to the lower five to ten miles of the atmosphere, the troposphere. Over the oceans the atmosphere may contain as much as 4 percent water vapor. There are 95,000 cubic miles of water vapor in circulation in the troposphere.

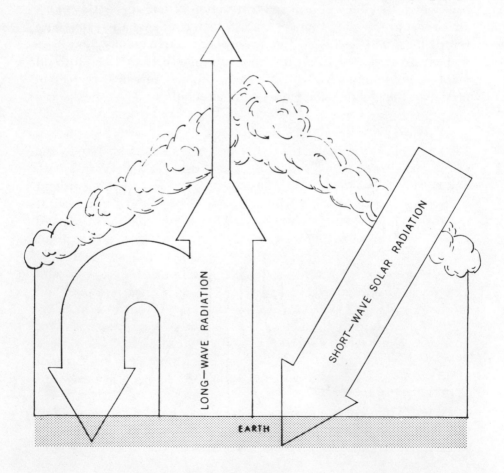

Of this total, 80,000 is evaporated from the oceans, 15,000 from the land. Water vapor condenses when its molecules become less agitated, when the surrounding air cools, so that the slower moving molecules, when striking particles of dust or salt, adhere and condense to form water droplets or, at low temperatures, ice crystals. Air is said to have a dew point, a temperature at which the number of water vapor molecules present will conglomerate sufficiently for condensation to occur. Warm air accommodates more water in vapor form as the more rapidly moving molecules are less likely to adhere. The dew point of a given mass of air is thus dependent upon the amount of water vapor present. When the temperature falls to a point at which the molecules present begin to adhere (when the dew point is reached) condensation occurs, the molecules aggregate rapidly, and the energy of their previous kinetic activity is released into the surrounding air. Particles of some sort (chiefly salt) suspended in the air are necessary to condensation. Four times as much water vapor can be accommodated in air free of particles, but no such air exists in nature. Condensation usually takes place when air is lifted or pushed upward where it is cooled to its dew point and droplets form on particle nuclei. The resistance of the surrounding air molecules is sufficient to keep such miniscule droplets aloft in the atmosphere—as clouds.

Although water vapor acquires some heat directly, the atmosphere is largely heated from the surface of the earth, which is the chief recipient of the sun's radiation. A decrease in temperature with height is thus the normal state of the atmosphere and this gradient is known as the lapse rate. The agitated molecules of air heated at the surface push each other farther apart causing the air to expand in the direction of least pressure—upward. Cooler, more dense air alongside such a column of heated, less dense air will move laterally into its base. Cycles of airflow are thus established both locally and globally as air heated over one section of the earth's surface rises and flows outward aloft while cooler air moves inward at the surface toward the heat source. Such vertical cycles (convection cells) of airflow account for the thermal lift-off that produces the local sea breeze as well as the great global circulation that causes equatorial air to move aloft toward the poles and polar air to move equatorward at the surface.

The horizontal elements of this vertical convection are the winds in which we sail. Horizontal movement of the atmosphere is known as advection. Small-scale circulations are usually associated with rapid horizontal and vertical airflow, while large-scale circulations are usually associated with slow horizontal and vertical airflow. The atmospheric engine transforms heat into the energy of air motion, both vertical and horizontal, energy necessary to overcome the frictional resistance of individual molecular and particular motion. The direct force involved is the difference in pressure at various levels in the atmosphere consequent to differential heating. This is known as the pressure gradient and winds derived from large-scale pressure gradients are often called pressure gradient winds. The other forces that modify the pressure-gradient-induced flow are the angular momentum induced by the earth's rotation, the friction of the earth's landform, and, in unusual circumstances, centrifugal force. Weather maps indicate the locus of sites of equal pressure by lines called isobars. The closer the isobars are spaced the more rapidly pressure changes with distance, the greater is the pressure gradient, and the greater is the resultant wind flow. Pressure gradients relate to pressure differences at the same level. A pressure gradient may induce flow in one direction at one level and in the opposite direction overhead (or below) at a different level. Such an occurrence is characteristic of convection cells in which the pressure gradient and the direction of wind flow are in one direction aloft and in the opposite direction at the surface.

The rotation of the earth profoundly affects the movement of the water and the atmosphere on and above its surface. As the surface of the earth at the equator is moving at a velocity of approximately 1000 miles per hour, but is stationary at its poles, an angular velocity is imparted to the movements of all substances not fixed to its surface. Anything attached to the earth's surface at the equator is initially moving eastward at 1000 miles per hour. If it moves northward toward a site on the earth's surface which is moving at a lesser velocity, it will pass to the east of its destination. Coriolis force, the resultant effect, causes a deviation to the right of all motion in the Northern Hemisphere and a deviation to the left of all motion in the Southern Hemisphere. The rotational effect deviates motion in proportion to distance above the earth's surface. The lower levels of the atmosphere are held to the earth's surface by friction and are therefore minimally deviated. The upper levels, freed of frictional attachment, are maximally deviated. The lower levels respond to and move in the direction of the pressure gradient; the upper levels are deviated so that the direction of flow ultimately becomes parallel rather than perpendicular to the isobars. Above 1500 to 3000

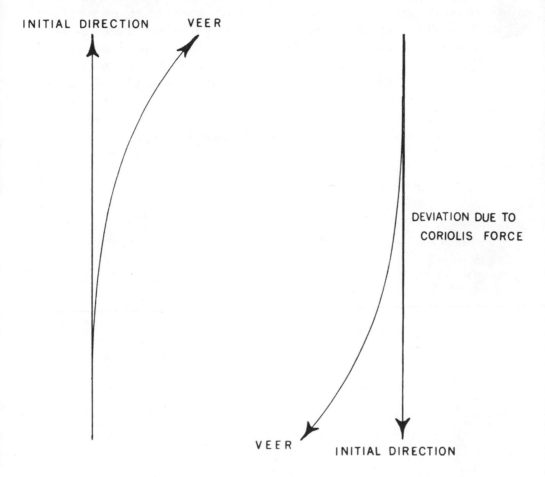

feet the pressure gradient force and Coriolis force result in a flow channeled as if between the "banks" of the isobars at a velocity inversely proportional to the width of, the channel.

Wind is therefore a vertical mixture of flows and in the northern hemisphere is backed in its lower levels, veered in its upper. The magnitude of the deviating Coriolis force increases not only with height but with the velocity of the wind flow and with the degree of inclination of the earth's surface to its polar axis. Its effect is greatest in the higher latitudes, absent at the equator.

The friction of the earth's surface modifies wind flow by inducing turbulence in its lower levels. Turbulence is proportional to the initial velocity of the flow and to the irregularity of the terrain. Turbulence causes additional friction within the airflow itself, reducing its velocity. It also brings segments of upper airflow to the surface to mix with lower-level airflow. Segments of upper airflow are usually of higher velocity as they are less slowed by friction and are (in the Northern Hemisphere) veered to the direction of the lower flow. Gusts are characteristically veered, lulls backed. Over water, where friction is minimal, airflow is markedly deviated by Coriolis force and is therefore aligned within 10° of the isobars. Over land, where friction is greater, the airflow will be more affected by the pressure gradient and deflected from 20° to 45° from the isobars.

B. Prevailing Winds and Global Currents

"When the wind is in the south,
The rain is in its mouth;
The wind in the west
Suits everyone best."

Heated air tends to rise, to elevate the pressure levels aloft by expansion, and to flow outward toward areas of lower pressure in the upper levels of the troposphere. Above a heated surface the total weight of the air column is reduced (surface pressure is reduced), the density of the air is reduced, and the pressure at a given level aloft is increased. Thus, when low pressure, compared to surrounding pressure at the same level, exists at a heated surface, high pressure, compared to surrounding pressure at the same level aloft, exists above it. Over cold surfaces high pressure exists at the surface, but because the overlying air is more dense, the pressure gradient with respect to height is increased and overlying pressure is lower than surrounding pressure at the same level aloft. Convection airflow is determined by these relationships. Warm air flows out from high pressure above the heat source aloft and cold air flows into low pressure at the surface.

This circulation essentially describes the global airflows set in motion by the atmospheric engine. Heat production at the equator causes upper-level flow poleward, and cold polar air tends to flow equatorward into the low pressure at the heated surface. While the atmosphere is being circulated, pressure gradients within the oceans induced by temperature differences, and resulting from changes in density, cause a similar horizontal flow of water. The result is climatic moderation as heat is transported to the cold latitudes and moisture is transported from the equator to the dry lands.

The major oceanic currents are the superficial evidence of a great convection system that tends to dissipate the temperature differences between water masses at the poles and at the equator. Cold, dense water, being heavier, tends to sink and move laterally beneath areas of warmer, less dense, lighter water while the latter tends to float and move laterally above areas of cold, dense water. A convection circulation is established as the ocean waters along the equator are heated, expand, and spread along the surface toward the poles while cold, dense Arctic and Antarctic water moves along the ocean bottom toward the equator. This circulation acts as a great thermal blanket for the continents, cooling those that might otherwise become too hot and warming those that would otherwise be excessively cold. The resultant circulation at the surface is, of course, not nearly so simple, particularly because flowing water, like air, is affected by Coriolis force. Thus, instead of moving directly toward the poles from the equator, the surface flow is deflected in each major ocean into a major clockwise gyral in the Northern Hemisphere and into a major counterclockwise gyral in the Southern Hemisphere. This flow pattern is esentially similar to the atmospheric flow about the great subtropical highs that permanently reside over the major oceans to the north and south of the equator. The wind flow from these high-pressure systems, aligned with the water flow beneath, increases the velocity of currents initiated by internal convection.

The circulation of the atmosphere is not simple either, because the pressure-gradient flow is deviated by Coriolis force and because heated air loses its heat in the upper troposphere long before it reaches the poles. The upper airflow spreading poleward from each side of the equator is in fact cooled so rapidly that it sinks back to earth (cooling results in an increase in density) at approximately 30° north and 30° south latitude. This sinking air creates the great, rela-

tively permanent circulations known as the subtropical highs. Because of the variability of the surface of the earth, instead of forming a continuous band about the earth, this sinking air forms isolated cells of high pressure over the oceans. Air reaching the surface after subsiding in the subtropical highs flows outward in all directions, poleward and back toward the equator. The residue of the upper airflow which does not subside and the poleward flowing portion of

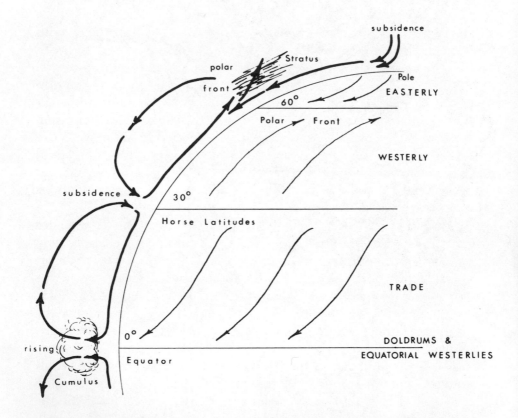

the subsiding air continue poleward and are deviated by Coriolis force into the prevailing westerlies of the mid-latitudes. Cold air flowing outward at the surface from the poles is warmed and rises to form the subpolar lows. Polar air, deviated easterly, meets the residue of equatorial westerly flow along the polar front, the site of recurrent cyclone formation in the mid-latitudes. The largest mass of the atmosphere is in a continuous westerly flow, at all levels in the mid-latitudes and aloft above the surface easterlies of the equatorial and polar zones. At the 700 millibar level (about 10,000 feet) the pressure gradient is high over the equator, low over the poles, the reverse of the surface gradient, resulting in poleward, deviated westerly, flow over the entire globe. The surface pressure belts shift poleward in summer, equatorward in winter, resulting in a transfer of atmospheric mass and a steepening of the pressure gradients in the winter hemisphere.

The lifted, heated equatorial air cools as it moves poleward, subsides above the subtropical highs and diverges in all directions at the surface. The sinking air becomes compressed as it sinks and gains heat due to its compression. As the air immediately over the relatively cool surface of the ocean is cooler than the subsiding air above, a sharp level of temperature change between the two layers results. As an increase in temperature with altitude is unusual it is known as an inversion. Inversions are typical of subsiding air and limit convection to the layers beneath the inversion level. The air above is dry and protected from penetration by moisture. Over the subtropical highs skies are clear and pressure gradients are minimal (except at the periphery of the high pressure cells where the wind velocity is increased).

A major subtropical high exists north and south of the equator over each of the major oceans. Over the continents, heating from below disturbs subsidence and prevents the development of an organized subtropical cell. About the oceanic subtropical cells in the Northern Hemisphere air flowing outward is deviated into a clockwise circulation around the center. From the poleward side of the high, air flows north and is deviated to become a southwesterly. From the equatorial side, air flows south and is deviated to become a northeasterly. This northeasterly flow is known as the trade winds and occupies an immense zone which circles the earth between the subtropical highs and the Equatorial Convergence Zone. On the eastern flanks of the subtropical highs subsidence is particularly strong, the airflow is northerly, and the inversion is distinct and low, at about 1500 to 3000 feet. The heated, sinking air above the inversion is extremely dry and the inversion prevents significant lifting and condensation from below. Thus the western margins of the continents neighboring the subtropical highs are deserts (the Sahara, the Sonora, the Mojave) except for a narrow strip of shoreline influenced by the low-level marine air beneath the inversion. On the western flanks of the subtropical highs subsidence is less strong, the

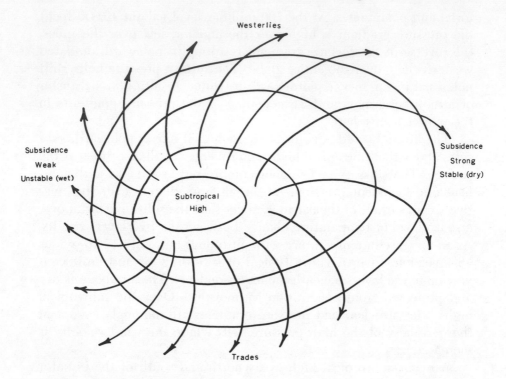

airflow is southerly and moist (water vapor acquired after long passage over the warm equatorial ocean), and the inversion weak. The eastern margins of the continents neighboring the subtropical highs have moist, warm climates with much rainfall (the Caribbean, the Gulf of Mexico, Indochina). Along the western margins of the subtropical highs warm southerly airflow is lifted above cool northerly airflow from an adjacent high-pressure cell contributing to condensation and rainfall.

The northeast trade winds which flow equatorward from the subtropical highs are stable, dry, non-buoyant winds. Near their origin at the center of the subtropical highs they are associated with clear skies. Here subsidence is marked, the inversion is marked, and little rainfall is possible. Along their eastern oceanic margins the trade winds are steady at 10 to 15 knots; racing sailors can depend upon their presence day in and day out. Farther south they acquire moisture (and latent energy) as they pass over the warm ocean and approach the equatorial lows. Here the trades become more unstable, the inversion disappears, and deep, convectional activity appears. The trades bring the fuel for the equator's atmospheric engine, picking up water vapor in their thousands of miles transit over the oceans.

Two-thirds of all the water evaporated on the globe is condensed in the Equatorial Convergence Zone. Hundreds of times more energy is released by condensation here than in all the other global winds combined. The trades are not really as steady as their reputation implies. They are particularly erratic near the western margins of the subtropical highs where their moisture is associated with convective disturbances.

Poleward from the subtropical highs the mid-latitudes (30°–60°) are characterized by the prevailing westerlies. Equatorial air flowing northward over the subtropical highs, between them, and escaping

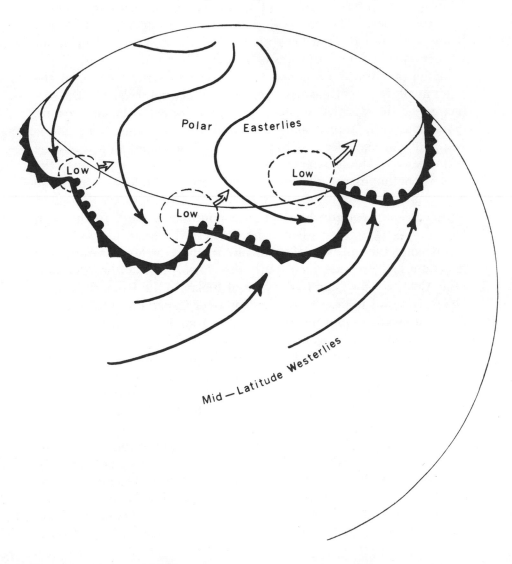

from their western flanks is deviated into a southwesterly and westerly flow. The westerlies are highly variable in both strength and direction. Continental monsoon systems and frontal systems characteristic of the mid-latitudes distort the regular westerly flow. In the Northern Hemisphere the marked variation between the surface temperatures of adjacent continents and oceans produces major convectional disturbances. In the Southern Hemisphere, however, the prevailing westerlies flow true to form, undisturbed by obstructing land masses, in the "roaring forties," "furious fifties," and "shrieking sixties." Gale force westerlies blow almost continuously in the Northern Hemisphere winter, resembling the year-round pattern of the Southern Hemisphere. The pressure gradients are steeper in the winter hemisphere and the northern margins of the continental polar air masses reinforce the basic westerly flow at this time of year.

High pressure is presumed to be present at the surface of the poles at all seasons. Dense, cold air diverges equatorward at the surface while the warmer, westerly flow sinks into the lower pressure aloft, constantly replenishing the outflow. The dense cold air is warmed as it subsides and as it moves south, depending upon the surfaces over which it flows and upon the season. In summer the heated continents set off convectional activity while in winter the oceans are relatively warm and low pressure develops over the water. Subpolar low pressure develops in a continuous band in the high latitudes of the southern hemisphere where there are no continents to interrupt the out-flow of polar air. In the Northern Hemisphere in winter low pressure recurrently develops south of the Aleutians (the Aleutian Low) and to the west of Iceland (the Icelandic Low). Deep masses of high pressure develop over Canada and Siberia and flow southward as continental polar (cP) air in winter. In summer these lows and highs are barely discernible. The result of the periodic emergence of these polar lows and highs is erratic collision with the mid-latitude westerlies, the polar front. As a consequence, the weather in the high mid-latitudes is an alternating sequence of high- and low-pressure systems ranging around the world ahead of the prevailing westerlies.

The surface westerly flow in the mid-latitudes opposes the easterly flow on either side of it. Equatorward the subtropical highs separate the westerlies from the trades, but poleward the southwesterly mid-latitude flow meets the northeasterly polar flow head on. Strong, sporadic air exchanges occur as masses of continental or maritime polar air thrust equatorward and masses of tropical air thrust poleward. There are long vertical waves in the upper-level westerly flow which result in sequential pressure variations at the 500 mb (10,000-foot) level. These pressure changes seem to be the determinants of polar air mass thrusts. Continental polar air surges down from Canada into the United States in the rear of troughs in the westerly wave pattern. The sequence of troughs and ridges in the upper troposphere creates great areas of high and low pressure through convergence and divergence at the surface. Meteorologists in the mid-latitudes utilize charts of the 500 mb pressure level to predict the major sequential variations in the polar front.

The prevailing winds, which derive from the global circulations described, operate in the upper levels of the troposphere. The trade winds, derived from subsiding air over the subtropical highs, reach the surface across wide bands of the low latitudes. In the mid-latitudes, however, the prevailing westerlies flow steadily above the chaos of the polar front. The weather system winds which reach the surface generally flow only below 20,000 feet. The weather systems themselves are carried steadily eastward by the prevailing westerlies but the latter are never evident at the surface. Their flow is revealed by the movement of high-level cirrus. The alto clouds between 6000 and 20,000 feet reveal the circulation of the weather system and the surface pressure gradient. Local persistent winds, such as the sea breeze, only function at the lowest levels, usually below 5000 feet.

The major effect of the great global currents is to moderate climate. The North Atlantic Current makes Europe warm in winter while the California Current makes our west coast cool in summer. The influence of these currents upon continental climate depends upon whether they flow near a windward or a leeward coast. The prevailing westerly wind of mid-latitude Europe carries the warm air from above the North Atlantic Current far inland. As the prevailing winds are offshore along the North American east coast at the same latitude, the average winter temperatures are some 30° to 40° colder than Europe's. The western coasts of the continents are close to the strong eastern ends of the subtropical highs where cold water from northern segments of the current gyrals is sweeping back toward the equator. The strong, persistent low-level inversion above the cold water along these coasts dampens convection, produces fog and stratus in the low-lying marine layer which extends a few miles inland, and prevents any significant transfer of moisture from the ocean to the overlying air. In the mid-latitudes the western coasts have marine climates. Here the prevailing westerlies bring the cool, moist ocean air ashore. The Olympic Peninsula and British Columbia, like England, are known for their mild winters, heavy rainfall, and small seasonal variations in temperature.

The eastern coasts of the continents have climates essentially opposite to their western counterparts. Here the subtropical highs are weaker and both wind and current are bringing heated air and water from the equator to the south. In the subtropics, such as along the Gulf and southern Atlantic coasts of the United States, this results in hot summers and warm winters with much rainfall. In the mid-latitudes the east coasts are more akin to their continental interiors as their winds are westerly, emanating from the heart-lands to the west. If the coasts are sufficiently far north so as to be associated with a cold current flowing south, winters will be cold but the heat of summer will be moderated.

In addition to their major effects upon climate, the warm currents determine the development of the great cyclonic systems. Hurricanes develop in summer where eddies of the warm equatorial currents meet with surrounding cooler water in the presence of major convective atmospheric changes. The western North Pacific and the western North Atlantic are notorious cradles of cyclone development in winter. Tropical energy is transported north in the warm water of the Gulf Stream and the Japan Current and in the latent heat of the water vapor carried in the warm air overlying them. Temperature gradients are steep in winter off the eastern coasts of the continents when continental polar air sweeps offshore to meet the warm air and water of northerly flowing currents. Strong convection of the warm surface air laden with moisture through the cold air aloft generates the great winter low-pressure systems of these latitudes.

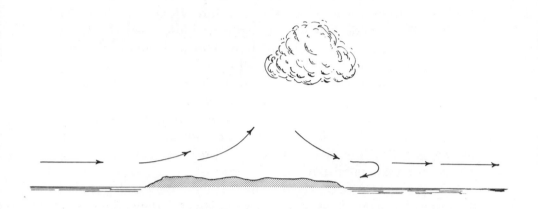

C. Vertical Airflow

"Men judge by the complexion of the sky
The state and inclination of the day."

Horizontal air movement (wind or advection) is the consequence of vertical air movement (convection), therefore an understanding of vertical airflow is fundamental to an understanding of wind. As temperature is the major determinant of air density and weight, temperature differences resulting from uneven surface heating produce pressure differences and initiate airflow. The surface of the earth is heated unevenly partly because the surface is unevenly exposed to the sun's heating and partly because different surfaces respond differently to exposure. Uneven exposure results in the great global air circulation previously described and accounts for local air movements which result when neighboring surfaces are screened to varying degrees by cloud and water-vapor cover. Where the temperature is dry—over the deserts and about the subtropical highs—surface heating is intense and heat loss is rapid. Marked temperature, density, and pressure differences result each night and day. Where the atmosphere is saturated with water vapor or is occupied by extensive cloud cover (condensed water vapor), surface heating is blocked and heat loss is restricted. Diurnal variation in temperature, density, and pressure is minimal over the oceans and is reduced in the Equatorial Convergence Zone. More significant to local wind flow, however, is variation in surface heating consequent to variations in the response of the surface to radiation exposure. In general, land gains and loses heat rapidly while water gains and loses heat slowly with variation in exposure to solar radiation. This unevenness of surface heating must be detected by the racing sailor because the vertical airflow that results will provide the wind in which he will sail.

Surface heating alters two major characteristics of the overlying air which must be recognized separately. Not only is the *pressure* of the overlying air changed directly but the *buoyancy* of the overlying air changes, which indirectly affects the pressure. Both factors contribute to horizontal airflow.

The pressure at the surface (which is more or less described by the values given on the usual weather map) is not dependent merely upon the temperature at the surface but upon the sum total of the temperature and density at *all* levels above that surface. Although pressure at the surface (total pressure) may be higher (or lower) than neighboring areas at the surface, pressure at various levels above the surface may deviate from the surrounding pressure in the opposite direction. Frequently where the pressure is high at the surface the lower levels of the atmosphere are dense and pressure throughout the lower levels is higher than in the surrounding air. However, the upper levels may be considerably less dense and pressure throughout the upper levels may be lower than in the surrounding air. The result is that horizontal airflow at the surface is divergent from the high while horizontal airflow aloft may be converging over the high. Such continuous inflow at upper levels is essential to the maintenance of high pressure and is characteristic of persistent high-pressure systems from the huge subtropical highs to the high-pressure dome which accumulates over a body of water and results in a sea breeze.

Heating of the surface results in heating of the adjacent levels of the atmosphere. As air is heated, it expands; a given mass of heated air then occupies a greater volume. It moves outward from the heat source laterally and vertically. The mass of air in the column overlying the heated surface is reduced as air is added to columns of air neighboring it. This lateral displacement of air mass results in a reduction in total (surface) pressure over the heated surface and a rise in total (surface) pressure over the surrounding surfaces. Vertical expansion over the heated surface means that the vertical extent

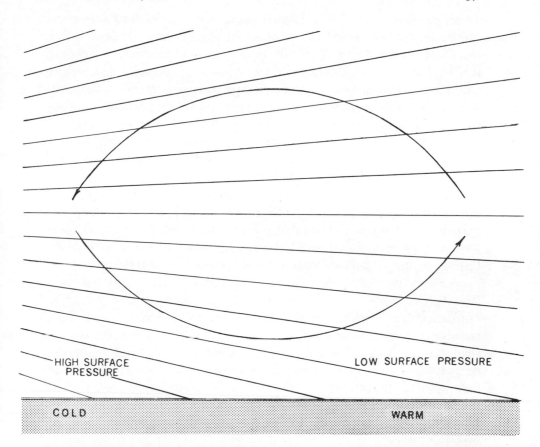

HIGH SURFACE
PRESSURE

LOW SURFACE PRESSURE

COLD

WARM

of a given mass of air is increased and that each pressure level above the surface is elevated above its original position. Thus although the total pressure over the heated surface falls and the surface pressure is reduced, the pressure at various levels in the upper atmosphere above the heated surface is increased. At comparable upper levels, pressure over the heated surface is higher than over surrounding surfaces so horizontal outflow results. As air is added to the columns overlying surrounding nonheated surfaces (at the surface by direct expansion, aloft by pressure elevation and outflow) their total (surface) pressure is increased. Consequently, at the surface, horizontal inflow develops from surrounding high pressure toward the heat source. This pattern is characteristic of the development of low-pressure systems which are usually temporary or episodic features. Total pressure is reduced in such systems but aloft flow is divergent, away from the site of low pressure, and at the surface flow is convergent, toward the site of low pressure.

Expansion of air over a heated surface is one form of a general phenomenon of vertical air motion, lifting. There are four major causes of lifting: thermal lift (the one discussed above), orographic lift, frontal lift, and lift due to convergence. Orographic lift results when horizontal airflow is deviated upward by a terrain elevation. Frontal lift is the consequence of the elevation of a warmer air mass by a cooler one. Convergence results in lift as horizontal airflow is compressed, usually by the meeting of two horizontal airflows, resulting in deviation upward. Regardless of the cause, lift is associated with expansion of the lifted air due to the reduced pressure at the elevated level. Expansion is associated with cooling (and compression with heating). A standard rate of cooling results from lifting and this is known as the Adiabatic Lapse Rate. This rate is modified by the amount of moisture in the rising air as when, after cooling has been sufficient, condensation occurs, the air will be heated.

As indicated previously, heating of the surface results not only in a direct change in overlying pressure but also in a change in the buoyancy of the overlying air. In the atmosphere the pressure surrounding any given small mass of air is essentially the same except that it is slightly increased beneath, greater by the weight of the mass itself, and slightly reduced above, lesser by the weight of the mass itself. If the density of a segment of air is different from that of the surrounding air, the pressure upon it will cause it to be displaced. If it is less dense, the surrounding pressure will be greater and as the pressure beneath will be the greatest, it will be displaced upward. If it is more dense it will exert a downward pressure greater than that of its surroundings and will sink. Heating causes air to become less dense, and if it becomes less dense than its surroundings, it will rise. Any mass of heated air will rise until it reaches a height at which its density is equal to that of its surroundings. The height at which this will occur depends upon the Adiabatic Lapse Rate and upon the lapse rate of the surrounding air.

If the lapse rate of the surrounding air is less than the Adiabatic Lapse Rate (the rate of change in density and temperature with lifting), then the heated air will rise but a short distance before it reaches a level of equal density and will cease to rise farther. When an inversion, a zone of negative lapse rate or heating with elevation, exists in the surrounding air, heated air will cease to rise at the inversion. If the lapse rate of the surrounding air is greater than the Adiabatic Lapse Rate then heated air will rise and will continue to rise so long as the lapse rate of the surrounding air is greater.

The Dry Adiabatic Lapse Rate is 1°C. per 100 meters; when the air is saturated (at levels above condensation) the Adiabatic Lapse Rate is approximately one-half as great, or 0.5°C. per 100 meters. The average lapse rate of surrounding air is 0.66°C. per 100 meters. Lifting, therefore, usually causes lifted air to cool more rapidly than

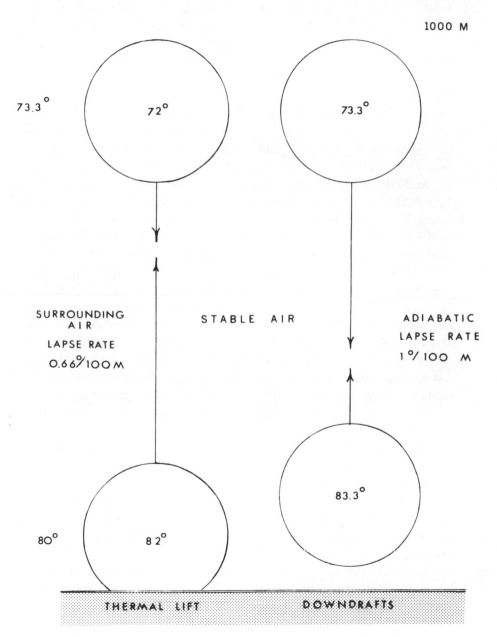

1000 M

73.3°   72°   73.3°

SURROUNDING
AIR   STABLE   AIR   ADIABATIC
LAPSE RATE   LAPSE RATE
0.66%100 M   1%100 M

83.3°

80°   82°

THERMAL LIFT   DOWNDRAFTS

the surrounding air and is self-limiting. Air is considered stable if its lapse rate is less than the Adiabatic Rate because air segments lifted within such air will soon cool to a lower temperature, be compressed to a greater density than their surroundings, and will sink back. The atmosphere is stable when the lower levels of the atmosphere are relatively cool, such as they are over the land at night and over the water almost all the time. The atmosphere is unstable when the lower levels of the atmosphere are particularly hot, such as they are over land exposed to sunlight. Then, when the surrounding lapse rate is greater than the Adiabatic Lapse Rate, lifted air will not cool as rapidly as the surrounding air and will continue to rise in the atmosphere until a level is reached where the lapse rate is less than 1°C. per 100 meters. Instability is characteristic of the lower levels of the atmosphere and is particularly evident during the daytime, over land, and when the overlying airflow is relatively cool.

Stability is a major determinant of surface flow. Stable air resists being lifted, whatever the genesis of lift, and therefore flows in layers much like water. If an opening in a shoreline or a mountain pass is in the line of flow, the air will flow at a high rate through the opening and will not rise, except in wave fashion, to surmount the obstacle. Stability may vary greatly at different levels within the atmosphere. The lower hundreds of feet of a sea breeze, particularly when flowing over land, may be quite unstable, but the upper portion of the sea breeze (and the sea breeze flow as a whole) is stable relative to the air above it. A sea breeze behaves like water, flowing around obstacles and channeling along shorelines. Stability is characterized by the presence of dense air beneath less dense air. When the density change is dramatic there is said to be an inversion at the level of the change, an abrupt rise in temperature and fall in density with height. Inversions are characteristic of subsiding air, the lower levels becoming increasingly heated as they descend, and of the advection of warm air over a cold surface, tropical air masses flowing over winter land or cold ocean currents. Stable air is characterized by reduced surface airflow, as friction retards surface flow and the upper, more rapidly moving layers fail to mix with the surface air, and by the absence of the oscillating shifts which characterize unstable airflows.

Unstable airflow, on the other hand, is characterized by strong, gusty surface flow and by frequent oscillations in direction, the consequence of a mixture of upper and lower airflows reaching the surface. Lifted air within such an airflow is buoyant, readily lifts above

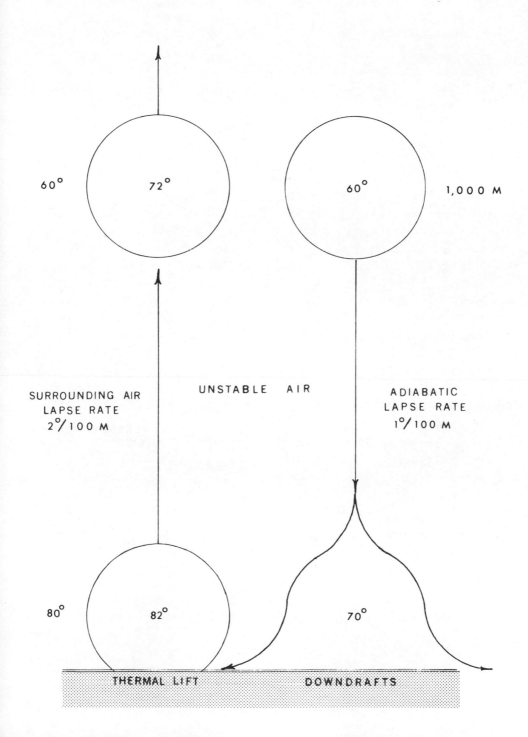

SURROUNDING AIR
LAPSE RATE
2°/100 M

UNSTABLE   AIR

ADIABATIC
LAPSE RATE
1°/100 M

60°   72°   60°   1,000 M

80°   82°   70°

THERMAL LIFT   DOWNDRAFTS

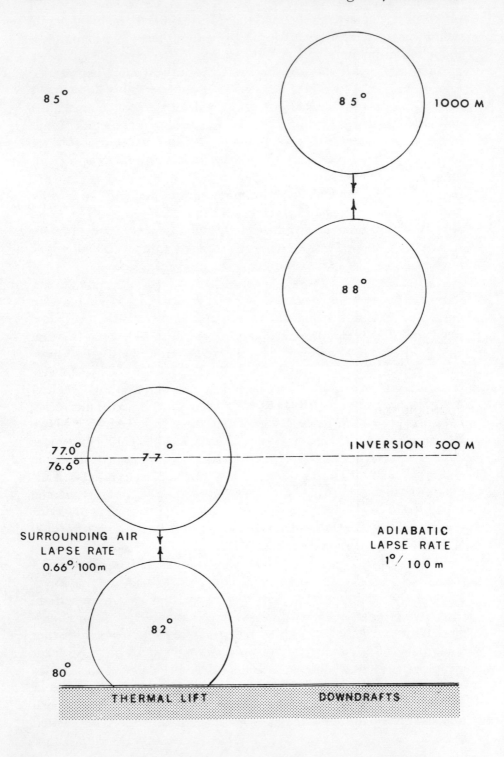

85°

85°   1000 M

88°

77.0°   77°   INVERSION 500 M
76.6°

SURROUNDING AIR   ADIABATIC
LAPSE RATE   LAPSE RATE
0.66°/100m   1°/100m

82°

80°

THERMAL LIFT   DOWNDRAFTS

obstacles encountered, and continues to rise until it reaches a height where the surrounding air lapse rate is less than the Adiabatic. A reduction in pressure will occur over segments of the surface when air is heated or lifted by impinging upon an obstacle. Neighboring segments of air of greater density will rush downward and inward to restore the pressure reduction. As air sinks it gains in temperature and loses density at the Adiabatic Rate (1°C per 100 meters) while in the surrounding air temperature is gained and density is lost at the unstable, higher lapse rate. Thus a downflow of air replacing a rising air segment will be gaining heat and losing density less rapidly than its surroundings and will continue to sink until it hits the surface with a splash—the gust characteristic of unstable airflow. The sailor alternately meets segments of surface airflow slowed and held to the surface by friction and gusts of rapidly moving upper airflow which have rushed to the surface to replace the buoyant columns.

Lifted air becomes progressively less and less dense in comparison with its surroundings the higher that it lifts in unstable, buoyant air. Thus the higher it lifts the more readily it continues to lift and to expand. The higher the instability persists, the higher the buoyant air can lift and the greater will be the reduction in density and pressure over the site of origin. The more marked the pressure reduction, the more violent will be the replacement inflow. In airflows such as the northwesterly outflow from a cold continental polar air mass, instability (a relatively high lapse rate) may be present far above the surface so that rising air columns may reach 5000 feet or more before they sink back. Lifting through such great distances results in a marked reduction in pressure and a violent replacement gust. Lifting due to surface heating in an overland sea breeze flow is restricted to the lower one to two thousand feet (as stability is present above the sea breeze), and therefore surface pressure reduction is limited and replacement inflow less dramatic.

When land surfaces are exposed to sunlight, heating of the immediately adjacent air regularly produces instability in the lower levels of the atmosphere. As indicated above, this has an immediate direct effect upon overlying pressure but whether it will be associated with a dramatic pressure reduction depends upon whether heated air can separate from the surface and rise through buoyant air to great heights. When this occurs marked changes in the density of the lifted segment and *of the entire overlying air column* occur which result in major horizontal airflow. Air tends to remain in position and heated air tends to remain attached to an underlying heated

occurring in the vicinity, giant cumulonimbus cloud formation will develop. Finally, the release of the heat of condensation of the moisture in the vertical flow aids further lifting and expansion until a typical summer thunderstorm appears. In dry air masses, even though buoyant, the initial effect of the surface lifting force is soon dissipated so that the vertical extent of lifting is relatively limited. It is the release of the latent heat of condensation in moist airflow that permits lift to upper atmospheric levels. And it is this lift over great vertical distances associated with marked expansion that results in major reductions in surface pressure. The giant convective systems associated with dramatic pressure drops, the hurricanes and typhoons, occur in summer over warm, moist oceans and are dependent upon the massive release of heat in the condensation of huge masses of water vapor at heights above 30,000 feet. Thus the greater the moisture content of a given mass of lifted air, the greater will be the height of the resultant lifting and the greater will be the pressure reduction and the velocity of replacement inflow at the surface.

Lifted Air (Thermal updrafts)	Temperature reduced Density increased	At Adiabatic Lapse Rate– 1°/100m
Sinking Air (Downdrafts)	Temperature increased Density reduced	At Adiabatic Lapse Rate– 1°/100m
Stable Surrounding Air	Temperature and density change with height	At lapse rate less than 1°/100m
Unstable Surrounding Air	Temperature and density change with height	At lapse rate greater than 1°/100m

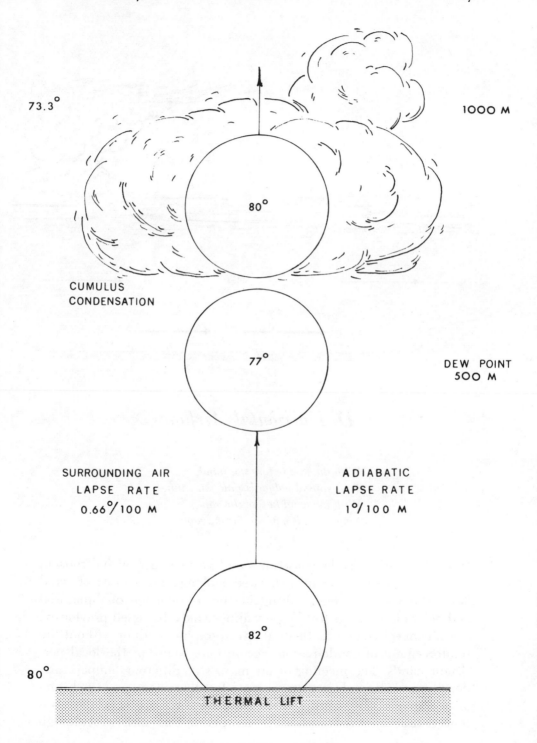

73.3°

1000 M

80°

CUMULUS
CONDENSATION

77°

DEW POINT
500 M

SURROUNDING AIR
LAPSE RATE
0.66°/100 M

ADIABATIC
LAPSE RATE
1°/100 M

82°

80°

THERMAL LIFT

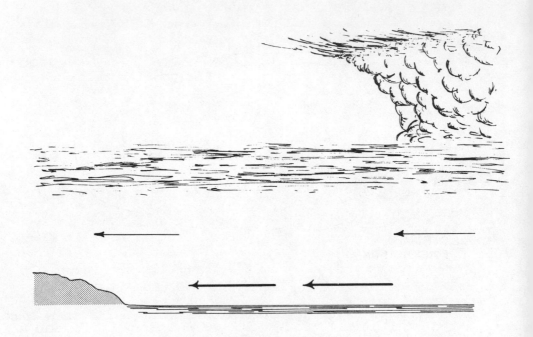

D. Horizontal Airflow

"With the rain before the wind,
Your topsail halyards you must mind;
With the wind before the rain,
Your topsails you can hoist again."

Horizontal airflow is the consequence of vertical airflow and thus all
the causes of lifting (and associated sinking) are causes of wind
flow. Major convection resulting in the interchange of equatorial
and polar air accounts for the prevailing winds discussed previously.
Local convective effects, thermal or orographic, with or without the
reinforcement of condensation, account for many of the local persistent winds. The meeting of air masses of different temperature,
density, and internal circulation create frontal systems and the lifting
of one air mass by another creates the low-pressure (cyclone) systems that account for much of the temperate-zone airflow. Although

these vertical phenomena are the initiators of horizontal airflow, the direction and velocity of surface flow and the occurrence of shifts are dependent upon a variety of modifiers. These modifiers are the factors listed in the first chapter. They are dependent upon the following:

The weather system and its movement

The presence of a local persistent wind and the interactions between it and the weather system wind

The stability and turbulence of the airflow

Diurnal variations in the vertical distribution of the airflow

Terrain features which modify the velocity or direction of the airflow

Air flows horizontally from a region of higher pressure to a region of lower pressure at the same elevation. Low-level airflow responding to the pressure gradient is essentially attached to the surface by friction and therefore its direction is unaffected by the rotation of the earth. At greater distances above the surface, however, the atmosphere becomes detached from such frictional effects. At these levels the airflow retains the velocity of the earth's surface at its site of origin and flows with a combined velocity and direction due to both the pressure gradient and the earth's rotation. Airflow at progressively higher levels above the surface is progressively deviated from its direct course from high to low pressure by Coriolis force. In the Northern Hemisphere this means that flow in the upper levels of the atmosphere is increasingly veered as compared with surface flow. When elements of upper airflow reach the surface, wind at the surface will be veered relative to its original direction. Upper airflow will reach the surface when the velocity of the total airflow increases (mechanical turbulence) and when thermal lift-off brings downdrafts of upper airflow to the heated surface. Thus surface airflow will veer increasingly with time in a strong airflow and will be increasingly intermingled with veered segments in an unstable airflow.

Strong surface winds are present near the periphery of new high-pressure systems and near the center of low-pressure systems, small or large. Strong surface flow may also be produced by the alignment of two separate wind-generating systems, a pressure-gradient wind, and a thermal wind. When two airflows of different origin are present in the atmosphere, one may alternate with the other at the surface or one may be present in one portion of the racing area while another is present elsewhere. A local wind may transiently appear at a particular time of day, replace a pre-existent wind, and in turn fade and be replaced by the original wind. Calms are occasionally consequent to the absence of a significant pressure gradient near the center of a high (or in the very center of a low). Usually calm is a surface phenomenon, however, consequent to vertical stability. The other common cause is a conflict between two winds flowing in opposing directions. Convergence in the meeting ground between the sea breeze and the offshore weather system wind often obliterates the surface airflow.

THE ORIGINS OF WIND

The unique winds listed as local persistent winds are the major winds of many of our racing areas and are subject to the same modifications as the major pressure system winds. All respond to pressure gradients, all are horizontal consequences of vertical motion, all are modified by temperature, moisture, and stability. And all are altered in direction and velocity by the various terrain features they encounter.

PREVAILING WINDS

Polar easterlies	High latitudes
Westerlies	Mid-latitudes
Trade winds	Subtropics
Equatorial easterlies	Equator

EPISODIC WINDS

Cyclones	Low-pressure systems
Anti-cyclones	High-pressure systems

LOCAL PERSISTENT WINDS

SHORELINES

Sea breezes	Onshore convection
Land breezes	Offshore convection

MOUNTAINS

Transmountain winds	Dry, hot, downflow residues of
Chinook	weather system wind
Santa Ana	
Upslope anabatic winds	Upslope convection
Downslope katabatic winds	Downslope convection

Valley winds   Combined convection in valleys
Drainage winds   Cold air drainage from high
Bora   plateaus

STABILITY AND TURBULENCE

The mixture of elements of upper airflow through some form of turbulence causes an increase in surface flow velocity. The magnitude of the turbulence and the degree to which elements of the upper airflow reach the surface depend upon the velocity of the airflow, the irregularity of the terrain, the stability of the air, and the temperature of the surface. Friction between the ground and the air results in a series of eddies developing in the lower portion of the air stream. Friction is less over water than over land and therefore airflow is always stronger at the surface of the water than at the surface of adjacent land. Over the open ocean a strong wind meets little friction, creates its own turbulence, and brings high-velocity flow to the surface. Near shore and over confined water surfaces instability of the airflow (a high lapse rate due to the presence of heated surfaces) is the best inducement to strong surface flow. When the air is unstable the racing sailor seeks the windward shore. Here thermal turbulence brings elements of the upper airflow to the surface. A few miles offshore the wind velocity may be but half as great.

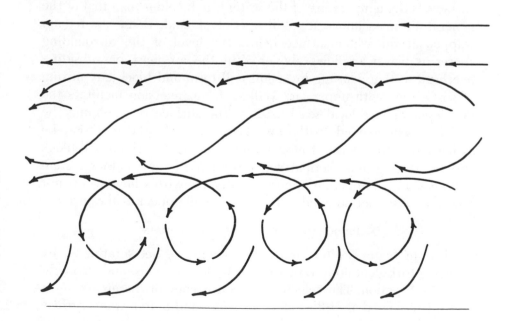

In stable conditions wind flow may be entirely separated from the surface. This is particularly likely to be the case in winter when the water is very cold and in summer when warm air may flow from shore to shore above a cool lake or bay for hours without reaching the surface. Stability is determined by the temperature of the surface of the water and of the neighboring land and the temperature of the air that is flowing over it. Surface temperature is dependent chiefly upon exposure to the sun and the interference with such exposure by cloud cover. The temperature of the air is dependent upon the origin of the wind flow and the temperature of the surfaces over which it has recently flown. Each day the temperature of the land and its overlying air changes with the sun. Stability is characteristic of the night when the surface is cold and an inversion develops aloft. Instability becomes progressively more evident with the day as the surface heats and the lapse rate increases in the lower levels of the atmosphere. There are characteristic variations in surface and air temperatures with the changing of the seasons as well. In general, winter, with its cold surfaces, is a season of stability, summer of instability, but variations in surface heating and airflow temperature can modify either.

On each racing day the racing sailor must evaluate the characteristics of the surface and of each layer of the atmosphere to determine the stability of the airflow and the likelihood of flow at the surface. Is the temperature of the water much colder than that of the general air mass above it? Will a pool of cold, dense air remain trapped at the water surface below the level of the surrounding shores as warm air flows above? Will the air mass be subsiding overhead so that a strong inversion will form and block any mixing of surface air with upper air? Will such an inversion facilitate the development of a local sea breeze at the surface by confining the weather system wind to the air above? Or will the inversion be associated with a dense stratocumulus cloud cover which will block surface heating and thermal generation? Will the weather system wind flow in the upper air oppose or interfere with a low-level sea or land breeze so that no wind or two winds will appear at the surface?

MODIFICATIONS OF WIND BY TERRAIN

Terrain features alter airflow by slowing or accelerating it, by inducing turbulent eddy formation in its lower levels, and by modifying its direction. The velocity and consistency of the air stream is abruptly changed as airflow emerges from land onto a water surface and as it meets land along a leeshore. An offshore flow will be modified differently depending upon whether it is stable or unstable. In vertically unstable air the surface wind is enhanced near the windward shore. If the airflow is stable it will tend to continue out from shore at the level of the shore or of the top of the barriers (trees, buildings, etc.) that protrude above the shoreline. The full force of the wind will not appear at the surface until it has passed twenty or more times the height of the shore to seaward. Closer to the shore only eddies will reach the surface, reduced in velocity and highly variable in direction. If the barrier is partially open so that some wind flows through without impedance there will be a consistent though reduced flow over the water within a distance equal to five times the altitude of the barrier. Farther out the direct flow is confused by eddies from the overflow. The wind is therefore more disturbed and less useful to the racing sailor between five and twenty altitudes from shore than it is closer in.

As wind approaches a leeward shore it tends to assume a straight line trajectory, aiming for the top of the barrier ahead from about nine altitudes to windward. Between this position and the shore the flow eddies downward from its main stream; the resultant surface wind is highly disorganized and reduced in velocity. When sailing in a channel across which a wind is blowing, both the area within twenty altitudes to leeward of the weather shore and the area within nine altitudes to windward of the leeward shore should be avoided if possible. In many sailing areas this includes the entire water surface so that a compromise must be made. In general one would deviate toward the weather shore in an unstable wind flow and toward the leeward shore in a stable wind flow. In the latter circumstance a course two-thirds the diameter of the channel to leeward of the weather shore should provide the least interference from either shore.

The airflow is also deviated horizontally as it emerges off or approaches a shoreline. If it leaves a shoreline at an oblique angle the wind front will change heading so that it becomes more perpendicular to the shoreline. This refracting effect is evident up to a half mile offshore, the distance affected being proportional to the velocity of the flow. Such refraction is most pronounced in a vertically stable wind. As the wind obliquely approaches a leeward shore, particularly if that shore is high, it will tend to change direction to flow more parallel to it (as well as lift to flow over it). This channeling effect is most pronounced in a stable wind flow such as a sea breeze.

It causes the flow to follow the contours of a lake or bay and to turn with the bends in a river or other elongated water mass. Channeling is evident in the entry of a sea breeze into a bay and in its turning to flow into the extremities of the arms of a harbor. Channeling is also evident in the flow parallel to the long axis of a valley of a katabatic downslope wind or a dense bora drainage wind.

TABLE OF COMPARATIVE
WIND-VELOCITY TERMINOLOGY

BEAUFORT FORCE	VELOCITY		SEAMAN'S DESCRIPTION OF WIND	U.S. WEATHER BUREAU TERMINOLOGY
	MPH	KNOTS		
0	1	1	Calm	Light
1	1–3	1–3	Light air	Light
2	4–7	4–6	Light breeze	Light
3	8–12	7–10	Gentle breeze	Gentle
4	13–18	11–16	Moderate breeze	Moderate
5	19–24	17–21	Fresh breeze	Fresh
6	25–31	22–27	Strong breeze	Strong
7	32–38	28–33	Moderate gale	Strong
8	39–46	34–40	Fresh gale	Gale
9	47–54	41–47	Strong gale	Gale
10	55–63	48–55	Whole gale	Whole gale
11	64–72	56–63	Whole gale	Hurricane
12	73–82	64–71	Hurricane	Hurricane
13	83–92	72–80	Hurricane	Hurricane
14	93–103	81–89	Hurricane	Hurricane
15	104–114	90–99	Hurricane	Hurricane
16	115–125	100–108	Hurricane	Hurricane
17	126–136	109–118	Hurricane	Hurricane

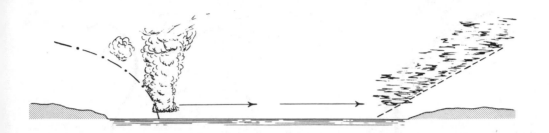

E. Sequential Weather System Movement—
The Polar Front

"Glass high, heave short and away;
Glass low, let your anchor stay."

The establishment of a general westerly airflow in the north temperate zone to the north of the subtropical highs has already been described. This general movement of warm air opposes the easterly flow of cold air flowing at the surface from the pole toward the equator. Where these opposing flows meet the polar front is formed. The flow of warm westerly air up and over the cold polar air creates the sequential pressure cells that characterize the weather conditions of the United States and the temperate zone in general. At any one location along the globe-circling polar front the weather is determined by the character of the air involved. Air that is swept into these pressure cells derives from the great air masses that accumulate over the oceans and the continents. Homogeneous masses of air form over large uniform surface areas and persist over these areas until pulled into the circulation of the cells forming along the polar front.

The major air masses that affect the United States are the continental polar (cP), the maritime tropical Gulf (mTg), the maritime polar Pacific (mPp) and the maritime polar Atlantic (mPa). The polar front across the continental United States is usually formed between the continental polar and the maritime tropical Gulf air

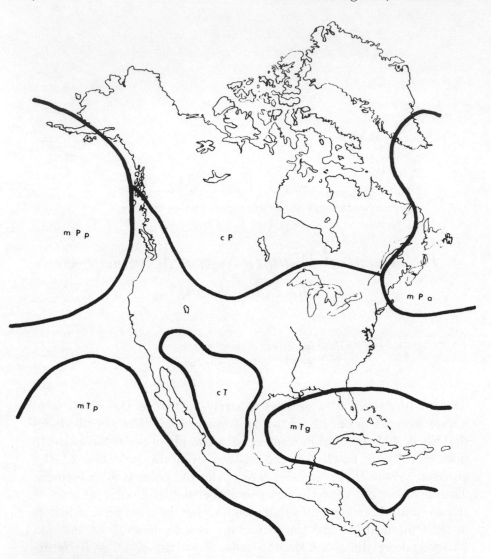

masses. Maritime polar Pacific air periodically invades the Pacific
Northwest but maritime polar Atlantic only occasionally reaches into
the United States from the east. Each air mass accumulates air and
therefore becomes a dome of high pressure within which air sinks
to the surface. Periodically segments of this air spread peripherally
and form satellite high-pressure centers. The continental polar air
mass is formed over cold snowfields in northern Canada. Its cold
dense air is heated as it sinks to form an inversion at several thousand feet. As this cold, stable air flows south its lower levels become
heated and it becomes unstable. At some position, depending upon

the position of preceding weather systems and the season, the south-ward flowing continental polar air meets the maritime tropical Gulf air. The latter air mass has formed over the warm, moist Gulf of Mexico at the western end of the Atlantic (Bermuda) subtropical high. The southerly flow at the western end of this high-pressure cell causes segments of mTg air to flow north to meet the cP air and form the polar front. To the north of the polar front, cP air is flowing from the east about a high-pressure center while immediately to the south mTg air is flowing from the west about a high-pressure center. The front forms as an interface between two air masses of differing temperature, stability, humidity, and flow direction.

Theoretically a "stationary" front between the two air masses could persist but in fact it rarely does. Continental polar air periodically surges southward and maritime tropical air surges north so that the polar front is, in fact, rarely stationary. Jet streams, which are high-speed rivers of air embedded in the generally westerly flow at 40,000 to 50,000 feet, seem to parallel the surface polar front and determine the surges of cP and mTg air which constantly alter the position of the polar front. These jet streams expand and contract toward and away from the pole every four to six weeks. In Stage 1 the northerly jet streams and the polar front are far north, flowing parallel to the equator; in Stage 2 the jet streams move equatorward and waves form in their course; in Stage 3 large waves appear accompanied by thrusts of polar air southward and tropical air northward; in Stage 4 large masses of polar and tropical air are isolated in inappropriate latitudes creating maximal temperature contrasts and major cyclonic disturbances. In winter the polar front is farther south than in summer (often as far south as the Gulf of Mexico) and the excursions of polar air travel correspondingly deeper into the subtropics. In summer the polar front is across the Great Lakes (or farther north) and excursions of tropical air regularly cross the Canadian border.

Low pressure develops along the polar front as warm tropical air lifts above cold polar air. Tropical air penetrates and a kink to the north develops in the polar front wherever lifting of warm air is stimulated. This may occur by thermal means where the surface is warmer than its surroundings (the Great Lakes in winter, the Plains in summer) or by orographic means when a mountain range intrudes. Once warm air wedges into the cold air it is squeezed aloft. Pressure at the surface decreases beneath the rising air and as the surrounding air at the surface flows in toward the center, Coriolis

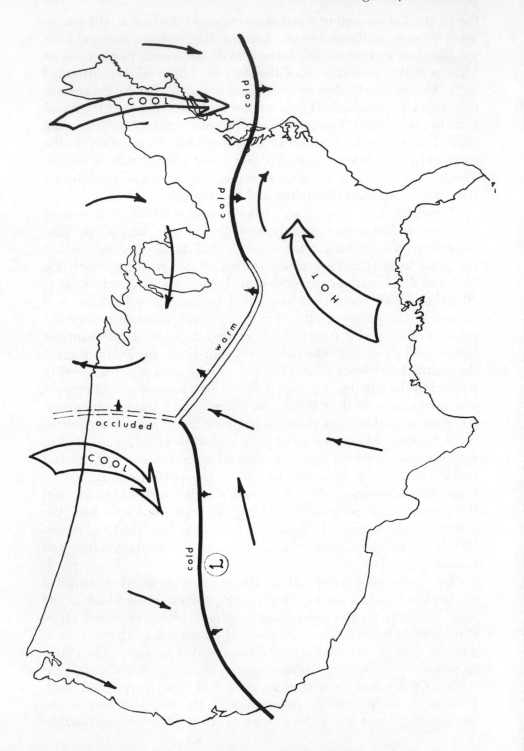

force deviates it into counterclockwise circulation—a cyclone is formed. Warm mTg air to the south of the kink, flowing westerly as a consequence of its position relative to the center of pressure in the mTg high, rises slowly above the cold cP air, resulting in a wide band of clouds, rain, snow, or sleet—the warm front. Cold air to the north and west of the kink moves rapidly in toward the low pressure, wedging under and lifting the warm air, to produce a narrow band of heavy showers, thunderstorms, and gusty winds—the cold front.

A low-pressure center (**depression**) migrates along the locus of the polar front moving in the direction and velocity of the wind in its

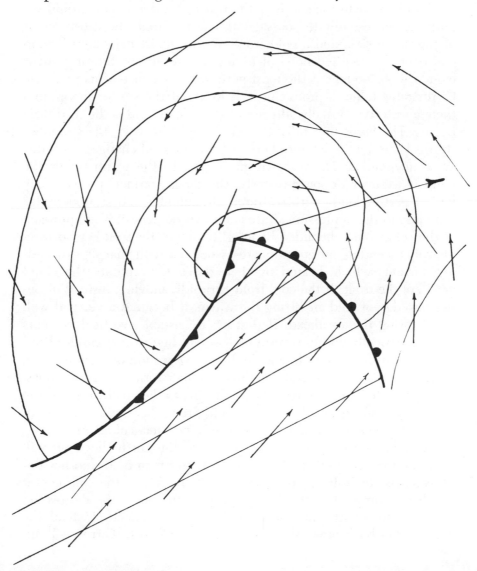

warm sector (the segment of mTg air between the leading warm
front and the trailing cold front). Large depressions move very
slowly but small ones may race eastward at 60 knots. All lows migrate across the United States in a general east–west trajectory
aimed toward the New England coast. Lows beginning in the Pacific
northwest migrate along the Canadian border across the Great Lakes
and out into the Atlantic; those that originate farther south or in the
Gulf reach the Atlantic off the Carolinas and migrate up the coast.
Their ultimate position and tendency to linger off the coast result
in the classical "three-day northeasters" of New England.

An observer to the south of the track of a depression would experience successively the passage of a warm front, the warm sector
of the depression, and a cold front. Warm, moist mTg air rides up
and over the inverted bowl of high-pressure cP air, forming cirrus
clouds at 40,000 feet as the most peripheral evidence of its invasion.
Cirrostratus follows, producing a halo about the sun or moon, and
then altostratus. Finally altocumulus appears and a light drizzle
begins. The barometer falls, the wind begins to veer, black nimbostratus looms on the western horizon and low scud changes to stratus
or stratocumulus. The warm front passes. In the warm sector the
wind is westerly or southwesterly, the air is warmer, the sky may
be but partly cloudy with scattered altocumulus and stratocumulus
but close to the depression stratus and drizzle persist. The approach
of the cold front is heralded by a lightening of the weather horizon.
Sharply ascending air currents are associated with sharply descending currents which, heated by their descent, evaporate the cloud
ahead of the front. If the cold front is rapidly moving, instead of being a wedge of cold air lifting the warm, it becomes a vertical wall
compressing the air ahead. If that air is unstable, vertical currents
rise dramatically within it forming a squall line twenty miles ahead
of the actual front. This line is the breeding ground of vicious gusts,
sharp showers, black cumulonimbus, thunderstorms, and tornadoes.
The barometer rises, the wind veers sharply to the northwest and the
front passes abruptly. Behind the cold front the sky is clear with
only scattered cumulus in the outflow of a new mass of cP air.

If high pressure persists and passes to the north the wind will
continue to veer—NW to N to NE to E to SE to S. If another depression is to follow, the wind will back as the barometer
steadies or drops. If instead of passing to the north the depression
passes to the south, no fronts would be experienced. Instead the
wind would back progressively SW to S to SE to E. Cirrus will ap-

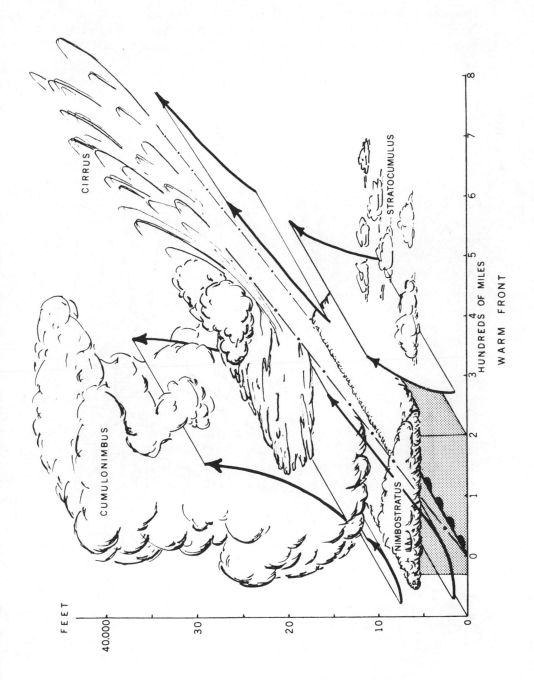

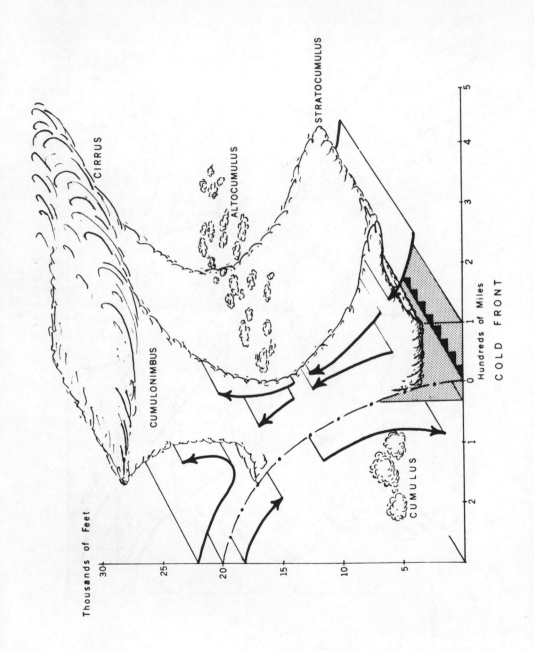

pear 400 to 500 miles ahead of the depression center, followed by altostratus, stratocumulus, stratus, and drizzle close to the center. Showers may be present after passage of the depression but no sharp front line appears. Near the center of the depression, where the isobars are tightly curved, the wind responds to the gradient and blows almost directly into the low-pressure center. Farther from the center the wind follows the isobars flowing from the eastern quadrants as the depression passes to the south.

Elements of the polar front move erratically eastward under the influence of the prevailing westerlies. High pressure from each air mass surges across the average position of the polar front, its outflow moving rapidly ahead but its center moving slowly behind. High pressure is characterized by sinking air, which heats due to compression as it sinks, and by inversions which form as the heated air layers above the cool air below. Such stable conditions are characterized by lack of cloud (or cloud melting as the land heats each day), light winds at the surface, and the development of sea and land breezes and mountain and valley winds.

Interposed between the slowly moving highs are the lows. A ridge of high pressure tends to invite a low to move into the pass or col between two highs. Lows move at the speed of the winds in their warm sectors, and new ones tend to move more rapidly than old ones. Trailing cold fronts move more rapidly than the warm fronts ahead and so tend to catch up, producing an occluded front. Precipitation is the consequence of rising air, cooled by expansion and is therefore characteristic of low pressure. The degree of precipitation and velocity of airflow depend upon the stability, temperature, and moisture content of the air behind a warm front and upon the stability of the air ahead and the rate of movement of a cold front.

The typical relationship of high- and low-pressure systems depends upon the direction of the circulation about the high. Air from a neighboring system may be drawn into its circulation. Lows tend to move around the periphery of high pressure along the course of its clockwise circulation. Maritime polar Atlantic air may be drawn into the northerly circulation of cP high pressure as it approaches the North Atlantic coast. As cP air moves eastward mTg air is drawn into the southerly circulation on its back. The northward surge of mTg air meets a new outflow of cP air to the north and west of the original cP high center and a new segment of the polar front is formed. Low pressure rushing across the mid-continent draws mTg air into the southerly circulation ahead of it, creating some of the best southwesterlies of the East Coast. Continental polar air is drawn southward into the northerly circulation behind a low, pressing the cold front on to overtake the warm front ahead.

Typical sequences of weather systems traversing the United States and crossing the East Coast are as follows:

cP High Passes to the North

First day	Northwesterly (cP outflow)
Second day	Northerly–Northeasterly (circulation ahead of high)
Third day	Easterly–Southeasterly (circulation to the south of high—sea breeze frequent)

mTg High Passes to the South

First day	Westerly–Southwesterly (circulation to the north of high)
Second day	Southerly (circulation to the west of high—sea breeze frequent)

Low Passes to the North

First day	Southerly (mTg air drawn into circulation ahead of low)
Second day	Westerly (warm front passes followed by warm sector)
Third day	Northwesterly (cold front passes followed by cP outflow)

Low Passes to the South

First day	Southeasterly–Easterly (circulation ahead and to the north of low)
Second day	Northeasterly (circulation to the west of low)
Third day	Northeasterly (circulation to the west of low persisting off coast—may continue for three days)

III. *A Classification of Wind Shifts*

Persistent and oscillating shifts—their causes and recognition.

Persistent and Oscillating
Wind Shifts

"And may there be no moaning at the bar,
When I put out to sea."

PERSISTENT SHIFTS

1. *Movement of the weather system:*

   As the center of a high- or low-pressure system moves past the racing area, the direction of the outflow or inflow determined by it will change.

   If the pressure gradient is large and the wind flow strong, this change is usually associated with a gradual progressive veer or back.

   If the pressure gradient is small and the wind flow weak, or if the weather system is moving rapidly, this change is often abrupt and associated with erratic oscillating shifts.

   A mass of flowing air cannot change direction abruptly without turbulence due to wind shear. The initial flow must cease and a period of calm must ensue before flow can commence from a new direction.

   Frequently, when calm is followed by the brief invasion of a new wind, the initial flow returns for a few minutes before it is finally replaced. Experience suggests that this is the usual pattern. The shift back after the initial calm and shift is to be expected. This sequence is a set of oscillating shifts and must be managed as such.

2. *The appearance of a new air mass:*

   The passage of a warm front usually results in a gradual veer from southerly to southwesterly or westerly.

The passage of a cold front usually results in an abrupt veer from westerly to northwesterly.

3. *The appearance of a low-pressure system:*

    A major low-pressure system is often associated with frontal changes. Its passage over a given area is predictable by the "cross winds rule" (a variation of Buys Ballot's law) which indicates that low pressure is approaching from the west in the Northern Hemisphere when a surface southerly flow is associated with a westerly flow aloft and that low pressure is receding when a surface northerly flow is associated with a westerly flow aloft.

    A focal low-pressure system (thunderstorm, hurricane, etc.) is characterized by an abrupt downdraft outflow ahead followed by a counterclockwise surface flow around a calm center. The initial wind is usually directly away from the center of the low. The direction of the subsequent wind will depend upon the position of the center of the low relative to the observer, i.e. upon which segment of the counterclockwise peripheral flow is present at the site. If the low passes over the observer, a period of calm will be experienced and this will be followed by a persistent shift to the direction of the segment of counterclockwise flow on the opposite periphery.

4. *The appearance of a sea breeze:*

    The sea breeze flows from the periphery of a dome of high pressure which develops over the water and moves as a cold front (cold air beneath warm) toward the shore and inland.

    The nature of the persistent shift is dependent upon the alignment of the sea breeze with the weather system wind. If the weather system wind is minimal, the sea breeze first appears from a period of calm near the shore and is directed onshore. If the weather system wind is offshore, the sea breeze first appears offshore and pushes a zone of calm and erratic oscillating shifts ahead of it as it progresses toward the shore. If the weather system wind is more or less parallel to the shore, the sea breeze first appears offshore and progresses toward the shore accompanied by oscillating shifts between the weather system wind and the sea breeze.

5. *The appearance of an offshore local wind*—a Santa Ana, a bora, a katabatic wind, a land breeze:

Offshore local winds will outflow over the water to produce a persistent shift from the previous wind direction.

The site, degree, and persistence of such a persistent shift will depend upon the vertical stability of the flow—marked temperature differences may be associated with an inversion which separates the new wind from the old—and upon alignment of the offshore flow with the original flow.

Frequently, the offshore flow is associated with an onshore sea breeze flow. Then a zone of erratic oscillating shifts and calm develops at the surface a short distance offshore between the two wind flows. This intermediary zone frequently persists in a fixed location in contrast to the migration toward the shore characteristic of the advance of the sea breeze front beneath an ordinary offshore weather system wind.

6. *Vertical variation in wind direction:*

Lower-level airflow is held to the surface by friction and therefore responds but minimally to the Coriolis force induced by the earth's rotation. This means that in the Northern Hemisphere airflow is progressively veered with height as it is freed from friction and increasingly affected by Coriolis force.

Coriolis force varies directly with velocity; therefore, all airflows tend to veer as they increase in velocity and back as they decrease in velocity.

Vertically unstable airflows are mixtures of airflows derived from varying levels; therefore, at the surface they appear as a random mixture of airflows of widely varied direction and velocity. Additions of upper airflow to the surface mixture depend upon surface heating and thermal lift-off; therefore, such flows veer with diurnal heating and back with cooling.

7. *Breakthrough of an inversion:*

Vertically stable airflows are often associated with an inversion which isolates warm airflow above cold. A persistent shift will occur when surface heating dissipates the inversion and brings the upper airflow to the surface.

Offshore sea breezes are associated with overlying inversions (cold marine air beneath air heated ashore). With increasing surface heating the sea breeze near the weather shore shifts increasingly to the direction of the overlying weather system airflow.

An upper-level subsidence inversion may permit the isolated development of a low level sea breeze and separate it from weather system airflow above. With the breakthrough of such an inversion, the low-level sea breeze may be dissipated to be replaced by a new, reorganized sea breeze, backed to the initial sea breeze, or by a weather system wind. With the reappearance of such an inversion, the weather system or sea breeze may be eliminated to be replaced by a new, low-level sea breeze.

8. *Geographical effects—channeling:*

Surface airflow tends to follow the contours of the shorelines, particularly if they are significantly elevated. The denser (colder) the airflow (northerlies, sea breezes, boras), the more it tends to deviate around surface elevations and flow like a liquid.

Onshore flows, such as sea breezes, seek low-level entrances to heated surfaces ashore and therefore channel into harbor openings and subsequently diverge and converge with the shorelines.

Offshore flows tend to channel down valleys and along river beds. They increase in velocity over water (decreased friction) and deviate to follow the long axis of a river at each bend.

A series of persistent shifts, which result from a series of headlands along a shore or bends in a river, creates a set of oscillating shifts which should be handled as such.

9. *Refraction:*

As air flows off a shore at an oblique angle, the resultant change in velocity causes the flow to be refracted to a direction more perpendicular to the shoreline.

The more rapid the flow, the more stable the flow, and the more irregular the surface (tree-covered), the greater will be the degree of refraction and the farther offshore (usually within a quarter of a mile) will it persist.

Oblique onshore flow begins to slow in advance of its traverse of a shoreline; therefore, in a zone up to a quarter of a mile offshore it will be refracted more perpendicular to the shore.

Anabatic flow is directed perpendicular to the slope which is creating it and therefore may deviate flow over the nearby water to a direction more perpendicular to the shoreline.

10. *Velocity shifts:*

Coriolis force causes moving air to be deviated in proportion to the velocity of its flow. As a wind flow (of any origin) increases in velocity it veers (in the Northern Hemisphere), and as it decreases in velocity it backs.

Sea breezes are characterized by a slowly progressive veer as their generation increases with heating of the land, and a rapidly progressive back as their generation subsides with cooling.

Sea breezes tend to be veered near the shore they are invading, as there they are composed of upper-level, peripheral, rapidly moving airflow, and backed farther from shore, where they are composed of low-level, central, slowly moving airflow (the fan effect).

OSCILLATING SHIFTS

1. *Unstable airflow:*

Buoyant airflows are associated with vertical movement within the horizontal flow due to turbulence both thermal and mechanical. Upward movement of surface air is associated with downward movement of upper-level air. As upper airflow (in the Northern Hemisphere) is veered to surface airflow and of higher velocity, mixing of the flows results in gusts, which are usually veered, and lulls, which are usually backed. This relationship may not be evident to an observer, however, unless he is directly ahead of a downdraft gust.

Cold northerly airflows which pass over warmer land are associated with large vertical lapse rates, buoyancy, mixing of airflows derived from various levels, and oscillating shifts between the veers and backs.

Many initially stable offshore flows become vertically unstable and associated with oscillating shifts as the land surface is heated with the sun and thermal uplift causes mixing of flows from different levels.

The sea breeze is vertically unstable as it flows over warm, often shallow, water and particularly as it flows over land and emerges offshore over an inland bay, harbor, or lagoon. It emerges as a mixture of heated upper and lower sea breeze flow and may include weather system flow from above the sea breeze inversion as well. In this instance gusts may be backed (or veered) depending upon the direction of the weather system airflow.

When partial, low-level cloud cover—cumulus or stratocumulus—exists, downdrafts which are melting the cloud and updrafts which are forming the cloud may be presumed to be present. Downdrafts, which appear in association with segments of clear sky, will bring elements of veered, upper-level airflow to the surface, while updrafts, associated with cloud cover, leave backed, lower-level airflow at the surface.

2. *Mixtures of two winds:*

As a new airflow develops in an area, the old flow must lift or deviate or subside before it can be replaced. It often does this erratically so that a series of oscillating shifts occurs between the new wind and the old before a persistent shift to the new wind finally develops. Oscillating shifts are most likely to occur when the two wind flows are flowing at 45° to 135° to each other. (Such oscillations are extremely difficult to predict.)

Typical examples:

A sea breeze replacing a weather system wind or another sea breeze.

An inversion breakthrough/weather system airflow reaching the surface intermittently.

Weather system movement.

3. *Channeling effects:*

Alternate shifts on either side of a series of headlands along a shore or bend in a river, particularly in a dense, stable airflow such as an onshore sea breeze.

IV. *The Winds of the World*

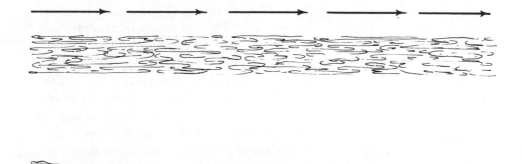

A. The Weather System Winds—
United States East Coast

1. Diurnal Wind Variation
and the Inversions

"The more rain, the more rest;
Fine weather's not always best."

All wind is derived from pressure differences induced by thermal variations. Therefore the diurnal temperature changes induced by periodic exposure of the earth's surface to the sun regularly modify the wind. The sailor needs to understand these basic modifications as they are often the major determinants of the direction and velocity of the surface wind. The nature of the weather system airflow determines the timing and the likelihood of appearance of the varying diurnal effects, but the basic pattern is always evident. Offshore, over thermostable water, diurnal variations are slight. Along shore and inshore (where most racing sailors sail), over thermolabile land, variations are marked. "Local knowledge" is largely an understanding of the diurnal variations in wind flow induced by local land masses. It remains for each sailor to apply this "local knowledge" of

95

diurnal variation to the circumstances of a particular weather system airflow to predict the surface wind flow at a particular time on a particular day.

Temperature changes in the lower layers of the atmosphere are induced from the surface upward. Thus a temperature/pressure change in the air, which induces a wind or a modification of an existing wind, is initiated by heating or cooling of the surface. The temperature of the land changes significantly throughout each day, whereas the temperature of the water (unless it is very shallow), because of diffusion within, varies very little. The surface is heated largely by radiation from the sun. Although the sun's infrared radiation is obstructed by clouds, its major shortwave radiation is not obstructed and thus the surface is heated (though to a lesser degree) even under cloud cover. The surface is also heated by conduction and this becomes most significant with the advection (horizontal flow) of air of differing temperature. Cooling of the surface is caused chiefly by longwave radiation. Such radiation is obstructed by cloud cover. Maximal surface heating thus occurs when the sun is overhead on a clear day, and such a clear sky will permit maximal cooling during the evening and night. Cloud cover will, on the other hand, reduce heating but delay cooling and thus be associated with less diurnal variation—cooler days and warmer nights.

The normal relationship of temperature to altitude, the lapse rate, falls steadily with distance above the surface. This "normal" relationship rarely exists, however, as variations in surface heating and the advection of airflows of differing temperature cause marked variations in this gradient. An increase in temperature with height—cold air below warm air—is called an inversion. The most common inversion occurs on most nights over the land due to cooling of the surface by radiation. The radiation inversion is particularly likely to develop when the sky is clear (no cloud cover to limit radiation), dry (no moisture to limit radiation), and calm (no wind to diffuse the low-level cooling). An inversion may also be produced by the advection of warm air over a cold surface—the characteristic result of a southerly airflow over cold water in winter. Inversions are also integral to subsidence and occur in the lower 2000 to 5000 feet of large high-pressure air masses such as the subtropical highs and pressure systems derived from them. Turbulence in the lowest levels of subsiding air systems keeps the inversion above the surface. In warm anticyclones, such as the Pacific high that affects the California coast, the inversion is so strong that the air is that of a hot desert

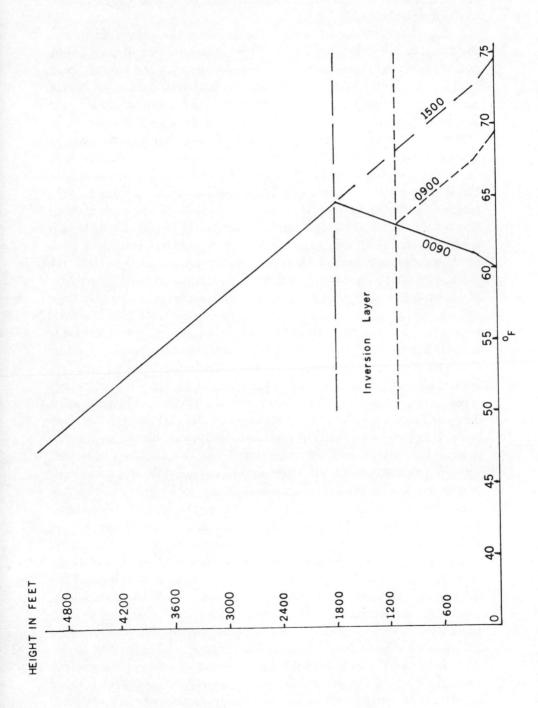

above but filled with salt and moisture and, over Los Angeles, smog in the marine layer below.

Though inversions are common to radiational cooling and subsiding air anywhere, they are also evident in the absence of such conditions whenever warm air flows over cold air. In a sea breeze front, cold sea air flows inland near the surface below an outflow of heated air from the land. Warm air flowing over cold water creates a very low-level "conduction" inversion. The sea breeze as it flows over its water source often has an inversion in its lowest levels separating the flowing air from the dense, stagnant air within a few (tens or hundreds) feet of the surface. This accounts for the reduced velocity of the sea breeze as one moves offshore and for its low velocity at the surface off the Maine and northern California coasts where it flows toward the shore over a cold surface current. It also accounts for the tendency of an offshore sea breeze, one which has traversed some land and become heated en route, to lift progressively above the surface of cold water with distance from the windward shore. One of the major causes of calm in summer, when most sailors do their sailing, is the inability of the sea breeze to penetrate this low-level inversion over the harbors, bays, and lakes it encounters en route inland. Long Island Sound and the Chesapeake are characterized by this problem along their inland sides, particularly when the sea breeze air is derived from warm, subsiding mTg air and particularly when, in the spring or after a flood tide, the water is unusually cold. The sea breeze may be flowing strongly at the surface over the land when one throws the sails in the back of the car, but there may be none at the surface over the water where the race is to be conducted.

The existence of an inversion demonstrates stability, and stable conditions tend to persist. An inversion layer separates upper airflow from the surface and prevents turbulence, thermal or mechanical, from below from reaching into the upper airflow and thus bringing it to the surface. Thus inversions are usually the foe of the racing sailor as they prevent the development of a strong wind flow in the surface air in which he sails. Inversions can occur at any level of the atmosphere and are often present at several levels simultaneously; each successively prevents the airflow above from reaching the surface. The lowest and most significant is the *conduction* inversion (cold air that has subsided to the lowest level and is further cooled by conduction) which bars sea breezes and weather system winds from the lower 10 or 20 or 100 feet above cold water. Above this a sea breeze or weather system wind of only slightly warmer tempera-

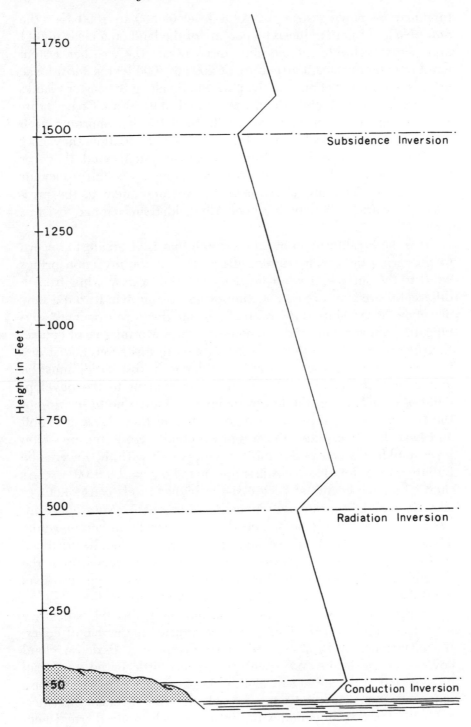

ture may be flowing strongly. At a level of 300 to 1000 feet the *radiation* inversion (induced by cooling of the land on a clear night) may persist well into the morning and separate the weather system wind from the surface. Farther up, at 2000 to 5000 feet, a *subsidence* inversion may exist continuously, particularly along the eastern flanks of the subtropical highs. Along the United States East Coast, however, subsidence inversions tend to "burn off" in late morning each day and to return each night. Prior to their dissipation they may separate a sea breeze below from a weather system wind above or prevent a low-level sea breeze from full generation into upper air levels. At any level an *advection* inversion consequent to the presence of a warm airflow over a generally colder surface may exist as well.

It is the breakthrough of an inversion that is of greatest concern to the racing sailor. The sudden dissipation of the inversion brings wind to the surface, a wind in place of calm, a new wind from a different source, or a reorganization of an existing wind from a new direction. These shifts may be baffling but they are extremely significant in determining the outcome of a race. Morning is, of course, the time to be alert to the breakthrough of an inversion, and if one is presumed to be present, a wind shift due to its dissipation must be anticipated. Inversion breakthrough is consequent to the development of turbulence in the lower air layer, usually due to heating of the land surface. The progressive generation of thermals that lift-off and heat the atmosphere above will eventually erode the inversion layer until finally convection mixes the upper air with the lower. The radiation inversion dissipates first and may be gone by 8:00 A.M. As thermal mixing occurs at progressively higher levels consequent to the elimination of a radiation inversion, a co-existing subsidence inversion may eventually be breached as well, usually in late morning. The low-level conduction inversion over the water cannot be breached by heating from below, its dissipation therefore depends upon the development of mechanical turbulence in the increasing low-level wind flow that follows the rupture of the higher inversions.

If stratocumulus is present, it has probably formed beneath a subsidence inversion. If chinks of blue appear in this cloud cover, the inversion may be presumed to be dissipating. If dense cloud cover persists, the inversion will persist and little or no wind can be expected at the surface. A cloudy day in winter is the worst case of inversion persistence. An upper-level advection inversion may persist with dense stratocumulus beneath it which limits thermal gen-

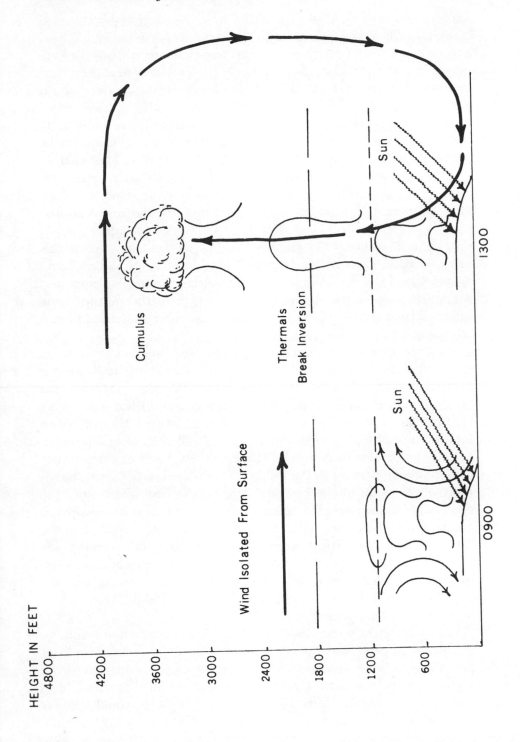

eration, and the low-level conduction inversion over the water may block all surface wind throughout the day. Strong winds and cloud cover can only persist together around low-pressure systems. In high pressure, if the wind becomes strong, turbulence destroys the inversion and dissipates the cloud cover. Under an inversion the cloud is either total or absent.

The most important sign of inversion breakthrough is a change in wind velocity or direction, and this is particularly significant in the breakthrough of an upper-level subsidence inversion. The weather system wind previously separated from the surface may appear for the first time. A sea breeze (which is only a few thousand feet deep at full generation) may have developed beneath the inversion and have been present from 7:00 to 8:00 A.M. As the subsidence inversion burns off at 11:00 A.M. the organization of such a sea breeze disintegrates and must be reestablished. At Marblehead and on Long Island Sound this typically results in a marked drop in velocity and a gradual back as the sea breeze dies, and a further abrupt back followed by a steady increase in velocity and veer as the sea breeze reorganizes (see subsequent chapters).

If a weather system wind instead of a sea breeze is flowing at the surface early in the morning, and the conditions indicate the presence of an advection or subsidence inversion overhead, the breakthrough of the inversion will be associated with a major veer in the weather system wind. A light northeasterly at the surface in the presence of high pressure to the north will change to a stronger easterly as the inversion breaks. Upper airflow freed of surface friction is flowing parallel to the isobars; lower-level airflow is responding more directly to the pressure gradient flowing away from the center of high pressure. The thermal turbulence which has dissipated the inversion thereafter mixes the upper-level flow with that at the surface; the entire airflow increases in velocity and veers. A sea breeze that has been unable to develop under the protection of the inversion will not appear as it dissipates. If a sea breeze is to develop on such a day it will only do so later, under the influence of maximum thermal generation.

Not infrequently inversion breakthrough is uneven and results in the bizarre appearance of winds from inexplicable directions for brief periods as airflows at various levels are mixed and brought to the surface for the first time. Gradients induced by local thermal influences, temporarily disrupted by inversion breakthrough, and weather system gradients overlying a persistent surface conduction inversion in the lowest 10 or 20 feet, may result in transient zephyrs from any or every quadrant. All this characteristically occurs at about 11:00 A.M. (when a subsidence inversion usually dissipates), a time when many race committees want to start a race! Because of this timing, upper-level subsidence inversions are most significant to racing sailors. Their breakthrough often determines the outcome of the first beat—and the race.

The upper-level subsidence inversion may also be significant in the late afternoon or early evening when it reforms due to the combined presence of warm advection and surface cooling by radiation. Its return may be associated with an abrupt drop in weather system wind flow or sea breeze. But, just as in the morning, following an abrupt back and drop in wind velocity, a new, stronger wind may appear. This will be a low-level sea breeze which, protected by the inversion from the wind shear of a malaligned weather system wind or the opposition of an offshore wind, is able to generate an organized circulation for the first time.

THE UPPER-LEVEL SUBSIDENCE INVERSION

Typical precursors:

High-pressure system—"sinking" air

Clear skies—facilitate longwave radiation and cooling of the earth's surface at night. A radiation inversion aids the formation of a subsidence inversion

Warm airflow—northeasterly, easterly, southeasterly flow from thermostable (nocturnally warm) water toward thermolabile (nocturnally cool) land along the East Coast and southerly flow. An advection inversion reinforces a subsidence inversion

Characteristics:

Clear sky (or)

Stratocumulus cloud cover pre-existing in the morning—due to sinking air from above, heating (due to compression) as it sinks, but precipitating its moisture as it cools just below the inversion (or)

Stratocumulus formation during the morning—consequent to warm convection from the surface precipitating below the inversion and spreading out beneath it, temporarily increasing the cloud cover

Light wind flow (without gusting)—weather system wind backed
to predicted direction or a low-level sea breeze

Breaking through:

Skies clear (if cloudy)—usually from the shore toward the water
and usually abruptly. Cloud cover is burned off by thermal lift-
off and by absorption of longwave radiation from the heating
surface below. Clearing is blocked by additional cloud cover
aloft—frontal systems, etc.

Wind velocity drops initially—as radiation cooling is abruptly increased by the dissipation of the cloud cover, surface air cools
and briefly decreases surface airflow. Disorganization of the
upper sea breeze circulation interrupts the lower-level flow

Wind velocity increases and wind veers. The surface is heated
by longwave and shortwave radiation after the cloud cover dissipates and rapidly warms the air above it. The warmed air
rises, mixes with the veered, higher velocity air aloft and brings
it to the surface. Sea breeze circulation reorganizes on a larger
scale and a new sea breeze commencing from a direction approximately perpendicular to the shore appears and subsequently veers—or a weather system wind previously separated
from the surface (partially or completely) appears for the first
time or strengthens and veers

DIURNAL WIND VARIATION AT ANNAPOLIS

An outline description of a typical day at Annapolis, Maryland
follows. The timing and degree of change indicated would be most
typical of a clear, dry airflow (northerly, high-pressure system) in
the summer or fall. Cloud cover resulting from a warm or moist airflow would modify this sequence, as would the colder water surface
of winter and spring which often prevents the wind from penetrating
through the cold, dense layer overlying it. The pattern is present
whether detectable or not; cooling of the surface and the lower air
occurs each night and heating each day. The weather system airflow
may never get to the surface but it exists at higher levels. The sea
breeze may never develop but it is induced. The pattern may be
clearly evident and on time as described, it may be completely absent, or, most likely, it may be obscure in both degree and timing
yet extremely significant in modifying surface airflow in both direction and velocity.

8:00 P.M.–7:00 A.M. Radiation inversion (unless weather system wind very cold). Land cooler than surface air and water.
SURFACE AIR: temp.—cool; wind—land breeze, light.
UPPER AIR (above inversion): temp.—air warmer than surface; wind—weather system.

7:00 A.M.–8:00 A.M. Radiation inversion dissipating. Land warming to same temperature as surface air and water.
SURFACE AIR: temp.—warming; wind—absent, *Calm.*
UPPER AIR: temp.—slightly warmer than surface air; wind—weather system.

8:00 A.M.–11:00 A.M. Radiation inversion breakthrough. Descent of the weather system wind or appearance of low-level sea breeze beneath subsidence inversion. Land warmer than surface air and water.
SURFACE AIR: temp.—warm, rising thermals break radiation inversion; wind—low-level sea breeze or weather system.
UPPER AIR: temp.—slightly cooler than surface air; wind—weather system.

11:00 A.M.–2:00 P.M. Subsidence inversion breakthrough. Invasion of the upper level sea breeze. Land considerably warmer than surface air and water.
SURFACE AIR: temp.—thermal lift-off occurring over land; wind—sea breeze (low or upper level) begins near shore or above shore—flows perpendicular to shore.
UPPER AIR: temp.—cooler than surface air; wind—weather system.

2:00 P.M.–4:00 P.M. Sea breeze deepens and veers. Land hot.
SURFACE AIR: temp.—thermal lift-off widespread, rising into upper air; wind—*sea breeze,* moderately veered, with oscillating shifts due to mixtures of upper and lower airflows.
UPPER AIR: temp.—cooler than surface air; wind—sea breeze, veered.

4:00 P.M.–7:00 P.M. Sea breeze moves inland. Land cooling: still warmer than water but cooler than upper air.
SURFACE AIR: temp.—cooling, thermal lift-off limited to lower (surface) air; wind—*sea breeze,* fully veered, shifting minimal—moves inland.
UPPER AIR: temp.—warmer than surface air forming inversion at

a few thousand feet; wind—weather system (above inversion).

7:00 P.M.–8:00 P.M.   Radiation inversion returns. Land cool: cooler than surface air, same temperature as water.

   SURFACE AIR: temp.—cool, no thermal lift-off; wind—absent, *calm.*

   UPPER AIR: temp.—warmer than surface air; wind—weather system (above inversion).

If a local sea breeze is present flowing approximately perpendicular to the shore, near the shore, prior to 10:00 A.M., it is probably an isolated low-level sea breeze flowing beneath a subsidence inversion and can be expected to die as the inversion breaks at about 11:00 A.M. It will back as it dies and the sea breeze that replaces it will be backed up to 40° to the earlier sea breeze direction. If between 10:00 A.M. and 12:00 noon the wind is calm, the first wind to appear should be the weather system wind and one should tack toward it. If the weather system wind appears to change between noon and 2:00 P.M. (falter or increase depending upon its alignment) or has not appeared, the sea breeze should be expected and one should tack toward it. If the sea breeze has appeared perpendicular to the shore, it should progressively veer as it strengthens between 2:00 P.M. and 4:00 P.M. and one should keep to starboard of the fleet. When thereafter the sea breeze begins to falter, expect it to back toward its original direction more perpendicular to the shore. If it falters earlier than might be expected (usually associated with cloud cover), the weather system wind (if strong) may be returning and one should tack toward it. If it is clear, expect surface cooling to be rapid in the evening, the sea breeze to die abruptly, and a strong radiation inversion to develop overhead blocking the access of the upper-level sea breeze or the weather system wind to the surface. A low-level sea breeze may then reorganize beneath the inversion after a period of calm as the weather system wind is excluded above the inversion. Sometimes, on days such as described, an offshore weather system wind and the sea breeze fight each other to a standstill along the shore. No breeze may reach the surface until late in the day when the returning inversion blocks the weather system wind above and permits the sea breeze to flow in beneath—the "anchor breeze."

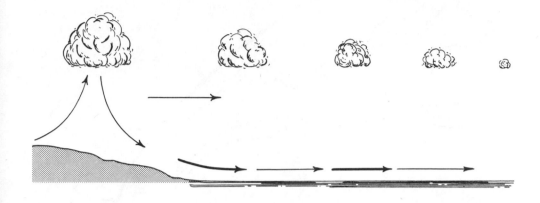

2. The Classic Northwesterly

"When freshly blow the nor'western gales
Then on courses snug we fly;
Soon lesser breezes will fill the sails,
And royals proudly sweep the sky."

Cold winds flowing offshore from warmer surfaces have similar characteristics all over the world. They are unstable and therefore are associated with marked vertical (convective) movements. At the surface they are mixtures of segments of upper, veered airflow and low-level backed flow appearing as gusts and lulls of markedly varied velocity. They are strongest near the windward shore and are subject to marked diurnal variation. Along the United States East Coast the classic example of this wind is the northwesterly, the outflow from a mass of continental polar air which has moved south from the Canadian interior. Along the coast the northwesterly appears with a sudden drop in temperature, crystal-clear air, "well-washed" blue skies, and fluffy cumulus heaps often organized into cloud streets. It provides the best of sailing—strong winds, oscillating shifts, and smooth water.

When a mass of cP air is drawn down across the United States behind a low-pressure system, it flows outward from its dome-like center in all directions. Obstructed by the Rockies from turning west, and dragged to the east by the upper-level westerlies, the 10,000–15,000-foot deep pool of cold, dense air turns southeastward. The cold front plows its way forward, thrusting the warm air ahead up-

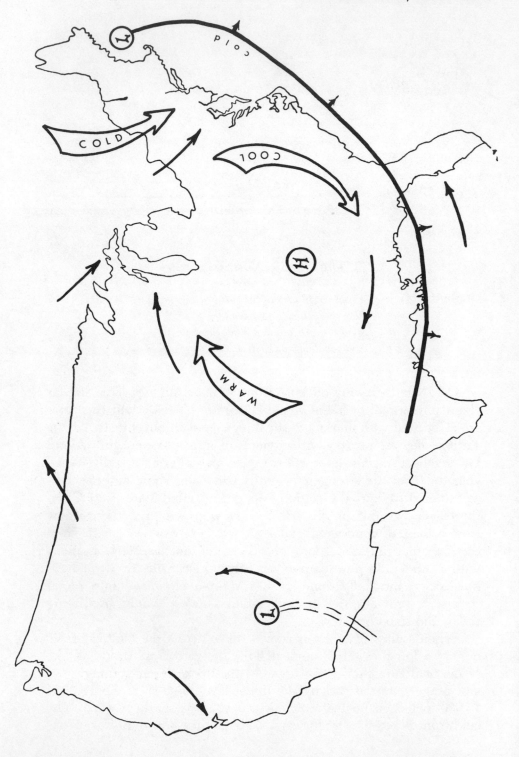

ward into thunderstorms, tornadoes, and drenching downpours. When breaks appear in the nimbostratus and a few rifts of sunlight appear on the western horizon ("Red at night, sailor's delight"), an abrupt veer in the westerly warm-sector wind appears. The temperature drops abruptly, the pressure begins to rise, and the surface airflow becomes northwesterly. If cloud cover is dense the northwesterly may be but light to moderate. Sometimes, however, it races across the water with the speed and fury of a locomotive, blue sky replacing black cloud, and 25 knots of northwesterly replacing 5 knots of westerly within a period of a few minutes. If a cold front passage is expected it is essential to be upwind to starboard of the fleet while beating to obtain the full advantage of the abrupt veer. If reaching or running, a position to leeward may provide a better sailing angle and will probably permit the receipt of the new wind as soon as a position to weather.

The northwesterly is not the same wind at its origin that it is at its dissipation. It begins dry and cold and dense. It adds warmth as

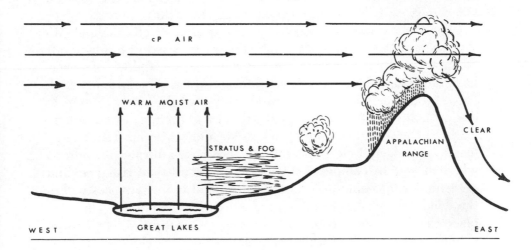

it travels south and moisture as it passes over the Great Lakes. Cumulus and stratocumulus appear as the dew point of the cold, moist air is reached when it is lifted above the Appalachians. Snow and rain in the mountains leave the air dry and clear upon its arrival over the coast. Passage over the Gulf Stream adds moisture once again so that over Bermuda the northwesterly builds huge cumulus towers and occasional rain squalls. In winter cP outflow reaches as far south as Florida and is still flowing at 35 knots when it is halted by opposing high pressure over the Gulf. In summer it barely reaches the Carolinas and, heated by the hot surfaces over which it has flowed, scarcely musters 10 knots when it limps off the Chesapeake shore.

Under clear skies, the land heats each day, creates a high lapse rate and marked buoyancy, thermal turbulence is high, and the high-velocity upper levels of the airflow reach the surface. At night under clear skies a radiation inversion develops that often excludes the air-flow from the surface entirely. Over heated land in summer, or warm water in winter, convection brings strong flow to the surface. Over cool water in summer, or snow-covered land in winter, the absence of convection minimizes surface airflow. In any northwester the sur-face wind increases with the heat of the day, reaching a peak in midafternoon and decreasing rapidly thereafter. When it blows 40 knots in the winter the only time for racing may be early in the morning or after three in the afternoon. The surface wind is stronger near the windward shore in summertime as the shore is the site of convection. Looking down at the Chesapeake from the Bay Bridge one may see whitecaps induced by a northwester along the western shore and near calm five miles away along the eastern shore.

The offshore northwesterly is composed of gust cells moving with the speed of the mean wind. Each cell is composed of a downdraft of upper-level, high-velocity, veered flow and an updraft of lower-level, low-velocity, backed flow. If an updraft rises sufficiently high (usually above 5000 feet), expansion will cool the rising column to its dew point and a cumulus cloud will form at the top of the column. Early in the day the cumulus are small and scattered. Later large masses appear and clear spaces between them indicate downdrafts which, heated by compression, melt the cloud away. A rising column exists under the center of each cumulus (and in many places within the wind flow where clouds fail to form) and downdrafts which re-place the rising air trail behind and along both sides of each rising column. The downdraft trails backward behind the cloud so that the strong gust at the surface often appears to be beneath the leading edge of a following cloud. The downdraft is warmed and slowed as it spreads across the surface, falls astern, and then rises as an updraft in the rear of the gust cell. Thus the gust cell which moves across the surface is recognized as a veered downdraft moving at one and a half to two-times the velocity of the mean wind, followed by a backed lull which is moving at less than the velocity of the mean wind. Gust cells appear at intervals of approximately three minutes in a 20-knot wind and at longer intervals, up to twenty minutes, in

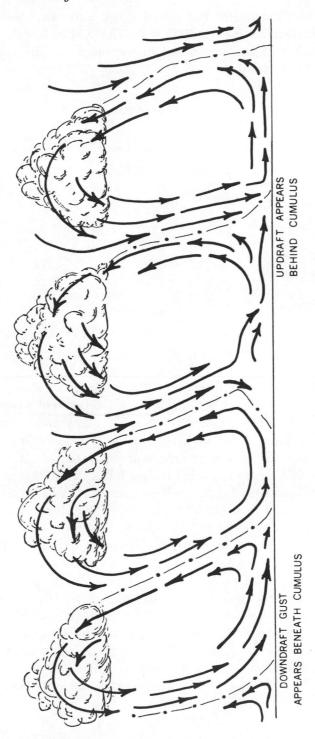

a wind of lesser strength. Individual downdraft gusts may persist along the surface for 500 to 1000 feet. The width, length, and velocity of each gust is proportional to the height of the convection column which initiated it.

GUST/LULL SEQUENCES

CONDITIONS	MEDIAN VELOCITY	CONVECTION HEIGHT	LENGTH OF GUST CELL	OSCILLATION RANGE	INTERVAL
Northwesterly (Strong, cold offshore weather system flows)	15–25 knots	Cumulus— bases at 5000 ft.	4000–6000 ft.	10°–30°	Short interval (medium eddies) Oscillation every 3–5 minutes
Offshore sea-breeze (moderate, cool offshore local winds)	5–15 knots	Strato-cumulus— bases at 2000 ft.	1–4 nautical miles	5°–10°	Long interval (medium eddies) Oscillation every 5–20 minutes

The surface wind shifts in an oscillating manner between veered gusts and backed lulls at varying intervals dependent upon the velocity induced by the gradient of the cP outflow and upon the instability of the surface air, which in turn is dependent upon the disparity between the surface temperature and the air temperature. This airflow is a mixture of short eddies induced by surface friction, medium eddies due to the gust-cell organization and long eddies due to variations in the convection lift-off inland. The short eddies are too frequent and too transient to be useful to the racing sailor, but they must be accommodated by constant changes in heading and traveler trim. The moderate eddies are usually about 4000 to 8000 feet apart and therefore produce oscillating shifts which can be utilized to shorten the distance sailed to the weather mark. The long eddies, often associated with cloud streets, are from five to fifteen miles apart and therefore produce persistent shifts which must be planned for and sailed toward if strategic gain is to be achieved. Gusts are free of short eddies as they are composed of freely moving upper air, while lulls are erratic as they are composed of surface flow modified by passage over surface obstacles.

Surface heating and convection lift-off, particularly if aided by anabatic flow up mountain slopes, is periodic. Convection within a rapidly moving air stream tends to occur in strips the width of which are twice the height of the convection. A strip of land lying across the wind flow heats until a sufficient temperature disparity results to permit separation of the heated surface air. The strip is then cooled by a replacing downdraft and an interval elapses before the strip is sufficiently heated to permit convection lift-off once again. Intermittent convection from such a strip produces the cloud street that flows downwind from the site of initial lift-off. Once initiated the circulation revealed by the cumulus cloud street is maintained by a continuous updraft from the land over which the street passes. As cumulus formation usually takes place between 3000 and 5000 feet, and the width of the streets are twice the height of convection, cloud streets are usually about 10,000 feet apart. Weak descending currents are present in the wide, clear sections between the cloud streets. Strong downdrafts are present behind and within the cloud streets and may be revealed by chinks of blue between the clouds.

The convection induced by the clear skies and cold air of the northwesterly, and revealed by cumulus formation, is a major inducer of sea breeze circulation. If the water and its overlying surface air is colder than the northwesterly, an onshore flow may develop beneath the offshore flow. In winter when the northwesterly is very cold and hugs the surface, onshore flow is rarely able to develop against it. In summer, however, when the northwesterly is weak and extensively heated by the land over which it passes, the sea breeze regularly undermines it. In winter a northwesterly may persist and blow strongly for two or even three days (although it tends to veer significantly during such a period). In summer it may not even last one day before it is usurped by a sea breeze. On the second day the wind will be around in the northeast and a sea breeze will certainly develop beneath it. When the sea breeze does fill in beneath the northwesterly (or northerly or northeasterly) the offshore wind may persist near shore or up channels which make away from the main body of water while the sea breeze flows over the surface offshore.

As the northwesterly departs from the shore it leaves the sources of convection behind. The cumulus clouds which characterize its sojourn over land begin to disintegrate as soon as the northwesterly emerges over the water. If a sea breeze forms along the shore an abrupt line of demarcation develops between the cloud-filled skies over the land and the clear blue over the water. This is the sea breeze front. Air sinking above the trough of cold, dense air over the water heats by compression and melts the cumulus as they leave the land. At St. Petersburg the imminence of the sea breeze is indicated by clearing of the cumulus and stratocumulus to seaward. Long before the sea breeze arrives at the water surface the zone of blue sky can be seen advancing from the Gulf across the St. Petersburg Peninsula. A tack toward the sea breeze may be timed to meet its first appearance along the peninsula shore.

STRATEGIC USE OF THE NORTHWESTERLY

The variations in the northwesterly which permit one boat to obtain an advantage over her competitors are differences in velocity in different portions of the course, oscillating shifts associated with the passage of the medium eddies of gust cells, and a variety of persistent shifts.

Differences in velocity are partially dependent upon proximity to shore. The surface flow is always stronger near the windward shore so that, except in extremely strong wind flows, this shore should be sought. Differences in velocity are also dependent upon the time of day. Sails and trim should be modified for the expected steady increase in velocity between morning and midafternoon and then modified again for a steady decrease in velocity from midafternoon onward.

Oscillating shifts, the major characteristic of the northwesterly, typical of all unstable airflows, must be managed by the principles indicated in the chapter "Utilization of Wind Shifts." The course to the weather mark can be significantly shortened by keeping to the tack lifted relative to the median wind. This requires tacking whenever the previously lifted tack is headed beyond the previously detected median so as to obtain the advantageous lift on the opposite tack. As distance to the side of the course from which a heading shift appears increases the gain to be achieved, it is better not to tack in a minor header or when in doubt as to whether a header has occurred. For the same reason sailing through heading shifts and continuing to a position near the layline provides an increased advantage if the final tack can be made and continued all the way to the mark in a shift to that side of the course. Once the layline is reached, however, no shift can shorten the course further and therefore such strategy entails a major risk. The stronger the wind, the shorter the interval between gust cells and therefore the less likely an oscillation will persist long enough to permit a long-approach tack in a single shift. In general the stronger the wind, the more frequently the boat should be tacked and the later the layline should be approached.

Gusts are veered and lulls are backed relative to the mean wind flow. Theoretically, therefore, gusts should provide a starboard-tack lift and lulls a port-tack lift. The outflow of a downdraft before it reaches the surface is certainly veered to the mean flow but as the gust hits the surface it spreads outward from the site of impact in a semicircular manner. A boat approaching such a gust from dead to leeward of it will receive a moderate veer usually 5° to 10° from the mean wind. A boat approaching the gust from a position to port of the gust's trajectory will receive a marked veer often up to 30° from the mean wind. This is the approach that results in capsize; the sudden appearance of a gust veered 30° to the mean wind flow (and possibly veered even more to the pre-existent lull) may completely back the jib of a boat on port tack or hit a boat on starboard tack broadside. However, a boat approaching the gust from a position to

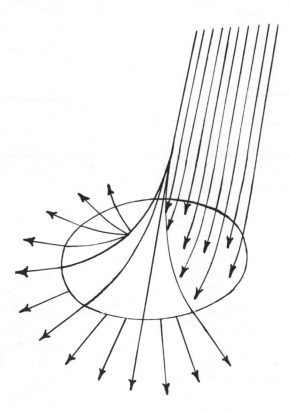

starboard of the gust's trajectory will receive a back, often a marked back (though rarely so great as the severe veer received by the boat approaching from the opposite side of the gust). Thus although starboard tack will usually be lifted in a gust, it may be headed (even severely). Lulls are backed to the mean flow but they are associated with short eddies due to surface friction and are therefore inconsistent. Changes in velocity induce changes in apparent wind direction so that *either* a lull or a gust may seem to be a back on one tack and a veer on the other. No general rule can be established to determine the preferred tack in gust–lull situations except that the preferred tack is the lifted tack. It is still possible to benefit from the probability that, in general, gusts will be veered and lulls backed, however. In light- to moderate-velocity flows, when the intervals between gust cells are prolonged, it may be possible to predict the

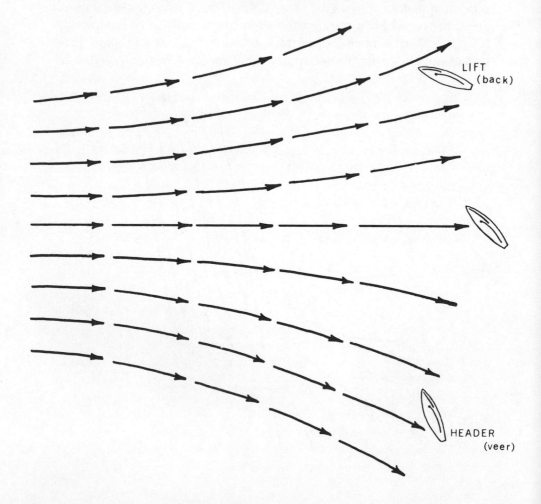

LIFT
(back)

HEADER
(veer)

likelihood of a persisting oscillation in one direction or another and to place oneself accordingly at the beginning of a windward leg. It may also be possible to predict whether a gust or lull will be present just before arrival at the weather mark and to acquire a position that will permit the final tack to be lifted.

As the strategic effects of oscillations tend to cancel each other, provided all competitors assume the lifted tack in each oscillation, the most important oscillations are those that initiate and terminate the leg. It is essential to start each windward leg on the lifted tack, and the only way this tack can be detected is by the compass. Before the start, a period of observation of starboard- and port-tack headings will permit the distinction of heading angles which are lifted. A starting plan that permits acquisition of the lifted tack immediately after the start must be undertaken. The lifted tack must also be selected at the beginning of subsequent weather legs. Any time spent on the headed tack not only takes the boat on a longer course during the duration of that tack but enters the boat into the sequence of subsequent tacks in a disadvantageous position referable to the remainder of the fleet. The compass is essential but once out on the beat, inasmuch as gust cells do not affect all boats equally or may affect some boats and not others, it is important to tack relative to competitors and not to follow slavishly the dictates of the compass. Whenever one's own tack is lifted relative to nearby competitors or to one's most significant competitors, the tack should be continued. Whenever one's own tack is headed relative to nearby competitors, when boats on the same tack are lifted relative to one's own course or boats on the opposite tack are headed relative to one's own course, the opposite tack should be assumed. In general, when the wind is strong and the interval between gusts is short or when the leg is short, tacking should be done relative to one's competitors. When an advantage is evident it should be consolidated by a tack. When a loss is imminent it should be mitigated by a tack. When the wind is light and the interval between gusts is long or when the leg is long, tacking should be done relative to the indications of the compass. Then competitiors are best ignored and the tack lifted to the median wind selected.

Two major problems exist for helmsman sailing in an oscillating northwesterly. One is reaching the layline too soon. Preoccupation with tacking in oscillations and with one's competitors may easily bring the boat to the layline far from the mark. From this position every shift benefits the opposition. It is better to sail through a

header or two to avoid reaching the layline early and to be to leeward of it near the mark. The final tack can then provide a conclusive
advantage consolidated by the rounding of the mark. The second
problem is failure to recognize a persistent shift within the maze of
oscillations. When the compass shows a lift (or a header) beyond
the range of expected oscillations, a persistent shift should be suspected. If the lifted tack is continued in a persistent shift, the boat
is sailing away from that shift and will lose progressively as she
sails away from it. If a persistent shift is suspected and/or as soon
as it is detected the boat must be sailed toward it. This means pur-
suing the headed tack longer than one's competitors or ignoring a
heading shift and continuing on into the next lift, working to the
side of the course from which the persistent shift is expected. Although oscillating shifts cancel each other, persistent shifts do not;
if a persistent shift occurs it will usually determine the outcome of
the race.

Persistent shifts are typical of the northwesterly, as typical as
oscillating shifts. The northwesterly tends to refract (slightly) more
perpendicularly off the windward shore, providing an advantage additional to enhanced velocity near that shore. It tends to be channeled (as is all cold, dense airflow) along the main axis of narrow
bodies of water, such as rivers and inlets, and around headlands protruding into a water body. This requires a position "inside at the
bend" whenever a channeled shift is expected. The northwesterly
may have such long intervals between oscillations that, for a short
beat, an oscillation becomes a persistent shift. In these circumstances
the compass is the only means of determining the advantageous tack
but its implications must be taken in reverse. If one long veer is
expected, port tack must be continued well into that veer after it is
clearly headed so as to be to starboard and inside of all competitors
when assuming the lifted starboard tack. A northwesterly may be
replaced by a sea breeze. If such a new wind is expected, one must
determine whether the next mark will remain in the northwesterly
or be overrun by the sea breeze. An appropriate position must be obtained in whichever wind will prevail. The zone of calm and erratic
shifts that intervenes between the two winds must be traversed and
subsequently avoided if the sea breeze is to prevail. It must be
avoided altogether or, if a portion of the course lies beyond it,
traversed as rapidly as possible to regain position in the northwesterly. Persistent shifts must be actively sought; preoccupation with
oscillating shifts in their presence is fatal.

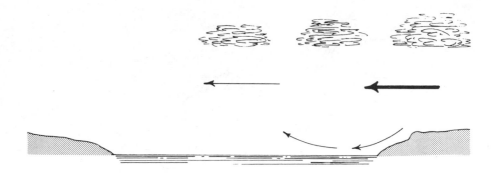

3. A High Passes to the North

"Evening gray and morning red
Make the shepherd hang his head."

After the passage of a cold front a high-pressure system dominates the region. If the center of the high passes to the north, the sequence of winds over a period of several days will be a progressive veer: northwesterly, northerly, northeasterly, easterly, and southeasterly. This is the typical pattern effected by the passage of a continental polar (cP) air mass across the mid-North American continent. Continental polar air rarely extends south of mid-United States in spring and summer and thus during the sailing season its leading edge, the cold front, approaches the east coast along an east–west axis. The first day after its arrival the wind will be the classical oscillating northwester, but as the center of the high moves eastward, the wind swings to the northeast within a day or less. Rarely in the summer does the northwester persist a second day as it characteristically does in the winter. The heated land of summer heats the polar air mass, induces rising airflows within it, and diminishes its elevated pressure, its penetration south, and the strength of its peripheral airflow. The appearance of the northeasterly indicates that the surge of the polar air south and west has been halted and that the high is passing to the north and deteriorating. Weather system winds will diminish progressively thereafter during the dominance of the polar air. After the northeaster the sailor looks to and can only hope for the local thermal wind, the sea breeze.

Memorial Day 1970 was a Friday. Early Thursday a cold front passed over Annapolis and the northwester blew throughout the day.

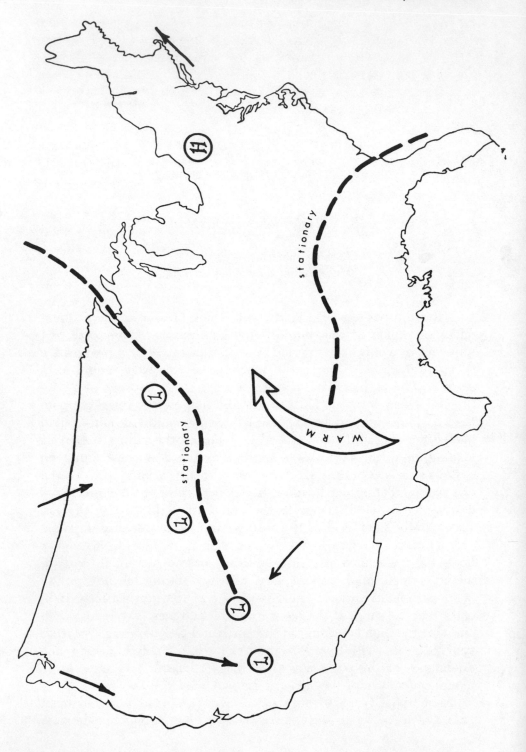

By Friday, the first day of racing for the 14's Warner Trophy, the center of the high was over New York, the sky was clear, and the wind was out of the northeast at 10–15 knots. In addition to oscillating shifts, characteristic of offshore winds in any of the northern quadrants, a persistent easterly shift of the median wind appeared and the wind diminished as the day progressed. This shift could have been due to further movement of the high, but as it was synchronous with heating of the land, it was more likely due to admixture of elements of the upper airflow with the lower. The northeasterly airflow was cold enough to reach the water surface early in the day but with increased heating of the land it was warmed, lifted, and, at the surface, progressively diminished. The now-warmed airflow was less able to invade the cushion of cold air above the water surface. Only wind brought down by thermal turbulence could reach the surface thereafter. The presence of this veered upper airflow resulted in the easterly shift. As the day began to cool the wind began to shift back to the north again, though never to its original direction, and diminished further. Reduced thermal lift-off over the cooling land resulted in less mixing of the upper airflow and therefore a backed and diminished flow at the surface. By 6:00 P.M. the wind was gone and the water a glassy calm.

We presumed that the following day would bring a good sea breeze from the southeast as the high moved farther east and its strength deteriorated further. Sea breeze flow tends to develop along the Atlantic Coast whenever high pressure brings clear skies and does not oppose the onshore flow with a strong weather system wind. To our surprise, however, the cool easterly in which we sailed to the starting line faded and by the time of the start at 11:00 A.M. there was not a breath at the surface. We lay on our backs in the bilges and watched the cumulus clouds racing overhead at about 20 knots from the east northeast. The clouds were large and rounded over the eastern shore but gradually disintegrated as they negotiated the seven-mile crossing of the Chesapeake. They were mere wisps when they crossed the western shore but began to fill out again as they moved inland. We spent the day drifting and hoping that the wind aloft would reach the surface; the racing was cancelled at 3:00 P.M. When we arrived ashore we were told that it was blowing 15 knots at the surface in the Miles River on the Eastern Shore and 10 knots at Round Bay five miles inland to the west!

The clouds explained the conditions of both Friday and Saturday. The air mass was heated progressively on Friday by radiation from

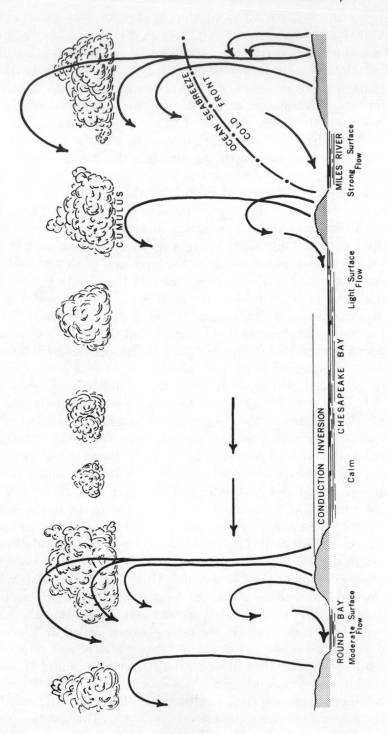

the land and never cooled to its original temperature. On Saturday the sun burnt through the morning inversion over the Eastern Shore early. Cumulus began to form by 10:00 A.M. and the easterly flow was progressively heated thereafter. Over the Eastern Shore the rising thermal columns which produced the cumulus clouds at their peak were bringing the strong upper airflow to the surface and warming the lower levels of the entire air mass. Racing would have been excellent within the Eastern Shore, on one of its rivers, or along the eastern margin of the Chesapeake on the leeward edge of the Eastern Shore. However, as that heated air flowed out over the cold, late May water of the Bay it lifted above the cold surface air and never returned to the surface until it reached the western shore. The absence of thermal generation, as evidenced by the deterioration of the cumulus, meant that no mixture of upper airflow and surface air could occur above the cold water surface. Over the western shore thermal generation again restored the upper airflow to the surface so that sailing wives at home 5 miles inland near Round Bay were amazed to hear that their husbands had been becalmed all day on the Chesapeake.

At 5:00 P.M. wisps of an easterly began to appear at the surface and by 7:00 there was a good sailing breeze. The day had begun to cool and a subsidence inversion had presumably begun to re-form over the Eastern Shore before 5:00. The warm upper airflow, excluded from the cool water surface all day, was even less able to reach the surface after thermal generation had ceased. A new wind source had appeared, bringing a cold airflow beneath the inversion across the Eastern Shore—the sea breeze had arrived. This was, of course, the ocean sea breeze bringing cold air from the Atlantic, a cold front burrowing beneath the warm weather system airflow and forcing its way across thirty miles of the Eastern Shore finally to arrive at the Chesapeake in early evening. This cold air, derived from the frigid North Atlantic of May, was dense enough to mix with the pool of surface air that had remained undisturbed between the eastern and western shores of the Chesapeake all day long. We had our breeze, and it was the sea breeze we had expected, but it had come far too late to do us any good.

Sunday dawned hazy but warm and clear. The center of the high was far away off the coast to the northeast and there was little strength left in it. The rising air columns associated with three days of clear skies and heated land had reduced the high pressure, the isobars were far apart, and there was little pressure gradient left to

produce a weather system wind. By 10:00 A.M., however, the wind
was steady at 5 knots from the southeast and increased steadily
thereafter to a peak of 15 at 3:00 P.M. The residue of weather system
wind was around to the southeast and the cool, low-level sea breeze
was up and flowing early in the day. This was, of course, the local
sea breeze, the movement of cold air from the water surface of the
Bay toward the heating land. On Saturday decreased pressure over
the land created by thermal generation had been restored by weather
system airflow. A strong flow from the east northeast carried the rising, heated air away inland. On Sunday, without a strong weather
system flow to maintain pressure ashore, heated air spread aloft
toward the unheated Bay and required surface movement toward
the shore. Onshore flow along the upper Chesapeake's western shore
aligned with the residual weather system southeasterly to provide
the best sailing of the weekend.

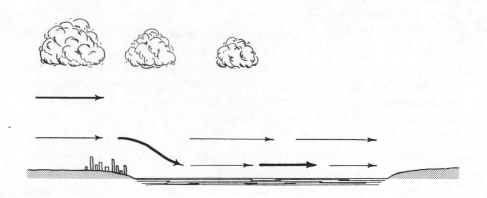

4. A High Passes to the South

"A red morn, that ever yet betoken'd
Wrack to the seaman, tempest to the field,
Sorrow to shepherds, woe unto the birds;
Gusts and foul flaws to herdmen and to herds."

On a Friday in July we drove from Annapolis to Ottawa and
passed through the entire range of sailing opportunities in that single
day. The eastern United States lay under a mass of mTg air flowing

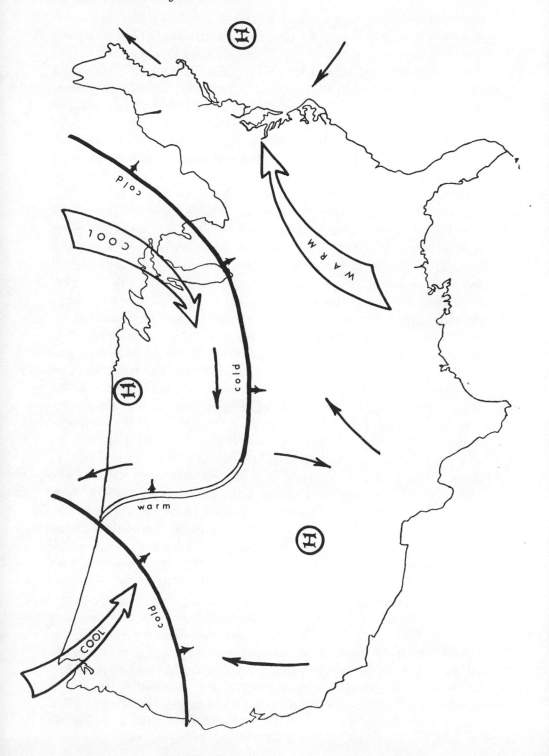

northeastward behind a high-pressure center off the Virginia coast.
A cold front was crossing the Great Lakes trailing behind a depression in the St. Lawrence Valley. The southerly flow of mTg air on
the back of the high was urged on by the southwesterly flow to the
south of the low. Pennsylvania and New York were in the warm
sector. The air had been clear the night before and surface cooling
had been marked. Early in the morning nothing stirred beneath the
radiation inversion. Farther aloft stratocumulus filled the sky beneath a subsidence inversion. We drove through Pennsylvania in a
dead calm. By 9:00 A.M. the radiation inversion had undoubtedly
dissipated but there was still no wind. North of Binghamton, N.Y.,
at about 10:00 A.M., the sky began to clear and a southwesterly of
about 8–10 knots appeared at the surface. The subsidence inversion
had broken aloft and the upper-level weather system flow was being
brought to the surface by thermal turbulence. As we approached
Syracuse an hour later, the stratocumulus had become dense overhead once again and the wind had died completely. Farther north
the cloud cover was burning off and there was a light southwesterly
blowing across the surface of Lake Oneida. As we approached Wa-
tertown and the eastern shore of Lake Ontario, the wind veered and
strengthened. Within a few miles of the lake the sky was clear and
the wind was westerly, sweeping inland at 20 knots. This was the
lake breeze strongly reinforced by the southwesterly warm-sector
flow and its upper-level circulation was dissolving the stratocumulus. As we crossed the Ivy Lea Bridge at 2:00 P.M. the St.
Lawrence was being whipped to a blue-and-white frenzy by the
Kingston lake breeze, funneling down the valley. At Ottowa the
westerly was blowing hard across Lake Deschennes and by 6:00
P.M. the first rain squall preceding the cold front had appeared.

Rain fell throughout Friday night but early Saturday morning
rifts in the cloud cover were appearing, as downdrafts, heated by
compression, evaporated the nimbostratus. The first race was held
in a markedly oscillating 10- to 12-knot northwesterly and the afternoon race in a steadier 20 knots under clear skies. On Sunday cumulus cloud streets were forming over the Gatineau Hills and sweeping
over the lake. At the surface the wind was down to 12–14 knots
backed about 20° to its Saturday direction and oscillating as markedly as it had on Saturday morning. As the new cP high moved past
to the south the wind backed to the west and by Monday was in the
southwest as a new cold front approached across the Great Lakes.
Again the eastern United States received an inflow of mTg air

pulled up from the Gulf behind the high and squeezed ahead of a cold front.

This sequence is typical of east coast summer. Continental polar air periodically invades the area behind successive cold fronts. Each invasion penetrates less deeply than its predecessor until in August the mTg air lingers for days on end before a weak cold front briefly pushes it out into the Atlantic. In June and July the cP highs drift easterly across New York and New England. For the Chesapeake this is high pressure to the north and the wind sequence veering north-west, north, northeast to east. For Long Island Sound it is high pressure overhead with little pressure-gradient wind at any level, glassy calm at the surface, and long waits for the only sailing wind possible, the sea breeze. At Marblehead it is high pressure to the south and, as the high moves out to sea, the probability of a southerly sea breeze reinforced by the pressure-gradient wind. In the St. Lawrence Valley it is high pressure to the south, a southwesterly flow across Lake Ontario, and the mighty Kingston lake breeze roaring through the Thousand Islands. There is good sailing someplace along the eastern seaboard on every spring and summer day. If we sailors were more mobile, we could reach one of these sites on every racing day and avoid the drifting matches of our home waters.

The simple wind sequence of high pressure passing to the south is backing—northwest, west, southwest to south. As many of our sailing sites have westerly, southwesterly, or southerly seabreezes this sequence provides good racing. Unfortunately, the sequence is infrequently so simple. On only two occasions during June and July 1971 was the passage of a cold front followed by this simple sequence as high pressure dominated the coast for three or more days. Cold fronts rarely penetrate farther south than Georgia at this season and sometimes falter long before they reach Virginia. On one occasion during this period in 1971 the cold front was halted by the northward thrust of maritime tropical Gulf air, became a warm front, and drifted back up the coast. For several days thereafter, as an mTg high lingered off the coast of the Carolinas, a southwesterly flow of hot, humid air depressed the northeast. Where the sea breeze is southerly, as it is in the Chesapeake, a strong southerly or south-westerly surface wind resulted. The wind sequence was northwest, north and east followed by the warm front passage and then south-west. On two other occasions during this period the cold front was of the "backdoor" variety. On these occasions continental polar air pushed south to the east of a depression which had stalled over the

Great Lakes. The warm front ahead of the low became a cold front, the cP air pushed down the coast until halted by the pressure of mTg air to the south and once again warm air rose over cold, and the front, reconverted to warm, once again retreated to the north. The wind sequence in these circumstances was west followed by the cold front passage, northwest and northeast, followed by the warm front passage, and west or southwest once again.

On two occasions the cold front disintegrated over the east coast as the cP air behind it became as warm as the mTg air ahead. The east coast experienced moderate to strong southerly airflow for three or four days and frequent afternoon thunderstorms. In some areas the strong heating of the surface resulted in sea breeze development sufficient to overcome the southwesterly weather system flow. Within Maryland's eastern shore at Cambridge on one of these days a 6-knot westerly was replaced by a 12- to 15-knot southerly as the ocean sea breeze filled in at about 3:30 P.M. Occasionally a new low formed along the cold front either under the influence of strong heating inland over Ohio or Kentucky or due to the addition of moisture as the front moved off the coast. Once established these lows migrated slowly up the coast resulting in "three-day northeasters." On two occasions a stationary front of cP air was precisely balanced by the northward thrust of mTg air.

For the greatest portion of the summer the eastern United States lies between a frontal system approaching along a southwest–northeast axis and a disintegrating high off the coast. The resultant flow of air from the Gulf produces the heat, humidity, and advection inversions typical of east coast summer. Inversions—conduction (at the water surface in early summer), radiation, advection, and subsidence—may persist throughout the day. Then the weather system wind will be excluded from the surface and the only surface wind will be the sea breeze, arriving erratically and disappearing and reappearing with the sequential breakthrough of each inversion. Once the inversions have broken, the weather system southwesterly may be brought to the surface by thermal turbulence, usually late in the afternoon. The strongest wind of summer in the Chesapeake is the southwesterly, a weather system flow aloft combined with a low level, veered southerly *Bay* sea breeze. The easterly *ocean* sea breeze along the Jersey coast and over Maryland's eastern shore opposes the summer weather system flow and thus abruptly replaces it (pushing a zone of calm ahead) in late afternoon. Both breezes may be strong on the same day. The weather system westerly provides an upper-level outflow toward the water which stimulates the sea breeze circulation and results in its own exclusion from the surface.

As a frontal system to the northwest approaches the coast the southwesterly airflow is compressed ahead of it and the southwesterly wind at the surface is increased in velocity. Often the strongest southwesterly is present when a depression formed in the frontal system (often over the Great Lakes) passes close to the north of the sailing site which then lies in its warm sector. On the Chesapeake, we expect our best southwesterly, the combined flow of weather system wind and sea breeze, to appear when the area lies in the warm sector of a low over Lake Erie or just ahead of a cold or stationary front and on the upper back of a high off the Carolina coast.

We had some fine racing under these conditions on the last weekend of July 1971. A stationary front settled along a line from Louisiana to New York and lay just to the west of the Chesapeake. Warm mTg air flowed rapidly parallel to and ahead of this front from the southwest. On both days the weather system air was down to the surface at 10:00 A.M. after dissipation of the radiation inversion. The Chesapeake was sufficiently warm and the airflow sufficiently turbulent, due to both mechanical and convective effects, that the wind in the sailing layer was 8–10 knots by the start of each day's racing at 11:00 A.M. There were holes in it and small oscillations, chiefly due to the persistence of a patchy conduction inversion over the water, the temperature of which remained at about 70° F. beneath an airflow of 85° F. The median wind was about 250° with some infrequent and irregular oscillations about 10° either side, probably associated with convective disturbances ashore. By midafternoon on Saturday large cumulonimbus clouds were forming inland to the northwest and showers were occurring nearby. Such thunderstorm activity is characteristic of the rapid lifting ahead of an advancing cold front and the ingress of very moist Gulf air ahead of a stationary front. As the convective activity increased at about 4:00 P.M. the southwesterly assumed a couple of large oscillations, gasped, deteriorated, recovered, and then died. To the south the ocean sea breeze could be seen advancing up the Bay, a hard line of dark water with a narrow zone of calm ahead of it. The wind backed to about 210°, the standard ocean sea breeze direction off Annapolis, and filled in to a solid, steady 15 knots.

On Sunday the wind was backed (relative to Saturday) to about 200° and was 10–12 knots by race time, 11:00 A.M. This wind resembled the ocean sea breeze but during the starting sequence for seven classes its direction backed further to about 180°. The early wind had been the southwesterly weather system flow, more southerly because of a kink in the front, and the back was the appearance of the local western shore Bay sea breeze. This breeze, at 180°, built and backed further to about 170° during the course of the first race as convective activity ashore increased and the local sea breeze (usual direction 165°–190°) strengthened. Between races, at about 1:00 P.M., a corner of a thunderstorm passed over the racing area and behind it the sea breeze built to 15 knots at approximately 170°. A modest veer to 180° became apparent by the last round due to the velocity increase. We went out for a sail in the Soling at about 5:30 P.M. because the breeze looked so great and by this time the wind was around to 200°. The ocean sea breeze had amalgamated with the local sea breeze and the weather system wind. Huge cumulonimbus heads towered behind us as we sailed southeast into bright sunlight and a glorious 18- to 20-knot southwester.

This was the best of summer sailing on the Chesapeake, a combined seabreeze/weather system southwesterly. The weather system flow was strong because the isobars were compressed close to the front. The sea breeze was strong because the convective activity ashore was so great. Heated columns were rising tens of thousands of feet into the air in each cumulonimbus tower and dozens were present. Most of this activity was drifting away to the northeast under the influence of the southwesterly weather system flow but heated air was constantly being fed into the sea breeze circulation at a few thousand feet as well. As each cumulonimbus passed nearby, additional heated air was added aloft to the high pressure over the Bay and low-level outflow was sucked into the surface low pressure ashore. Beyond the towers the spreading warm air aloft melted the cloud so that we could sail and race in bright sunshine, while ashore the "wind machines" heated, condensed, and generated great whirlpools in the air.

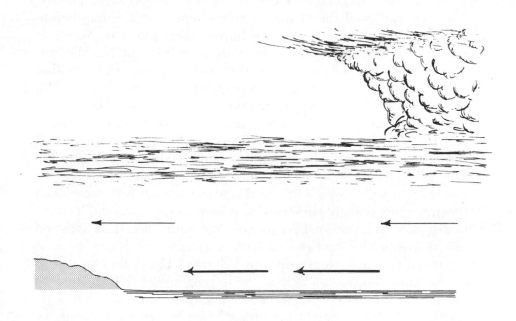

5. The Three-Day Northeaster

"A nor'wester brings a short storm,
A nor'easter brings a long storm."

There are people who shudder when they detect low pressure coming up the coast. They don't appreciate the heavy, overcast skies, the damp chill, the rain and the strong, relentless wind. To my mind the only wind better is a sea breeze in the spring (but the sea breeze is undependable) or a northwester in the winter (but the winter northwester is frigid).

On three successive weekends in May 1971, we raced at Annapolis in a northeaster. On the first weekend we had but one day of northeaster to race in but it was still present on Monday. The following weekend the northeaster arrived on Friday evening and continued until midday Sunday. On the final weekend the northeaster again appeared on Friday but this time it persisted until Monday, a full, classic northeaster. This was the best of racing—

dependably strong, steady winds, cool air, and relatively little sea for the strength of the breeze.

On the first weekend we raced in the 14 for the Avenger Trophy. They had called off the racing for the Tempests and Snipes before we started at about noon. In the harbor the wind was gusty but periodically light. We beat to a buoy up river from the Naval Academy and then reached down the harbor and out into the Bay. Within the harbor the wind averaged 10 knots with an occasional gust to 15, but as we passed Greenbury Point and entered the open Chesapeake, it abruptly increased to 25. One boat which had been close astern and 100 feet to leeward was left far astern thereafter as her wind did not increase until she had sailed considerably farther into the Bay. We had taken the lead at the beginning of the reach and increased it rapidly as, sailing into the stronger wind first, we planed down the increasingly large waves. Before we rounded the leeward mark, three miles down river, almost the entire fleet had capsized astern. We headed up the beat with a quarter mile lead. The next leg was a four-mile thrash up into Whitehall Creek in a steady 25 knots. The compass showed a small geographic shift related to channeling around Greenbury Point but there were absolutely no oscillations. Unfortunately the boom broke before we entered the more sheltered creek and we were forced to retire. The remainder of the fleet found the wind considerably decreased and fluctuating markedly in the creek, but the gale was still present when they reentered the Bay on the trip back.

We raced the Soling on the two subsequent weekends but on these occasions the racing was entirely on the Olympic Circle in open water. For an hour at a time the wind didn't shift more than 2° but it did vary in velocity between 15 and 20 knots. About four o'clock on the first Saturday, after the racing was over, a squall appeared and wind above 40 knots blew the tops off the white caps, although not a drop of rain fell. The squall persisted for about twenty minutes with winds veered about 10°. It dissipated gradually and the wind returned to its original direction. On the third weekend during the first round of Saturday's first race the northeaster was as steady as before but during the second round it veered about 10° as it increased in velocity. On Sunday it was the same old northeaster, cloudy skies and occasional drizzle, but backed about 10° from its Saturday direction. On both days it was slightly veered where the Bay was more completely open to the east of the course and a gradual header could be perceived as one held a long starboard tack to the west to escape the ebbing current.

Northeasters are characteristic of spring and early summer along the east coast. They are the consequence of low pressure developing over the mid-continent or the Gulf and subsequently moving off the Georgia or Carolina coast. This track is rarely evident in winter when the polar front is far south and low pressure moves out into the Atlantic off Florida, or in late summer or fall when the polar front is far north and low pressure from the Great Lakes moves down the St. Lawrence Valley. The Atlantic is cooler than the land in spring and summer and provides little support for low-pressure generation. Therefore, once low pressure moves off the coast at this time of the year it tends to deviate parallel to the coast. As low pressure migrating up the coast encounters colder and colder water and eventually meets the Labrador Current, it slows progressively. Off Maryland it hovers for a day or two, rarely three; off New England it often settles in for a "three-day northeaster."

To the north of these offshore lows the flow is from the east and along the coast from the northeast. As the low approaches from the south, the wind, usually in the south or southwest, backs progressively into the southeast, east, northeast, and finally north. Near the center of the low, where the isobars are tight, the wind at the surface, the gradient wind, blows directly into the low, and along the nearby coast this is a northerly or even a northwester. As the low approached on the final Soling weekend of May we noticed this back. On Saturday when the low was off the Carolinas starboard tack had been 350°; on Sunday when the low had moved up just off the Maryland coast starboard tack was headed to 330°.

High cloud, cirrus and cirrocumulus, appears when the low is about 500 miles away, to be replaced by altostratus as it approaches. Close to the center low stratus and stratocumulus fill the sky and drizzle begins to fall. After the low has passed and the wind backs west of north, showers and rain squalls appear in its wake. The easterly and northeasterly flow is stable, relatively cool air from the cool ocean flowing over colder land. The cloud cover prevents the usual diurnal heating of the land and thus blocks any instability that might otherwise be induced in the cool air flow. The northeasterly flow along the coast is strong because it is close to the center of the low and steady because it is stable. As the low passes farther to the north the flow along the coast becomes northerly or even northwest-

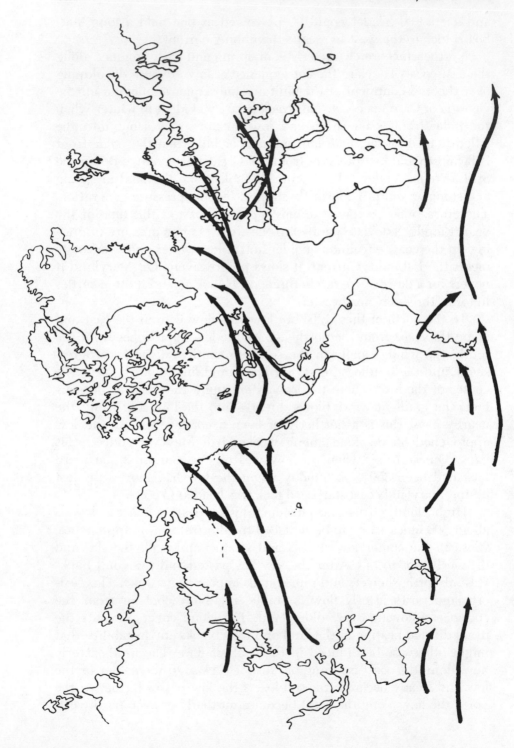

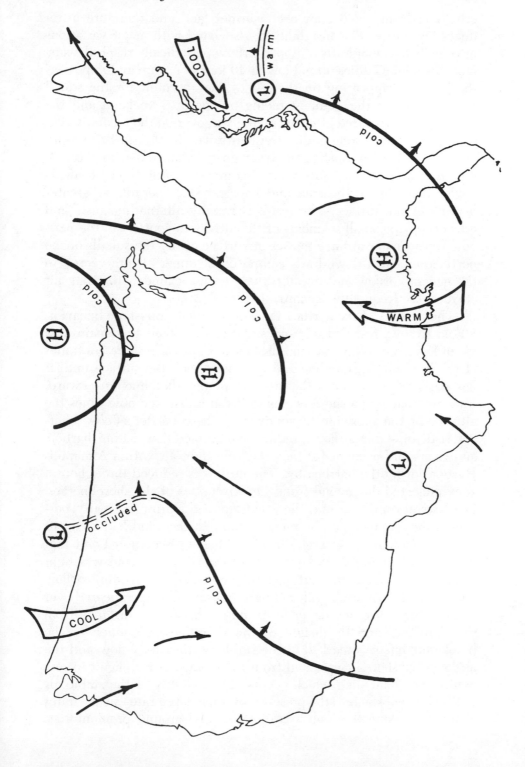

erly. This brings colder air over warmer land and therefore introduces instability. This instability is associated with major variations in velocity as downdrafts of upper airflow periodically reach the surface. Such long eddies often blow at 40 knots or more and appear as the low is disappearing up the coast. They account for the squall which blew out the Tempest racing on the first weekend and the squall which appeared after the racing was over on the second weekend of May. Such long eddies frequently last for ten to thirty minutes, in marked contrast to the brief gusts associated with the outflow northwester. The northwester, composed entirely of cP air, is colder than the northeaster, and its clear skies permit far greater heating of the surface. The result is rapidly alternating gusts and lulls occupying small segments of the airflow in contrast to the periodic replacement of huge masses of surface air by the squalls of the northeaster. Such downdrafts composed of upper air are veered to the general airflow and because they are associated with rising air currents are frequently accompanied by showers.

The stability of the northeaster determines its longshore behavior. Stable airflows resist lifting and sinking; they tend to remain at a given level and to flow around obstacles. Flow off a shore continues at the level of the shoreline and does not reach the surface until it has passed twenty times the altitude of the shoreline to leeward. Flow approaching a shore begins to lift at a distance nine times the altitude of the shoreline to windward. These barrier effects, characteristic of stable airflows, reduce the surface flow within harbors and rivers and account for the relatively light air within Annapolis Harbor during the northeaster. The airflow is reduced throughout a zone projected downwind from the extremities of the shoreline and increases abruptly beyond these extremities. During the early portion of the Avenger Trophy race we thought the wind had died but found as soon as we emerged from the lee of Greenbury Point that it was still blowing at 25 knots. Up in the river the wind was light but an occasional downdraft gust appeared as the overriding airflow eddied to the surface. Significant variations in velocity appeared over a small-distance range dependent upon variations in distance from the shorelines and the height of the shorelines. Inasmuch as the blanketing effect is marked in the stable northeasterly flow and the airflow near shore is separated from the surface, it is difficult to recognize the channeling which occurs. The inability of the stable air to lift above obstacles (the presence of a low lapse rate) necessitates channeling along the long axis of rivers and around promontories.

We noticed a modest difference between the direction of flow in the river (more in line with its long axis) and in the open Bay (veered to the general flow).

Squalls are associated with the nearby passage of the low and therefore although they are veered they follow a period of gradual backing. Veering is also associated with any increase in velocity which occurs during the period of stable airflow prior to the passage of the low. Over open water where airflow is less impeded by friction the wind is veered relative to its inshore direction. On each day of the northeaster we found that the farther we moved from the shore toward the open Bay, the more the wind was veered. Oscillations are scarcely evident; persistent shifts of small amplitude are typical.

6. The Thunderstorm

*"When the peacock loudly bawls
Soon we'll have both rain and squalls."*

Along the United States East Coast thunderstorms appear in the midst of hot, sultry mTg air, usually following a period of calm. Inland, particularly in the Mississippi Valley and across the southeastern states, thunderstorms appear ahead of cold fronts as cP air sweeps down from Canada pushing and lifting the hot Gulf air ahead. Such thunderstorms appearing ahead of a "Texas norther" may be the only sailing wind available to midwestern lake sailors. When cold air is moist, as it is when coming in from the sea, or when the land is very warm, as it is in September, thunderstorms may appear *behind* a cold front. Then lovely fair-weather cumulus become cumulonimbus and gentle showers are transformed into fierce squalls.

Thunderstorms are the ultimate form of convection. Tons of air and moisture are lifted 40,000–60,000 feet into the stratosphere and then dashed to earth at 50–75 knots. The basic ingredients are those of all convection: unstable air, a heated surface, and moisture. A high lapse rate (instability), a decrease in temperature with height of greater than 1° C/100 meters, is essential. A high lapse rate is composed of a hot surface to heat the surface air (usually to temperatures above 80° F.) and/or a cold air mass aloft. Parcels of air separate from the heated surface and rise through the cooler air above. So long as the temperature of the rising air remains above that of the surrounding air the parcel will continue to rise. Although air near a heated surface often has a lapse rate greater than the adiabatic which facilitates the lifting of the surface air, air at some higher level will usually have a lapse rate less than the adiabatic. When the rising air meets such a change in lapse rate its upward progress will be halted. Continued upward progress is then dependent upon a reduction in the lapse rate of the rising air. This is achievable if the rising air is moist and if it can rise sufficiently so that it cools to its dew point. The heat released in condensation and cumulus cloud formation reduces the lapse rate of the rising air to about two-thirds the dry adiabatic rate. The rising air continues warmer than its surroundings. Billows of new condensation on the upper surface of a cumulus cloud demonstrate its continued upward progress.

The reduced pressure induced by the first column of rising air attracts additional updrafts into the base of the cumulus if surface heating is sufficient. Soon, if the lapse rate of the surrounding air is sufficiently great, many columns or cells of rising air are attracted into the base of the cumulus cloud as it moves over the heated landscape. Early in the afternoon cumulus clouds, forming above the dewpoint level, at about 5000 feet, evaporate rapidly but add additional moisture to the upper air. The rising central core of the cumulus entrains additional air from alongside the column. If this air is moist it condenses additional cloud in the rising column. Eventually a persistent, billowing "cumulus congestus" may form over a column or group of columns of rising air a mile in diameter. Small water droplets bombard each other in the updrafts until large supercooled droplets form above 25,000 feet. A thunderstorm is underway as the updraft boils out of the top of the cumulus congestus to 30,000–40,000–50,000 feet and on into the stratosphere. Surface air from within an eight-mile radius is drawn into the base of the cloud, sucked up its central core, out its top, and down its sides.

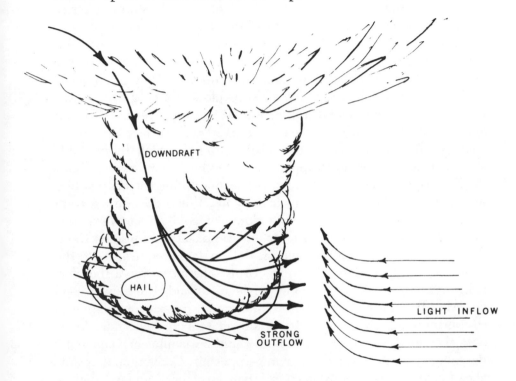

The supercooled water drops eventually freeze and hail forms within the updraft. When the weight of the large droplets and hail exceeds the upthrust of the rising air, a downdraft of droplets, ice, and air commences. Because the downdraft heats by compression as it descends the droplets and ice begin to evaporate and cool the surrounding air. Thereafter the downdraft heats at the moist adiabatic rate, considerably less rapidly than the surrounding air. As it descends the air in the downdraft becomes progressively colder and denser than the air surrounding it. Thus the downdraft accelerates until it roars out on the surface at 50 to 75 knots. An anvil of ice crystals is blown off the top of the huge cumulonimbus cloud by the upper-level westerlies as the updraft dissipates into the stratosphere.

Fifteen to thirty minutes after the development of the cumulus congestus the updraft blows itself out into the stratosphere and thereafter the thunderstorm is all downdraft. The cold surface blast and heavy rain change to a moderate breeze and drizzle. In another twenty to thirty minutes the entire cumulonimbus has evaporated. The local surface temperature has dropped ten or more degrees but nothing else remains of the giant storm.

Under certain circumstances instead of a single storm, a series of thunderstorms, a squall line, develops. These are vicious storms, far more dangerous and far more long-lasting than the single-cell variety. They usually appear when lifting is occurring for other reasons and when the air is particularly unstable. They often occur as warm air is lifted by the cold air snowplow of a cold front crossing the heated continental midsection. When an inversion is lifted ahead of a cold front or broken by marked surface heating, an extremely unstable air mass may result through which thermal lift occurs readily. Moisture trapped beneath the inversion lid is suddenly dissipated throughout the upper air inhibiting the evaporation of condensed moisture is rising air columns. When downdrafts from a single-cell thunderstorm push a dome of cold air outward, this miniature cold front lifts warm air and propagates additional thunderstorms ahead of it. Strong winds aloft may also contribute to the continuous propagation of thunderstorms. The air within a thunderstorm is a mixture of entrained upper-level air and rising lower-level air. Aloft the cloud is slowed in its horizontal movement relative to the surrounding air by updrafts of slower moving lower air. At its base the cloud is stimulated to more rapid horizontal movement by downdrafts of more rapidly moving upper air. Convergence results ahead of the more rapidly moving lower levels of the cloud. Divergence results ahead of the more slowly moving upper levels of the cloud. The effect is to stimulate rising air columns ahead of the storm and to suppress them behind it. If the surrounding air is unstable and moist, the cold outflow at the thunderstorm's base, the inversion ahead, and the wind shear aloft combine together to propagate storm after storm, the squall line.

SURFACE WINDS

The surface wind begins to be affected by a thunderstorm when it is approximately six to eight miles away. Convergence begins at this distance as a slow deep movement of surface air moves toward

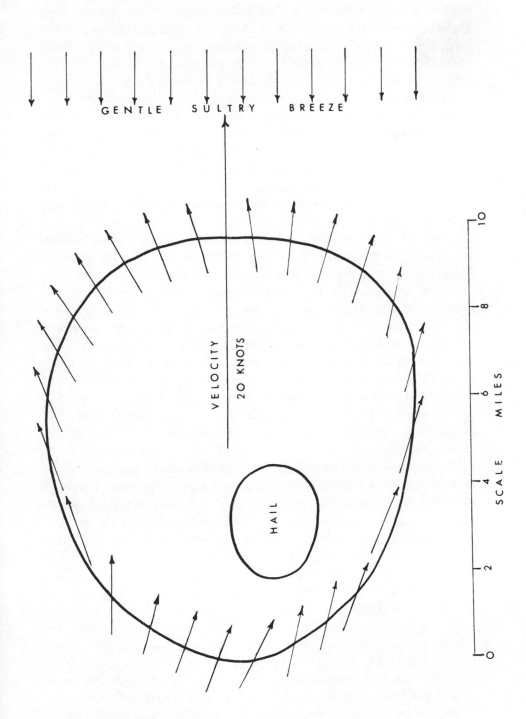

the low pressure beneath the cumulus congestus. If the surface wind has been toward the storm, as it is likely to be if a sea breeze is flowing onshore toward the site of convection, the surface wind will be strengthened. The development of thunderstorms inland is often an excellent stimulant of a weak sea breeze or one that has been kept from the surface by an offshore wind or has been obstructed by wind shear. If the pre-existing surface wind is away from the storm or perpendicular to its course, it will be diminished by the approaching storm and a zone of calm may result that will persist for ten to twenty minutes until the downdraft appears. In any case a zone of calm and erratic shifts can be expected immediately ahead of the downdraft as the cold outflow ahead of the storm converges with the surface wind.

The storm moves in the direction of its "steering winds" which are usually westerly at about 15,000–20,000 feet. The direction of movement of the storm will determine the duration of calm at a given site inasmuch as the zone of convergence extends six to eight miles in all directions from the storm center. The dome of dense cold air flowing out from the base of a mature thunderstorm which follows the calm is usually about 2000 to 5000 feet deep. Its strongest winds, flowing out from the storm center, may be 50 to 75 knots at an altitude of about 1000 feet. The duration of the downdraft is related to the quantity of rain or hail brought to the surface and varies from two to twenty minutes at a given surface site. The edge of the dome moves forward at about 15 knots or about five miles in twenty minutes.

When a cumulus congestus or cumulonimbus appears on the horizon, the first essential is to determine its trajectory. This will be in the direction of the steering winds aloft and in the temperate zone this usually means that the storm will advance in an easterly or northeasterly direction. If its trajectory will take it parallel to or away from the course, its only effect will be the reinforcement of a pre-existing wind toward the storm or a reduction of a pre-existing wind away from it. If its trajectory will bring it over the course, an abrupt reduction in wind flow as the storm approaches within about two miles will be followed by approximately three to five minutes of calm and erratic shifting. The boat must be worked toward the storm during the period prior to the calm so as to receive the downdraft ahead of the fleet. This is particularly important if the leg is already a beat and the downdraft will result in a continued beat with a persistent shift. The first evidence of outflow appears cold and strong, fully capable of capsizing a small boat which is unprepared, and slightly backed to the trajectory of the storm. It flows outward in all directions from the base of the storm but is deviated by the updraft at the storm's center in a counterclockwise direction. Therefore as the downdraft flows overhead it veers. The boat, kept between the fleet and the storm and on starboard tack initially, to benefit from the backed flow, must be tacked to port immediately after the arrival of the downdraft so as to accommodate the progressive veer. If the storm passes directly overhead the wind will rapidly drop in velocity to be followed by a period of complete calm under its center. The appropriate maneuver is to get as far "up-storm" as possible before the wind dies. The boat farthest up in the storm's center will be the first to receive the new wind on the storm's back.

If the trajectory of the storm carries it to starboard of the course, the wind will decrease in intensity but remain strong and veer gradually. If the windward mark remains to windward, port tack to windward of the fleet should be selected and continued in the progressive veer, a persistent shift. If the trajectory of the storm carries it to port of the course, the wind will back slightly and then veer rapidly as the center passes. Port tack is again the initially favored tack in this set of oscillating shifts to take advantage of the initial back, and a tack to starboard appropriate as the center passes and the wind veers. The flow behind the storm is almost perpendicular to its trajectory flowing from starboard to port (veered to its course). If the storm has been encountered on the beat this marked change in direction will turn the leg into a reach. The ideal position to deal with this shift is to leeward of the fleet, providing a close reach into the mark. Following passage of the center of the storm and a reduction in wind velocity, starboard tack should be assumed as this will place the boat to leeward in the final veer—of almost 90°. Behind the storm a zone of calm appears again between the downdraft outflow at its rear and the slow-moving flow converging toward it. Eventually the pre-existing wind returns. If an inversion has blocked surface flow prior to the storm the first wind of the day (other than the storm wind) may appear as the inversion is broken by the thunderstorm. This will be either the weather system wind from aloft or a strong sea breeze induced by the increased convection associated with thunderstorm development.

The sequence of maneuvers associated with successful use of a thunderstorm is as follows:

1. If its trajectory will cause it to pass near but not cross the race course, sail away from it so as to avoid the calm zone between the pre-existing wind and its downdraft.

2. If its trajectory will cause it to pass over the race course, sail toward it so as to receive its downdraft ahead of the remainder of the fleet.

   a. Sail on starboard tack so as to position oneself as far toward the storm center as possible before the zone of calm appears.

   b. As soon as the downdraft appears an initial back relative to the storm's trajectory will cause starboard tack to be headed and require a tack to port.

   c. Continue on port until the wind diminishes significantly (until the center can be presumed to have passed). If the storm passes to starboard the wind will veer progressively and port tack will be carrying the boat *toward* the new wind in a progressive shift. If the storm passes to port the wind will back farther after its initial back and port tack will be the lifted tack in an oscillating wind flow.

   d. As the center passes tack back to starboard, which should be progressively lifted in the persistent veer if the storm is passing to starboard, or the oscillating veer if the storm is passing to port.

4. Keep to leeward of the fleet after the storm passes, as an approximately 90° veer can be expected on its back which will cause a beat to become a reach.

5. Expect a zone of calm immediately behind the storm followed by the return or first appearance of the weather system wind or sea breeze thereafter. If the leg will continue to be a beat or become a beat, position oneself upwind of the fleet in the expected wind. If the leg will continue to be a reach or run or become a reach or run, position oneself downwind of the fleet in the expected wind.

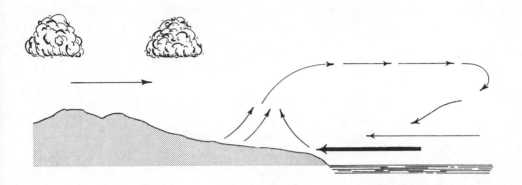

B. The Sea Breeze

Local thermal winds.
The simple onshore sea breeze.
Anabatic influences.
Sea breeze flow over interposed land.
Strong sea breezes associated with cold currents.
Sea breezes and inversions.
Combined ocean and bay sea breezes.
Onset and offset of the sea breeze.

1. The Nature of the Sea Breeze

"Glimpse you ere the green ray
Count the morrow a fine day."

Each day the temperature of the land changes periodically with the rising of the sun and the falling of darkness. The increase in the temperature of the air overlying heated land initiates a circulation which will be maintained in the presence of cool water. Water is thermostable; its temperature remains at some median level between the nocturnal and diurnal temperatures of the land. Redistribution of heated air from over the land adds to pre-existing high pressure, induced by cool, dense air, over the water. If vertically circular flow between low pressure above the heat source ashore and high pressure over the water can be maintained, the sea breeze will appear and the heat of the sun will maintain the flow. Every body of water will develop a sea breeze flow under circumstances peculiar to the geography of its shoreline.

Initiation of the sea breeze due to the rising temperature of the land:

1. Induction.

    Clear sky permits exposure of the land to sunlight.

    Uniform surfaces—sand, paving, grass—enhance thermal generation.

    Dark surfaces—plowed fields, asphalt—enhance thermal generation.

    Hills facing the sun are heated earlier and to a greater degree than flat surfaces.

2. Pressure change in the overlying air.

    Overlying air is heated by conduction and by convection.

    Generation of thermals—segments of heated air intermittently separate from the heated surface.

    Separation ("lift-off") is enhanced by the disparity between the temperature of the surface and the temperature of overlying air. Cold airflow enhances separation.

    Separation is correlated with increasing heating of the land —late morning or early afternoon.

    Anabatic flow—movement of surface air up hill sides— facilitates thermal lift-off as heated air is carried to higher altitudes where surrounding air is cooler.

    Flat, uniform surfaces along the shore with hills rising a few miles inland provide optimal conditions for thermal generation.

    Thermal generation heats the overlying air causing it to become less dense—a higher column therefore contains the same weight of air—and pressure at a given level aloft *rises.*

    A mass of air whose upper levels are at higher pressure develops over the heated land. The upper-level high pressure is constantly regenerated by heating from below.

3. Cumulus cloud development demonstrates thermal lift-off.

    Heated air cools as it rises and is unable to contain as much

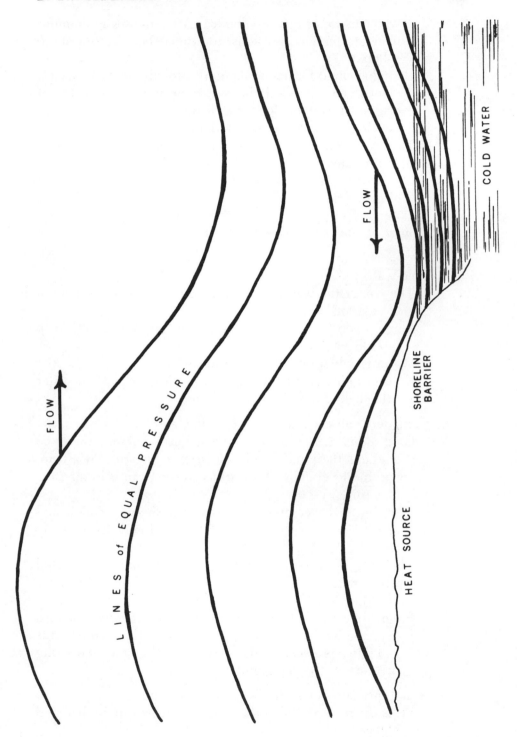

water in vapor form. Water vapor condenses in cumulus cloud formation and adds additional heat to the atmosphere.

Cumulus cloud formation demonstrates thermal lift-off. (If clouds move toward the water or hover over sites of origin—mountain ridges, dark surfaces, etc.—sea breeze development may be expected.)

Thunderstorm production (massive thermal lift-off from inland sites) is a major inducer of the sea breeze and a sign of its development (if the thunderstorm itself is not affecting the local area).

Development of the sea breeze due to the low temperature of the water:

1. Cold water.

    The colder the water the greater the likelihood of thermal circulation.

    Large, deep bodies of water—oceans, large lakes—tend to be colder.

    Water is colder in the winter and spring.

    Cold currents, flood tides, and upwelling of bottom water bring colder water to the shoreline.

2. Cold, dense air accumulates over cold water.

    Cold air is denser than warm—a lower column therefore contains the same weight of air, and pressure at a comparable level above the surface is *lower* in cold air than in warm.

    A trough of lower pressure exists over the water aloft and changes little with heating of the land and its overlying air.

    The rising mass of warming air over the land is associated with lower pressure at comparable levels over the water and therefore flows out over the water at upper levels.

    Progressive transfer of air from the rising heated columns over the land to the dense trough over the water results in falling pressure at the surface of the land and rising pressure at the surface of the water.

3. A high-pressure dome develops over the water.

    Pressure rises at the surface and increases at higher and higher levels with time.

    As pressure increases at low levels over the water, outflow

from the water toward the lower pressure at the surface of the land commences.

A dome of dense air develops over the water whose greatest depth is some distance offshore (usually 2–5 miles over large bodies of water) and whose height decreases at its shore periphery as outflow commences.

4. Onset of flow (sea breeze) from the high-pressure dome depends upon the height of the shoreline.

High pressure must reach a sufficient depth over the water so that pressure at the level of the top of the land barrier exceeds the pressure at the same level ashore.

The lower the shoreline the earlier sea breeze flow commences.

Breaks in a high shoreline barrier cause sea breeze flow to develop at that site earlier and at a greater velocity because pressure disparity is greatest at the lowest levels.

Flow is downward from the dome toward the surface.

Offshore there may be no flow at the surface but flow may be significant at higher levels (detected by boats with tall masts first). First indications of the sea breeze are detected ashore and within a few miles of the shoreline.

If the shoreline is high the sea breeze may only be apparent ashore. The cold, dense air at the surface of the water may remain trapped below the top level of the shoreline barrier and never stirred to motion.

5. A cold front develops as the sea breeze flows from above the cold water toward the heated land. The velocity of this flow varies with height above the surface and the direction of the flow varies with its velocity.

Cold, dense airflow resembles the outflow of sugar poured from a scoop. The lower levels move little if at all, retarded by friction. The upper levels flow rapidly downhill toward the periphery.

Occasionally in Maine and San Francisco sailors may be shrouded in stagnant fog at deck level but find their yachts moving at high speed in a sea breeze flow which only affects the upper half of their sails.

Stronger flow induced by strong thermal lift-off will involve the lower air levels sooner and will produce stronger surface flow offshore.

Surface flow (beginning ashore or near the shoreline) pro-

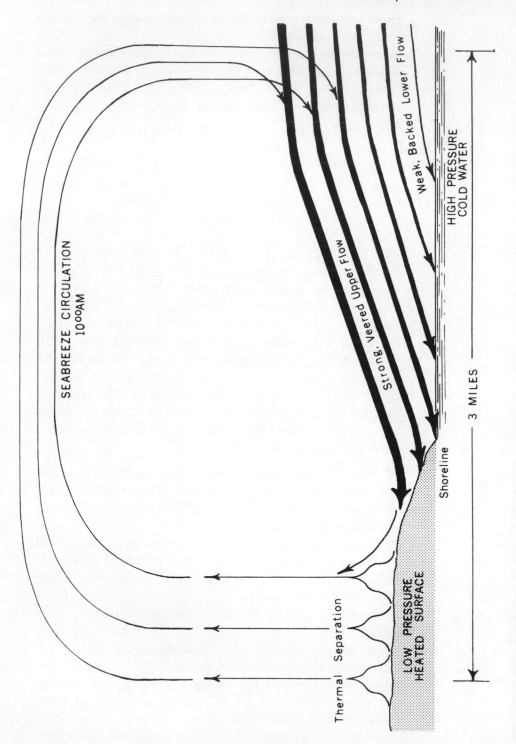

SEABREEZE CIRCULATION
10⁰⁰AM

Weak, Backed Lower Flow

HIGH PRESSURE
COLD WATER

Strong, Veered Upper Flow

3 MILES

Shoreline

Thermal Separation

LOW PRESSURE
HEATED SURFACE

gresses in a retrograde manner to involve the water surface farther and farther offshore with increasing thermal generation. Ocean sea breezes rarely extend more than 5–10 miles off shore, however.

A steady increase in sea breeze flow may be expected concomitantly with increased thermal generation ashore and a steady decrease in flow may be expected commencing an hour or more after the time of peak thermal generation. Outflow from the high-pressure dome once established will continue for a significant period after thermal generation has ceased and until pressure at comparable levels over the land and water is equal (usually early evening).

Sea breeze flow can be considered to be composed of two vertical segments—lower airflow and upper airflow with differing velocity and direction.

Upper airflow, free of surface friction and moving at higher velocity, responds to Coriolis force and therefore instead of flowing directly toward low pressure ashore (as does lower-level airflow) is veered in proportion to its height and its velocity.

Increased turbulence due to increased velocity brings veered upper airflow to the surface and veering increases in direct proportion to velocity.

Late in the day the entire airflow is veered and oscillations between segments of upper and lower airflow disappear.

Land masses intervening between the cold water and the sailing site—harbors, lagoons, etc.—generate thermal lift-off which rises into the upper airflow of the sea breeze and brings segments of the upper airflow (downdrafts of high-pressure cold air to replace rising "balloons" of heated surface air) to the surface.

"Offshore sea breezes" (which pass over intervening land) are mixtures of low-velocity, low-level sea breeze flow; upper, veered sea breeze flow; and, sometimes, if thermals rise through the entire sea breeze flow, weather system airflow. They are therefore highly variable in velocity and direction, composed of gusts and lulls and oscillating shifts which sometimes veer and sometimes back as they gust.

Surface flow farther from the shore is low-level flow in the high-pressure dome and is therefore determined by the pressure gradient and directed perpendicular to the shore. Flow nearer the shore is peripheral flow derived from higher levels and is therefore of higher velocity and more veered.

As velocity increases during the afternoon, turbulence is increased and upper airflow becomes increasingly mixed with low-level flow. Therefore the sea breeze as it increases in velocity becomes increasingly veered and as it decreases in velocity becomes increasingly backed.

If cloud is present in the weather system flow or forms above the thermal columns of intervening land surfaces, sea breeze flow will be modified by variations in the cloud cover. As cloud moves over the shore thermal generation will be reduced, sea breeze flow will be reduced and will consist only of lower-level flow perpendicular to the shore. With clearing flow velocity will be increased and veered upper flow will be brought to the surface.

Continuous vertical circulation between land and water:

1. Continuous heating ashore and high-level flow offshore must continually replace the pressure and density lost in sea breeze outflow.

    In the absence of weather system wind the ideal flow pattern will develop—heated air flowing from land to water at high levels and cold air flowing from water to land at low levels.

    Flow will continue so long as high-level pressure is higher over land than water and low-level pressure is higher over water than land.

2. Offshore weather system flow aids sea breeze development.

    Although pressure reduction at the surface ashore may be limited by high-pressure weather system flow, if the air mass is relatively dry and sinking, skies will be clear and thermal generation will be stimulated. If the offshore flow is cool thermal lift-off will be enhanced.

    Offshore weather system flow will carry the heated air out over the cold, dense air above the water, enhancing the upper-level sea breeze circulation.

The seabreeze front will be distinguished by a sharp line of cumulus clouds, derived from thermal lift-off ashore, moving seaward but evaporated at the shoreline by the heated upper-level sea breeze flow.

The cold, dense air of the sea breeze front will move shoreward beneath the warmer offshore flow lifting it above the surface as it progresses.

The colder and denser is the weather system offshore flow (such as in a northwesterly behind a winter cold front), the less likely will the sea breeze develop beneath it. If the weather system air is actually colder than the air over the water surface, no sea breeze will appear.

Where the sea breeze cold front, moving landward, meets the offshore flow and displaces it upward, convergence and "wind shear" occur. (Marked turbulence occurs whenever airflows of significantly differing direction and velocity meet.)

A zone of turbulence due to convergence appears at the leading edge of the sea breeze front. This zone is usually about 100–400 yards wide, a mixture of calm and frustrating drastic oscillating shifts between the two winds.

The sea breeze front in an offshore weather system wind flow instead of being first evident ashore appears initially at the surface several miles offshore and gradually progresses toward the shore pushing the zone of convergence ahead of it.

3. Onshore weather system flow aids sea breeze development.

Onshore weather system flow is oriented to surface high pressure over water and low pressure ashore which enhances the pressure gradient necessary to sea breeze flow.

Circulation is maintained as sea breeze outflow is replaced by weather system inflow and thermal lift-off is carried away inland.

Turbulence created by aligned weather system flow brings the dense air at the water surface into the general airflow.

The resultant wind is an oscillating mixture of lower and upper levels of sea breeze flow and of weather system flow.

Approximate alignment of weather system airflow and sea

breeze flow within 45° produces a strengthening of the resultant wind with oscillating shifts between the two extremes.

As the sea breeze strengthens and veers with increasing heating of the land it becomes steadier. If the weather system wind is veered (up to 45°) from the onshore sea breeze flow the late afternoon sea breeze will be further strengthened. If the weather system wind is aligned with with the fully veered sea breeze flow the strongest sea breeze of all is created.

If the weather system wind is backed up to 45° from the onshore flow, after a period of oscillation between the two winds, the sea breeze will veer and decrease in strength.

4. Weather system flow parallel to the shore impairs sea breeze development.

Weather system flow perpendicular to the sea breeze flow dissipates the organization of low pressure at the surface ashore and high pressure at the surface of the water. Sea breeze circulation cannot be maintained.

Wind shear develops where the weather system wind overflows the sea breeze front. Turbulence at this meeting zone disturbs organized airflow resulting in a chaotic mixture of shifts between the two flows.

Resultant wind flow when the weather system flow is between 45° and 135° of the sea breeze flow is reduced in velocity and extremely flukey. Often no wind appears at the surface as the weather system wind flows on above the cold, dense air overlying the water surface.

5. Surface wind perpendicular to the sea breeze (parallel to the sea breeze front) may develop in the zone between an offshore wind and a sea breeze.

A warm offshore wind is lifted above an advancing sea breeze front. A cold offshore wind denser than the sea breeze air will not lift and will prevent sea breeze development.

Pressure over the water surface will fall immediately ahead of the sea breeze front as an offshore wind lifts to flow above it.

Lateral flow may commence into the zone of reduced

pressure perpendicular to the opposing offshore and on-shore flows.

Usually such lateral flow is transient and veered to the initial offshore flow. As the sea breeze front moves progressively shoreward the surface flow veers progressively until it amalgamates with the sea breeze flow perpendicular to the shoreline.

Occasionally when the temperature of offshore and onshore flows are nearly the same a prolonged period of calm will develop and cover the entire water surface within a few miles of shore. This calm is usually broken by the appearance of the sea breeze but may sometimes be associated with transient (5–60 minutes) eddies of the offshore flow and/or flow perpendicular, *backed* or *veered,* to the offshore flow and the sea breeze.

When the sea breeze flow fills into such a zone of calm, it develops almost simultaneously throughout the area, although the first visible evidence of its presence is a dark line of ruffled water advancing from seaward.

6. An upper-level subsidence inversion may aid the development of a morning sea breeze.

An early morning (8:00–11:00 A.M.) local, low-level sea breeze protected from the weather system wind may develop beneath the overlying subsidence inversion. Full circulation may be readily established as dissipation aloft of high pressure above the heated land is blocked and upper-level outflow is channeled out over the water by the inversion lid.

Breakthrough of the inversion layer is associated with dissipation of the organized sea breeze circulation and deterioration of the sea breeze. A weather system wind or a new sea breeze will appear to replace the the initial low-level sea breeze. If a new sea breeze appears it will take 15–30 minutes to reorganize, including air above the dissipated inversion, and will appear from the initial sea breeze direction perpendicular to the shore, backed up to 40° from the direction of the already veered, previous, low-level sea breeze.

7. An upper-level subsidence inversion may aid the development of an evening sea breeze.

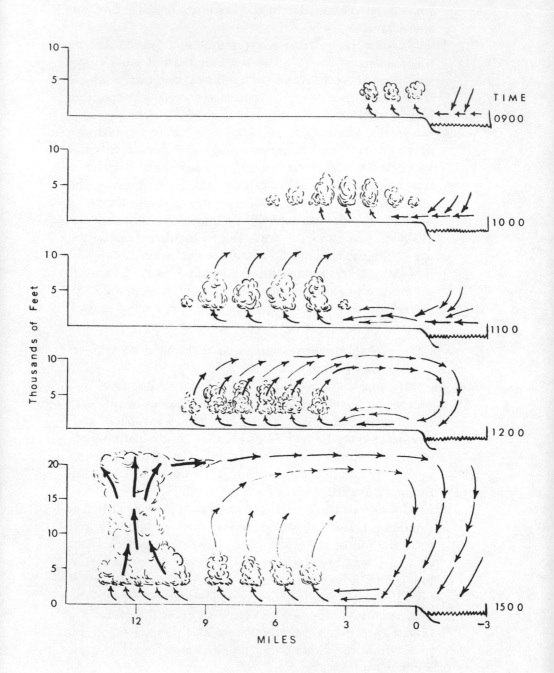

When the weather system wind has been opposing the sea breeze because it is offshore or approximately parallel to the shore, an inversion reduces the opposition. The inversion confines the weather system airflow to the upper air above the level of abrupt temperature change. Wind shear is abolished as the sea breeze and the weather system wind are no longer in contact.

Often on clear days when the water has been calm through the afternoon, the sea breeze appears suddenly and builds rapidly at 4:00 to 5:00 P.M. This is the "anchor breeze," an airflow which has been about to appear all day but was unable to achieve an organized circulation until freed of the weather system wind.

Once established, the anchor breeze will persist long after the land has cooled and until the high pressure developed over the water surface is dissipated.

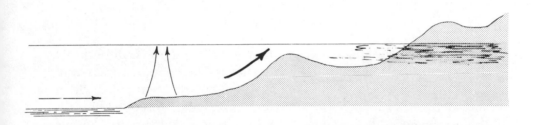

2. *The Southern California Sea Breeze*

"A veering wind brings fair skies,
A backing wind to be despised."

One of the most impressive aspects of southern California is the regularity of its wind flow. Diurnal and geographic variations are predictable almost to the hour and the mile on most racing days. A huge high-pressure system lies in the Pacific to the northeast of Hawaii and its outflow provides the air which flows ashore along this coast. This mass of sinking air, heating as it sinks, rests above the cool, moist ocean and creates an inversion layer above an altitude of approximately 1000–2000 feet. Below this inversion the marine layer floods shoreward as the sea breeze develops each day and ebbs back each night. The major variation in southern California's airflow occurs as the North Pacific high shifts southward in the winter and northward in the summer. In winter the outflow from the high is westerly along the coast, which means that moist air and a series of depressions are brought ashore with accompanying cloud cover and rain. In summer, as the high shifts northward, its outflow along the coast is northwesterly, which means that it has been well dried out by passing above the cool waters of the California Current en route to southern California. Its Pacific moisture has been dumped on British Columbia, Washington, and Oregon. In the summer the inversion created by this dry sinking air protects the marine layer from the weather system northwesterly above and permits dependable sea breeze generation at the surface. Rarely is any other wind evident at Los Angeles. The Santa Ana blows on about six days of the year and very rarely maritime tropical Gulf (mTg) or maritime tropical Pacific (mTp) air invades the region to produce major thunderstorms.

THE SEA BREEZE

The cool, moist marine layer that gives southern California its delightful, stable climate and creates its fertile coastal strip is confined like a huge lake, 1000–2000 feet deep, by the mountains which rise a few miles inland. Little mixing takes place through the subsidence inversion between this moist air below and the dry, hot air above so that stratus, fog, and smog are trapped in the dense, cool air below. Each day heating of the land creates major thermal liftoff over the inland deserts and gradually heats the marine layer along the coast. By midmorning (or sooner) the stratus deck which has formed at night beneath the inversion at the top of the marine layer is melted away. Thermal updrafts break through the inversion and a steady outflow of hot, dry air from above the heated surfaces ashore moves out over the ocean. As pressure rises offshore due to this mass addition, the sea breeze begins to flow shoreward at the surface. A sloping cold front develops whose periphery is initially at the shore where surface airflow first appears. The sea breeze cold front moves inland at 5–10 knots associated with a 500-foot bulge in the top of the inversion layer. The forward progress of the sea breeze front and the velocity of the surface airflow within it is en-

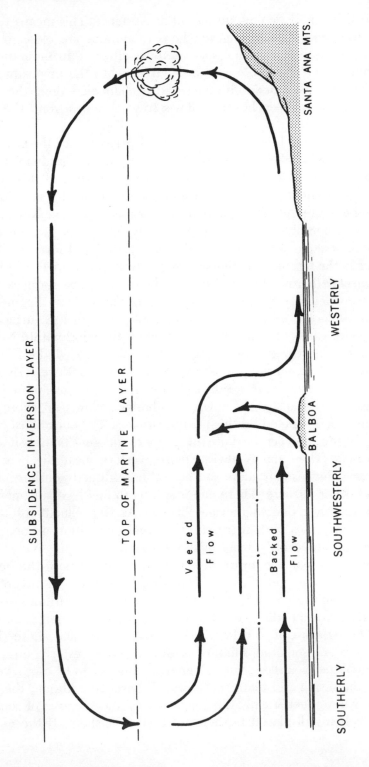

hanced by anabatic flow up mountain surfaces. This means that sea
breeze flow will be strongest where mountains are close to shore;
thermal lift-off from their peaks is most effective in inducing early
onshore flow. The stable air, confined beneath the inversion above,
deviates to pass around obstacles and is channeled along the face of
bluffs, hills, and beaches as it flows toward and beyond the shorelines.

The morning breeze is the low-level periphery of the sea breeze
cold front which flows, in response to the pressure gradient, directly
onshore. On most summer days in Newport Harbor this onshore
flow is evident at 8:00 A.M., replacing whatever nocturnal wind may
have been present after a period of morning calm. Off Newport the
initial onshore flow is from approximately 200°, strongest but patchy
near the beach and gradually filling in farther and farther offshore.
Later in the morning, as the sea breeze front moves over the Balboa
Peninsula, thermal lift-off from its heated surface induces downdrafts which bring upper-level flow to the surface. Segments of
higher velocity, veered upper-level flow come to the surface over
and to leeward of the peninsula and cause the wind within Newport
Harbor to be stronger and more westerly than the wind offshore. At
Newport, after, finishing a 5.5 race in a 4-knot southwesterly a mile
offshore, we would often sail back into the harbor to find a 10-knot
westerly blowing straight down the channel. Flow near shore in the
ocean is also affected by this mixing process. The entire onshore airflow begins to veer offshore in preparation for its transit of the
peninsula. The wind is always more westerly near the beach and
becomes increasingly more southerly, more directly onshore, as one
goes farther offshore. There one is sailing in low-level air unaffected
by turbulence due to thermal lift-off. As the velocity of the sea
breeze increases with increasing thermal generation ashore, it develops progressively farther offshore and veers progressively so that
in late afternoon the entire flow within a few miles of the beach is
westerly. If one goes far enough offshore, however, an area of more
southerly flow will always be discovered where airflow, of lesser
velocity, is responding directly to the pressure gradient.

During most of the day in the racing areas near shore the sea
breeze is an oscillating mixture of upper, more westerly, and lower,
more southerly, airflow, with a general tendency to be more westerly
near the beach and more southerly offshore. In addition, the entire
airflow in a given area is shifting westerly and the area of southerly
flow is being displaced farther and farther offshore. If the morning

clouds fail to clear or the land fails to heat as usual, the low-level onshore wind may persist all day. At Newport this means a 4- to 6-knot southerly (185°–230°) with marked oscillations as occasional gusts of the veered flow aloft intermittently reach the surface. Oscillation between 200° and 230° in midmorning may be replaced by oscillation between 250° and 260° in late afternoon. The afternoon flow becomes progressively more stable with less-frequent and less-marked oscillations. If the start is in a south-westerly in the early morning, the persistent shift to be sought is the more southerly wind offshore. This requires an initial starboard tack followed by a port tack to weather of the fleet in what, hopefully, will be a progressive lift. Later in the day (unless one is starting far offshore) the area of southerly flow is beyond the racing area and the wind is progressively veering as it increases in velocity. The persistent shift to be sought is the westerly wind near shore which requires an initial port tack, followed by a starboard tack near the layline, to weather of the fleet, in what, hopefully, will be a progressive lift. It is essential to avoid becoming so preoccupied with tacking in the oscillations that a really significant persistent shift is missed.

In addition to the persistent shift determined by time and velocity there may be local shifts associated with channeling and altered velocity near headlands or coastal mountains. A major increase in velocity occurs as the westerly flow is funneled between Santa Catalina and the Palos Verdes Peninsula. This section of the San Pedro Channel is known as Hurricane Gulch and is responsible for the stronger and more veered wind flow characteristic of Alamitos Bay as compared with Newport. Here the westerly shift is evident early in the day as the velocity is high and there is no significant southerly shift offshore as the entire area is under the influence of the Hurricane Gulch channeling. Off Marina Del Rey the onshore flow is westerly as it is channeled around the western end of the Santa Monica mountains and flows eastward along their faces. Offshore the wind channeled by Santa Catalina is flowing more parallel to the general shoreline, i.e., northwesterly. A persistent veer as one goes offshore and a reduced tendency to veer near the beach—the reverse of the situation at Newport—results. The early port tack is essential at Alamitos where the wind veers early over the entire course. It may be equally important off Marina Del Rey because port tack is directed more offshore than elsewhere along the coast and leads to a channeled veer farther offshore.

Upper-level flow all along the coast is a combination of the

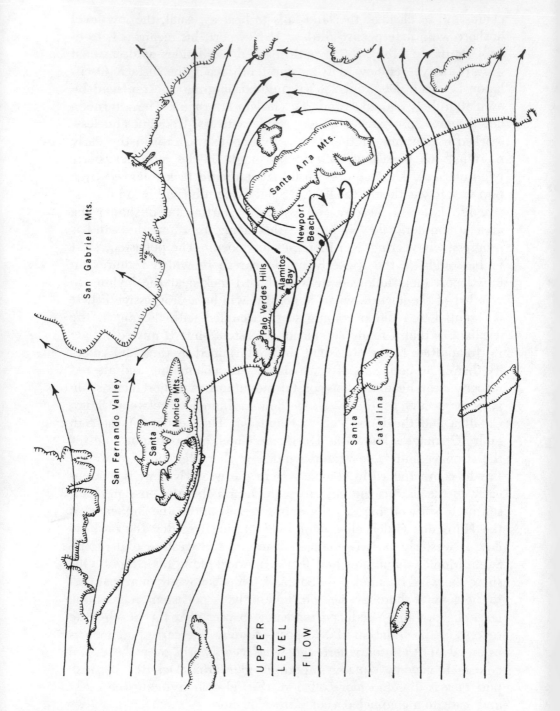

San Gabriel Mts.

Santa Ana Mts.

Newport Beach

Alamitos Bay

Palo Verdes Hills

San Fernando Valley

Santa Monica Mts.

Santa Catalina

UPPER LEVEL FLOW

northwesterly outflow from the North Pacific high and the veered upper segments of the sea breeze. The westerly shift that results as the upper airflow is brought to the surface, associated with a major increase in wind velocity, tends to reach the surface initially in the west and to progress down the coast. This means that the boat farthest to the west on port tack, receives the new stronger, more westerly wind first. The strong, upper airflow is brought to the surface first by the land protruding farthest into the ocean to the west, Point Fermin. Although anabatic effects enhance sea breeze flow, surface velocity close to shore is inversely proportional to the height of the shoreline toward which the flow is directed. The 9h effect reduces the flow immediately off a mountainous coast while channeling increases the flow at low-level openings. Surface velocity is greatest in the vicinity of Long Beach where nearby mountains stimulate lift-off and the flat shoreline permits the entrance of low-level flow into the Los Angeles basin.

The mixture of upper- and lower-level airflow is most evident off the Balboa Pier where the races at Newport are usually held. The strong westerly flow aloft may only be brought to the surface near the thermal columns which rise from the heated shore, and then only those boats that tack up the beach on port receive its heading effect. Boats that initially hold port usually do well, but when they tack offshore they may sail out of the westerly into a header, the low level southerly.

The 5.5 Meters raced about two miles off the Newport jetty to the west of Balboa in their 1968 Olympic trials. The wind before the start of each race shifted west from approximately 180° to 230° by race time and often shifted farther west to approximately 250° during the race. The westerly shift created by the strong westerly aloft had to be reckoned with in every race and it never paid to sail significantly to port of the rhumb line to the weather mark. However, the local southerly was always present offshore and the farther offshore we went the more it was evident. Races were won and lost as the surface wind (and the boats) oscillated back and forth between the upper-level westerly, most evident at the surface inshore and to the west, and the lower-level southerly, most evident offshore and to the south. Several races were won by the boat that continued farthest on starboard into the southerly shift offshore and then tacked to windward of the fleet in a progressive lift. During the trials we kept praying that the westerly would finally settle in, as it does elsewhere along the coast, and simplify our strategic problems. The Race Committee had managed to find the one spot in southern California where the early port tack "down the one-way street" often failed to pay.

THE CURRENT AND THE OCEAN SWELL

The California Current and the typical westerly sea breeze, funneling through the channel between Santa Catalina and the mainland, combine to produce a current parallel to the coast which runs generally northwest–southeast. Port tack in the prevailing westerly sea breeze is therefore upcurrent and in many areas carries the boat into less adverse current, close to shore. The boat tacking to port immediately after the start remains in the less adverse current along the shore (until she tacks offshore on the layline) and moves upcurrent of the fleet (an advantageous position in a dying wind). As the depth of water increases rapidly offshore, small increments of distance from the shore are associated with large increments of current velocity. Boats continuing on starboard before tacking end up falling in line astern of the first port tacker when racing just off the Balboa Peninsula.

Both at Newport in the 5.5's and at Santa Monica in the 14's we discovered days when although there was no significant current (or even a slight current to the north at Santa Monica) and no persistent westerly shift, the initial port tack was still advantageous. As direct wind waves were small and inconsequential the only other influence that could have been relevant was the ocean swell. The large swells off the California coast in the summer are initiated by the prevailing northwesterly (characteristic of the subtropical highs at this latitude) and are reinforced by the regular westerly thermal wind described above. These swells have a length of 50–75 feet and are therefore moving at 10–15 knots, forward in the crests and aft in the troughs. Although the boat does not attain the full effect of this movement its speed through the air and thus its apparent wind are markedly affected by its position in the swell and its angle of approach to the swell.

When sailing to windward against the direction of the swell movement the boat rapidly crosses successive crests and troughs. As its forward speed increases in the backward-moving water of the trough, its apparent wind increases dramatically. The boat surges ahead and tends to heel as both driving force and heeling force increase. If the wind is veered to the course of the swells, the apparent wind for a boat on port tack will shift aft in the troughs, which permits the boat to be headed up abruptly (as soon as the crest passes beneath the hull). As the apparent wind decreases and shifts forward in the crest of the swell, driving force and heeling force decrease, the sails luff and the boat slows and comes erect. To avoid this slowing and luffing the boat must be headed off to increase the angle of incidence and the limited aerodynamic force available. If the true wind is backed to the direction of movement of the swells (the boat is headed closer than 45° to them), the effect will be reversed, i.e., the boat will be headed in the trough and lifted in the crest. In a small boat, when the wind is veered to the swells, the crew will have to hike hard in each trough, move inboard in each crest; in all boats marked variations in heading must be utilized with each swell to maintain sail efficiency and make optimal progress to weather.

One tack will provide a more favorable relation to the swells than the other whenever the swells are not moving directly downwind (as they rarely are). Boats on the tack which tends to meet the swells nearly head on will be exposed to abrupt and frequent recurrent variations in the strength and direction of the apparent wind which may be impossible to compensate for through heading changes. The advantageous lift will appear in the crest when the apparent wind velocity is reduced and the advantageous apparent wind increase will appear in the trough to be negated by the associated header. Boats on the tack which tends to meet the swells more obliquely, however, will meet fewer swells per unit time and have more time to adjust to each segment of the swell. Then, as the apparent wind increases in the trough, its direction shifts aft improving both boat speed and pointing simultaneously. As the apparent wind decreases in the crest its direction shifts forward, impairing both boat speed and pointing simultaneously. This problem can usually be managed satisfactorily, however, as when sailing obliquely to the swells additional time is available. One tack is almost always oriented more obliquely to the swells than the other and along the southern California coast that tack is usually port.

The swells move southeast down the San Pedro Channel under the influence of the strong westerly which blows strongly for many hours each day off Long Beach. As the swells approach the beaches farther down the coast, they swing to the east as bottom friction retards their inshore ends. As with all significant waves, they eventually strike the shore perpendicularly. This means that a boat sailing on port in the westerly parallel to and near the northwest–southeast shore is sailing obliquely (or occasionally parallel) to the swells. A boat sailing on starboard near the shore is meeting the swells nearly head on. Offshore the swells are maintaining their initial southeast course and near shore they are moving easterly or even northeasterly. As the wind veers with the day, port tack becomes progressively more oblique to the swells. When port tack is the initial tack, the boat sails progressively into swells which are more and more oblique as it approaches shore. Then on starboard, after meeting the seas near shore almost head on, she meets them more and more obliquely as she moves offshore. By contrast the boat taking the starboard tack initially never has an advantage, she always meets the swells at approximately the same angle as she did at the start.

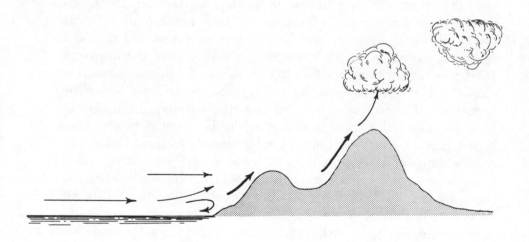

3. The Wind of Acapulco

"No weather is ill
If the wind be still."

The wind of Acapulco is a sea breeze chiefly because the climatic conditions of the southwestern coast of Mexico are stable and a significant temperature disparity exists between the cool ocean offshore and the hot hills ashore. Usually a high-pressure system rests languidly over the interior of Mexico to the north (which has but a minimal pressure gradient at its southern periphery) and a huge air mass (maritime tropical Pacific—mTp) sits stably offshore to the west. Acapulco rests between the two, little affected by either. In October 1968, when the Olympics were conducted, these conditions prevailed. Thermal winds were present for six of the seven races and modified the seventh.

Acapulco lies at the eastern periphery of the huge subtropical high that continually hovers over the low latitudes of the North Pacific. This warm air is constantly sinking, heating, and drying. The presence of such air accounts for the desert climates of the lands bordering the eastern margins of the oceans in the low latitudes—the Sahara and the Sonora. The continual sinking results in a persistent subsidence inversion over the ocean and the strip of coast bordering the ocean. The turbulence, mechanical and thermal, in the lowest 2000–3000 feet of the atmosphere prevents the subsidence from continuing to the lower levels. In the marine layer beneath this inversion, protected from the weather system airflow above, the sea breeze develops each day. Only when the weather system wind is unusually strong, as in the presence of a depression, is the inversion swept away. At other times the sea breeze, generated beneath it, continues unabated throughout the day; no inversion breakthrough such as is typical of the United States East Coast ocean sea breeze occurs at midday to interrupt its progressive generation.

I surveyed the records of the winds of October in Acapulco for the previous ten years and easily distinguished three patterns. The most common wind developed at approximately 210° (between 1100 and 1300 hours) perpendicular to the coastline, and gradually shifted to approximately 270°; this was the Acapulco sea breeze. Another wind commenced at approximately 145° and shifted toward, but never past, 180°. This was the result of the southeasterly flow from the offshore depressions typical of October in this area. The few remaining days displayed strong offshore and onshore winds, presumably from weather systems whose gradients prevented the development of the thermal wind.

The records of the sea breezes showed a shift west by increments, veering west by 20° in one hour and then backing 10°–15° in the next. If the wind veered past 235° by 1300, it would almost certainly back between 1300 and 1400. It increased in velocity as it veered west. The first few days of practice sailing revealed that the wind was more southerly offshore, more westerly along shore, and was of higher average velocity offshore. Before the Olympics started we felt that we were dealing with a predictable situation quite comparable to the known conditions off the southern California coast.

It soon became evident, however, that the wind of Acapulco was more complex. This was primarily due to the super-imposition of widespread oscillations of approximately 10°–15°, lasting approximately 5–10 minutes. These oscillations often affected the entire area of the course, but more often only affected one side or the other, or even a smaller portion, of the beat. In addition, marked variations in velocity occurred within a small portion of the area. In general, the gusts were veered and the lulls were backed. There was less oscillation when the wind was strong and after it had veered well around to the west. Thus there was more oscillation early in the afternoon (the racing started at 1300) and more when it was light and remained more southwesterly. The wind was generally stronger to the east of the course (as well as offshore).

The sea breeze flow during the Olympics was stronger than expected. The expectation was apparently derived from the unusually light air experienced the preceding October and possibly from misreading of the widely published record of October winds in Acapulco which was given in meters/second (numerically less than half the value in knots). The thermal winds (contrary to some reports) were never strong (maximum velocity recorded at the surface during a race was 16 knots) but were never light (the lightest day of thermal wind during the series averaged 6 knots). The usual wind increased from approximately 8 knots at 1300 to approximately 12 knots at 1600.

On the first day of racing at Acapulco the thermal wind began to develop before 1100 and had swung around to 270° by the time of the start. A high-pressure system was located offshore so that the basic flow was already from the west. The sun had no sooner warmed the hills ashore than the thermal wind was up and in the west and relatively steady. On the second day the high had moved closer, providing a relatively strong onshore drift. This unusual situation produced the strongest wind of the series (increasing to 16 knots by 1600) with little deviation from the expected sea breeze direction. As the high moved inland the thermal was left to its own devices on the thrid day of racing. It didn't appear until near noon, obliterated the slight offshore wind of the early morning, produced a zone of calm for half an hour, and then filled in abruptly at about 8 knots.

On the fourth day an offshore depression appeared to the southeast with a slight easterly flow in the area of the racing. The thermal wind rose gradually and was centered at about 210° at 1300. Large infrequent oscillations between 200° and 230° occurred during the race and the wind never went farther west than 230°. The fifth race was conducted with the offshore depression so close that an oblique onshore flow from the southeast was evident in the area. This flow, almost 90° to the direction of the sea breeze, received little or no support from it, but was deviated to near 180° and was characterized by large swings between 155° and 180°—the typical result of the combination of an easterly weather system wind with a southerly sea breeze. The sixth race was held in a moderate sea breeze of abrupt onset with marked oscillations between 210° and 230° but which never went west of 230°. There was a moderately dense cloud cover ashore associated with a warm northerly flow from a low to the northeast. The typical thermal wind, unaffected by any significant weather system wind, returned for the finale, appeared abruptly at about 1100, and veered to approximately 255° by the time of the start. The wind velocity rose to an unusual 12 knots in the presence of a dense cloud cover offshore and brilliant sunshine inland despite the absence of any supporting onshore weather system flow.

Acapulco demonstrates the effects of weather system wind/sea breeze mixtures. In the presence of strong weather system flows aloft sufficient turbulence may occur to break through a subsidence inversion. It the weather system wind, as it breaks into the marine layer, is backed to the sea breeze direction it creates wind-shear effects which disturb and reduce the total flow. This was the result when easterly flow from an offshore depression invaded the area on the fourth day of Olympic racing. When the weather system flow was opposed to the sea breeze but relatively isolated above it the resultant wind was the sea breeze, reduced in velocity and less veered because of the cloud cover and associated with large, infrequent oscillations. On the fifth day of racing, when the weather system wind had broken through the inversion, the surface wind was markedly reduced and associated with large swings between the weather system wind at 155° and the low-level sea breeze at 180°. When a strong weather system wind veered to the sea breeze direction is present and breaks through an inversion it reinforces the sea breeze flow. As the sea breeze velocity increases with heating and veers it becomes more and more aligned with such a weather system wind. The wind resultant from the combination of a strong westerly high pressure-gradient flow with the southerly sea breeze on the second day of Olympic racing produced the best sailing of the series.

The variable mixing of the strong westerly flow aloft and the weak southerly flow at the surface contributes to the oscillation of the sea breeze so characteristic of Acapulco. The gusts, being upper air surging to the surface, are veered to the west. The entire flow swings gradually to the west as the day progresses but, in addition to its gusting, oscillates between a surface, more southerly flow and an upper-level, more westerly flow. When, usually late in the day, it finally swings to approximately 270°, it becomes steadier as upper flow is then almost entirely replacing surface flow. The other determinants of the oscillations in the Acapulco sea breeze are the mountains which rise above 1000 feet along the shoreline. These mountains modify the sea breeze through their barrier effect and through their effect upon convection. Coastal mountains act as barriers to the sea breeze and cause it to lift above the surface. Lifting commences at a distance to windward nine times their height. At Acapulco this is nearly two miles from shore and includes a significant portion of the race courses. Within this range the sea breeze lifts, heading for the peaks of the mountains ashore, and comes to the surface chiefly as intermittent eddies. This barrier effect accounts for the evident reduction in wind velocity near shore. At the same time the sea breeze is deviated by the high shore and tends to channel more parallel to it. This accounts in part for the more westerly wind which we found near shore. The sea breeze seeks, is channeled into, and, of course, is less restricted by low barriers along the shore. As the shore to the east of the 5.5 Meter course was low, the surface wind to the east of the course was stronger and the wind tended to channel more westerly along shore to seek this break in the barrier.

Even more significant to the confused surface flow offshore at Acapulco is the enhancement of thermal convection by the mountains. The development of the sea breeze is delayed until approximately noon as the west-facing slopes of the coastal mountains delay the heating of the shore. Once the sun breaks over the peaks, warm air accumulates along the beaches and in the valleys. Air tends to remain attached to the ground and does not break its attachment until it reaches a significantly higher temperature than the air above. Thereafter, it tends to break away intermittently and to move along the surface laterally to areas of decreased pressure, i.e., to higher

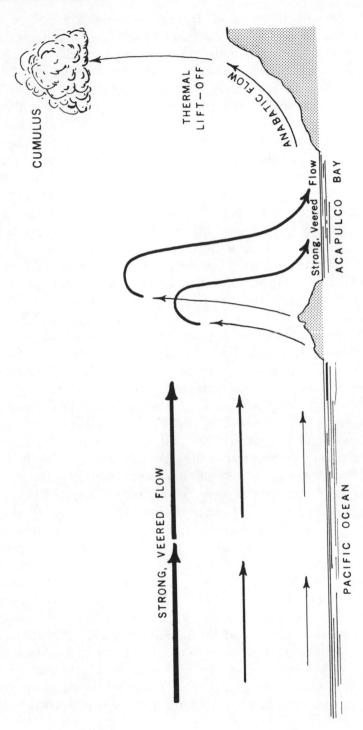

altitudes. This is the origin of the anabatic wind, the flow of warm
air along the surface and up the slopes of hills and mountains. Rising
slopes near the shore thus help to initiate the convection of air over
the land and aid in the induction of the sea breeze which replaces it.
The anabatic wind moving up the valleys induces the sea breeze to
follow its trajectory, bringing it ashore into the mouths of valleys
which open toward the sea. Anabatic flow brings warm air to the
peaks at an altitude where the surrounding air is cooler. At the peaks
because of the greater temperature disparity, the warm air readily
breaks away from the surface and condenses overhead to form the
characteristic cumulus clouds of the thermal wind. Cumulus formation is thus both a stimulus to the sea breeze, as it is associated with
the breaking away of warm surface air which encourages replacement, and a sign that the sea breeze is developing.

The differences in wind strength and direction on various parts
of the Olympic courses, the changes in strength and direction as
the day progressed, and the frequent appearances of gusts from
farther west are now readily understood. As yet unexplained is the
periodic oscillation at five- to ten-minute intervals which permeated
the sea breeze days until the wind had settled in the west. This was
apparently due to the intermittent breakthrough to the surface of
the more westerly flow aloft and an intermittent return of the local
surface flow perpendicular to the shoreline. Early in the day these
oscillations were between 210° and 230°, later between 230° and
250°, and finally between 250° and 270° before stabilization at
270° (with only gusting remaining). As demonstrated by the formation of "cloud streets" (strings of cumulus clouds across the direction
of wind flow, separated by intervals of clear sky), convection lift-off
from mountain peaks is intermittent and in addition is coordinated.
This means that the sea breeze-inducing pressure reduction ashore
is fluctuating over a large area in a periodic manner. In periods of
increased induction, the entire sea breeze flow is strengthened and
the surface winds, dragged along by the westerly flow aloft, veer
west. In periods of decreased induction, the surface flow reverts to
its low-level basic direcion more perpendicular to the shoreline.

The gradual swing west by increments (with oscillations back
whenever the swing went more than 20°) was occasioned chiefly by
the gradual strengthening of the sea breeze which then dragged the
surface flow into the trajectory of its upper levels. In Acapulco Bay
where the upper airflow was brought down by thermal columns

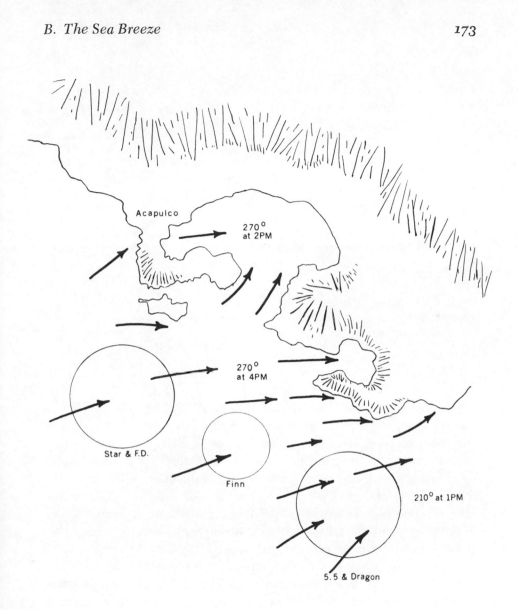

rising from the warming of the peninsulas and offshore islands, the wind was westerly early in the afternoon and to the north of west when the fleets returned in the evening. This same effect was gradually achieved several hours later offshore. Cool westerly airflow from aloft was the rule at the surface in late afternoon and little oscillation remained as the local perpendicular flow had been all but eliminated.

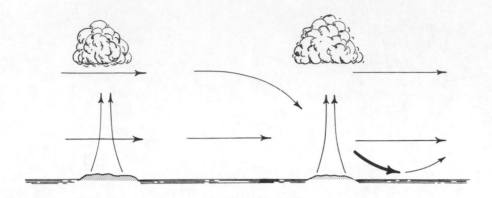

4. Galveston Bay—
The Offshore Sea Breeze

*"When the wind's in the south
The rain's in its mouth."*

Every day of the 1970 North American Soling Championship was spent sailing in, or waiting hopefully for, the offshore sea breeze of Galveston Bay. An offshore sea breeze is characteristic of Long Island Sound, Barnegat, and Chesapeake Bays and landlocked harbors such as that at Newport Beach, California. Although they retain many of the basic characteristics of simple onshore sea breezes, their sojourn over land produces modifications often baffling to the racing sailor. The basic breeze is inherently erratic, filled with gusts and holes due to mixture with weather system wind.

In the absence of other wind flow a sea breeze commences near the shore toward which it is directed. The dome of high pressure over the water pushes inland toward the low pressure at the heated surface ahead. As the sea breeze cold front progresses over warm land it is vertically unstable and buoyant. Its lapse rate is high so that heated air lifted from the surface readily rises through the entire sea breeze flow. Above the cold, dense air of the sea breeze warm air is spreading seaward and the weather system wind is flowing in the direction of the general pressure gradient. An inversion exists at the interface between the sea breeze and the warm air above. Early in the inland progress of the sea breeze thermal lift-off is limited to the unstable cold air mass and is unable to break through the inversion. For each column of rapidly rising air a neighboring downdraft rushes upper-level sea breeze airflow to the surface. Thus at the surface ashore the sea breeze is gusty and strong long before it has reached significant velocity offshore to windward.

Ultimately the surface of the land is heated sufficiently above the temperature of the overlying airflow that buoyant columns rise through the inversion. Heating to this degree usually requires a long sojourn overland and clear skies. Thus the farther the sea breeze penetrates inland, the more the inversion deteriorates. If the air mass is moist, stratocumulus cloud cover may form beneath the inversion and delay heating of the land. As heating is delayed, breakthrough of the inversion is delayed and burning off of the cloud cover may not occur until late in the day. Once the inversion has been broken, downdrafts are partially composed of the weather system airflow from above the inversion. After prolonged heating, surface airflow over the land is composed of a mixture of upper and lower sea breeze airflow and weather system airflow. This is the air that flows out from the land onto any inland water surface, the offshore sea breeze.

The offshore sea breeze is composed of segments of air moving in three different directions, the low-level sea breeze flow moving perpendicular to the general orientation of the shoreline, the upper-level sea breeze flow freed of surface friction and veered by Coriolis force, and the weather system airflow moving in response to the general pressure gradient. In addition to these changes in direction, as the sea breeze comes ashore it is progressively heated both by heating from below and by admixture of the weather system flow from above. Thus the sea breeze becomes progressively stabilized; although the inversion is lost the lower levels are progressively heated, the lapse rate is reduced and buoyancy is decreased. The now-warmed air flows in layers out over segments of cool water below. Where the initial sea breeze flow is derived from cold water —cold current and deep-ocean sea breezes—it retains its coldness and instability far inland. To leeward of the islands in Maine, and at Edgartown in the lee of Martha's Vineyard the sea breeze flow reaches the surface strong and gusty. On a clear day in summer the ocean sea breeze crosses forty miles of the Delmarva Peninsula to emerge at maximum velocity along the Chesapeake's Eastern Shore. Earlier in the year, when the Bay water is colder, heating of the ocean sea breeze may be sufficient to create a stable airflow as it emerges from the Eastern Shore. On Long Island Sound a flood tide

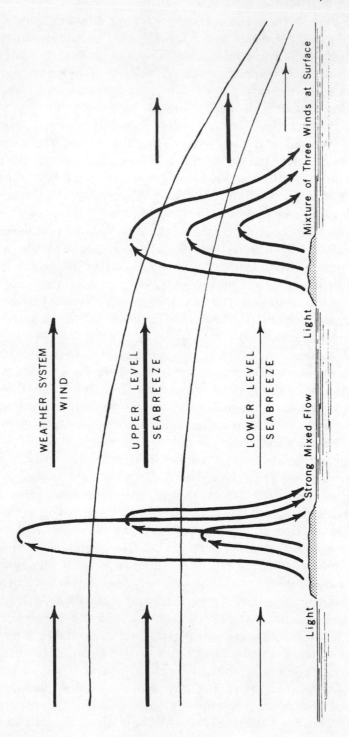

WEATHER SYSTEM WIND

UPPER LEVEL SEABREEZE

LOWER LEVEL SEABREEZE

Mixture of Three Winds at Surface

Light

Strong Mixed Flow

Light

may bring in water so cold that the heated ocean sea breeze will flow stably off the Long Island shore and only reach the surface well offshore where it reinforces the local Connecticut shore sea breeze. Where the water is warm, such as it always is in summer in shallow Galveston Bay, the offshore sea breeze mixes readily with the warm air in the sailing layer and provides a strong and gusty airflow close to the windward shore.

The windward shore is usually favored in a vertically unstable offshore airflow as thermal turbulence over the land enhances the surface flow while the leeward shore is favored in a vertically stable offshore airflow as distance offshore diminishes blanketing and may be associated with a local onshore sea breeze. When the offshore airflow is a sea breeze which has been extensively heated by its passage overland, heated above the temperature of the underlying water, its velocity at the surface will diminish progressively with distance offshore.

In Texas we experienced some of the typical manifestations of offshore sea breezes. The southeasterly flow from the Gulf began regularly during the period of maximum heating of the land, gradually increased in velocity to a peak in late afternoon, and gradually (if erratically!) veered to the south as it increased in velocity. Although the wind developed in the early afternoon of the first two days of racing, its appearance was significantly delayed on the following two days, necessitating the cancellation of the race on the final day. On the fourth day there was no wind at all until after a thunderstorm. There were always marked holes in the wind flow as well as sudden variations in direction.

As the polar front rarely reaches down to southern Texas in the summer, Galveston Bay lies immersed in maritime tropical Gulf (mTg) air within which pressure variation is minimal. Therefore, local sailors rely on the sea breeze for their summertime wind. As the Texas coast runs northeast-southwest, the sea breeze is (initially) a southeasterly. The subtropical high (sinking air) from which the mTg air derives is centered over Florida in the summer and produces a monsoon-like, southerly, onshore flow all along the United States Gulf Coast. A large area of low pressure (rising air) persists throughout the summer over the deserts of northern Mexico. These two weather systems combine (the front of the low and the back of the high) to produce the characteristic southerly flow over the Texas coast. When the center of the high is far away over the United States East Coast, the pressure gradient is derived chiefly

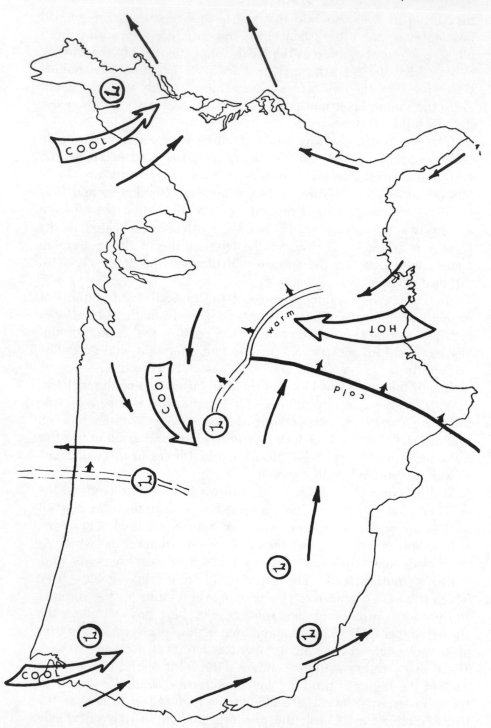

from the low and brings relatively dry air from Mexico in a southerly or south-southwesterly flow over the Texas coast. When the high is near, the pressure gradient produces a more southeasterly flow of moist air resulting in dense cumulonimbus and thunderstorm formation.

Galveston Bay is a shallow body of water inland of the large bar on which lies Galveston itself. The sea breeze flows from the Gulf across this bar and becomes a mixture of upper and lower southeasterly and weather system airflow as it emerges over Galveston Bay. The racing area of the Texas Corinthian Yacht Club is in the bight created by the protrusion of Eagle Point. It is downwind of that point and therefore the sea breeze in which racing is conducted has traversed two land masses en route which produce marked thermal mixing. If the pressure-gradient wind flowing above the sea breeze is southerly (hot, dry air from the low over Central Mexico) as it was on the first two days of Soling racing, it produces a strong sea breeze in which both gusts and lulls are veered and the median wind veers progressively with time. Surprisingly, however, the intermittent veers are often associated with a drop rather than an increase in velocity. The lull is produced by elements of the light weather system airflow brought to the surface by convection ashore. With increasing distance to leeward of the shore the airflow becomes steadier but reduced in velocity. While the competitors drifted in the center of Upper Galveston Bay each afternoon awaiting the sea breeze, the spectators at the yacht club enjoyed its presence and, noticing the fresh wind on the water near the shore, wondered why the races were not being started.

Thermal updrafts from the land readily induced the breeze to cross Lower Galveston Bay, but farther north in Upper Galveston Bay the shallow water was cooler than the sea breeze and could induce no convection. Ultimately, further heating of the land farther north induced the sea breeze front to cross Upper Galveston Bay and to escape in the convection produced inland. Until strongly induced to move on, however, it was unable to fight its way down to the surface.

If the pressure-gradient wind is an easterly or southeasterly from the back of the subtropical high over Florida, as it was on the last two days of racing in the Soling North Americans, surface wind is often delayed in appearance and reduced in velocity. This is partially due to a decrease in the heating of the land as moist Gulf air brings in an extensive cloud cover and to the minimal pressure-

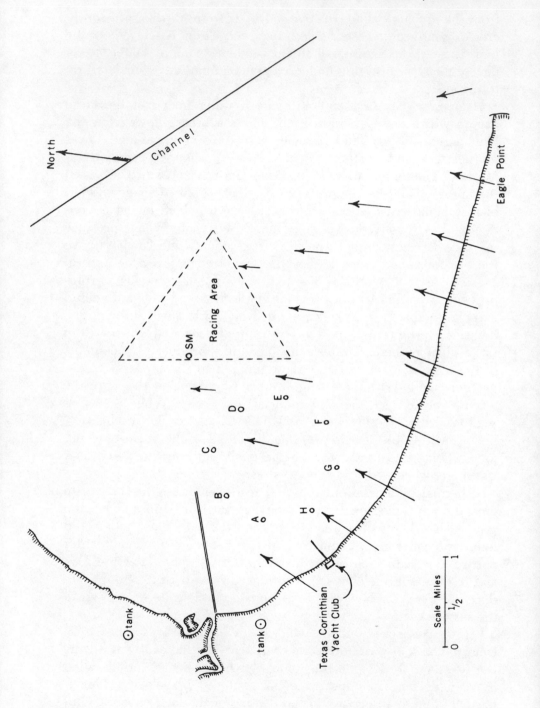

North

Channel

Racing Area

SM

D
C
E
B
F
A
G
H

tank

Texas Corinthian
Yacht Club

Eagle Point

Scale Miles
0   1/2   1

gradient flow associated with the sinking mTg air. Most significantly, the southeasterly weather system wind is progressively malaligned with the veering sea breeze. In contrast to the enhancement of sea breeze flow by a weather system southerly, a southeasterly interferes with sea breeze generation and does so increasingly with time, surface heating and veering of the surface flow. On the final day of racing in the Solings with an easterly pressure-gradient wind the sea breeze did not appear until 5:00 P.M. and even then was light and fitful. When the pressure-gradient wind is southeasterly it brings ashore massive amounts of moisture from the Gulf and, although cloud cover may then delay sea breeze formation, ultimate thunderstorm development will dramatically stimulate it in late afternoon.

Offshore sea breezes have the following characteristics:

1. They are strongest and most veered near the windward shore.

2. They are mixtures of sea breeze and of overlying pressure-gradient wind so that at the surface they are composed of random segments of low-level sea breeze, veered upper-level sea breeze and pressure-gradient wind. Gusts and lulls may be veered or backed depending on the velocity and direction of the overlying pressure-gradient wind.

3. They are delayed in appearance compared with the time of onset of the initial onshore breeze.

4. Their velocity is dependent upon their alignment with the pressure-gradient wind, being strongest when the pressure-gradient wind is veered relative to the initial sea breeze direction.

5. They are reduced in velocity offshore as their airflow has been heated in its passage over land and becomes more stable and less inclined to sink to the surface with distance to leeward of that land.

5. Maine and San Francisco—
Cold Current Sea Breezes

"The wind in the west
Suits everyone best,
The wind from the northeast
Is good for neither man nor beast."

The coldest water in the North Atlantic Ocean south of New-foundland is immediately adjacent to the coast in the Gulf of Maine. Thermographic charts of the North Atlantic show little change in temperature over vast areas offshore and then a dramatic and pro-gressive fall in temperature close aboard the coast. The same pat-tern is detectable along the California coast off San Francisco; the coldest water at that latitude lies immediately adjacent to the coast. In the summertime this apposition of cold water and warm land results in a strong, predictable sea breeze. On almost every racing day in both Boothbay Harbor and San Francisco Bay the onshore wind appears in late morning and builds with the heat of the day. The disparity of temperature between land and water which creates the sea breeze also produces the characteristic fog of these coasts. Warm air flowing over the cold offshore water precipitates its mois-ture in the advection fog that flows inland across the Maine islands and over the hills of San Francisco.

The cold water of the Maine Coast is due to the distribution of water from the Labrador Current. This current is the southerly flowing portion of a counterclockwise eddy in Baffin Bay to the west of Greenland. It brings Arctic water down to the Grand Banks of Newfoundland where it confronts and eddies with the northeastward flowing Gulf Stream. This meeting accounts for the dense and persistent fog of the Grand Banks. The residue of the Labrador Current separates the Gulf Stream from the Atlantic coast and spreads southward to Cape Cod eddying into the mouth of the St. Lawrence, the Bay of Fundy, and the Gulf of Maine en route. Coriolis force, deviating southerly flows to the west (in the Northern Hemisphere), deviates the Labrador Current toward the Maine coast, keeping the coldest of the water against the very edge of the land.

The cold water of the northern California coast is consequent to the southerly flowing portion of the North Pacific Current which, after crossing the Pacific from Japan, divides at Vancouver Island into the Alaska Current and the California Current. The North Pacific Current is an easterly flow of relatively warm water, a continuation of the gyral whose south portion is the westerly flowing North Equatorial Current. It warms and determines the mild climate of the Pacific Northwest. Compared with the warm climate of central and southern California the California Current is cool, but its temperature is scarcely cool enough to explain the cold water which floods into the Golden Gate. The Coriolis force, which deviates the Labrador Current toward the Maine coast, deviates the California Current away from the California coast. As current deviates surface water to the west, away from the coast, sea level is restored by an "upwelling" of cold bottom water from the depths of the Pacific. The shoreside water may therefore be several degrees colder than the California Current itself. Upwelling is particularly prominent in the spring and summer as the prevailing wind is from the northwest at this time. This wind accelerates the current; its increased velocity results in increased deviation to the west, upwelling is increased, and the coastal water becomes increasingly cold. Thus the shoreside water grows colder as the shore grows warmer. As summer wanes and the northwest wind subsides, the coastal water warms and the sea breeze decays. The famous sailing breeze of San Francisco Bay appears in June and July, not September.

Warm air over cold water produces stable airflow with little vertical mixing. Cold coastal water and warm summer air create an advection inversion separating weather system airflow from the surface, an ideal condition for the development of a local thermal wind. The prevailing surface wind in the summer in Maine is, therefore, a southerly (veered southwesterly by Coriolis force) flow of cold air from the surface of cold water offshore toward the hot land inshore. This wind appears on about 80 percent of the days of summer. It overcomes all but the strongest of high-pressure weather system winds. Only the strong northwesterly, which appears on the first day after the passage of a cold front, regularly overcomes it. When low-pressure systems appear, their rising air is attended by cloud formation which obscures the sun and blocks the thermal generation that induces the sea breeze. But lows are rare in summer and the Maine coast sailor can plan on the southwesterly almost every racing day. So regular is this wind flow that many of the northwest to southeast passages in Maine are known as reaches. In addition to famous Eggemoggin Reach, there is Fiddler's Reach up the Kennebec and The Reach, the western approach to Carver's Harbor on Vinalhaven. In the summer one can almost guarantee a dead reach in both directions through any of these passages.

When fog is present in Maine, the wind to be expected is the southwesterly, and when fog is present in San Francisco the wind to be expected is the westerly. The airflow will usually be light and variable at the surface offshore of the islands and peninsulas. As the sea breeze develops during the day the lower levels are stirred and the offshore fog is distributed throughout a deepening layer of air. The more turbulence is created (the stronger the airflow which develops), the more the fog thins and the higher the fogbank becomes. The strong westerly sea breeze of San Francisco bay dissipates the fog into a thick haze. The better the sailing, the less fog obscures the surface; and the faster one sails, the more visible become the hazards ahead. Rarely, however, will the fog be completely dissipated as the sea breeze is a cold airflow which cannot sustain much water in vapor form. In Maine the result is the "smoky" southwester.

The major variation in fog density is occasioned by local geography. Where the water is warmer the fog will be less, i.e., the fog rarely reaches far up the many rivers which flow southward to the coast in Maine or empty into San Francisco Bay. The fog is less in such inshore channels on the ebb tide. On the other hand, one must expect the fog to be dense in the deep water passages such as the Golden Gate where tidal change produces little temperature variation and in open bays where the water temperature is the same as in the ocean.

The islands in Maine and the peninsulas in San Francisco are the major determinants of fog and wind variation. They affect the air

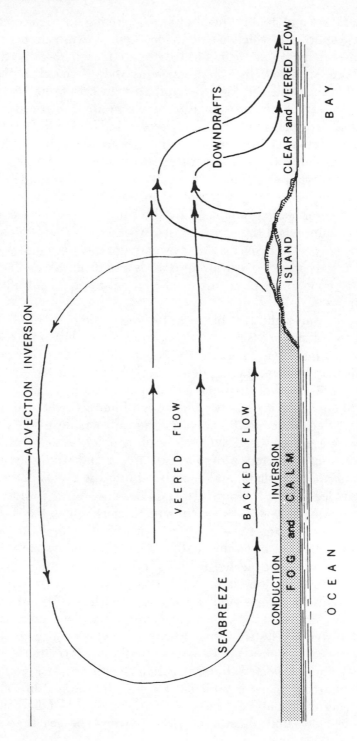

temperature and modify the ability of overlying air to accommodate water vapor. Air which passes over them is warmed by thermal columns rising from their surfaces heated each day by the sun. Downdrafts, heated by compression as they descend, replace the updrafts and melt the fog over and to leeward of the island. The air to leeward becomes a mixture of warm air from the surface of the land, segments of cool sea breeze and downdrafts of warm weather system air from aloft. Although an island has little affect upon the temperature of the water surrounding it, during the daytime it always warms the air above and to leeward of it. The degree of warming is directly proportional to the size of the island and to the degree of heating produced by the sun. Heating is, of course, at its maximum when the sun is most directly overhead—midsummer —and when cloud cover is least. Maximum clearing and maximum wind at the surface to leeward of islands and peninsulas will occur in midafternoon and will persist until thermal updrafts subside in the evening.

As the only wind that blows in the fog is the onshore sea breeze, the leeward sides of islands and peninsulas are always their inshore sides. And inshore is where the fog is least. To windward of an island the air may be cool, the fog dense, and the wind at the surface 1–3 knots. To leeward of the same island, perhaps a half mile away, the air will be warm, the sun shining from a blue sky overhead, and the wind at the surface 9–10 knots. As one sails amongst the islands of Maine one passes successively through a patch of calm and fog to the south of an island, a dramatically clear and windy area to the north of another island, and then back into the fog as one emerges from its lee into open water. In the "thoroughfares" inshore of the major islands of Maine, as within San Francisco Bay, the weather is dependably clear and warm while "outside" it is foggy and cold.

In the absence of an unusually strong weather system wind, the sea breeze can be expected in the summertime in either San Francisco Bay or along the Maine coast. It is particularly likely to appear when weather system winds are light and when they are excluded from the surface by an inversion. Inversion will be present whenever the weather system brings warm air to flow over the cold water along shore and will be associated with fog formation. The sea breeze can be expected to develop beneath this inversion whenever heating farther inland is sufficient to generate thermal lift-off. Thermal generation may be expected in the presence of high pressure and the associated absence of cloud cover. The sea breeze front

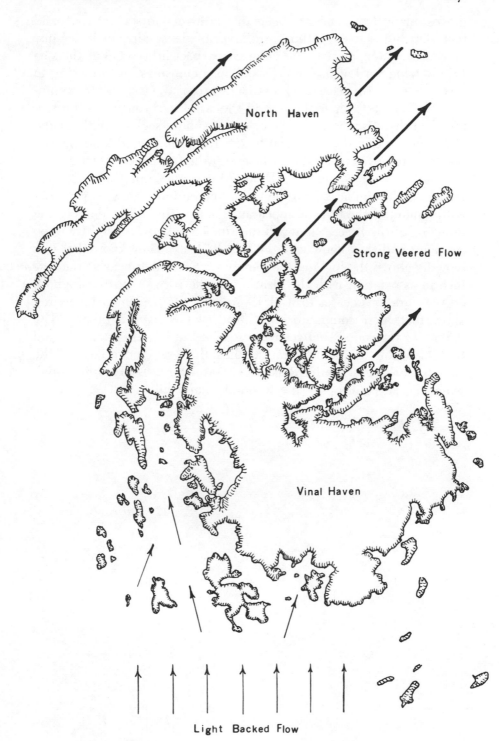

moves inland from offshore beneath the inversion several thousand feet aloft but above the thin, cold layer of dense air which lies just above the water surface. The sailor can expect little wind at the surface to windward of the outer islands or peninsulas, or in the fog to be expected in these areas. Only to leeward of the islands and peninsulas and close to their shores will the wind be brought to the surface and there is where the racing sailor should seek it. Without the turbulence induced by thermal lift-off from interposed land the sea breeze may never reach the surface and the fog never clear.

Those who have sailed in both Maine and San Francisco will recognize the similarities in the sailing conditions. They can predict within minutes the time of appearance and within a few degrees the direction of the breeze they will race in. They know where it will be strongest and they know where it will be least. They know that it is blowing above the fog and they know that it will appear at the surface in association with the clearing of the fog. When the foghorn on the Farallons ceases to wail, those on boats becalmed in the fog know that their competitors near the islands have a breeze. The difference, of course, between the sea breeze in San Francisco and that in Maine is that the former has the great energizer of the deserts to the east of the Bay to generate the pressure differential, while the latter has only the wooded inland hills.

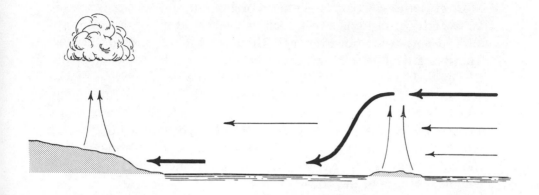

6. Marblehead and Buzzard's Bay—
The East Coast Ocean Sea Breeze

"When the glass falls low,
Prepare for a blow;
When it rises high,
Let all your sails fly."

Marblehead and Buzzard's Bay seem to have little in common other than their presence in Massachusetts, but in fact they share the same wind, the ocean sea breeze, flowing from the same ocean toward the same heated shore. Marblehead Harbor is in fact a miniature Buzzard's Bay. The sea breeze, veered to its initial course offshore, flows strongly at the surface in late afternoon within each. Outside to the south and east the same wind blows far more quietly and far less consistently. Buzzard's Bay has the reputation (justifiably) of being the best racing site on the East Coast. Marblehead Harbor, if it was a bit larger and sheltered a few less yachts, might have a similar reputation.

The characteristics of Buzzard's Bay are those of all great sea breeze areas. Its onshore wind flow appears at midday, increases steadily in velocity to a peak in late afternoon and is directly proportional to the disparity between the heating of the land and the coolness of the water. Although local sailors claim their breeze peaks at approximately 20 knots visitors suspect it blows at a considerably greater velocity. Its high velocity is consequent to the alignment of the Bay with the southerly weather system flow. High pressure lin-

gers off the coast in summer providing such flow for long periods.
Most of the East Coast is aligned north-south and its sea breeze is
an easterly. Protruding capes such as Cape Cod and Cape Ann are
aligned east–west, however, and their sea breezes are southerlies.
The Buzzard's Bay sea breeze also benefits from the presence of the
Elizabeth Islands between its waters and the ocean source of the
sea breeze. This interposed land provides the thermal turbulence
which brings down upper sea breeze flow and thus increases its
surface velocity. Finally Buzzard's Bay has relatively high shores
which converge progressively from mouth to head. This means that
the cold, dense sea breeze flow is funneled at increasing velocity as
it moves inshore to the north.

At Marion the sea breeze, the "smoky southwester," appears
regularly in late morning or early afternoon on most summer days.
It is most likely to be present when a high-pressure system has
passed to the south and east and hovers out in the Atlantic. If low
pressure exists simultaneously over the Great Lakes (as it frequently
does), southwesterly flow in its warm sector enhances the resultant
flow. The strongest sea breeze is present in late spring and early
summer when the temperature disparity between the cold ocean and
the heated land is at its greatest. The intensity of flow in Buzzard's
Bay is affected by the tide. The ingress of cold ocean water markedly
enhances the sea breeze if maximum flood coincides with the afternoon heating of the land.

The recommended course after starting in the sea breeze at
Marion is port tack to the line of buoys off Converse Point and the
earliest possible port tack across the Point. The sea breeze channels
around each of the protruding points along the north shore and into
the harbors. A persistent veer occurs to the east of each point as at
Converse and the first boat to the veer has the advantage. Beyond
Converse the wind backs to its main flow direction and therefore the
wise helmsman takes starboard tack out from the end of Converse
Point. If the mark is off Angelica, port tack should be resumed to
reach shore just short of the point and obtain the advantage of the
veer beyond it. This channeling is characteristic of all sea breezes
as they move inshore and can be expected to obtain around all of
the promontories of the Bay. The mainstream flow, southwesterly
off New Bedford, becomes more southerly off Marion and even
southeasterly as it deviates into the inlets of the north shore. Success
at Marion depends upon ability to sail in a big breeze and appropriate use of the persistent geographic shifts. Oscillating shifts are

present as they are in any offshore (in this case from the Elizabeth Islands) sea breeze but they are modest in extent and insignificant to strategy when compared to the persistent shoreline deviations.

Marblehead Harbor, like Buzzard's Bay, is aligned southwest–northeast, parallel to the prevailing weather system southwester, and protrudes into the sea on the south shore of a large cape. It has Devereaux Beach across its southern end to provide a thermal turbulence similar to that created for Buzzard's Bay by the Elizabeth Islands. It has high shores which gradually converge toward its northern end. And it has a strong afternoon seabreeze, often 8–10 knots stronger than the breeze in the racing area outside and veered 20°–30° to the offshore wind direction. Enhancement of surface sea breeze flow by interposed land is, of course, characteristic of most of the great sea breeze areas of the world—Barnegat Bay, Great South Bay, San Francisco Bay, Galveston Bay—and strong, veered flow is characteristic of sheltered harbors along ocean coasts—Newport Harbor, Acapulco Bay, Boothbay Harbor. An area of abrupt calm is regularly present at the entrance to Marblehead Harbor. This is a convergence zone where the channeled flow from within the harbor and the channeled flow entering Marblehead Channel meet and have no place to go but up.

Unfortunately racing at Marblehead does not take place in the harbor but outside to the southeast of Cat Island where the sea breeze is weaker, backed, and far more erratic. On a typical summer racing day when a high lies off the coast to the east and the predicted weather system flow is southwest 10–15 knots, the first breeze is evident within the harbor and close to the outer shores. At the time of its first appearance off Cat Island about 7:00 to 8:00 A.M., it is blowing at about 4 knots from 140° to 150°. By the time of a race start at 10:00 A.M. it has increased to 6–8 knots (occasionally more) and has veered to 180° to 190°. Within the harbor it will usually increase in velocity at a steady rate and veer further to about 200° or 210° in the late afternoon. Not so in the racing area. This first sea breeze is but a teaser and cannot be relied upon. On each of the days on which we raced the 1971 New England Soling Regatta, after a start at 10:30 A.M. the sea breeze gradually died and backed while it died. On two of the mornings (before the pattern became evident) we had tacked out on port hoping for a progressive veer with an increase in velocity. In both instances we were rewarded by a gradual back to about 160° either before the start or halfway up the first beat. Then, after a few minutes of very light

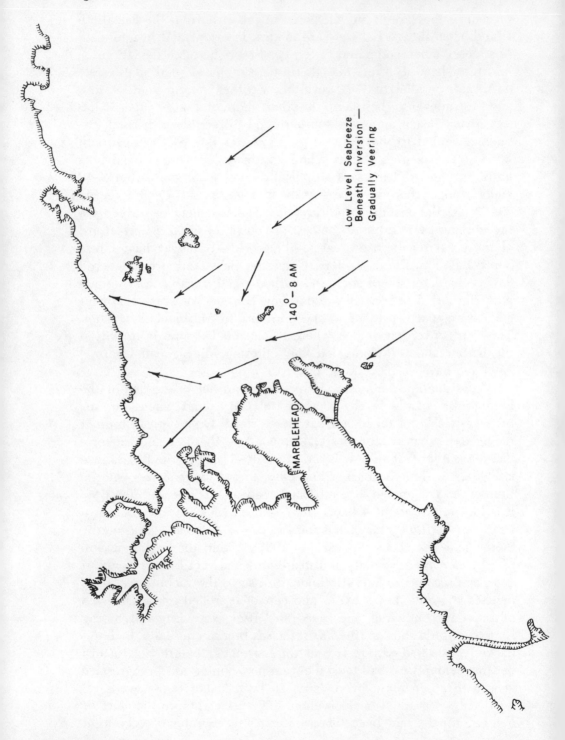

Low Level Seabreeze
Beneath Inversion —
Gradually Veering

140° — 8 AM

MARBLEHEAD

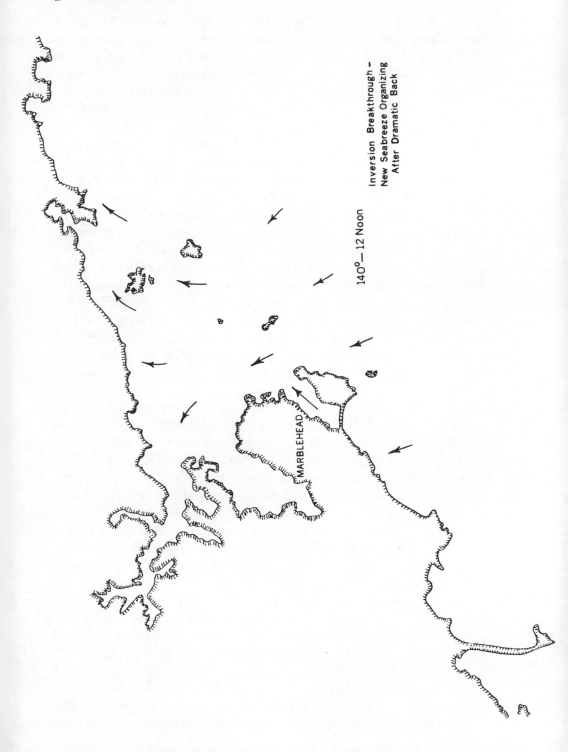

Inversion Breakthrough –
New Seabreeze Organizing
After Dramatic Back

140° — 12 Noon

MARBLEHEAD

air at 160°, the wind rapidly backed to approximately 140° and then progressively increased in velocity. Once we salvaged second at the weather mark as the 40° back lifted us to the mark by the great circle route; once we were left far on the wrong side of a 40° back which had done its first 20° of backing before the start.

The new breeze, which appears between 11:00 and 12:00, steadily increases in velocity and gradually veers. By the end of a morning race, at 12:00 to 12:30, it is often up to 8–10 knots and has veered to 155°. During the pause preceding a race at 2:00 P.M. this wind veers further and may build to 10–12 knots. A 2:00 P.M. start is likely to be conducted in a sea breeze from 165°. During the first beat or two of an afternoon race gradual oscillations between 165° and 175° appear and recurrent tacks to take advantage of such oscillations are useful. An abrupt veer to approximately 185° to 195° occurred at approximately 4:00 P.M. on each sea breeze day of the 1971 Soling Regatta. In one instance this occurred on the final beat and we gained considerably by being to the west of the fleet; in the other it occurred on the final run and we lost two boats who had taken starboard jibe to the east of the fleet and came roaring back high on port jibe to nip us at the line. Thereafter the veered flow built further and within the harbor upon our return was gusting to 20 knots.

This same pattern—a dying morning sea breeze followed at about noon by a replacement sea breeze backed 40°—is also typical of Long Island Sound and the Chesapeake. It seems evident that one sea breeze is progressively generated from 7:00 to 11:00 A.M., builds, veers, and decays. Another replaces it at about 12:00 noon from the same initial direction, builds and veers progressively throughout the afternoon. An abrupt veer in late afternoon is followed by a further increase in velocity before the breeze deteriorates at dusk. A simple rule for dealing with this phenomenon is to take starboard tack when the sea breeze is dying (particularly in late morning), expecting a back, and to take port tack when the sea breeze is building (particularly in late afternoon), expecting a veer. This technique is also appropriate to dealing with the seabreeze under intermittent cloud cover—backing and dying under cloud cover and increasing and veering under clear sky—and suggests that the pattern has something to do with the breakthrough of an inversion.

The initial sea breeze direction at both 7:00 A.M. and 12:00 noon is approximately perpendicular to the general alignment of the shore. Thus the beginning sea breeze represents initial outflow from

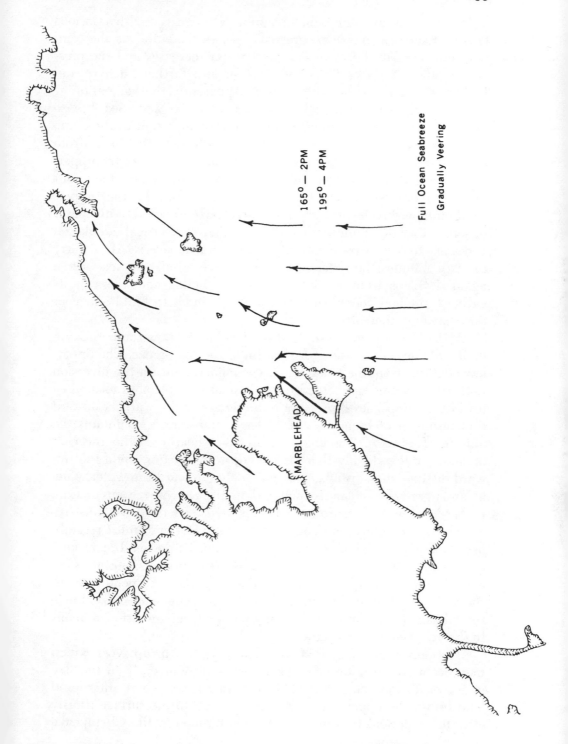

165° — 2PM
195° — 4PM

Full Ocean Seabreeze
Gradually Veering

MARBLEHEAD

a dome of high pressure which has not yet been veered by Coriolis effects. Each sea breeze progressively veers thereafter as the temperature disparity between land and water increases and the pressure gradient induces flow from farther and farther offshore and higher and higher above the surface. Apparently the generation of the morning sea breeze falters at about 11:00 A.M. Sea breeze maintenance depends upon the constant replenishment of the dome of high pressure over the water by outflow toward the water from above the heated land. Although heating and elevation of the upper-level pressure must be continuing ashore, outflow toward the water must temporarily cease in late morning. This suggests that upper-level outflow directed toward the water early in the day dissipates in some other direction temporarily and that the vertical circulation necessary to sea breeze maintenance temporarily ceases. After thirty to sixty minutes, however, circulation is restored, the sea breeze again develops from its initial direction, builds and veers to its earlier force and veered direction and continues to build and veer unremittingly thereafter.

At 11:00 A.M. the morning inversion breaks down and this undoubtedly accounts for the dissipation of the sea breeze. The upper-level outflow from the heated land is confined beneath the inversion until late morning, prevented from dissipating aloft, and channeled toward the upper-level pressure reduction over the water. Constant replenishment of high pressure at the water surface maintains the morning sea breeze. The inversion breaks as heating of the lower air increases and suddenly there is no lid, no restriction upon the upward dissipation of rising air, no channeling toward the water. Now a far larger mass of air is included in the sea breeze circulation. Upper-level high pressure must be restored over the land, must reestablish an organized outflow toward the water, and must reestablish the dome of high pressure over the water before sea breeze flow commences again at the surface. A new sea breeze is established and like all new sea breezes it commences its flow perpendicular to the shore, backed 40° to the end of the morning sea breeze. Once reestablished, generation is continuous; no other inversion remains to disturb the organized flow.

The only remaining dramatic change is the abrupt veer which may occur in late afternoon. This veer is present early in the day in Buzzard's Bay and within Marblehead Harbor where interposed land brings the upper veered sea breeze flow to the surface shortly after its inception. It is present in midafternoon in the Chesapeake

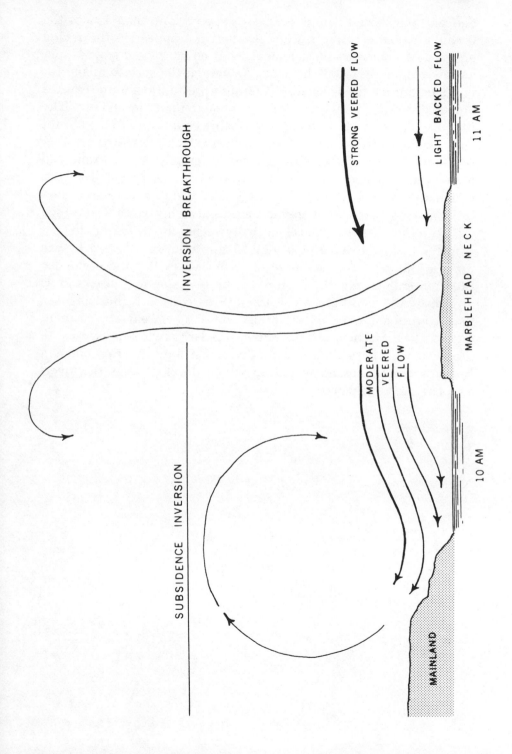

and on Long Island Sound as the interposed land mass brings the ocean sea breeze to the surface. It does not appear in the racing areas off Marblehead until late as there is no interposed land. Upper airflow veered 190°–200° has been flowing at the surface inland for hours before the lower levels of the high-pressure dome to seaward are finally dragged along with the veered upper-level flow. The irregular shoreline at Marblehead probably contributes to the abrupt and seemingly erratic late afternoon veer which often appears over but limited areas of the offshore surface initially. This abrupt and temporarily isolated change is in contrast to the progressive veer which occurs when upper-level flow is included in a more organized fashion along a straight shoreline such as at Long Beach, California.

There are two sea breezes in many racing areas, frequently dependent upon the superimposition of an ocean or lake sea breeze upon a local or harbor sea breeze. At Buzzard's Bay the ocean sea breeze usually awaits the rupture of the inversion and breaks in as an apparently uniform flow (although a light early morning sea breeze is often present in the harbors and dies before its replacement arrives). At Marblehead there are regularly two sea breezes—a morning sea breeze beneath the inversion and an afternoon sea breeze several thousand feet deep which develops after the inversion has been dissipated.

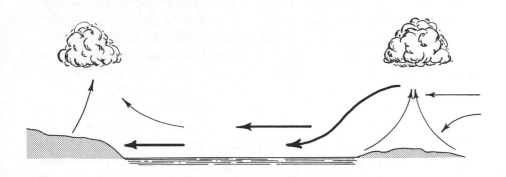

7. The Chesapeake and Long Island Sound— Combined Sea Breezes

"When the sun sets clear as a bell
There'll be an easterly wind, as sure as hell!"

Summer sailing in the Chesapeake and on Long Island Sound is notorious for its light air (Don Doyle calls Annapolis the "Light Air Capital of the World"). Weather system winds are light in the summer because the air masses have dissipated their high pressure long before their airflows reach the east coast. Cyclone formation, except in the form of thunderstorms, is infrequent in the summer because heated land surfaces do not provide enough associated moisture to develop a significant reduction in pressure and the oceans are cool relative to the overlying airflow. Chesapeake Bay and Long Island Sound rely on the appearance of the sea breeze to provide their only decent summer sailing. But they have few of the attributes of the great sea breeze areas and many of the defects that delay or prevent the appearance of a sea breeze in otherwise appropriate conditions. Long Island Sound is distinctly the more advantaged of the two areas, however, as it runs east-west and so aligns its onshore sea breeze with the prevailing southerly winds of summer. In addition, Long Island interposes a land mass but half as wide as the Maryland–Delaware Peninsula (the Eastern Shore) between the sea breeze and the racing.

The best sea breeze of 1970 in the upper Chesapeake occurred on June 17. Other excellent sea breezes were noted as early as

March 28 but no really strong sea breeze occurred during racing hours after July. The maximum strength of midday sea breezes in summer and fall was about 15 knots and even this strength was infrequent. On ideal spring days, the southerly developed in late morning, reached a peak of approximately 25 knots in midafternoon and did not subside until sundown. Spring, of course, provided the ideal circumstance of cold ocean and Bay water, retaining the chill of winter, in the presence of intensely heated land. On June 17 a high was centered over South Carolina and on the other great sea breeze days a high was centered off the coast of Virginia or the Carolinas. These highs were derived from continental polar (cP) air and were thus composed of dry, clear air through which thermal generation was readily achieved. On each of the days of strong sea breeze flow a frontal system lay along a southwest to northeast axis from Texas to the Great Lakes. The frontal system moving rapidly east, compressed and reinforced the southerly flow on the back of the high. The strong weather system flow thus aligned with the southerly thermal flow to produce the best sea breezes of the year.

The Chesapeake is characterized by a local sea breeze emanating from a dome of cold, high-pressure air overlying the Bay itself and by an ocean sea breeze derived from a far larger ridge of cold, high-pressure air over the ocean. The easterly onshore flow which appears in late morning along the Chesapeake's western shore is a local sea breeze outflow from high pressure over the Bay. It may be associated with a westerly onshore flow along the Eastern Shore. Outflow from this dome of high pressure over the cold Bay develops in all directions except toward the open water to the south. Here the ocean sea breeze enters the Bay unimpeded by an intervening land barrier and, channeled between the entrance capes, provides a strong southeasterly onshore flow in the "Southern Bay." The ocean sea breeze entering the lower reaches of the Bay provides the initial impetus to set the high-pressure air over the Bay moving to the north. As outflow of the dense surface air is impeded to some extent by the land barrier of each shore this impetus is readily converted into a general northerly movement. The excess heating produced by the large city of Baltimore at the head of the Bay aids the trend to northerly deviation. As the velocity of flow increases with additional heating ashore, the characteristic veer induced by the earth's rotation appears, deviating the southeasterly onshore flow along the western shore to a southwesterly. All of these influences combine to produce the characteristic southwesterly sea breeze flow of the Upper Bay's western

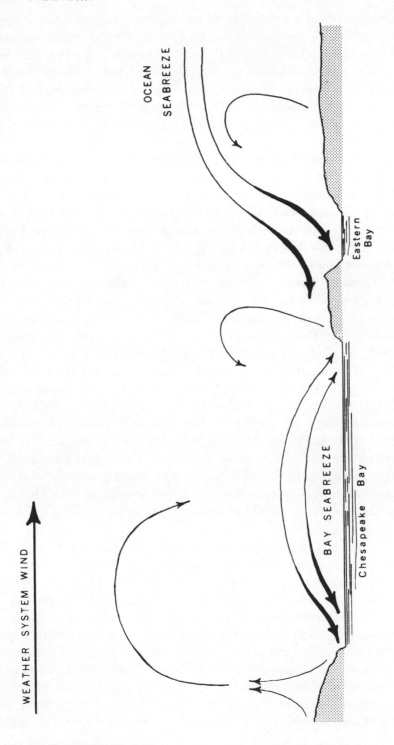

shore. The local Eastern Shore sea breeze, on the other hand, is progressively diminished as veering of the initial westerly flow to northwesterly causes increasing malalignment with the channeled flow from south to north. An onshore flow from the west along the Eastern Shore is, in fact, rarely seen except in unusually light conditions and then only within the Eastern Shore where interposed land may transiently bring a light thermal down to the surface of the tidal rivers.

Looking down from the Bay Bridge at midday one will notice the Bay sea breeze beginning as an easterly flow from mid-Bay toward the western shore. The eastern half of the Bay will be a glassy calm. By midafternoon, however, the sea breeze now deviated southeasterly, fills the entire Bay and the strongest wind is flowing offshore along the Eastern Shore. This heralds the appearance of the ocean sea breeze. By late morning a strong easterly onshore flow has appeared along the ocean coasts of Delaware and Maryland which provides good sailing in the lagoons behind Ocean City and similar beach resorts. The cold front of this ocean sea breeze progresses inland to the west aided by thermal generation ahead as it crosses the Delmarva Peninsula. As a sea breeze cold front progresses at about 10 knots, it may be late afternoon before the ocean sea breeze traverses the thirty to forty miles of intervening land between the ocean and the Upper Bay. This land is extremely flat and thus creates little barrier to the frontal movement. By the time the front has traversed the land its velocity is sufficiently great to be associated with a large southerly veer. Thus as it comes off the Eastern Shore it aligns well with the Bay sea breeze and, reinforcing it, produces the strong southwesterly of late afternoon. This is the "anchor breeze" in which we plane home after waiting all day for a breath of air.

Sailors who race within the rivers of the Eastern Shore receive the best of the ocean sea breeze. At Oxford and Corsica River they receive it sooner and they receive much more of its strong upper flow. Thermal columns rising from the heated land interposed between these rivers and the sea breeze induce downdrafts of upper sea breeze air so that a strong veered flow reaches the surface in the gusty fashion characteristic of these racing waters. Fifteen miles away in Annapolis there may be no wind at the surface, however, as the sea breeze flow, warmed by its long traverse of land, glides over the cold, dense surface air of the Bay. If one were racing a long-distance race on the Bay one would seek the western shore early on

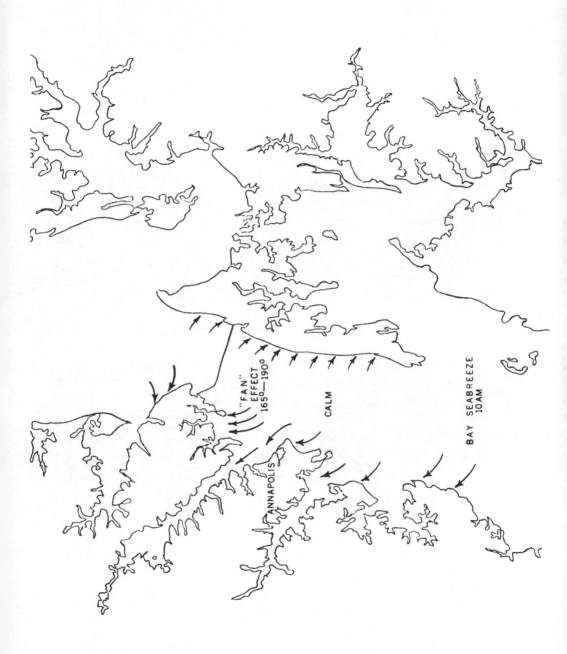

"FAN"
EFFECT
165°—190°

CALM

ANNAPOLIS

BAY SEABREEZE
10 AM

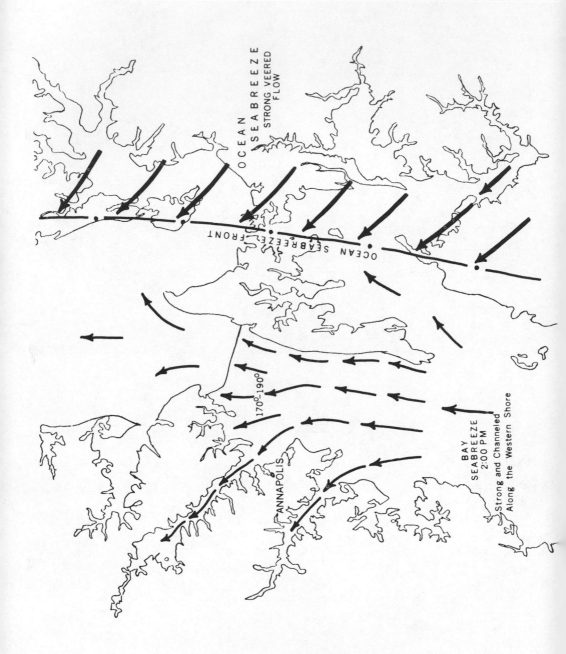

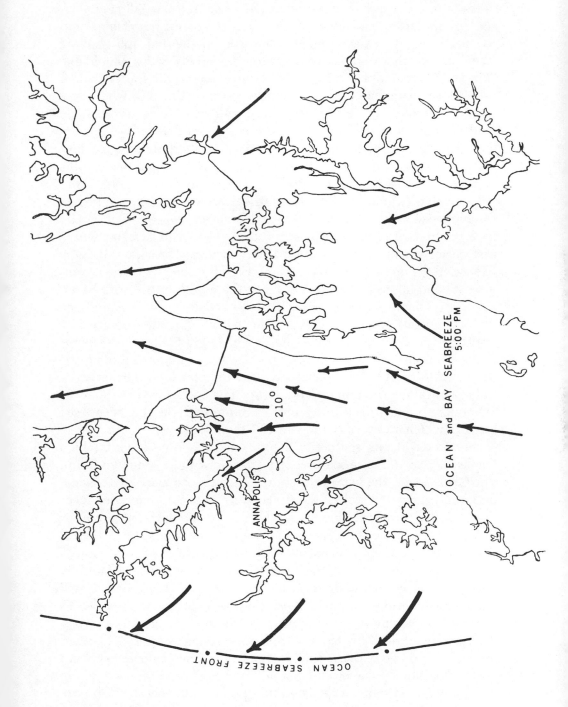

a sea breeze day as here is where the Bay sea breeze will first appear. But by midafternoon the ocean sea breeze should be offshore and strong, brought to the surface by interposed thermal uplifts along the Eastern Shore, and this is where the racing sailor should be. The sea breeze will last longer into the evening on the Eastern Shore for the same reasons. In the southern part of the Bay where less land is interposed, the Eastern Shore will provide less advantage and, in fact, the reinforcement of the ocean sea breeze by the easterly flowing Bay sea breeze along the western shore usually provides an advantage to the west. This is particularly true at the mouths of the major southeasterly flowing rivers of the western shore (Tidewater Virginia) where the southeasterly ocean-Bay sea breeze is channeled between high banks at increased velocity. One of the best sea breezes of the east coast is found below Mobjack Bay where the ocean sea breeze, channeled between Cape Charles and Cape Henry and unobstructed by any intervening land, is further compressed and intensified as it rushes into the mouth of the York River.

Long Island Sound is also characterized by a local Sound sea breeze and an ocean sea breeze. The early Sound sea breeze is a southerly along the northern shore which gradually veers southwesterly. It first appears (in spring, early in the morning) along the northern shore at a time when there may be some light northerly onshore flow along the Long Island Shore. The Sound sea breeze never amounts to much, however, unless reinforced by the ocean sea breeze which rarely fills in before 2:00 P.M. in the summertime. Thereafter a strong southerly, a combined sea breeze flow, which backs the North Shore sea breeze may persist until sundown. As in the Chesapeake, the best of the summer sea breeze, once established, is found along the Long Island shore as thermal generation over Long Island brings the ocean sea breeze to the surface. Again, as with the Eastern Shore, there may be a good southerly in Oyster Bay when the Sound is glassy calm. If the weather system airflow is warm and the Sound cold, the warmed sea breeze, further heated by mixing with thermal updrafts from the surface of Long Island, will pass imperceptibly over the dense pool of cold air at the Sound's surface. No sea breeze may appear at this surface despite a strong flow overhead until too late for the racing sailor to use it. The wind may come and go with the tide, increasing on the Connecticut shore as the flood tide enhances the Sound sea breeze and diminishing on the Long Island shore as the flood tide prevents the ocean sea breeze from reaching the surface. The minimal tidal changes of the shallow Chesapeake rarely demonstrate these effects.

The ocean sea breeze/Bay sea breeze combination will vary with the seasons as the strength of each varies. Variations in ocean temperature are limited to a narrower range and are delayed compared to variations in Bay or Sound temperature. In winter the ocean is warmer than the Bay and considerably warmer than the land. In spring the ocean is but little warmer while the Bay is considerably warmer. By summer the ocean has warmed considerably but not nearly as much as the Bay and is far cooler than the land. In the fall, the ocean still holds the heat of the summer while the Bay has already cooled considerably and approximates the average temperature of the land. By winter, the Bay is very cold, frequently cooler than the air which flows above it while the ocean retains its warmth and is almost always warmer than the land and the air which flows above it. The Bay or Sound sea breeze, therefore, reaches its maximum velocity in the spring when the temperature disparity between the land and the inshore water is at its maximum, flows at a lesser velocity in the summer, and is weak or absent in the fall. The ocean sea breeze reaches its maximum strength in summer when the temperature disparity between land and ocean is at its maximum, diminishes in the fall, is absent in the winter, and becomes barely perceptible in the spring.

SEASONAL VARIATIONS IN THE ANNAPOLIS SEA BREEZE

	LAND TEMPERATURE (RELATIVE)	OCEAN TEMPERATURE (RELATIVE)	BAY TEMPERATURE (RELATIVE)	OCEAN SEA BREEZE	BAY SEA BREEZE
WINTER	Cold	Warm	Cold	Absent	Rare
SPRING	Warm	Cool	Cold	5:00 P.M. Weak Southwest	12:00 noon Strong South
SUMMER	Hot	Cold	Cool	3:00–5:00 P.M. Strong Southwest	1:00–2:00 P.M. Weak South
FALL	Cool	Cool	Warm	5:00 P.M. Weak Southwest	Absent

In the spring the local Bay or Sound sea breeze is present alone and, when strengthened by a strong southerly weather system flow aligned within 45°, can be an excellent racing wind. The spring sea breeze, being the local sea breeze, will begin in late morning or early afternoon, will be less veered as it travels but a short way to shore, and will fade as soon as the sun begins to fade. In late spring, the ocean sea breeze appears and in June the combination of a reinforced Bay sea breeze and an ocean sea breeze produces the best sea breeze of the year. In summer, when the local sea breeze is weak, the onshore thermal wind, the ocean sea breeze, develops later in the day, often not until 4:00 or 5:00 P.M. It is more veered than the local sea breeze as it has been moving rapidly over a long distance before it arrives at the water surface and it persists well into the evening as it is a massive airflow that must continue long after its generation ceases. In the fall, little sea breeze formation can be expected and then only when the land has been strongly heated and the air is crystal clear (usually on the second or third day after the ingress of cP air behind a cold front). The only likely sea breeze will be the ocean sea breeze, appearing late in the day and usually too late to race in.

The logical season to race in the Chesapeake or on Long Island Sound is in the spring when most sailors are still painting their boats. The logical time to race in the summertime, if that's when we must race, is after five o'clock as that is when the breeze comes in.

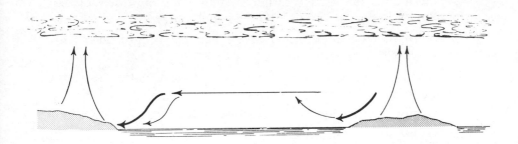

8. The Chesapeake and Long Island Sound—
Shifts in the Sea Breeze

"Winds at night are always bright,
But winds in the morning,
Sailors take warning."

An onshore sea breeze is a stable airflow, cool air (cooled by
the water over which it has accumulated) flowing over cooler water.
It does not oscillate so long as its course is over the cool water. Only
after it traverses land or heated shallow water does it become
vertically unstable and begin to oscillate. An offshore sea breeze,
particularly near the windward shore, is a markedly oscillating flow.
On Long Island Sound and in the Chesapeake such oscillations are
frequent and of brief duration near the Long Island or Eastern
Shore. Elsewhere, in the center of these bodies and along the Connecticut shore and the Chesapeake's western shore, shifts in the sea
breeze are often protracted. Frequently these shifts persist for the
duration of entire windward legs and are therefore properly termed
persistent. Often they last for only five to ten minutes and, for
typical around-the-buoys racing where windward legs last for twenty
minutes or more, are properly termed oscillating. This distinction,
dependent largely upon the duration of the leg, is of utmost significance in determining windward strategy.

Shifts in the sea breeze, in addition to the oscillations characteristic of offshore instability, are consequent to the following causes:

1. Onset, replacing a weather system wind or another sea breeze.
2. Offset, being replaced by a weather system wind or another

sea breeze, often after the breakthrough of a subsidence inversion.

3. Alternation between weather system wind and sea breeze aligned between 45° and 135° to each other.

4. Alternation between upper and lower sea breeze flow associated with intermittent cloud cover.

5. Veering, with increase in velocity and proximation to shore due to inclusion of upper airflow.

6. Backing, with decrease in velocity and distance from shore due to absence of upper airflow.

7. The fan effect, due to the combined veering and backing indicated above.

8. Channeling, along shoreline elevations, around promontories, and into harbors and inlets.

9. Refraction as the onshore flow prepares to traverse the shoreline or the offshore flow leaves the shoreline.

ONSET AND OFFSET

Sea breeze generation is accurately predictable and recognizable in the presence of strong northwesterly or northerly outflow from high pressure and when a high moves past to the south resulting in wind from the westerly quadrants. Then a dramatic zone of calm develops in the offshore weather system wind (along an east-facing coast) before it is replaced by the invading sea breeze from the opposite direction. Surprising shifts perpendicular to the sea breeze may then appear, however. Frequently a new wind, veered or backed to the apparently dying offshore wind, appears for a period of a few minutes to an hour. At Annapolis a dying northwesterly is often replaced by a light northeasterly which gradually veers to an easterly, a southwesterly, and only after an hour or so shifts to the classic southwest sea breeze (210°). At CORK '71, while awaiting the development of the sea breeze against a light northeasterly, a light westerly appeared, persisted for an hour in early afternoon and was finally replaced by the true southwest sea breeze at about 4:00 P.M. On Long Island Sound as the morning sea breeze beneath the inversion dies, it is often replaced by a brief easterly and/or (rarely) a westerly prior to the appearance of the afternoon sea breeze. Lifting of the offshore wind above the dense sea breeze air produces an area of reduced pressure ahead of the sea breeze front

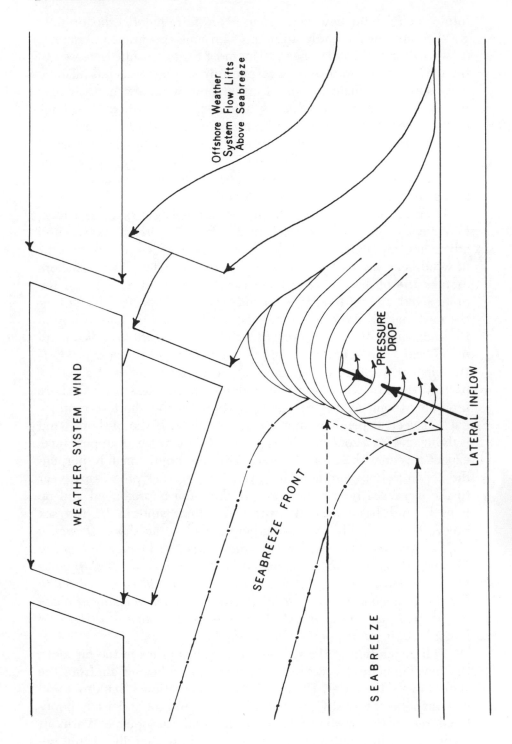

Offshore Weather System Flow Lifts Above Seabreeze

WEATHER SYSTEM WIND

PRESSURE DROP

LATERAL INFLOW

SEABREEZE FRONT

SEABREEZE

into which lateral flow may occur. Not infrequently the original wind returns momentarily after the transient appearance of such a new wind, and then disappears. The most common shift is veered to the offshore wind, probably in response to the more veered offshore flow aloft. The amalgamation of an offshore wind and a sea breeze *which are present simultaneously* is often accomplished by a back in the offshore flow (if the sea breeze is only moderately backed to the offshore wind). However, if a zone of calm has been present and/or if the sea breeze is not yet evident, the likely shift will be veered to the offshore wind even though this may require a 270° swing to the ultimate sea breeze direction.

If an offshore wind dies during or immediately prior to a race, look for evidence of the sea breeze. If it is already active and advancing rapidly toward shore, expect the passage of a brief zone of windshear and replacement by the sea breeze flow. Move offshore or take the offshore tack to receive the new wind first. If, on the other hand, the sea breeze is advancing slowly and it is likely that the next mark will remain in the offshore flow, sail inshore to stay in the old wind. *Alway seek to obtain the best position in the wind which will be present at the time of your arrival at the next mark.* If the offshore wind is strong, the sea breeze is strong, and a stable, narrow zone of windshear which does not progress toward shore separates them, expect an amalgamation by the shortest route, a back or veer, depending upon their alignment. If the offshore wind is dying and/or a zone of calm is present following its disappearance, expect a veer with an initial new wind flow approximately perpendicular to the offshore flow, followed by a further progressive veer to the usual sea breeze direction. If the calm is prolonged and no lateral wind has appeared, expect the first wind to be the sea breeze itself, initially flowing perpendicular to the shore. *If such a shift is expected to be moderate so that a beat will remain a beat, or to cause a reach or run to become a beat, sail toward the shift so as to be upwind in the new wind. If such a shift will cause a beat to become a reach or run, or a reach or run to become a changed reach or run, sail away from the shift so as to be to leeward at the best possible sailing angle in the new wind.*

Full generation of the sea breeze requires order in the air aloft, the development of a consistent movement of heated air from the shore toward the water. The increasing construction of buildings and pavement, as the East Coast becomes more and more densely populated, results in persistent heating of the total atmosphere. Warm air incorporated in weather system flow, already heated and lifting because of its low density, does not permit the development of a simple low-pressure system over the land toward which cool sea air can flow. Low pressure along the shore from any of these sources, instead of enhancing the sea breeze, permits the dissipation of the upper-level offshore flow in rising currents over the land. In the absence of organized outflow from the heated shore the dome of high pressure accumulating over the water soon disintegrates and the sea breeze disappears or is replaced by a residue of weather system wind. When the dome of high pressure reaccumulates the sea breeze reappears, but in such conditions usually not for long. The result is the typical summer weekend on Long Island Sound or in the Chesapeake, drifting sailboats on placid water, alternating appearances of sea breeze and weather system wind at the surface, and races won and lost by inexplicable persisting and oscillating shifts. Summertime east coast racing is deteriorating just as it is on Galveston Bay, where the increasing expansion of Houston has progressively reduced the development of the once-famous sea breeze.

A significant change in wind direction is regularly associated with a change in wind strength. A significant change in wind strength (increase or decrease) is often associated with a change in wind direction, but this is less often recognized. It may be the first indication of a new wind source. It may mean the appearance of a squall within the weather system, a new weather system, or the sea breeze (or the restoration of the initial wind after the appearance of a new wind). A cursory evaluation of the weather map and the sky should indicate whether a squall or a new weather system is likely to appear. In the absence of such conditions a general alteration in wind strength along the east coast indicates either a movement of the existing weather system or the appearance or disappearance of a superimposed sea breeze. An abrupt alteration almost certainly indicates the latter. A new wind flow, even if it results in an ultimate reinforcement, usually disturbs and reduces the existing wind before any directional alteration is detectable. The ultimate change in strength or direction is determined by the relative strength of each wind but even minimal thermal generation may cause a slight shift in the existing flow.

ONSET AND OFFSET WITH WEATHER SYSTEM WIND

While waiting at about 2:00 P.M. for the start of the second race of the 1966 Fall Invitational Regatta off Annapolis, we noted a significant drop in the strength of the moderate weather system easterly. The sun was shining brightly, the temperature ashore was rising into the high seventies, and it seemed reasonable to expect that the southerly Bay sea breeze had finally appeared. We took off from the starting line on port, were the first to receive the 15° veer to the south, and in a stronger breeze tacked across the fleet and won with ease. The breeze dropped again at the end of the race and then just before the start of the third race, at 4:00 P.M., began to fill in again. We (unfortunately) concluded that this was merely a variation in the sea breeze and/or that the weather system had moved far enough to reinforce the southerly. After some difficulty in moving past a Canadian who felt (correctly) that our overlap did not entitle us to room at the weather end of the line, we took off again on port. This time the wind swung back to the east and we, far away on the outside of the shift, rounded the weather mark next to last and were lucky to salvage a tenth at the line. Instead of an increasing sea breeze we had met with an increasing weather system easterly. We should have realized that a sea breeze would be unlikely to strengthen at 4:00 P.M. on an October afternoon. Instead its decrease with the sinking sun had permitted the return of the overlying weather system easterly.

ONSET AND OFFSET WITH INVERSION BREAKTHROUGH

Off Greenwich, Connecticut, during the 1971 Long Island Sound Soling Championship, the early appearance of a local sea breeze was regularly followed by a decrease in velocity and a back in late morning. During the first beat of the first race on four successive days the boats that initially continued out on starboard to near the layline arrived at the weather mark first. On three occasions this advantage was associated with a general back over the entire race course as a new sea breeze filled in and backed the entire wind flow. As, in the Chesapeake, I was used to a progressive veer as the local sea breeze developed, in three of these four races I was on the wrong side of this general shift. The morning sea breeze first appeared close to the north shore within its harbors, built, spread and veered (from 175°–215°) steadily throughout the morning and then at about 11:00 A.M. abruptly backed and died. Thereafter a new sea breeze appeared and provided a light flow at opproximately 175°, veered slightly to the perpendicular to the general Connecticut shoreline, but backed as much as 40° to the earlier sea breeze flow. Thereafter as the ocean sea breeze amalgamated with the local flow the wind

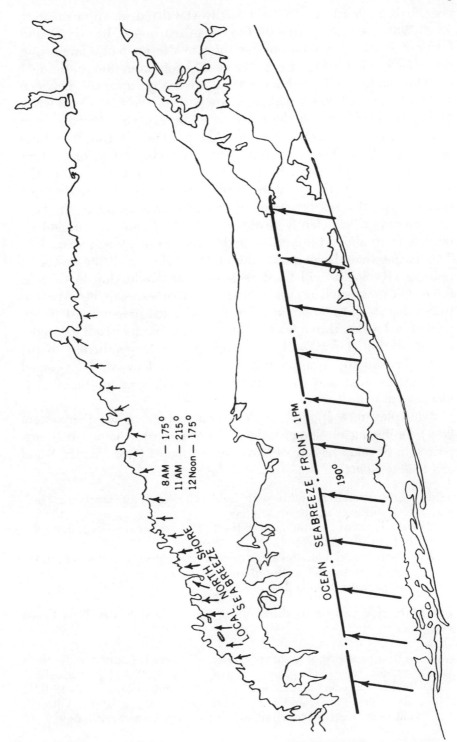

veered through 10° to 15° and finally stabilized at approximately 190°. With increasing strength the ocean sea breeze has fewer and fewer oscillations. In mid-sound in the late afternoon of a late spring day at high tide it reaches a steady 15–20 knots from due south.

This major shift, which characteristically appears between 11:00 A.M. and 12:00 noon along many parts of the East Coast when high pressure hovers off the coast, must be expected when a local sea breeze appears early in the day. The presence of a local onshore flow before 8:00–9:00 A.M. means that overlying inversions, either advectional or subsidential, are protecting the lower levels of the atmosphere from the weather system wind and facilitating the organization of a sea breeze circulation. When heating of the land has progressed sufficiently to destroy the inversion, the organized outflow from above the heated land is temporarily dissipated aloft. This means that the onshore flow at the surface will die and as it reduces in velocity will back because of the reduction in Coriolis force. On most such occasions a new sea breeze can be expected to develop in 15 to 60 minutes but this new sea breeze must be expected to develop through all the stages that characterized its predecessor. Its initial flow will be approximately perpendicular to the shore (backed 40° from the fully veered flow of the well-developed early sea breeze) and its subsequent flow will veer gradually as it increases in velocity.

The rules to be applied (in the absence of strong weather system flow) for racing on summer days along a coast which can be expected to develop sea breeze flow are as follows (from Watts, *Wind and Sailing Boats*):

(1) Big scattered cumulus with light wind—sea breeze comes in fast and goes a long way inland.

(2) Small puffs of cumulus over the hills—sea breeze not hindered but not greatly helped.

(3) Warmth and cloudlessness or a cloud layer (stratocumulus) which "burns off" in the morning—sea breeze comes in slowly and perhaps erratically.

The latter rule can be modified along the United States East Coast as follows:

(3) In the presence of an advection or subsidence (upper-level) inversion, sea breeze comes in early (by 9:00 A.M.) gradually builds and veers and then abruptly at about 11:00 A.M. to 12:00 noon dies, backs, and is replaced by a new sea breeze whose initial flow is backed up to 40° to the earlier sea breeze flow.

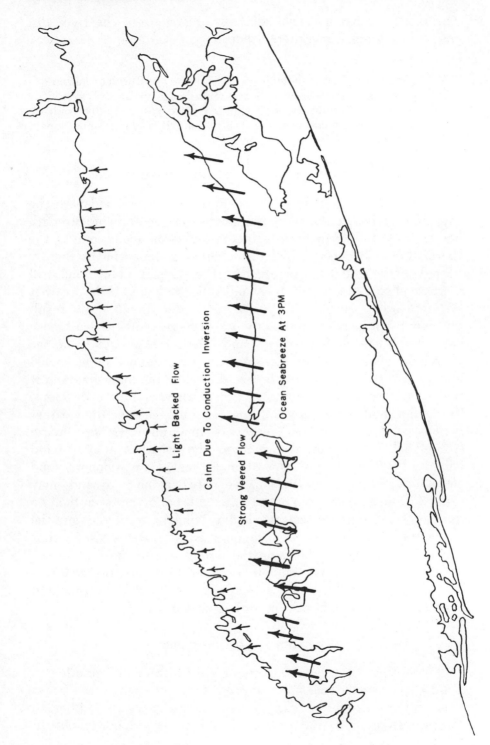

The tactical principle which derives, analogous to the rules discussed below regarding intermittent cloud cover and the fan effect, is:

> When the sea breeze is dying, expect it to back and in late morning to back severely and abruptly. Assume starboard tack.
> When the sea breeze is building, expect it to veer but only gradually. Assume port tack but watch for prolonged backing oscillations if it is offshore and beware the fan effect.

ALTERNATION WITH THE WEATHER SYSTEM WIND

If the weather system wind is approximately aligned with the expected sea breeze direction, an increase in general wind strength and a modest shift to the sea breeze direction will occur as the thermal wind is generated. If the weather system wind is slightly veered to the initial sea breeze direction, the resultant wind will increase in strength progressively and shift gradually. If the weather system wind is backed to the initial sea breeze direction, the resultant wind will increase in velocity early, decrease as the sea breeze veers with increasing generation, and then increase again from the veered direction. If the weather system wind is aligned between 45° and 135° to the expected sea breeze direction, the immediate effect will be a reduction in wind strength as the sea breeze develops. Thereafter light air and large alternating shifts between the weather system wind and the sea breeze continue until the sea breeze strengthens sufficiently to overcome the weather system wind completely. If sea breeze generation is weak (late summer, cloud cover, etc.), an approximate balance between the two winds may result with five- to twenty-minute shifts alternating between the two sources. This circumstance is particularly difficult to predict and the alternating shifts may be so infrequent as to create persistent shift effects, disaster for the boats on the wrong side of the beat. If the weather system wind is essentially opposed to the sea breeze direction, no wind or shifting confusion appears in the meeting zone and persists until one wind or the other becomes dominant.

INTERMITTENT CLOUD COVER

Among the many determinants of sea breeze flow, variation in cloud cover usually goes unrecognized. Often the sea breeze backs after an initial veer, or backs and veers sequentially in addition to its gradual veer as the day progresses. When we tack out on port in early afternoon only to find that the wind has backed to favor the starboarder tackers, we should probably look up for the explanation rather than ahead.

During the Fall Soling Bowl Regatta at Annapolis, we experienced marked variation in the southerly sea breeze's direction. Starboard tack varied between 120° and 165° and port tack between 210° and 255° during the course of Sunday's racing. There at first seemed little reason for these major shifts which often persisted for ten to fifteen minutes. I was on the wrong side of several of them (with disastrous consequences) before I realized that when the sun was shining the boats that went off on port were favored and when the Bay turned gray the starboard tackers had the advantage. We had been towed to the starting line and at 11:00 AM. there had been a heavy cloud cover with absolute calm at the surface. Between 11:00 A.M. and 12:00 noon a light and fitful southeasterly appeared, the faint evidence of the weather system airflow which had provided the moist air for the cloud cover aloft. As the day warmed, breaks in the cloud cover began to appear overhead. The southeasterly filled in more steadily and began to veer—starboard tack about 120° by noon. As the surrounding land surfaces gradually warmed, the cloud cover overhead dissipated and the wind aloft was brought increasingly to the surface. We looked for stronger wind offshore at the start of the first race but found that the wind, far from settled, veered further to a starboard-tack heading of 150° during the first beat. As it veered the sky cleared, the sun shone, the water turned blue, and the wind velocity increased to about 10 knots. By the start of the second race the cloud cover had returned, the sea and sky were gray and starboard tack was back down to 120°. There was little wind remaining at the surface as the fleet crept away from the starting line. Again blue sky began to appear overhead, the wind strengthened and veered, and the fleet, which initially took off on port again crossed the starboard tackers with ease.

The pattern was clear:

Cloud cover: velocity—light
                direction—backed

Clear sky: velocity—increased
              direction—veered

Breaks in stratocumulus cloud cover indicate downdrafts which, heating by compression as they descend, melt the cloud. The presence of stratocumulus cloud cover indicates updrafts which are cooling to their dew point and precipitating their moisture. Under a segment of clear sky upper-level sea breeze flow is descending to the surface. Under a segment of cloud cover lower-level sea breeze flow is isolated. Under the cloud cover boats are sailing in a light, shallow, low level sea breeze; in the sunshine boats are sailing in a strong, deep, veered downdraft of upper airflow. If cloud cover persists or reappears after the initiation of the sea breeze, look for significant shifts in the racing area. If blue patches begin to appear overhead, expect a veer, tack off on port to be inside of the fleet when it appears. If after a period of strong airflow the clouds return, expect a back, tack off on starboard to be inside of the fleet when it appears.

DIURNAL SEA (OR LAKE)

BREEZE VARIATION

	WIND VELOCITY	WIND DIRECTION
Early morning under subsidence inversion	light	perpendicular to shore
Morning under stratocumulus cloud beneath inversion	light	perpendicular to shore
Morning under breaks in cloud cover beneath inversion	moderate	veered 20°–40°
Late morning as inversion breaks	light	backed-perpendicular to shore
Early afternoon	moderate	veered 20°
Later afternoon	strong	veered 40°

Sea breezes back as they die, veer as they strengthen.

This progression—from minimal, perpendicular to the shore sea breeze to increased velocity, moderately veered sea breeze—is accomplished prior to breakthrough of the subsidence (or advection) inversion. The stratocumulus below the inversion is melted by thermal generation but the cooling induced by this evaporation postpones the inversion breakthrough. An hour or more later (or never) increased surface heating under the now generally clear sky breaks

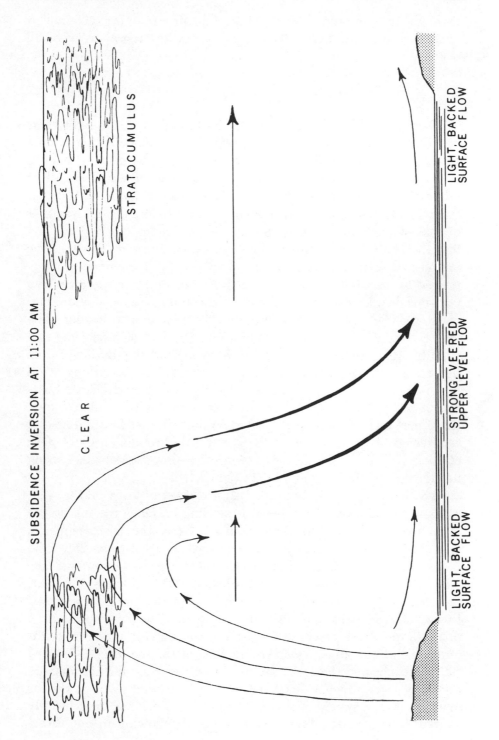

SUBSIDENCE INVERSION AT 11:00 AM

STRATOCUMULUS

CLEAR

LIGHT, BACKED SURFACE FLOW

STRONG, VEERED UPPER LEVEL FLOW

LIGHT, BACKED SURFACE FLOW

through the inversion layer. Then sea breeze reorganization is necessary—the wind dies, backs, and starts its progressive veer all over again.

THE FAN EFFECT

Sam Merrick and I first detected the fan effect about eight years ago during a fall International 14 regatta at Annapolis. Sam and I were the first in the fleet to break away from the starting line on port and soon found ourselves on the leebow of the fleet, all of whom had assumed the port tack to avoid the increased current farther out. The boats to windward began to lift on our weather quarter while Sam fell away to leeward. As we approached the lay-line the boats farthest to weather were pointing 5° or more above me and those in between had lifted in varying increments proportionate to their initial distance to windward. Relief in the form of a port-tack header was obviously not forthcoming; we came about and on starboard experienced a progressively increasing header. The fleet had sailed along the spokes of a fan. On port each boat pointed slightly higher than her neighbor to leeward and slightly lower than her neighbor to windward. We had sailed within a curving wind flow which backed progressively with distance to port. Those boats which delayed their tack to port were rewarded with an increasingly lifted port tack. Those which tacked to port early sailed in a header relative to their competitors to windward throughout the length of their port tack and then experienced a progressively increasing header during their inevitable starboard tack.

The fan is always associated with the onset of a sea breeze—not at its very initiation, but while it is settling in. Once the sea breeze is well established at near maximum velocity the fan disappears. Our port-tack heading in the race described above was 255°; the boats to windward were sailing at 250°. During the subsequent race when the sea breeze was well established at 12–15 knots, the port-tack heading was 265°, a typical heading for the late afternoon sea breeze at Annapolis, and the fan was gone. The fan represents a phase in the development of the sea breeze. The initial sea breeze is a movement of cool air along the surface of the sea directly toward the nearby heated shore. As the sea breeze extends farther offshore (operates over a longer distance), strengthens, and involves the air mass at progressively higher altitudes, it becomes increasingly veered. In order for a breeze that is initially flowing in one direc-

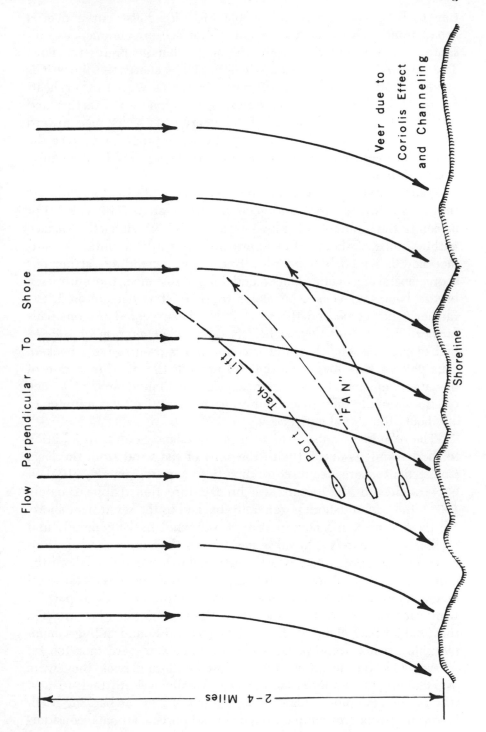

tion to be deviated to another, the air mass must curve over a broad front. Where the movement of surface air commences, offshore, it moves directly toward the shore that generates the flow. The farther it flows, the closer it approaches shore, the more it is veered. As the temperature disparity increases with further heating of the land, the site of sea breeze generation moves farther and farther offshore and thus the rate of veering with distance toward shore becomes less and less as the afternoon progresses. Over the area of the average race course, near shore, the wind ultimately flows in a uniform direction.

Near shore at Annapolis the local sea breeze fills in at about noon from approximately 185° and veers progressively to 210°–220°. For fifteen to thirty minutes it blows from 185°–190° along the surface within a mile of shore. After approximately thirty minutes the surface flow is joined by upper-level flow and, extending farther offshore, operating over a longer and longer distance, the entire sea breeze begins to veer. The closer to shore it is encountered, the farther it has come and the more it has been veered. As one sails farther offshore and approaches the area of generation of the sea breeze more closely, the wind encountered is progressively backed. This pattern is probably present throughout the day but a rate of deviation sufficient to be significant in the limited area of a race course is usually only evident during the period fifteen minutes to one hour after initial generation.

The fan effect is also evident in Long Island Sound. In addition to the backing associated with the shift of the wind from the local Connecticut shore sea breeze direction (approximately 210° off Greenwich) to the ocean sea breeze direction (approximately 190°), the wind offshore is generally backed to the wind near shore. On the first beat in a new sea breeze the wind backs generally and oscillates moderately. On subsequent beats the range of oscillations is reduced to approximately 10°, but the farther one is offshore the more it is backed. It almost always pays to take an initial starboard tack away from the leeward mark and then to tack back to port, to windward (south) of the majority of the fleet so as to be inside in this gradual back. During the '71 Long Island Sound Soling Championships, boats would occasionally continue starboard tack too far so that with the addition of a modest oscillating back they were overstanding. In midafternoon it was usually wise to tack to port when the mark could be laid on a heading of 220° as backing oscillations to this degree frequently permitted port-tack boats, considerably to leeward of a major portion of the fleet, to lift up to the mark. The fan effect here was compounded of veering due to low-level channeling and veering due to thermal generation along the Connecticut shore relative to the undeviated flow in mid-Sound and thus was less and less prominent as the flow strengthened to include all levels of the airflow in a single mass. Experience at Greenwich confirms the experience at Newport Beach where when the windward mark and the course are near shore an initial port tack is favored, and when the windward mark and the course are well off-shore an initial starboard tack is favored.

In addition to the shifts discussed above, which occur offshore and are only indirectly related to the shore, the sea breeze shifts as it encounters the shore. As discussed in other chapters, because it is a cold stable flow it is markedly channeled by the landforms it encounters and because it changes velocity as it begins to traverse the shore, it is refracted more perpendicular to the shore on its approach.

C. The Lake Winds

The small lake breeze.
The large lake breeze.
Weather system winds and lake breezes.
Anabatic and katabatic winds.

1. Saratoga—Small Lake Winds

"A dappled sky like a painted woman
Soon changes its face."

The winds of small lakes are distinctive chiefly in that all weather system winds are offshore and all local, thermal lake breezes are onshore (and sometimes in every direction). Every weather system wind must reach a lake by passing over land and land is subject to marked diurnal temperature variations. Marked variations in surface temperature are associated with radiation and conduction inversions and such inversions are characteristic of small lakes. When the weather system wind is stable it is often excluded from the surface. Calm reigns or a weak lake breeze, facilitated by an overlying inversion, develops weak onshore flow toward each shoreline. The weather system wind that reaches the surface is unstable, has advanced over a heated surface, has a high lapse rate, and is a mixture of upper- and lower-level airflow. Thus small lake winds, if strong, are gusty and shifty and, if weak, are associated with light winds flowing in markedly differing directions on different parts of the lake.

Land, subject to typical diurnal temperature variation, surrounds a lake. Each night a radiation inversion excludes the weather system wind from the surface. No wind ruffles the glassy surface, with the possible exception of a faint land breeze flowing from the cool land toward the warm water. Over shallow lakes whose waters become tepid with the passage of summer the land breeze may become sufficiently strong to persist into the morning and reappear early in the evening. As the radiation inversion disappears in midmorning the weather system wind may reach the lake surface. If the lake is deep and cold, however, a conduction inversion over its surface may exclude all but an unusually cold weather system flow. Ultimately if the offshore wind is sufficiently unstable and the land becomes sufficiently heated, thermal turbulence ashore will be sufficient to send downdrafts of the weather system wind through the conduction inversion. If the land heats sufficiently and the weather system wind is warmer than the lake water (to be expected for large lakes and particularly for deep lakes), an onshore thermal wind, the lake breeze, will develop between the cold water and the heated land. If the weather system wind is strong, unstable, or cold, as it is in the outflow from a new cP high, it is likely to overcome the attempted lake breeze generation and persist until the radiation inversion reappears in late afternoon. If the weather system wind is weak, stable, or warm, as it is in the presence of the typical summer mTg air of the United States, the lake breeze will develop beneath it and persist until the land cools and the radiation inversion reappears in late afternoon. The simultaneous presence of both winds at the surface is characteristic of large lakes and is discussed in other chapters. On small lakes it is rare for both wind sources to generate surface airflow simultaneously. Instead a period of calm intervenes as the weather system wind dies in late morning to be replaced by the lake breeze and in late afternoon as the lake breeze dies to be replaced by the weather system wind (or by a persistent calm or the ultimate appearance of a land breeze).

The lake sailor must look to the weather maps to determine the temperature and stability of incoming weather system air. If the expected airflow is cold relative to his lake's water temperature and instability in its lower levels can be expected from heating of the land surface under clear skies, he can expect a strong, gusty surface flow. This flow will be backed up to 30° from the isobars on the weather map as the small lake receives wind modified by the frictional resistance of the surrounding land. Little increase in velocity can be expected as the flow emerges over the lake surface inasmuch as it is slowed equally by the surface friction of both shores. If the pressure gradient is great, frictional turbulence induced by the strong airflow may be sufficient to break up low-level inversions even in the presence of a relatively warm, stable air mass. Cloud cover contributes to the stability of the lower air levels and will mitigate against the development of surface airflow unless the gradient is strong. Warm, stable airflows may be expected to be separated from the lake surface by intervening inversions. Then the lake sailor must rely upon local wind development to overcome the usual morning calm. Unless some unique local wind source is available, the only remaining source of wind generation will be the lake breeze. The lake breeze depends upon low-level instability, however, and will only develop significant flow in the presence of clear skies and thermal lift-off. Faint zephyrs of the lake breeze develop beneath the protective inversion which is associated with stable conditions and cloud cover, however, and in the absence of other surface flow may permit the experienced lake sailor to glide across the glassy surface to his chosen mark.

THE LAKE BREEZE

Some lakes are located where persistent winds of other than local thermal origin affect them. Near the seacoast or large lakes, such as the Great Lakes, the sea breeze or the large lake breeze may extend far enough inland to affect small lakes in the vicinity. Such breezes move inland gradually, rarely more than ten to fifteen miles, and arrive over such lakes only late in the day. If the weather system wind is light and/or stable, such a sea breeze may be expected and may replace a light local lake breeze or calm at the lake's surface at the end of the afternoon's race. Other lakes, such as Garda, located close to tall mountain peaks, have anabatic winds flowing up mountain slopes each afternoon and katabatic winds flowing down them each night and morning. In the absence of strong, unstable weather system airflow these winds may be regularly expected at the lake surface. Only lakes with large mountains close by develop such distinctive winds, but many lakes with moderate-size hills nearby obtain some enhancement of their local lake breeze by anabatic effects.

During a typical summer day the air overlying a lake's surface is cooler than the air overlying the surrounding heated land. A mass of dense, cold air develops over the lake and begins to outflow at the shoreline toward the falling surface pressure ashore. As is true of all thermal onshore ("sea breeze") flows, the surface wind is first evident at the shoreline. It spreads inland as the lake breeze front moves ashore, and lakeward as more and more of the surface air over the lake is caught up in the circulation. If surface heating ashore is marked, outflow from the shore will spread toward the lake at a few hundred to a few thousand feet, sink into the mid-level trough and add to the high surface pressure. Such heating will result in the gradual development of onshore flow over the majority of the lake's surface. In the absence of strong surface heating, the lake breeze may only develop near the shoreline in a band extending but a few yards or a few hundred yards offshore, leaving the center of the lake in total calm. Regardless of the extent of the flow its greatest surface velocity will be at the shoreline.

The most distinctive aspect of the lake breeze is its emanation from the lake's center and its spread in all directions toward the shoreline. This is divergent flow from sinking air in the center of the lake high. If the lake breeze alone is determining surface flow the center of the lake will be calm. If there is wind all over the lake, including its center, some other wind-generating factor in addition to the lake breeze must be present. Small lake breezes are weak, rarely more than 4–6 knots, as the air mass that generates them is small. In settled conditions, when the weather system gradient is minimal, however, they can provide good sailing. They are too weak to overcome unstable weather system flows in the manner of the coastal sea breeze. Thus, they are rarely associated with a meeting zone of calm and the presence of a lake breeze in one portion of the racing area and an offshore wind in another. If conditions are favorable and the center of the lake is calm, or nearly so, the wind can be expected to be onshore near *all* shorelines. Regardless of other influences, under stable conditions the lake breeze will be stronger the closer it approaches the shore.

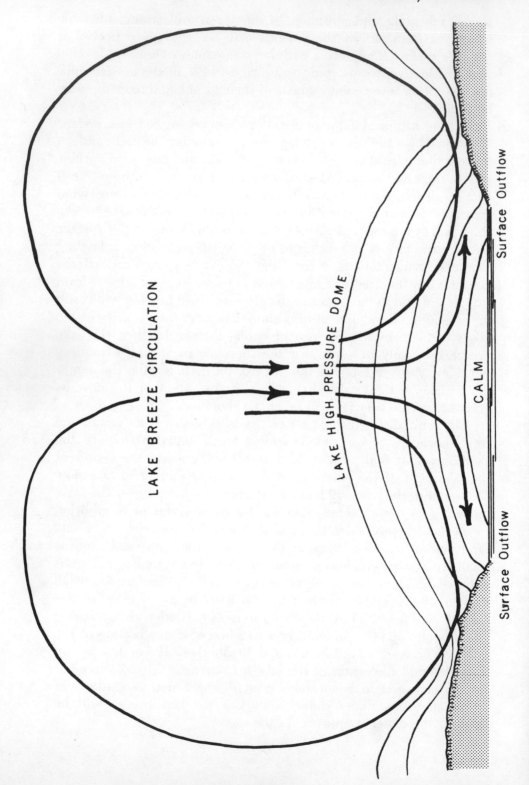

Only in light conditions, when cloud cover has dampened thermal generation, is the lake breeze so simple, however. In most circumstances other influences will cause the flow to become organized in a single general direction over at least a major portion of the lake. If the lake breeze has formed beneath an inversion, as it is likely to have done, intermittent breakthrough of the inversion will permit elements of the weather system wind to reach the surface periodically. When this occurs the lake breeze will be strengthened and will spread farther offshore along the shore toward which the weather system wind is flowing and be weakened and disturbed along the opposite shore. An unstable offshore flow which has been able to reach the surface will be strengthened by lake breeze development along the leeward shore of the lake and weakened along the windward shore for the same reason. If broken cloud cover is present, inversion breakthrough can be expected in the clear areas which indicate downdrafts and elimination of weather system flow under the clouds which indicate updrafts. When the lake lies in shadow the lake breeze will be relatively pure and the wind perpendicular to the shoreline; when the lake is bathed in sunlight the

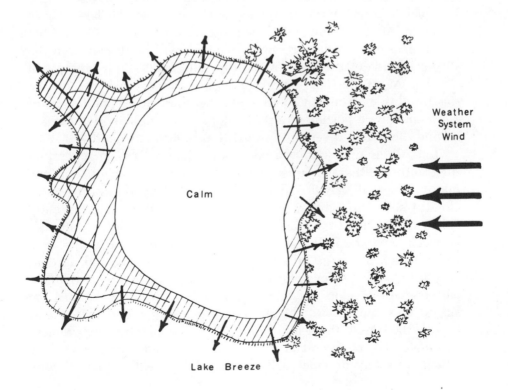

lake breeze will be deviated from its expected path or replaced by the addition of weather system flow.

Lakes that have steep shorelines develop anabatic and katabatic flow as well as lake breeze flow. Upslope (anabatic) flow will reinforce the lake breeze, downslope (katabatic) flow will diminish it. Each morning surface air begins to move up slopes which are heated by the sun as the pressure decreases near the surface of the hills more rapidly than it does over the lake (or valley) at the same altitude. A circulation is initiated as thermal lift-off from the hilltops cools and sinks back toward the pressure trough above the surface of the lake. This, of course, contributes to the lake breeze circulation and means that lake breeze flow will be enhanced by steep shorelines if (1) the hillsides are heated and (2) if the dense, cold air over the lake's surface can flow horizontally as well as vertically. The latter requires that the lake be sufficiently large so that its pool of cold surface air can escape or that, ideally, the immediate shoreline be low and that the hills be located a moderate distance inland. Earliest and strongest outflow will occur along that portion of the lake where the immediate shoreline is meadow, sand, or shingle and where the largest hillside is a few hundred or more yards inland. Unequal heating of the shorelines will also skew the lake breeze direction. Anabatic flow will develop on east-facing slopes long before it does on west-facing slopes. Thus air will be drawn from the shadowed side of the lake toward the sunlit side and a breeze will develop across the lake—weak and offshore (or onshore) on the shadowed side, strong and onshore on the sunlit side. If partial cloud cover shadows a portion of a sunlit slope, anabatic flow will deviate around the patch, diverging toward the sunlit areas nearby.

Large hills surrounding a lake will enhance thermal separation sufficiently so that cumulus cloud formation will occur, and the intermittency of that lift-off will be indicated by the formation of cloud streets. Surface flow over a nearby lake will be intermittently enhanced by such thermal separation and depressed in the intervals between separation. If the lake is elongated because it lies in a valley which has large hills or mountains at one end, and particularly if the valley extends far beyond the end of the lake, axial flow patterns will develop. Anabatic winds will be strongest toward the largest hills and toward the large area of rising slopes that extend beyond the lake to the head of the valley. The lake then experiences a combination of lateral and axial anabatic and lake breeze flow which is usually dominated by the axial flow with some skewing

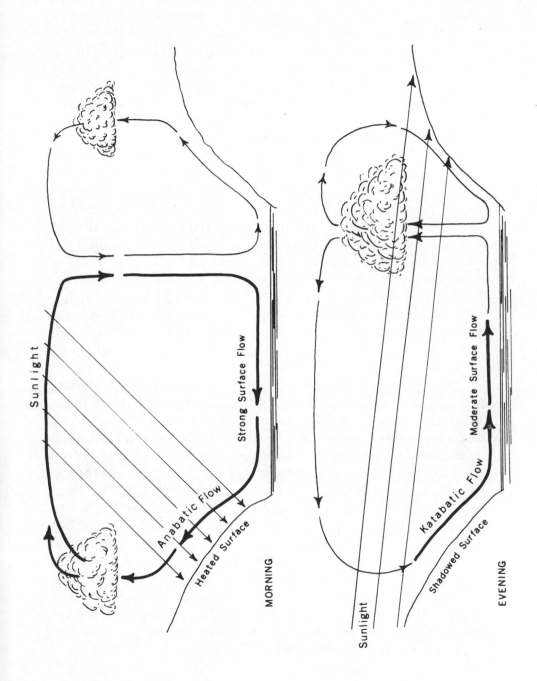

MORNING

Sunlight

Strong Surface Flow

Anabatic Flow

Heated Surface

EVENING

Sunlight

Moderate Surface Flow

Katabatic Flow

Shadowed Surface

toward the sunlit side of the lake. As the lateral slopes are closest to a valley lake, lateral upslope influences are the first to be evident in the early morning. Flow will be across the lake to the sunlit side. Thereafter, as the distant slopes at the head of the lake draw in the surface air, the initial wind will gradually shift to an axial direction skewed toward the sunlit side. In midafternoon when all surfaces have been heated to a maximum intensity and all are sunlit, flow will be toward the head of the valley but deviated more perpendicular to each shoreline, as the shoreline is approached, by refraction as well as by thermal influences. As the sun sinks behind the western hills local upslope flow will have ceased on the east-facing slopes and the axial wind will be deviated toward the west-facing slopes. Soon downslope flow from the shadowed side (essentially a land breeze) will add to this deviation to the east. The axial wind will persist beyond all the local upslope winds but eventually it too dies and the lake is calm. After dark, if the lake is deep and cold, a light katabatic offshore flow will be recognized along all the shorelines. And if the hills at the end of the valley are large enough a katabatic axial wind will appear in late evening to overcome the local downslope winds. On mountain lakes this downslope wind may persist well into the morning and provide ideal sailing conditions for the early risers.

With or without axial winds and terrain enhancement of anabatic flow, the lake breeze is modified by the contours of the lake's shore. In whichever direction the lake breeze is flowing it is relatively cold, dense flow seeking escape from the lake's surface toward low pressure ashore. Such stable flows cannot rise above obstacles but instead must deviate to flow around them. Thus although the lake breeze may attempt to move directly from lake to shore, it will be channeled parallel to high bluffs and directly into coves and inlets. Wherever a high promontory protrudes into the wind flow, the flow will be deviated and accelerated as it passes that promontory. If an entire shore rises abruptly, flow along this shore will be deviated to a more parallel direction and increased in velocity while flow along the opposite shore will be more perpendicular to that shore and diminished in velocity. Wherever a cove breaks into the shoreline, the lake breeze has an opportunity to escape so that flow is accelerated and deviated into the mouth of the cove.

STRATEGY ON THE LAKE

The lake sailor has the advantage of "local knowledge" and it is generally conceded that on his home lake the gifted sailor is almost impossible to beat. Local knowledge is compounded of a recognition of all those factors enumerated above. Involved are the recognition that (1) certain weather system winds and the lake breeze result in specific wind flow patterns on a particular lake, (2) that the time of day modifies these patterns as sunlight alters thermal flows in a predictable manner, and (3) that terrain features modify the direction and velocity of whatever flow develops. The visitor must attempt to overcome the local expert's experiential advantage by analyzing these factors as carefully as possible. He should prepare a time schedule indicating the variations in thermal flow which will occur consequent to the progression of sunlight across the terrain. He should also superimpose diagrams of the expected direction of the various possible wind flows on a chart of the area. Such a chart should indicate the channeling effects of shoreline features as well as the modifications induced by axial and lateral anabatic flows and variations in slope exposure to sunlight.

I was a newcomer to Saratoga when we raced the 1969 International 14 National Regatta there. Fortunately, I had had two days of racing and four races behind me when I prepared for the final and decisive fifth race. A 1¼-point lead over St. John Martin and a 10-point lead over the third boat meant that the finale would be a match race dependent upon strategic considerations. I had learned that Saratoga was typical small lake, that unstable weather system winds reached its surface, and that in stable conditions a lake breeze was to be expected. Axial flow developed not because the Adirondacks were close but because the lateral shores of the lake were steep while the shore at the end of the lake was flat. Outflow from the lake breeze was facilitated at the end of the lake and was channeled more parallel to, and accelerated along, both shores. A mile up the southern shore the axial flow was deviated and accelerated as it turned into the mouth of a deep cove. The lake breeze was weak or absent in the center of the lake, stronger along both shores. The weather system wind had been southerly throughout the series and as the land heated toward midday this flow penetrated to the surface. Early in the morning the lake was calm; by 11:00 patches of weather system wind were breaking through the conduction inversion and ruffling the surface. By midafternoon the onshore lake breeze was reinforcing the weather system wind along the leeward shore or replacing it all along the periphery of the lake.

We went out to the start early and determined that the wind had shifted about 20° from its standard of the previous two days, that the weather mark would be along the starboard shore of the lake rather than the port, that port would be the long (or major) tack and that, consequent to the enhancement of flow near the shoreline by the lake breeze, there was more wind along the port shore. This dictated that we stay to starboard of St. John after the start, on his lee bow, so that the advantages of being ahead and to leeward on the major tack would be ours, not his. Just before the start and for a short while thereafter the compass indicated that we were sailing in a 10° starboard-tack header which, of course, made port tack and the starboard side of the course all the more attractive.

Harassment of St. John before the start, if it accomplished nothing else, might at least prevent him from noticing some of these details. At the five-minute gun we were on St. John's tail on port tack heading up the line from the leeward end. At the starting gun we were fifty feet to leeward of the middle of the line with St. John dead in our blanket. As soon as he could, however, St. John tacked away and in the light air we were a little slow in responding. He now had clear air on our lee bow, heading for the preferred side of the course! By the time we sorted out a number of starboard tackers, St. John had gained considerably. Fortunately, as we finally broke clear of the fleet, St. John tacked back to cover us. Would he have us? He would. Would he tack on our lee bow or would he let us pass astern? He would let us pass astern! We were on his port-tack lee bow! We tacked back and forth at least three times to stay close to each other and each time we tacked on his port-lee bow. Finally a port-tack header became evident as we rounded a bulge in the shoreline and the better breeze along the shore began to tell. After we crossed the mouth of the cove we tacked back to starboard and were able to tack three boat-lengths dead ahead of St. John.

We gradually pulled away in the better breeze which was channeling into the cove. Each time St. John tacked out on starboard we tacked with him, but always came back just a little before he did. As we approached the shoreline tangentially the wind became more and more perpendicular to the shoreline and provided a port-tack lift. We tacked on the lee bow of another boat when almost on the port-tack layline, forced her about and she tacked back dead on St.

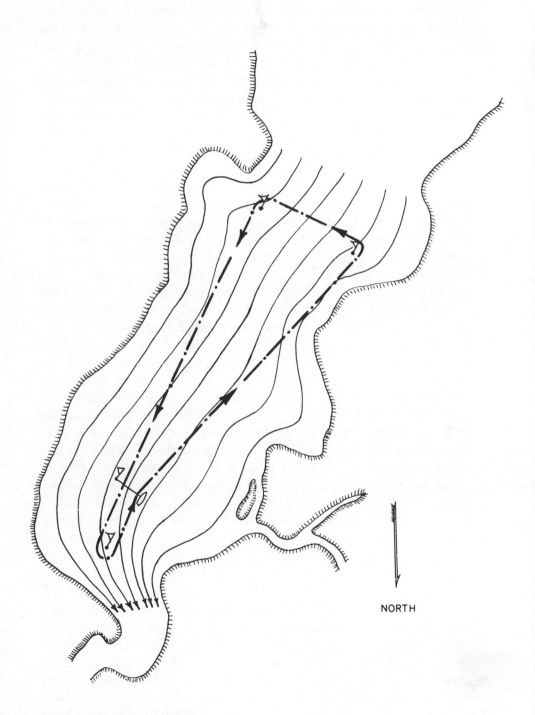

NORTH

John's wind. He tacked, *out* from the layline, to clear his air and we let him go. (It *never* [almost never?] pays to tack on the layline, on a "one-leg beat.") At the weather mark we were twenty boat-lengths ahead of St. John. We were twelfth, he was fifteenth.

St. John closed up on the second leg, a close reach, as we sailed out from the shoreline into the calm in the center of the lake. We needed to make the right choice so as to obtain clear and stronger air on the third leg, a long slow run, or St. John would be close astern, blanketing us, and all of our hard-won gains would be for naught. The entire fleet ahead was off on port jibe at a 30° angle to the rhumb line, their spinnakers sagging in that "center of the lake calm." Did we dare go for the starboard jibe at variance with the entire fleet? In such conditions clear air was the *sine qua non;* it couldn't be obtained in the midst of that colorful nylon, and starboard jibe would take us nearer the opposite shoreline. We went straight off on starboard, while St. John jibed in the midst of four others, jibed back a short while later to cover him (by which time we had doubled our lead), jibed back to starboard after St. John did, and passed boat after boat to leeward. At the end of the run, by keeping nearer shore than the remainder of the fleet, we were fifth, and St. John was thirty boat-lengths astern, in about tenth.

Thereafter, in the protracted hours necessary to completion of the final three legs of an Olympic course in little or no wind, we covered St. John assiduously. When he tacked out from the layline or sailed perpendicular to the run in hopes of finding some wind toward the center of the lake, we merely kept directly between him and the mark. When he sailed toward the shore we always went as far or farther in than he did. In so doing we gained and gained. When the wind finally disintegrated completely near the finish line a new local lake breeze appeared. St. John was astern rounding the final mark near the shore as we sailed offshore but we were far enough ahead that it didn't matter. At the finish we were still fifth and St. John was eleventh. We had won the National Regatta.

1. If the weather system wind is strong and/or unstable it will reach the surface. Expect the lake breeze to combine with the weather system wind along the leeward shore.
2. If the weather system wind is light and/or stable, expect the lake breeze to replace it.
3. If the lake breeze is present, expect it to be strongest along the shorelines and weakest or absent in the center of the lake.
4. Expect the lake breeze to channel parallel to high shorelines,

particularly if axial valley wind flow or axial weather system flow is present, and to be perpendicular to the shore near low shorelines.

5. Expect the lake breeze to be strongest near segments of low shoreline, at the entrances of coves and inlets, and particularly where a low shoreline is backed by hills at a moderate distance.

6. In a lake breeze keep to leeward and nearer the shoreline, when reaching or running. Keep to the tack nearer the shoreline when beating so as to benefit from the stronger wind near the shoreline and the expected lift as the wind flows more perpendicular to the shore near the shoreline.

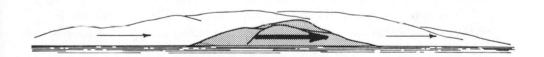

2. Kingston, Ontario—
Channeling of the Lake Breeze

"When the smoke goes west
Gude weather is past;
When the smoke goes east
Gude weather comes neist."

Kingston provides a great lake (sea) breeze and that lake breeze is at its best in August and September when CORK and the Olympics have been and will be conducted. But, as in all other sailing areas which advertise their dependably great sailing winds, the promise exceeds the actuality; lesser winds are common. A survey of the winds at Kingston during the latter part of August reveals that the lake breeze, a southwesterly, has been the most common wind during racing hours for the past several years. However, during the remaining one-third of the days a weather system wind predominated. In summer the polar front, the meeting ground between the continental polar (cP) air mass and the maritime tropical Gulf (mTg) air mass, is at the latitude of the Great Lakes. Depressions (cyclones) spawned by the polar front and fueled by the moisture of the Great Lakes migrate eastward down the St. Lawrence Valley. These depressions bring cloud cover and rain to Kingston. As their centers usually pass to the south of Lake Ontario and hover off the New England coast, their most persistent winds are from the east and northeast. These northeasters constitute one of two common summer weather system winds at Kingston. They average about 10 knots but occasionally reach 15 knots and usually persist for thirty-six to forty-eight hours. The other common weather system wind at Kingston is the northerly and northwesterly outflow from a continental polar (cP) high. Although the outflow from these domes of high pressure over central Canada is usually dissipated by the time it reaches the United States East Coast, significant flow velocity persists over the Great Lakes. Summertime northwesterlies in the Chesapeake are weak and transient; at Kingston they are often strong and may persist for several days.

The major question the racing sailor asks at Kingston relates to when and whether the southwesterly lake breeze will appear. Records (1959–1966) show that a southwesterly was present 38 percent of the total time during August and 26 percent of the total time during September. More important, it appeared at sometime during the hours of racing on two-thirds of all the days of August and on over 80 percent of the clear days of August. Only one clear day appears in the records of 1966 and 1967 during which a southwesterly failed to develop. When the sky was clear and the wind in the morning northwest to west, the lake breeze filled in early, usually before noon. Even when the sky was cloudy or partly cloudy, if the morning wind was in the westerly quadrants, the onshore southwesterly developed. When the morning wind was east or southeast (usually associated with high pressure to the north and east but at times with low pressure to the south and west) the southwesterly only appeared if the sky was clear or partly cloudy and was delayed until 1:00–2:00 P.M. Often on days of high-pressure easterly flow the wind swung gradually east, southeast, south, and finally southwest with a steadily increasing velocity.

Once the wind became southwest it tended to persist from this direction. If the lake breeze alone accounted for the onshore flow, it held southwest until approximately 8:00 P.M. and then returned to its morning direction. If, as was true of the best lake breezes, the weather system wind and the lake breeze were aligned, the southwesterly persisted through the night and continued through the lake breeze period of the following day. The southwesterly and westerly have the highest average velocity of Kingston's winds because of this reinforcement of two wind-generating sources. In summer the usual weather system is high pressure derived from maritime tropical Gulf (mTg) air centered off the east coast. Flow around such a high produces the characteristic southerly flow of the midcontinent. At the latitude of Kingston, however, this flow is from the southwest and this is a major factor in the production of the famous Kingston southwesterly. All southwesterlies are not lake breezes however; one of the best of 1967 was derived from an approaching low center, 16 knots in the rain.

The northeasterly is the wind most resistant to lake breeze development. There was but a single occasion in 1967 when a northeasterly which had been present throughout the night (associated with high pressure, an inversion, and morning stratocumulus) dissipated before 8:00 A.M. to be replaced by a southwesterly by 10:00 A.M. On all other occasions the northeasterly (associated with low pressure and dense cloud cover) persisted throughout the day. The dense cloud cover blocked sea breeze generation and the northeasterly or northerly flow directly opposed the development of onshore flow. Such airflow was stable, free of oscillating shifts, and usually of moderate velocity, 8 to 10 knots.

Northwesterly flow usually associated with the clear skies of continental polar (cP) air usually persisted and prevented lake breeze generation when it was strong. If it was less than 7 knots at 8:00 A.M. it was usually replaced by a southwesterly by early afternoon. Not infrequently the transition was protracted and associated with erratic and surprising shifts. When a lake breeze develops beneath an offshore northwesterly flow a calm transition zone develops at the leading edge of the low-level cold front. Convergence takes place here where the advancing periphery of the cold dense air moves from the lake toward the shore. On August 19, 1966, the northwesterly dropped from 10–17 knots during the night to 4 knots at 8:00

A.M. and then swung north, northeast, and briefly southeast, fluctuating between calm and 10 knots at the surface. The lake breeze finally filled in at 8 knots at 2:00 P.M. and increased to 16 knots at 4:00 P.M. On the other hand, when the northwesterly persisted at its early morning strength and direction or increased in strength as the morning progressed, it continued throughout the day.

IN KINGSTON BAY

Lake and sea breezes are channeled by the shores they flow toward and this channeling is characterized by modifications in both direction and velocity. Upward movement of the lake breeze is restricted by the warm air above (except for waves flowing across the interface). As the mainstream flows beneath this surface it is obstructed by elevations which rise along the shore. Calm at the surface will be evident wherever the shore is steep. This is partly due to the "9h effect" requiring the air to begin to lift from a distance offshore nine times the altitude of the shoreline. The stable lake breeze shows little tendency to lift, however, and instead spreads to bypass a shoreline elevation wherever a lower-level opening appears. Unable to top the cliffs, the flow angles toward the gaps. In valleys running back from the shoreline the flow is increased in velocity and directed along the axis of the valley. The airflow is concentrated in the gaps in the shoreline; the mass is compressed by the higher elevations and escapes at high velocity wherever the obstruction is at a lesser elevation. Even where the shoreline is relatively low, even along a sandy strip, the lowest levels of the airflow are deviated parallel to the shoreline and tend to drag the levels which are significant to the sailor along with them.

The most significant breaks in the shoreline which channel the lake breeze are those at water level. Where a river enters a bay, or a harbor entrance appears, the lake breeze will turn to flow directly into the opening. As the flow is constricted by shoreline elevations on either side of the opening, its velocity increases. The best sea breezes in the world are the products of constriction due to passage along or around a hilly shore or into a gap in a high shoreline. Sea breezes in the temperate zones are not expected to reach velocities above 15 knots but in the presence of channeling influences do, in fact, often flow at velocities above 25 knots. In Hurricane Gulch, near Long Beach on the southern California coast, the approaching sea breeze channeled between Santa Catalina and the Santa Monica Mountains is deviated around the high bluffs of Point Fermin and often reaches 25 knots. A few miles farther south, at Newport Beach, the onshore flow rarely exceeds 15 knots. At Acapulco there are marked differences in velocity within the area used for the three courses in the 1968 Olympics induced by deviation and concentration about the mountainous shoreline. At San Francisco a huge mass of sea breeze air derived from the immense high-pressure dome extending up and down the Pacific Coast is funneled through the Golden Gate toward the hot deserts to the east. This flow blocked by the high land to the north and south of San Francisco roars through the Golden Gate at velocities in excess of 30 knots and is still flowing at 20 knots in the lower and upper reaches of the Bay. The same Pacific sea breeze rushing down the Straits of Juan de Fuca between the Olympic Mountains and the hills of Vancouver Island may still be blowing at 20 knots when it reaches the small-boat race course off Shilshole. In the lower Chesapeake the Atlantic sea breeze increases in velocity as it passes between Cape Charles and Cape Henry and then, funneled between the headlands surrounding Mobjack Bay, rushes up the York River at speeds in excess of 25 knots. Once deviated by a headland or an entrance channel the flow follows the contours of the shoreline. It turns into each cove or river entrance and eventually runs straight up the valley at the end of the indentation. As the shoreline deviates away from the main water body, the airflow turns to follow the deviation, and as the shoreline deviates back toward the main water body the airflow is compressed and deviated to seaward.

The surface flow of a sea or lake breeze is well described by streamlines drawn along the path of flow. As the flow deviates to bypass an obstruction it is evident that the streamlines are compacted together. As air flows through a gap in an elevated shore, such as the entrance of a river, the representative streamlines are tightly compressed together and extend along the direction of the channel. The closer the streamlines lie together the more compressed is the airflow and the greater is its velocity.

A chart of the Kingston area demonstrates that Kingston lies at the northeast corner of Lake Ontario at the head of a progressively narrowing cone. The north shore and its Prince Edward Peninsula and the eastern shore with its associated islands funnel a southwesterly airflow into Kingston Harbor. As the southerly onshore lake breeze along the north shore progressively increases in velocity with the heating of the land, it progressively veers to become southwesterly and is more and more directly aligned with the Kingston inlet. Outflow from the high-pressure mass over the lake seeks its lowest level outlet and this is obviously the St. Lawrence Valley. As the southerly, veered southwesterly, flow impinges upon the north shore it turns more and more to the east, parallel to the shoreline, seeking escape. The least obstruction is into Kingston's bay between the Thousand Islands of the St. Lawrence and out the flatlands of the Rideau Canal to the northeast. As the airflow is compressed between Simcoe Island and the north shore it progressively increases in velocity and deviates to follow the shorelines on either side of its funneled course. Along the north shore it turns northward into Cataraqui Bay and then back easterly and even southeasterly as the north shore bulges out in its path. Along Simcoe Island it is compressed to the north and then as the bay widens flows south and then easterly again before escaping into the narrowing passage abreast of Fort Henry. It channels along both shores at a greater velocity near each shore, but at maximum velocity along the northern shore where it is most deviated from its direct onshore path. As the bay narrows the flow velocity increases, particularly near a protruding headland. As the bay widens, flow velocity decreases. At each indentation in the shoreline the direction of the flow changes, paralleling the general course of that shoreline.

The strategic principles which underlie success in racing at Kingston are dependent upon these characteristics of lake breeze flow. In the first place the lake breeze must be expected on most of the racing days of summer, particularly if the sky is clear and the weather system wind is in the westerly quadrants. It will usually be present before the start of racing but it must be expected to develop thereafter if the early wind is in the east or northwest and the wind goes light or begins to oscillate beyond its earlier range. It will be strongest along the north shore unless the initial wind is off that shore when it will first appear offshore and progress toward the beach. The middle of the bay is to be avoided as the wind will be channeled to a greater velocity near either shore and will be deviated by both shorelines. Local knowledge confirms this expectation; Kingston Yacht Club sailors make for the shore (but all do not agree on which one!).

Beyond Snake Island channeling is minimal but within the bay the streamlines are converging on the St. Lawrence entrance to the east. This means that a gradual header is to be expected as one approaches either the north or south shores. If the shoreline being approached is converging relative to the wind (so that the channel is widening upwind) one must expect the header to be further en-

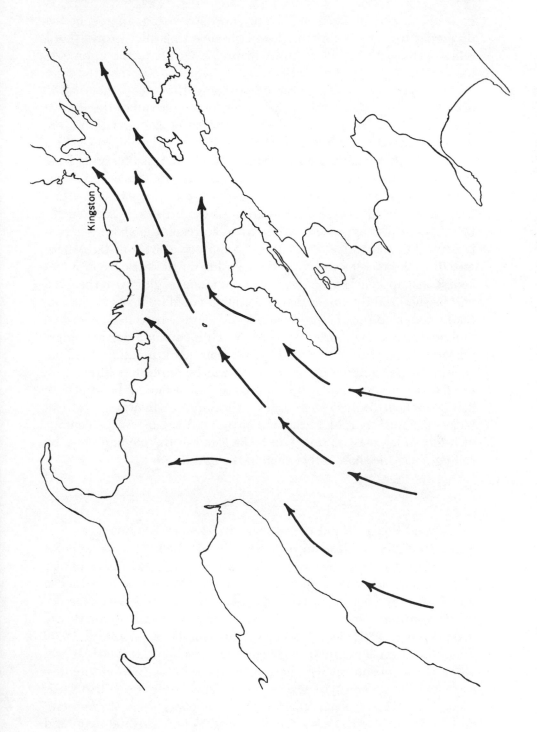

hanced close to the beach. If the shoreline being approached is diverging from the wind the flow, channeled parallel to the shore, will deviate with the shore and will provide a lift to the approaching boat.

If the starting line is nearer one shore than the other it will usually be beneficial to select the tack which approaches the nearest shore. This will provide an earlier acquisition of the course-shortening shoreline shift. Whichever shore is selected the approach tack must be made so that the beach is reached where it is diverging from the wind flow. Unless close to the layline the shoreline should be approached as closely (or more closely) as the competition so that the maximum advantage and duration of the lift is achieved on the tack back. If the approach tack is timed to reach the shore where it is diverging short of a headland, a progressive lift will be experienced on the tack in and a progressive lift on the tack back out. A course that approaches the shore where it is converging with the wind will be significantly longer than the course sailed by boats in the median wind, a course that approaches the shore where it is diverging will be significantly shorter. Whenever, while sailing along the shore, a header is experienced beyond the median wind direction, the boat should be tacked. So long as the boat can be kept on a lifted tack, relative to the median wind, approach tacks should be timed to bring the boat back to shore where the shore is diverging and exit tacks taken just short of a headland or point. A significant percentage of the total leg may be sailed on tacks lifted to the median wind by sailing along the shore rather than in the middle.

OUT IN THE LAKE

Beyond Snake Island the onshore breeze persists but usually at lesser strength. Against an offshore wind the lake breeze appears first out in the lake, but more commonly it develops inshore earlier and, consequent to funneling, more strongly. When the lake breeze develops early (before 10:00 A.M.) it may be presumed to have developed beneath an inversion. When it does so it may be markedly veered, up to 250°, by 11:00 A.M. Between 11:00 A.M. and 12:00 noon the inversion can be expected to break. As at Marblehead, when the inversion breaks, the lake breeze circulation deteriorates, the wind backs, and its velocity drops. Thereafter, prior to CORK race time at 12:00 noon, the lake breeze reorganizes, strengthens, and begins to veer. During the first beat, between 12:00 noon and

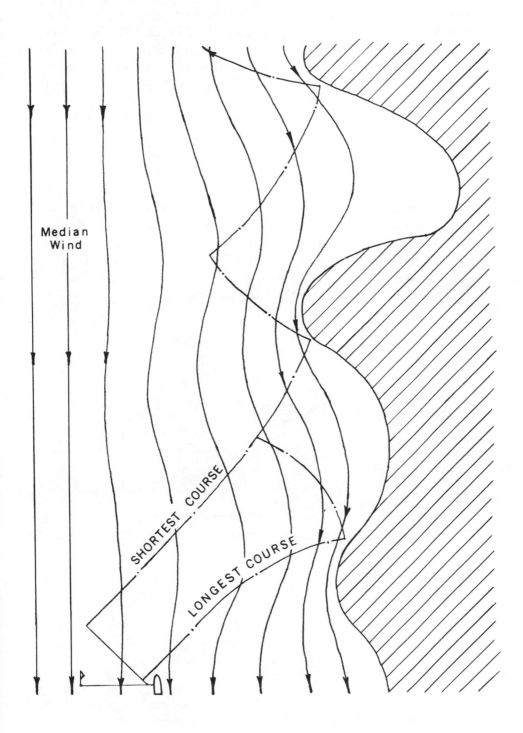

1:00 P.M., an abrupt additional veer frequently appears. The noon
lake breeze is usually from approximately 200° and the maximum
veer to approximately 215°. During the usual afternoon race oscillations between these extremes occur irregularly at ten- to twenty-
minute intervals. Often the majority of any one beat or run is sailed
in a persistent veer or back which favors one or the other side of the
course. Under cloud cover the lake breeze is weak. Then the lake
breeze may begin at 180°, veer, back, disappear, be replaced by a
brief westerly across the lake breeze front, and then fill in again at
200°. Under clear skies, and particularly if the temperature disparity between the lake (at 60°) and the air is great, the lake breeze is
strong but rarely above 18 knots. By about 4:00 P.M. the lake breeze
begins to die. As it dies it backs and holds more strongly offshore.
The beat at 3:00 P.M., in strong air, probably should be played for
the veer as lake breeze generation increases with the maximum heating of the day. The beat at 4:00 P.M., particularly if the wind is
dying, should be played for the back and the better breeze offshore.

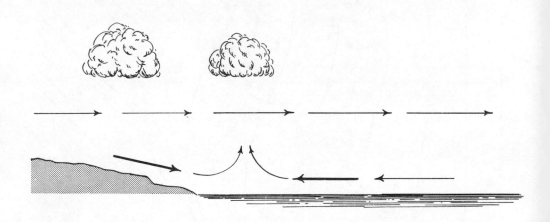

3. Chicago, Milwaukee, and Toronto— Two Winds Simultaneously

*"Evening red and morning gray,
Two sure signs of one fine day."*

I cannot remember a regatta on the Great Lakes in which there
was not at least one race when two winds were present simultaneously. The first time I raced in Toronto's Horrible Humber Bay I lost

a quarter-mile lead within a few hundred yards of the finish as we ran out of the lake breeze and into the zone of calm between it and the offshore weather system northerly. At Chicago, in the finals of NAYRU's match race series, we sailed in the lake breeze through almost an entire day only to meet the returning offshore westerly on the last beat of the last race at about 4:30 P.M. At Milwaukee, in the 1971 Soling Great Lakes Championships, we raced the beats in a 15-knot westerly and the reaches in a 10-knot southeasterly! The Great Lakes are the highway for the major weather systems of North America and each develops its own lake breeze which often appears simultaneously with the weather system wind. Race courses are usually set near shore in the meeting ground between two winds.

The Great Lakes, immersed in the plains, receive the best of the weather system winds. In summer the winds of high-pressure systems require convection to break through the usual inversions. The heated land surrounding the Lakes provides the necessary thermal turbulence to bring the wind to the surface and the low shorelines do little to impede its flow offshore. The polar front overlies the Great Lakes much of the year and low pressure, spawned by the front, tracks along the Lakes to the sea. These systems are enhanced by the moisture acquired in passage over the Lakes so that severe storms recurrently appear. In addition each lake regularly develops a local onshore thermal wind. The surrounding land is warm, often flat, and cleared of vegetation, ideal for the development of thermal lift-off, and the deep waters of the lakes are cold throughout the summer. The result is a tendency to lake breeze development whenever the sky is clear (and sometimes when it is not).

If the lake breeze is aligned with the prevailing weather system wind, as it is at Kingston, sailing breezes are strong and predictable. In summer, as high pressure passes to the south, the usual weather system wind is westerly and thus the eastern shores (and the eastern ends of the lakes) receive a combined weather system/lake breeze. Along the western shores, at Chicago and Milwaukee, as well as along the northern and southern shores at Toronto and Rochester, the weather system wind usually opposes the onshore lake breeze. The result is often no wind at all or a zone of calm between two opposing winds or two winds simultaneously and erratic shifts between the two. The stronger the weather system wind and the colder the air of which it is composed the less likely it is to be supplanted. The colder the lake water and the hotter the overlying air, the more likely the lake breeze will develop and prevail. A major indicator of the likelihood of lake breeze generation is the disparity between lake and air temperature, a figure readily obtainable from a local weather office or the newspaper.

The large cities contribute to the confusion between the two wind systems. The elimination of vegetation intensifies surface heating during the day, facilitating lake breeze development. The heated air spreads above the city and out over the water establishing an inversion. As the heated air, containing the city's smoke and other pollutants, sinks to the water's surface it cools and precipitates smog. The inversion traps the marine air below and results in the constant recirculation of the city's debris aloft over the city, down over the water, and back to the city in the lake breeze. At Milwaukee we saw the lake breeze as a smog bank 1000 feet high filling in against an offshore wind and engulfing the boats offshore. The inversion screens the surface from the weather system winds aloft and the heated paving stimulates thermal generation. Consequently the lake breeze appears more readily and opposes the offshore winds more frequently near the major cities. This means good racing when the lake breeze is unopposed but mass confusion when a weather system wind is attempting to reach the surface as well. It also means the exposure of the city to a high level of pollutants as, instead of being carried away by the weather system winds, these are constantly returned to the city's atmosphere by the lake breeze circulation.

Two days of racing in the Soling at Milwaukee illustrate some of the typical consequences of the presence of two winds simultaneously. On the first day a warm 10- to 15-knot southwesterly was present in the morning, strong and veered in the harbors where thermal turbulence brought it to the surface, but weak offshore. This wind veered with the day as thermal turbulence increased with the heating of the land. By 2:00 P.M. it began to fade and by 3:00 P.M. the lake breeze could be seen advancing at 45° to the shore, lifting the offshore wind ahead of it. Only a narrow zone of demarcation existed between the two wind flows: one at 210°, the other from the typical lake breeze direction, 160°. Within thirty minutes of its appearance the lake breeze had come ashore, the air was cool and moist, and the southwesterly was displaced above the inversion. The following day the weather system wind was around in the west, cooler and stronger, with gusts up to 18 knots near shore The lake breeze pushed to within two miles of shore by late morning and an abrupt line of demarcation, which traversed the race course, separated the two winds. The weather mark, up under the beach, remained solidly entrenched in the westerly while the jibing mark and most of the

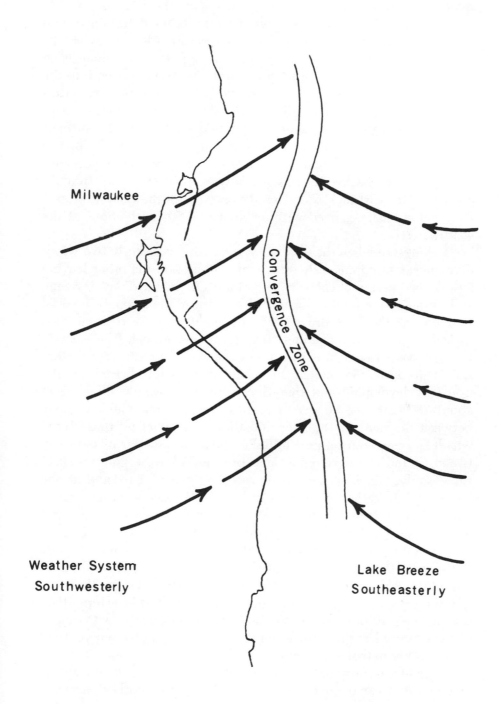

Milwaukee

Convergence Zone

Weather System
Southwesterly

Lake Breeze
Southeasterly

two reaches were in the moderate lake breeze. It was essential as soon as the beat commenced to work out of the lake breeze and into the westerly as position upwind in the latter determined race position at the end of the beat. As the leeward mark was in the lake breeze each helmsman had to accept a large port-tack header as he entered the westerly and resist the temptation to tack back into the starboard-tack lift until well clear of the lake breeze. By early afternoon increasing thermal turbulence ashore under clearing skies brought ever stronger elements of the cold westerly to the surface, destroyed the inversion that had earlier protected the lake breeze and swept it from the racing area. The stimulus to onshore flow persisted, however, backed the offshore flow to about 180° and strengthened it. Starboard tack was strongly favored on the final afternoon beat as the back occurred within the erratic 20° oscillations of the southwesterly.

At Kingston when the weather system wind is easterly two winds may appear simultaneously or one may obliterate the other leaving a prolonged period of calm at the surface. On the third day of racing at CORK '71 we made a beautiful start near the strongly favored port end of the line, drove over the boats to leeward, and then tacked to cross the remaining 80 percent of the fleet. The easterly weather system wind was dying and the sky was clear over eastern Lake Ontario. We knew that this meant that the lake breeze circulation was developing and that the "new" wind would fill in from about 180°–200°, a 90°–120° veer. It seemed reasonable to stay between the mass of the fleet and the mark, covering those boats which had gone out on port initially and were now far offshore between us and the developing lake breeze. We were going well in the easterly, which seemed to be receding ahead of us, and at one point must have had close to a quarter-mile lead over the nearest boats, those to leeward on port. We kept glancing back at the eight or ten boats (including some of the "gunslingers") who had maintained starboard tack and were working in toward the distant shore to the north. We recognized that they, nearer the shore, would hold what little remained of the dying offshore easterly longer than we, but we were steadily leaving them and, a half-mile astern, they scarcely looked threatening. We didn't feel secure as the last vestiges of the easterly left the surface but wouldn't have traded our position for any other in that glassy calm.

After fifteen to twenty minutes with almost no steerageway the lake breeze became apparent as a dark line on the southern horizon,

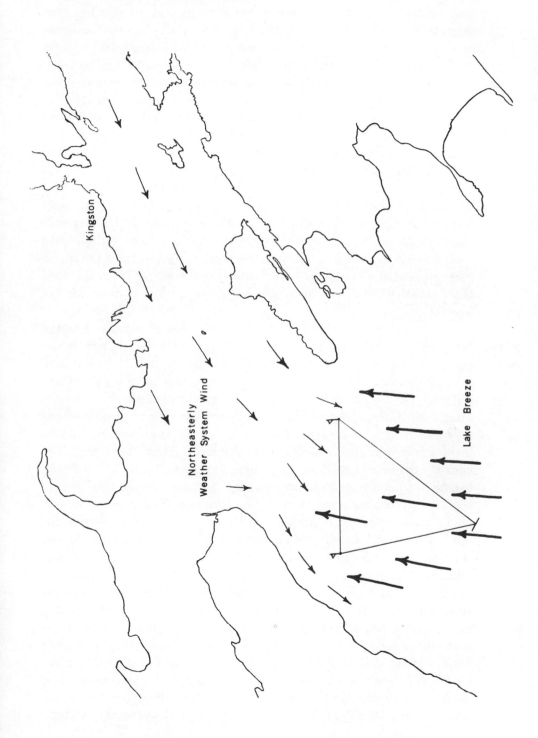

Kingston

Northeasterly
Weather System Wind

Lake Breeze

and moments later the tail-enders, between us and the starting line, were setting spinnakers in it. We began to worry about the boats on our lee bow who picked up a tongue of new wind and rapidly closed as we drifted helplessly. We began to move—at last—set our own spinnaker and, at a better sailing angle, moved ahead of the overtaking boats. Our lead had been cut drastically but we still had it—hadn't we? Preoccupied with the boats to the south we hadn't noticed that the boats inshore also had wind! Dave Curtis, who had taken a course halfway between us and the most inshore boats, was close-reaching into the mark at twice our speed and the others who had gone in even farther were now close-hauled in a wind as strong as our own. They would all reach the mark ahead of us. And now, in a breeze stronger than our own and at a considerably faster sailing angle, a pack of a dozen or more were spinnaker-reaching past us, a scant 200 yards to the north. We were twenty-fifth at the mark. We had beaten all the boats who had been nearer to the "new" wind than ourselves and lost to almost all those who had been farther away!

The easterly airflow had been relatively warm compared to the land surface (not nearly as cold as those northerlies whose dense air easily sinks to provide a strong, gusty surface flow). As the land heated, thermal turbulence mixed the hot surface air with the warm air aloft, decreasing the density of the entire offshore flow. As the heated air moved (in response to the weather system gradient) out over the trough of cooler, denser air, an inversion developed at a level a few hundred to a few thousand feet above the water. The easterly continued to flow above this inversion but was gradually excluded from the water surface. At the periphery of the pool of cold surface air near the shore and within Kingston Bay, it persisted.

Offshore wind flows, unless stabilized by an inversion over the land, are always strongest and most persistent near shore. Ashore thermal turbulence brings down gusts of high-velocity upper airflow and near shore these gusts are able to penetrate the surface air. As heated air from the shore accumulates above the water and the surface pressure ashore falls because of its departure, the cold surface air above the water begins to move shoreward. If the offshore airflow is strong and/or cold it will maintain flow at the surface near shore long after the surface air several miles from land has begun to move shoreward. Then a sharply demarcated zone of convergence and markedly reduced airflow occurs ahead of the advancing sea breeze front which lifts the offshore flow ahead of it. Two winds of markedly differing direction are present at the surface simultaneously, each of which may be strong. On the other hand, if the offshore air-flow is weak and/or warm it will lift above the cold air at the water surface shortly after daytime heating begins and its surface elements will recede progressively shoreward *prior* to the onset of the sea breeze. A dead calm then occurs and will persist until sea breeze generation is sufficient to cause the *entire* surface air mass to begin moving shoreward. There is no migrating zone between two winds and there is no abrupt shift, only the progressive development of a new wind throughout the area. The development of surface flow is spotty but it begins near the shoreline (depending upon the height of that shoreline) and develops its greatest strength near the shore-line.

It is evident that the starboard tack that took boats toward the shore away from the expected sea (lake) breeze was the preferred tack at the start of CORK's third race and that our pursuit of the dying easterly on port away from the shore was wrong. The easterly *should* have persisted longer near shore (though the boats that continued on starboard never got close enough to shore to benefit from this effect). The lake breeze *should* have developed near shore first, and it did, permitting the leading inshore boats to gain a half-mile before we regained steerageway. And finally when the inshore boats obtained the new wind they had a close jib-reach to the mark (the fastest point of sailing in light air) while we had a run.

Buddy Melges, who won the race, claimed that he stayed on starboard (the entire leg!) so that he could avoid being on port (a condition which had disqualified him the day before)! I suspect that his lake sailing background had long ago taught him that dying off-shore winds persist·longest near shore, that surface lake breeze flow begins near shore, and that when the new wind produces a shift greater than approximately 40° the position to seek is to leeward of the fleet. In very light air the speed of a boat sailing to windward may be twice that of a boat sailing downwind. If this speed differential can be obtained, one should sail *away* from the new wind.

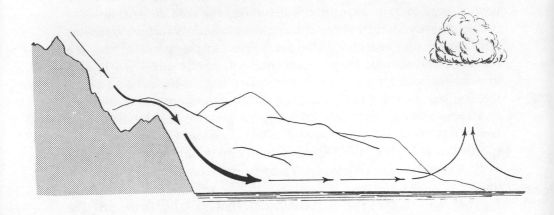

4. Garda and Huntington—Valley Winds

*"Rainbow at night, shepherd's delight,
  Rainbow in morning, shepherds take warning."*

One race a day is scheduled on Lago di Garda in northern Italy and it is started after 1:00 P.M. A fine southerly comes up the lake each day at this time, obviously associated with the heating of the land. But this wind is offshore from the heated plains to the south; it flows northwards toward the snow-covered Alps which rise 10,000 feet above the head of the lake! When the Tempest Class held its World Championship in September 1969, on Lago di Garda, six races had to be crammed into five days. As the southerly always died in late afternoon, the only possible time for a second race in one day was early morning. The Race Committee had the sailors rigging at 5:00 A.M. and being towed to the starting line by starlight in a flat calm at 6:00 A.M.! The starting line was three miles to the south of Riva where the boats were launched at the head of the lake. By 7:00 A.M., as the committee had expected, a 10- to 15-knot northerly was blowing down the lake and an excellent race was conducted to a weather mark near the shore to the east of Riva. It wasn't until 8:30 A.M. and the second round that the sun rose above the 1600-foot sheer cliffs along the sides of the lake. Once the sun was up the wind began to fade; it disappeared before 11:00 A.M. Thereafter the usual late-morning calm persisted until the southerly reappeared on schedule shortly after noon.

Lago di Garda is a forty-mile-long lake which receives the out-flow of several Alpine rivers. Within twenty miles of the northern head of the lake several Alps rise above 10,000 feet. Narrow valleys surrounded by lesser mountains lead from the lake to these peaks. The northern two-thirds of the lake is a three-mile-wide, flooded chasm eroded between sheer 1600-foot cliffs. The lower third of the lake spreads out into the plains of Lombardy completely free of the mountains which are its source. Garda is dramatic but not unique. Huntington (and other lakes of the High Sierras), the Swiss lakes,

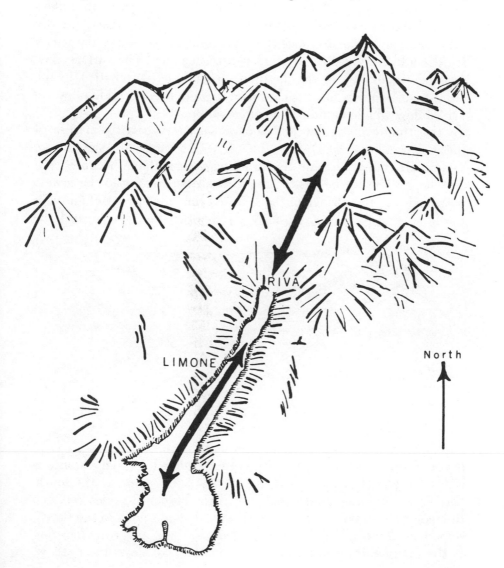

and many other lakes on which sailboats are raced are similarly positioned in the outflow valleys of a mountain range.

Such lakes have in common the development of two-way alternating thermal winds unique to valleys. Each night, as the slopes of the valley cool, the cold, dense surface air drains down the slopes and out onto these lakes from the neighboring mountains. And each day, as the slopes of the valley heat, the warm, expanded air flows up the slopes and from the lakes toward the neighboring mountains. Wherever major thermal differences in neighboring air masses occur, major changes in pressure result and air begins to flow. In valleys thermal differences are exaggerated as large surface areas rapidly heat and cool while air above the surface in the center of the valley is little affected by diurnal temperature changes. The surface flow upslope (anabatic) in the daytime, downslope (katabatic) in the night-time depends upon an associated upper-level, mid-valley reversed flow which maintains the circulation.

The timing of airflow at Lago di Garda reveals the nature of these thermal winds. During the night the mountain slopes cool rapidly (by radiation) and the air along their surfaces becomes cold and dense. This air begins to flow downslope, sinking to the lowest possible level, the surface of the lake. As the lake opens onto a plain the flow continues as a northerly wind down the lake toward the

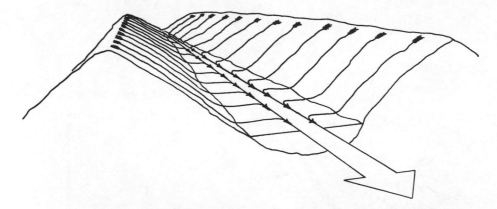

lower altitudes to the south. Its velocity, due to gravity alone, is but moderate and decreases further as the lake widens to the south. Circulation is maintained as cold air at the higher altitudes between the mountain peaks and between the valley walls adds to the downslope flow. Equilibrium is reached in the early hours of the morning as the minimal drop in altitude beyond the lake slows the outflow, surface cooling reaches its minimum, and the downslope flow is heated by compression at a rate which reduces its radiational cooling. Before dawn the lake is calm, pressure is the same throughout its length.

As the sun rises the plains to the south begin to heat, but the mountain slopes, in shadow, remain cold. As the surface air beyond the southern end of the lake is heated, surface pressure falls. By 7:00 A.M. the cold downslope flow is reestablished; outflow into reduced pressure occurs once again. At the southern end of the lake an onshore thermal lake breeze develops from the surface of the 60° lake toward the heated land. The combined downslope/sea breeze northerly flow builds to a peak of 15–20 knots at 8:00–9:00 A.M. by which time the plains are hot but the sun has barely reached the hidden mountain slopes. Above this surface northerly, high pressure is maintained by a deep gradual movement of heated air from the rising currents over the plains toward the lake and the mountains. When the sun finally reaches the mountain slopes above the lake and warms their surfaces, downslope flow ceases.

By 11:00 A.M. downslope flow has ceased; the air along the slopes is as warm as the air over the plains. The local onshore (northerly)

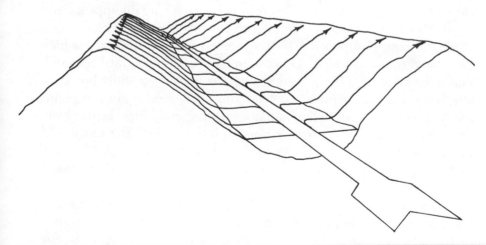

lake breeze at the southern end of the lake persists for a time but its overflow, instead of accumulating above the lake, is dissipated in the general expansion. By 1:00 P.M. the slope flow has reversed itself. The slopes are heating, the air above them warming to a greater extent than air at the same altitude in the center of the valley. Surface air begins to move upward along the course of least pressure,

upslope along the surface. Upslope flow continues along the surface
to an altitude where the temperature disparity between surface air
and surrounding air is sufficiently great to permit lift-off. The higher
the mountains, the higher the slopes can convey the surface air, and
the easier separation becomes. Soon airflow is moving upward along
all the slopes. Air from the lake is drawn into the upflow and begins
to move toward the highest mountains where lift-off takes place most
readily. The high lapse rate created by surface heating at high altitudes stimulates a rapid pressure fall and soon surface air over the
entire lake is drawn into the circulation at high velocity. By 3:00
P.M. the southerly is blowing at 20–25 knots in the upper part of the
lake. Its high velocity is due to its generation in thermal lift-off and
to the narrowing of the northern part of the lake which constricts
the total airflow. Cold air above the center of the lake continually
sinks to the surface to maintain the circulation, up along the slopes,
down in the mid-axis. The southerly is strongest at the northern end
of the lake, at the foot of the river valleys leading up to the snow-
covered peaks, and least at the southern end where the local onshore
lake breeze may persist or at least opposes the southerly flow.

Late in the afternoon as the slopes fall into shadow once again,
upslope flow decreases and finally disappears before dark. As the
slopes cool in early evening, downslope flow once again appears and
by 10:00 P.M. the northerly returns to the lake surface. The evening
katabatic flow is supported by the heated air over the lake which
flows onto the slopes aloft. Downslope flow continues until the cold,
dense, sinking air fills the valley and the heated air aloft forms an
overlying inversion which is not broken until once again the plains
are heated shortly after dawn. Slope cooling and slope heating depend upon clear skies and radiation as much as does the heating of
the plains. Cloud cover blocks both radiation cooling and heating
and therefore through the "greenhouse effect" obstructs all elements
of the valley wind.

Valley winds, like onshore sea breezes, are stable. The katabatic
wind is very cold, dense air flowing like a liquid over the cool waters
of the lake. The anabatic wind is much warmer, flowing from the
heated plains over the cool lake. Neither is associated with any
significant instability and therefore both tend to channel around
obstructions and along the face of steep shorelines. Long, narrow
valley lakes, like river valleys, tend to cause any wind to channel
along their main axis and to deviate parallel to any major deviations
in their course. As valley winds are aligned with the main axis of

the valley by virtue of their generation, they readily adapt to this channeling, deviating as the valley turns and increasing in velocity as the valley narrows. At Garda the Tempests discovered (what the local sailors knew) that in the afternoon southerly the first boat on port to the western shore would be the first to the weather mark. Just north of Limone the western shore bulges into the lake; its main axis more southwest–northeast below Limone becomes more north–south above. This change in axis causes a veer in the channeled southerly flow, a persistent shift to the west as the port-tack boats reach the western shore and round that bulge. According to Jim Linville this shift was minimal, however; the advantage of the western shore seemed to him to be due to an increase in velocity there. One might have expected an increase in velocity on the outside of the bend along the lake's eastern shore. At Garda, however, as the airflow enters the upper end of the lake, a 1600-foot vertical wall confines the airflow along the western shore. The air mass escapes and loses some velocity into the more gradually rising slopes of the eastern shore; the velocity of the confined flow along the western shore is increased by comparison. Such wind-velocity increases are as characteristic of sheer shorelines in narrow valleys as are current-velocity increases in areas of abrupt change in underwater contours.

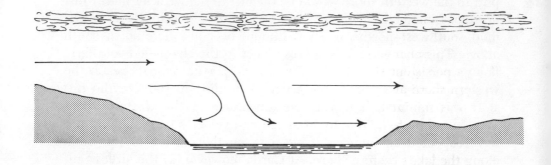

D. The River Winds

Refraction.
Barrier effects—blanketing and lifting.
Channeling.
The land breeze.

1. Tom's River—Surface and Barrier Effects

"The weary sun hath made a golden set,
And by the bright tracks of his fiery car
Gives token of a goodly day tomorrow."

Rivers and lakes imbedded in the land receive the winds of the land. When these winds are of weather system origin, they are modified by their passage over the land, by the friction associated with contact with the land surface, by diurnal variation in the surface temperature of the land, and by impingement upon obstacles protruding from the land. When these winds are of local thermal origin—the lake breeze (or river or sea breeze) and the land breeze —they are dependent upon the presence of the land and are modified in their strength and direction by the character of the land.

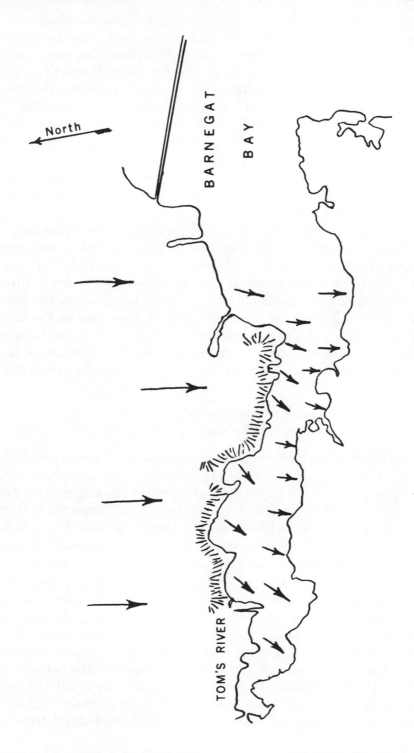

Variations in strength and direction induced by channeling over a
confined water surface are discussed in the chapter on the Severn,
modifications of the lake breeze induced by the terrain surrounding
a small lake are discussed in the chapter on Saratoga and the effects
of the shore upon the development of a land breeze are discussed
in the chapter "Winter on the River." The proximate effects of the
topographic features of the land, blanketing, lifting, mechanical eddying, and refraction, *when the airflow is essentially perpendicular
to the axis of the river*, are considered in this chapter. Although these
phenomena are evident in any offshore wind on any confined body
of water, they are determinants of racing success on a narrow river
when the wind is flowing across the river.

The surrounding topography of Tom's River is so varied that all
of these terrain influences are manifest at some point along its course.
The river is navigable for a distance of approximately two miles
from its entrance into Barnegat Bay up to the town of Tom's River.
Its upper reaches are narrow and winding, bordered on the north
by wooded hills that rise abruptly from the shore and on the south
by level terrain densely covered with houses and trees. Near its
mouth the southern shore becomes very low and terminates in a
large marsh which protrudes its sandy margins into the open bay.

BARRIER EFFECTS IN STABLE AIR;
SURFACE FRICTION AND REFRACTION

The lower levels of any airflow are slowed by contact with the
surface. Over open water the surface flow velocity is approximately
twice as great as over the land. Over smaller lakes and rivers it may
be minimally different from or approximately 1.5 times the velocity
over the land. Over mud flats, sand, or shingle, surface flow velocity
will be similar to its velocity over open water. Large trees and buildings reduce the surface flow to approximately half its velocity over
open water. The vertical velocity gradient is directly proportional
to the roughness of the surface, the velocity of the wind, and the
instability of the flow. Over open water the velocity gradient within
the sailing layer is minimal though the wind velocity at several thousand feet may be 1.5 to 2 times as great. Over long grass the wind
at 30 feet is twice what it is at 3 feet but changes little between 30
feet and higher altitudes. Waves, like long grass, move with the wind
and reduce the wind velocity in the sailing layer (below 30 feet)
by only about 20 percent. The strength of the airflow also determines

the degree of frictional slowing of the surface flow. The drag induced by solid projections is proportional to the square of the wind velocity. Instability due to a high lapse rate causes the surface flow to be a mixture of high-velocity upper-level and low-velocity surface flow and therefore minimizes the vertical velocity gradient. In the early morning and evening or under an inversion, when flow is stable, the surface wind velocity is markedly less than the upper-level flow. At midday the difference is minimal (if the wind strength increases according to its usual diurnal variation). In the spring when the water is cool the surface flow is less (compared with the upper-level flow) than it is in fall when the water is warmer.

At Tom's River the velocity of the wind in the open bay is usually twice its velocity in the upper river where passage over trees and buildings markedly reduces the surface flow. Where the wind is off the marsh at the mouth of the river, however, it is but slightly lesser in velocity near shore than it is in mid-bay. Here the wind rapidly achieves the full speed to be expected over a water surface. Up in the river the short distance from shore to shore permits little opportunity for a significant increase in velocity during transit. In the narrow river barrier effects are significant, friction slows the entire surface flow but tends to affect all boats equally.

Where the wind flows offshore onto open water with no land to leeward to modify its flow, a significant change in velocity and direction occurs. The change in velocity at the shoreline results in the phenomenon of refraction. The result is a band of wind near the shoreline which flows in a direction more perpendicular to the shoreline than the wind over the surface farther offshore. This effect is clearly evident when a windward mark is set up near the low Beachwood shore and requires that the tack toward the more perpendicular flow be selected initially.

The degree of refraction that produces such a persistent shift is proportional to the change in velocity that results as the airflow traverses the shoreline. If the land is rough, forested, or otherwise irregular, and its surface flow maximally slowed; if the shoreline is abrupt with no intervening beach or mud flat; and if the water to leeward is open, refraction will be marked. Refraction is greatest when the airflow is stable, least when instability mixes friction-free upper flow with low-level flow. The maximum shift is probably not greater than 10°. (Anabatic and katabatic effects where large hillsides reach the shore may cause greater deviations but refraction alone probably does not. A hillside heated by the sun may turn an

oblique weather system wind directly onshore while the katabatic
flow off a mountain may deviate an offshore weather system flow
directly offshore.) The refractive effect is not evident at the shoreline but becomes obvious 50–100 yards from shore. It persists up
to a half mile from the shore (a distance proportionate to the
velocity change). Farther offshore increasing mixture of unrefracted
upper-level flow restores the deviated surface flow to its original
direction.

Refraction results because the frontal breadth of the wind flow
is essentially incompressible. If a segment of flow speeds up as it
crosses the shoreline obliquely, it must do so without a change in its

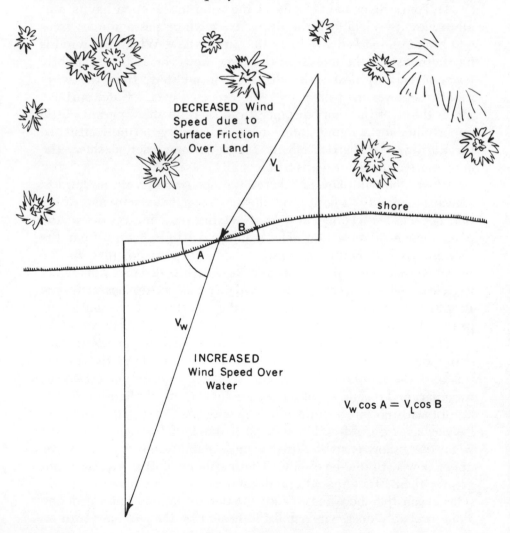

DECREASED Wind
Speed due to
Surface Friction
Over Land

V_L

shore

B

A

V_W

INCREASED
Wind Speed Over
Water

$$V_W \cos A = V_L \cos B$$

breadth. For such a segment to move farther in the same time (increase its velocity) it must change its direction so as to proceed more directly away (perpendicular) to the site of change. At the shoreline the front is moving in the direction of the frictionally retarded land flow; a hundred yards offshore it is deviated approximately 10°; farther out, with increasing amalgamation of upper-level flow, the surface flow deviates gradually back to its original direction. The result for a boat approaching a mark one hundred or more yards off a shore is a progressive shift, a shift which increases progressively toward the shore. In such a progressive shift the boat inside and to weather on an approach tack that just lays the mark gains the most. In order to achieve this position the initial tack must be the one toward the shoreline and the final tack must be taken short of the apparent layline to allow for the progression of the shift as the mark is approached.

WINDWARD BARRIER EFFECTS

Near shore the surface flow is affected by barriers to windward. The significant factors are the height and density of the barrier, the shape of the barrier, the presence of gaps in the barrier, and the direction of the offshore flow relative to the barrier. Any protrusion from the surface causes the airflow to deviate around it and to converge beyond it in an attempt to maintain the continuity of the airflow. Depending upon the instability of the airflow, its compliance with a stimulus to lifting, the flow will rise to surmount the barrier and eddy downward to leeward of the barrier. Studies of the effects of trees planted to protect vegetation from damage by wind flow have indicated the extent of eddying and convergence to leeward of such barriers. A dense barrier eliminates the wind flow completely just to leeward of the barrier and interferes with the wind flow to some degree for a distance 30 times the altitude of the barrier to leeward (30h). A 100-foot barrier typical of the tree-lined hilly shores of Tom's River affects the surface flow over a distance 3000 feet (half a mile) to leeward, the entire width (and more) of the river. At a distance 5h to leeward the wind velocity at the surface is approximately 40 percent of its velocity upwind of the barrier. At 15h to leeward, the far shore of the river in a northerly wind, the velocity is but 85 percent of its original strength.

Where the barrier is broken the effects are quite different. In the upper reaches of Tom's River the northern shore is marshland which extends to irregularly wooded hills many hundreds of yards away from the shore. The wind flows through such a medium dense barrier as well as over and around it. That portion of the flow which gets through the barrier meets the down and reverse flowing eddies from the overflow so as to reduce the flow at about 5h to but 20 percent of its original velocity. Immediately beyond the barrier the flow is composed entirely of air which comes through the barrier and is therefore stronger than the flow at 5h where the flow is a mixture of forward- and backward-moving air. The worst possible barrier is one which permits half the wind to flow through it and deviates the other half into overflow eddies which may cause the flow 20h to leeward to be but 60 percent of its original velocity. Even where the barrier is quite open, a few buildings or scattered trees, the eddy effect causes a significant reduction in the wind velocity, to 70 percent or less of its original speed, at 5h to leeward. If the river is narrow and an open barrier high, the strongest wind may be along the windward shore, up to 90 percent of its original velocity, and least along the leeward shore if that shore is approximately 5h beyond the barrier.

The distribution of such barrier effects is in a semicircle to leeward of the barrier. If the barrier is of limited breadth the zone of interference, though significant, may be quite narrow at a distance 20h to leeward. If the wind is at an angle to the barrier the semicircular zone of interference is skewed downwind. The more acute the angle of the flow is to the barrier, the less is the distance the blanket zone extends downwind. Only half as large a blanket zone results if the wind is 45° rather than perpendicular to the barrier. Convergence is maximal just beyond a barrier as the flow attempts to restore continuity beyond it. When reaching past medium-dense or dense barriers the sailor must avoid entrance into the zone within 5h

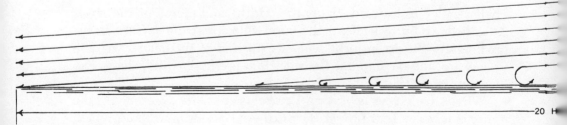

to leeward and if possible he should sail beyond 10h. Between 5h and 10h the blanket zone will be rapidly traversed; if the wind is other than perpendicular to the barrier, the area of reduction in velocity may be minimal. A lift will be experienced by a boat approaching the converged flow to leeward of a barrier and a header experienced as the boat emerges from its lee. If the windward mark is located off a shoreline barrier, the convergent flow resembles that associated with the widening portion of a river. Short tacks up the rhumb line best avoid the headers to either side, but deviation toward the side least obstructed by the barrier may be justified if a significant difference exists. (A race committee should know better than to place a mark within 5h of a windward barrier.)

The shape of a barrier modifies the degree of its interference to leeward. A wedge-shaped barrier whose blunt end is downwind—a slowly rising inland slope that terminates in a bluff at the water's edge—causes the wind to lift gradually and remain separated from the surface far downwind. A barrier which slopes down toward the water as trees give way to brush, and brush to beach, permits a gradual transition to the water surface and results in little interference. If the barrier is abrupt—a single line of buildings or trees along the water's edge—it is far more deleterious than if it is broad. The abrupt barrier produces a cushion of stagnant air to leeward over which the air must flow before it can rejoin the surface. It also causes the airflow to rise abruptly and so to initiate eddies which flow down beyond the barrier. A broad barrier, such as a large grove of trees, eliminates such eddies and smooths out the flow before it reaches the water to leeward. Thus a medium-dense barrier is converted into an eddy-free dense barrier and the resultant zone of interference is markedly reduced.

Observation of the constantly varying character of the windward

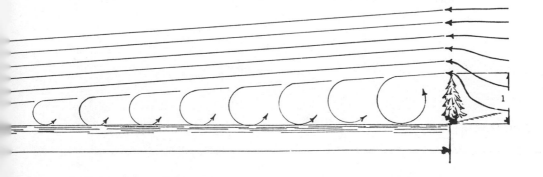

shoreline ahead should permit the river sailor to modify his intended course appropriately. If the river is more than five times wider than the average height of the windward shoreline, the ideal course will always be more than 5h from that shore. If the river is narrower than 5h a course close to the windward shoreline is appropriate if the barrier is open or only medium dense. When the barrier ahead is dense, a wedge-shaped shore terminating in a shoreline bluff for instance, the course should be as far to leeward as possible, up to 30h, so long as this does not result in an excessive lengthening of the course. The additional speed possible in the stronger air more than 5h to leeward compensates for the additional distance sailed when turning past a headland. A course farther out may be justified in very light air when modest increments of wind speed result in major increments of boat speed but would not be justified in a stronger wind. The ideal reaching course along the lower portion of Tom's River in a northerly is usually along the leeward shore (about 10–15h to leeward of the dense barrier of the hilly windward shore). Farther up the river, where the shoreline is lower, the barrier more open, and the river much narrower, a course along the windward shore is appropriate wherever the leeward shore is approximately 5h beyond the barrier.

LEEWARD BARRIERS

The optimal course along the river also depends upon the presence of barriers to leeward. The wind begins to lift as it approaches a barrier beginning approximately 9h to windward. Between this distance and the barrier the surface wind is reduced and disturbed by eddies which sink into the zone of reduced flow. Within this zone as in the blanket zone along the windward shore the wind shifts unpredictably. Fortunately the zone is less than half the length of the windward blanket zone. To windward of a dense barrier the

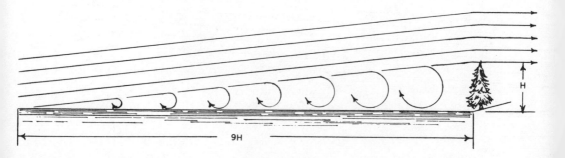

wind drops progressively from 100 percent at 9h to 80 percent at 5h, 40 percent at 2h and zero at the barrier. Open and medium-dense barriers modify the flow differently because, as is true of the barrier to windward, eddies reduce the flow to a greater degree at an intermediate position than they do at the barrier. Maximum reduction occurs at 2h (40 percent of the original velocity for a medium-dense barrier). At 5h the wind is always at least 60 percent of its original strength.

A course within 2h of a leeward barrier should be avoided unless the barrier is open and the river extremely narrow. If the river is wide the ideal course is at least 9h from the barrier. As the effects of a leeward barrier are only half as great as those of a windward barrier, on a narrow river a course two thirds the width of the river from the windward shore should be selected. If the river is more than 7h wide this should permit the avoidance of both the markedly detrimental 2h zone to leeward and the 5h zone to windward. Where the river is wider and the barriers vary, a course closer than one-third the way to a lower segment of leeward barrier or two-thirds the way to a lower segment of windward barrier will be appropriate. Where the river is narrower than 7h of the average barrier height the entire width of the river is adversely affected and marked variations in course to approach the windward shore or leeward shore closely, wherever the barrier becomes lower or more open, will be justified. In light air in a narrow river major increments of speed will be acquired by a boat able to obtain transient puffs of uneddied windflow close to a break in the windward barrier.

BARRIER EFFECTS IN UNSTABLE AIR

In unstable air, thermal turbulence induces vertical currents, updrafts, and downdrafts which result in markedly varied surface flow patterns. Over open water, downdrafts appear as gusts veered to the surface flow and of greater velocity than the surface flow. The direction of the mid-level or low-level cloud (cumulus or stratocumulus) movement indicates the direction of the gust flow. If this flow is approximately aligned with the long axis of a river or narrow lake, the cold descending air of the gust will be channeled in an axial manner and a standard gust/lull sequence will be observed. If the upper wind flow is approximately perpendicular to the long axis of a river or narrow lake, gusts will be partially obstructed by barriers along the shore. Where gaps appear in a hilly shoreline the gusts will be channeled along the axis of the gap and will appear at the water surface from the direction of the gap. Hills, trees, buildings, or other barriers may screen the water surface from the gusts as well as from the basic flow.

Gusts have a vertical velocity induced by the buoyancy of the surrounding air and dependent upon the higher lapse rate of the surrounding air. The higher the convection and the greater the temperature disparity traversed by the updraft, the more rapidly the gust will descend. The gust also has a horizontal velocity due to the flow of the air in which it is immersed. It therefore descends at an angle to the surface, the acuteness of which depends upon the degree of instability that created it. A barrier introduced into such a descending airflow will screen out gust elements in proportion to the acuteness of their angular descent. If instability is minimal and the gust is descending at a very shallow angle (nearly parallel to the surface) the barrier will prevent the gust flow from reaching the surface until it has passed nearly 20 or 30h to leeward, consistent with the screening effects of a barrier in a stable airflow. If instability is marked and the gust descends nearly vertically, the barrier will interfere minimally with the gust flow and the gust will reach the surface a mere 3–5h to leeward. Different gusts in a given airflow descend with different speeds; the most rapidly descending gusts contain segments of the highest velocity upper airflow and therefore have a maximum velocity due to both horizontal and vertical influences. As the highest velocity gusts are least obstructed by a barrier the gusts which reach the surface closest to the barrier are the strongest. The average gust reaches the surface about 10h from a barrier. Farther out the surface wind becomes increasingly composed of the full assortment of gusts of all possible velocities. In a narrow river, which may be but 3 to 10h wide, the only gusts which reach the surface are the strong ones. Here the wind is either light, reduced by the barrier, or very strong due to the presence of infrequent high-velocity gusts. This accounts for the danger in sailing in a narrow river or near shore in an unstable wind flow where the surface wind may almost instantaneously vary from 10 to 25 knots in velocity and why frequently it is safer to sail in open water in such a wind flow. Offshore the average velocity may be greater but the variations are far less extreme.

Variations in direction accompany these radical alterations in velocity close to the barrier. The basic wind, if oblique to the river, may be channeled along its main axis particularly by a high barrier along the leeward shore. If gaps appear in the windward shoreline

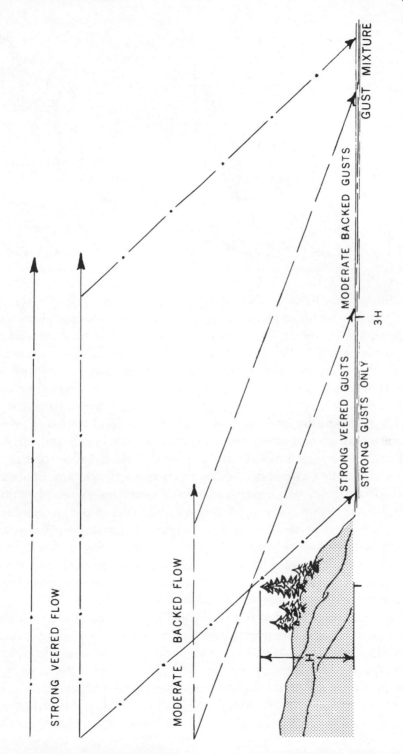

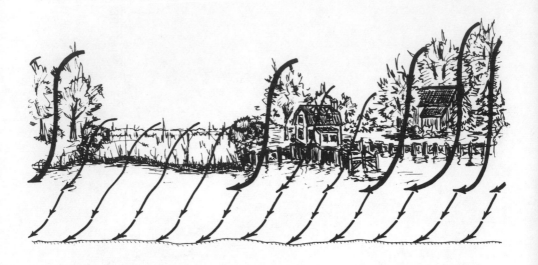

gusts may come through them at approximately right angles to the
axial flow. In addition gusts appear at the surface whose direction
is aligned with the isobaric flow aloft but which may be either
veered or backed to the surface flow on a particular river segment.
Along the windward side of the river the wind will be reduced in
velocity where there are barriers and if within 3h of the barrier de-
void of gusts except where gaps in the barrier appear. Here there
will be gusts and dramatic lifts. Farther out (5–10h) the basic wind
will be stronger, channeled more to the axial direction, and associated with infrequent but very strong gusts. Farther to leeward near
the lee shore the basic wind will be even stronger, its direction will
be axial and gusts will be frequent and varied in velocity, strong
as well as moderate. In very strong winds a course near the windward shore may be dangerous, but, for a boat beating up the river
in a channeled flow, will provide the most lifted course. In lighter
air the leeward shore, where the basic wind is stronger and most
gusts reach the surface, will be preferable even though the channeled wind will produce a significant header.

The course for the Tom's River Cup in 1965 was entirely in the
river in a stong unstable northeasterly. Few boats entered and fewer
boats survived. Dyke Williams, who eventually won, capsized less
often than the rest of us. In the narrow segments of the river vicious
gusts appeared infrequently but with disastrous consequences. As
the windward (northern) shore was blanketed by a dense barrier

(100-foot hills and dense trees), it was impossible to keep pace with boats to leeward by seeking its protection. The leeward shore, frequently but 10h away, provided the strongest mean wind and the mid-channel the most vicious gusts. Dyke, sailing his 14 with a marked reef in the mainsail, was able to tolerate the 25–30 knot winds along the leeward shore as well as the gusts that increased the basic wind force moderately. The gusts were generally veered to the average axial flow and thus channeled more northeasterly, particularly along the leeward shore. Where gaps appeared in the shoreline to the north the course along the river became a reach, where the shores were high and the river narrow, a beat. Where the river bent to the north a starboard-tack lift appeared, where it bent to the south the course became a run. I led for a considerable portion of the race with full sail but when approaching the finish after sailing twice around was unable to accommodate a dramatic gust in mid-channel and Dyke broke through to leeward. Here the gust was a major lift which just blew us over before we could release the sheets to accept it. Farther to leeward, where the mean wind was stronger, the gusts were more consistent with the mean velocity and more completely aligned with the mean direction. We probably could have managed one of these gusts more successfully than we did the mid-channel blast which was so dramatically different than the mean wind in both velocity and direction. Closer to the weather shore we would have sailed in a more lifted wind of lesser mean velocity but would have met such extreme gusts that we would probably not have survived the first round.

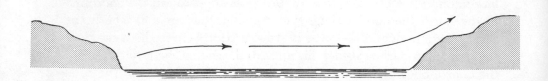

2. The Severn—Channeling

*"Rainbow to windward foul falls the day,
Rainbow to leeward rain runs away."*

At a river's surface, flow, whatever its origin, is usually stable. Even elements of unstable weather system airflows which reach the surface are cold and dense and therefore at the surface, stable. The lake or sea breeze that extends up an inlet of that lake or sea and may or may not be reinforced by anabatic flow is also cold and dense. Stable weather system airflows, unable to lift to surmount obstacles that they encounter, are channeled along the surface of a narrow water body. Flow spreads along the surface, deviates around obstacles, and seeks outlets wherever breaks in the shoreline appear. Beyond a zone of refraction or blanketing along a windward shore, decreased friction over the water surface and increased resistance created by the lee shore ahead result in deviation of such stable airflows along the main axis of the river. Anabatic and lake or sea breeze flows are aligned with the axis of the river initially and weather system flows tend to align themselves with the main axis regardless of their original direction. Thus in each segment of a river most wind flows tend to deviate along the main axis, bend as the river bends, and deviate to the greatest degree along the leeward shore. Such channeling is characteristic of winds that are flowing *parallel to the main axis of the river* but is evident in all wind flows that are stable at the surface.

A *cold, dense river wind* flows like water rapidly down the main channel, around promontories along the shore, out into coves and inlets which break the shoreline. Major deviations in direction result as this channeled flow meets various obstacles in its passage along the river. In the main channel the flow will (1) align itself with the long axis of each segment. (2) It will deviate outward into, and align itself with, the long axis of coves, creeks, and inlets making away from the leeward shore of the river. If the wind is completely aligned with the main axis, flow will deviate outward into coves on each side of the river. (3) Flow will emanate from, and be aligned with the long axis of the coves and inlets that emanate from the windward shore. (4) If flow is oblique to the main axis it will

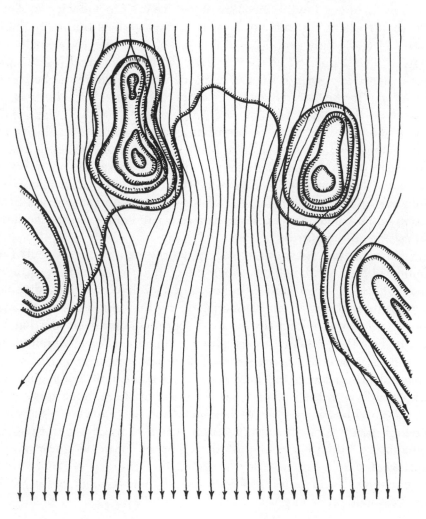

align itself more completely with the long axis of the river where the shores are particularly high. (5) Where a promontory protrudes into the river, flow will deviate around the obstruction paralleling the shore on either side of the promontory.

Variations in strength are associated with the variations in direction induced by the geographic factors enumerated. Wherever the cross-sectional area open to surface flow enlarges, the velocity of flow decreases; wherever the cross-sectional area diminishes, the velocity of flow increases. (1) Where the main channel of the river narrows, the velocity of flow increases; where the channel widens, the velocity decreases. (2) Where a headland protrudes into the channel, the velocity of flow increases at the tip of the headland. (3) If flow is aligned with the axis of the river, the velocity of flow decreases where the entry of a cove or inlet widens the main channel. (4) If the flow is oblique to the axis of the river, the velocity of flow will be increased as it exits from the main channel to leeward into a narrower cove or inlet or a segment of low shoreline between hills. (5) If the flow is oblique (or perpendicular) to the axis of the river, the velocity of flow will increase at a break in the windward shoreline. (6) Where high banks are present the velocity of flow increases and where a high bank is present on one shore and a low bank on the other, the velocity of flow is increased on the side with the high bank. (7) The velocity of flow will be particularly increased where a high bank confines the flow on the outside of a bend and particularly decreased where a low bank permits the flow to escape on the outside of a bend.

If the air flow is warm, it will leave the windward shore at the height of the shoreline, flow above the cold air at the river's surface, and lift readily to surmount the leeward shoreline ahead, unaffected by terrain features. Then blanketing along the windward shore and lifting prior to reaching the leeward shore, which are proportionate to the height of the shorelines, obscure the effects of channeling. *If the air flow is cold but perpendicular to the long axis of the river,* thermal lift-off along the heated weather shore will bring gusts of upper airflow to the surface near the weather shore. Such gusts will be most evident near the weather shore and particularly to leeward of high points along that shore from which thermal separation occurs most readily. Gusts of cold, dense air will flow along the river's surface and subsequently be aligned to the long axis of each water segment by the surrounding shorelines. Alignment (channeling) will be least evident where the wind is strongest and gustiest along the windward shoreline and most evident where it is weakest and steadiest along the leeward shoreline.

We frequently race in the rivers at Essex, at Annapolis, and in Washington. Once each year on New Year's Day, we race up the Severn River around St. Helena Island in Round Bay, and return, a distance of about twelve miles. The high shores of the river are indented by coves and creeks and by irregular promontories which channel the winds along the axis of the main channel. In 1965 we raced in a light, varying northwesterly which funneled down the river to provide a four-mile initial beat.

The starting line was established at the mouth of Weem's Creek which opens on the southwest bank of the river. Here the river wind was backed as a portion of the flow was channeled out of the creek. We started at the upwind (port) end of the line but were unable to break away to the port tack. Those who were able to do so were well to starboard of the fleet when the creek mouth was passed and the subsequent shift to starboard appeared. As we tacked up the straight main channel of the lower river in the oscillating wind we gradually improved our position by judicious use of the compass. As the river bent to the north we worked toward this bank and were rewarded by a persistent shift from this direction which gave us the lead. We tacked to cover the fleet and continued on starboard tack in the veer. *Goose* tacked off behind us, however, and, farther to starboard in the subsequent back off Luce Creek, was able to tack inside and ahead. We tacked behind her and rounded the next bend a close second. We were now faced with a gradual bend of the river to the west. We followed the gradual port-tack lift (back) waiting for an oscillating header to tack toward the port shore—but we waited too long. The back held, progressed, became marked; we lost three more boats, and were only able to recover one of these as we worked up under the next promontory on the north shore. The distance gained by the two leaders in the channeled shifts of the river was too great to be overcome in the subsequent beat across Round Bay or during the long run back down the river.

When racing in a river the competitor must be concerned with channeled deviations in the wind and must place himself in a position to take advantage of deviations resulting from promontories, creek entrances, or major river course alterations. When sailing to windward these "geographic" shifts always warrant primary consideration; and in a river race such shifts generally determine the outcome. The primary plan for racing to windward in a river must be based on being nearest to the side of the river from which the next geographic wind deviation will occur at each bend in the river. The general rule may be stated as follows: *Be on the inside of the fleet when rounding all major bends in a river* (or similar body of water). (Being on the inside, of course, must be accomplished with caution; if the shore at the bend produces significant blanketing it should not be approached too closely.) Protrusions of the shoreline that are followed by deviations of the river axis should be approached from beneath (downwind) on the most direct tack. This approach will permit tacking out from under the point, close aboard, on the tack which will be progressively lifted as the boat emerges into the new channel (or altered main axis). The boat making this approach will always be on the inside, to windward of her competitors, short-cutting across the great circle being sailed by boats on the outside of the bend.

Geographical shifts of this nature will effect all boats in the fleet and will not be counteracted by a shift back in the opposite direction unless the river bends back. These shifts thus take precedence over all other wind shifts. The presence of an oscillating wind superimposed upon the terrain shifts will require modification of tacking to conform to such temporal deviations, but should never prevent adherence to the fundamental rule given above. If I had paid less attention to the superimposed oscillations indicated by the compass and more to being in the right location to take advantage of the shifts created by the deviations of the river, less carrying on in a lift on the outside of the river's bends and more tacking, in an oscillating header if necessary, to be inside at the bends, I might have won the Ice Bowl again.

As these shifts are persistent (at least for a given area), relationships with other boats become meaningful indicators of progress—and such indications should be utilized to determine the need for covering tacks. If boats on the same tack are being lifted as compared to your course (particularly those behind and to windward), you are sailing in a relative header—tack and cover them, i.e., get inside for their lift. If boats on the opposite tack are sailing at an angle greater than 90° to your course, you are again sailing in a relative header—tack and cover them, i.e., get inside for your lift. Disregard nearby boats whose courses will be determined by the

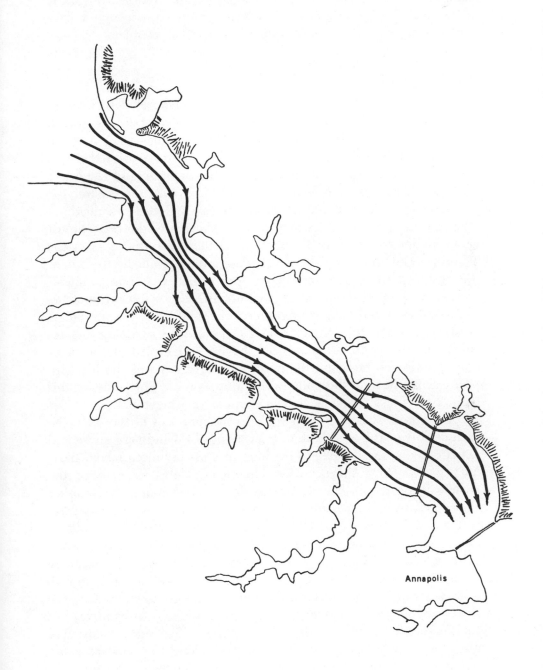

same wind and the same oscillations which effect you. Look for boats at a distance and utilize their experiences to indicate what is to be expected. Don't allow yourself to become preoccupied with neighboring competitors and immediate tactical problems.

LOCAL TACTICS

Basic strategy for sailing in a river in a channeled wind is to sail farther to the side of the course than one's competitors toward a persistent shift which is presumed to be present ahead. A channeled shift induced by a bend in a river is progressive for the boat emerging around the point which marks the beginning of the bend. The farther she emerges from the lee of the point, the greater the lift becomes. The boat on the inside of the lift gains on all those who sail the greater circles outside her. Therefore, the boat closest to the layline to the shoal off the point or the protruding pier or the offshore rock will receive the greatest advantage. In order to acquire this inside position she must have approached the shore immediately downwind of the point as close aboard as possible without being blanketed and have tacked when she could just lay the outermost obstruction to navigation at the point. By so doing she receives the maximum advantage of the lift to leeward of the point on the approach tack and the maximum advantage of the lift (opposite shift) beyond the point on the other tack. (The basis for this technique is also discussed in the chapter on Kingston.)

If the basic airflow is at an angle to the long axis of the river, the surface flow at the mouth of an inlet along the windward shore will deviate to emerge parallel to the long axis of the inlet. A boat beating up river in a surface wind channeled along the axis of the river will receive a lift as it approaches an inlet along the weather shore and usually an increase in wind velocity. This effect will result not only from an inlet but also from a valley between hills or any similar break in a high shoreline. The maximum effect of such a lift will be evident close to the windward shore and minimally along the leeward shore where the river channeling will prevail. A tack should be made close aboard the point downwind of the inlet entrance so as to emerge in the lift inside and to windward of the fleet as the mouth of the inlet is passed. The surface flow will also deviate where an inlet enters a river along the leeward shore but here the direction of flow will be from the river into the inlet. This deviation also creates a lift for boats beating in the river but will be maximal along the leeward shore and minimal along the windward shore. The mouth of such an inlet should be approached to leeward of the fleet where the greatest lift will be present and the lifted tack continued to the upriver point beyond the mouth. As the return to channeled river flow beyond the point will be associated with a header (relative to the lift at the inlet mouth), it is essential that the exit tack from the inlet mouth be taken close aboard the point to round it "inside and to windward at the point." The basic rule holds for dealing with points at the mouth of inlets along either shore. Along the leeward shore a gain can be made on the inlet-crossing tack, which is lifted, and on the tack that rounds the upriver point, which is lifted. Along the windward shore a gain is made at the downriver point as the windward boat emerges in a lift, but an equal loss may occur as the boat subsequently reenters the river flow in a header beyond the upriver point. The lift will in any case provide a gain over boats along the opposite shore which miss it altogether. *Take the shore from which the point protrudes or along which the inlet emerges.*

If a stable wind is flowing straight down the axis of a river (or approximately so), it will outflow into inlets on either side and deviate away from the main axis wherever an inlet appears. The presence of an inlet causes the river to widen; upwind and downwind of an inlet mouth the main channel narrows. The effect of an inlet entering a river (when the flow is parallel to the main axis of the river) is therefore similar to the effect of a diverging shoreline along any body of water over which a channeled wind is flowing. Wherever the river widens the wind diverges from its basic axis toward each shoreline, and downwind of the site of widening the wind converges toward the basic axis. When beating through a river segment of varying width the boat should be kept to the lifted tack, tacked whenever it is headed. This means that upon entering the widened portion of the river tacks will be made frequently, close to the central rhumb line, and upon entering the narrowing portion of the river beyond the widened zone tacks will be withheld until the shoreline is reached. The narrowing portion of the river corresponds to the presence of any protruding point or the upriver point beyond an inlet into which channeled flow is exiting—and requires an approach close aboard so as to be "inside at the bend." (The basis for this technique is also discussed in the chapter on Bermuda).

If the windward mark lies in a portion of the river that is widened, the wind downwind of the mark will be converging to-

ward the center of the river from both shores. A header will be experienced as the boat sails in either direction from the center line.
The farther the boat sails in either direction, the greater the header
it will experience as deviation increases with distance from that
center line. The shortest course to the mark, if it is located in the
middle of the channel, is achieved by a series of short tacks up the
center of the channel. The boat that sails far to the side of the
widening channel experiences, relative to the axial wind, a progressively increasing header all the way to the shore and a progressively
increasing header all the way back to the center line.

If the windward mark lies in a portion of the river which is
narrowed, the wind downwind of the mark will be diverging from

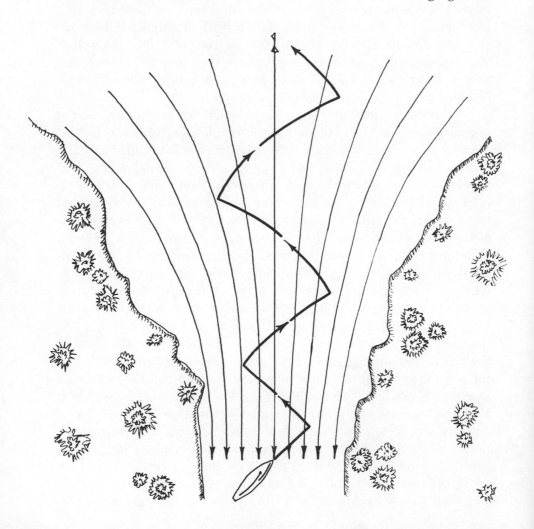

the center of the river toward both shores. A lift will be experienced as the boat sails in either direction from the center line. The farther the boat sails in either direction, the greater the lift it will experience as deviation increases with distance from that center line. The shortest course to the mark, if it is located in the middle of the channel, is achieved by a few long tacks, each continued to the shoreline. Not only is a progressively increasing lift experienced all the way to the shore but a lift is experienced all the way back to the center line. The boat that short tacks up the center line misses the big progressive lifts along the shores and sails a far longer course.

The major determinant of success between two boats, each of which understands the basic principles of sailing in channeled

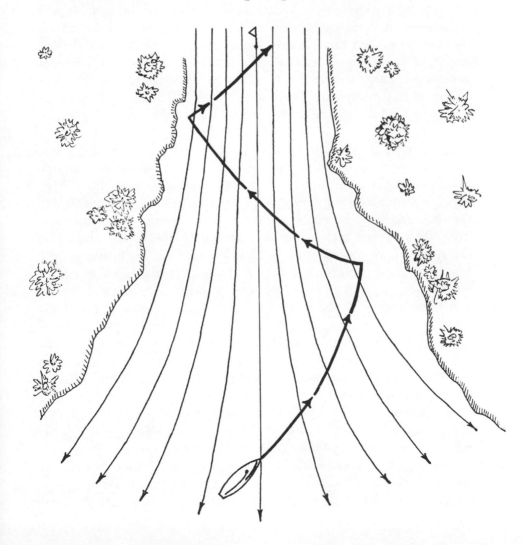

winds, is the position of their approach tacks relative to a bend in the shoreline, a protruding point, or a headland beyond an inlet. Being inside and to windward on the lifted approach tack to the headland is advantageous. It is tempting to hold out in the channel and to take an approach tack between the fleet and the channel. If, however, by carrying the boat to the tip of the headland, the approach tack misses the location of maximum deviation, a lesser lift will be experienced. If the approach tack is taken early, into the shore before that shoreline starts its divergence, the approach-tack lift may be missed altogether. And where the approach tack reaches the shoreline determines the position of the exit tack. If this is not farthest upwind, closest to the point (relative to the competition) as the point is rounded, the maximum advantage of the exit lift will be missed. In some circumstances, after reaching the shoreline on the ideal approach tack, it may be necessary to tack out and then back to the shoreline so as to acquire the inside position as the point is rounded. Large differences in distance sailed result from modest differences in position on both approach and exit tacks. It pays to take a few extra tacks, if necessary, to insure the optimal position for each.

Although the primary concern as one beats up a winding river, or a river with significant variation in its width, is to achieve a position inside and to windward in a variety of advantageous lifts, there are circumstances when being ahead and to leeward is beneficial. If the river gradually bends, a gradual header for one tack will occur. The advantageous tack is the one toward the persistent shift, i.e., the headed tack which must be continued until the heading shift has terminated. This means that as soon as a point, intermediate mark, or entrance to an inlet has been passed (close aboard, "inside and to windward"), the boat should be tacked (or continued) toward any subsequent gradual bend in the river. If the gradual bend is toward the same side as the point that has been rounded, an immediate tack is necessary to prevent a competitor from acquiring the ideal ahead-and-to-leeward position in the expected gradual header. If the gradual bend is toward the opposite side from the point that has been rounded, the rounding tack should be continued across the river and that side of the river adhered to until a bend back or a protruding point on the opposite side appears.

So long as a river bends back in the opposite direction after a single bend, the channeled shifts induced by the bends may be treated as oscillating shifts. To windward this means that the boat is kept to the lifted tack and tacked when headed beyond a prede-termined "median" direction. This technique is consistent with the principle of being "inside at the bends" and with the recommenda-tions for tacking in areas of converging or diverging shorelines. Where, however, the river makes a bend which is not followed by a subsequent bend or where, during a race, the windward mark lies beyond that final bend, the shift occasioned by that bend becomes a persistent shift. Then the boat must be sailed toward that persistent shift as soon as the boat emerges from the shore at that bend, point, or headland. This is a headed tack and must be continued on into the persistent shift until the shift is completed or the layline is reached. The final tack to the mark can then be taken inside-and-to-windward of competitors astern.

The same considerations are appropriate to sailing downwind with the axial river flow astern. So long as additional bends are ex-pected ahead each channeled shift may be treated as an oscillating shift. The boat is kept to the headed jibe and jibed whenever a lift beyond the "median" wind appears. Where, however, the river makes a bend which is not followed by a subsequent bend in the opposite direction the shift at that bend becomes a persistent shift and must be managed as such. The boat must assume an approach jibe that carries it away from the final shift and that jibe must be continued until the layline is reached or until the opposite jibe will carry the boat to the area of termination of the shift.

One must learn to think ahead and to distinguish the final shift before the layline or the final bend in the river and to plan to manage it in a manner distinct from the shifts associated with previous bends. Having emerged into open water from close aboard that last point, the headed tack or the lifted jibe must be assumed or continued so as to obtain an optimal position in that final shift.

The velocity differences induced by channeling are probably more significant when sailing downwind than to windward. Wher-ever the channel narrows or deviates, a local increase in velocity occurs. If the shores are elevated the velocity increase is accentu-ated. All of the air confined beneath the level of the banks in a channeled wind flow must deviate with each channel deviation. If a shoreline is low or an inlet appears, the air mass can escape from the channel and the expected velocity increase will be minimized. If a steep bluff is present along the outside of a bend, a major ve-locity increase will occur in front of it. We won the 1972 Ice Bowl in a warm, stable southeasterly by jibing downwind into areas of maximum velocity at the bends in the Severn. This stable wind flow had difficulty getting down through the conduction inversion over the cold water. Marked velocity differences occurred along different shores of the river and these were evident as we sailed up the lower river to the starting line. It was evident that the airflow attempted to follow a straight-line trajectory and was strengthened and brought to the surface as it impinged upon a shore which bent across its path. As we passed the Naval Academy there was no wind on the southwestern shore and 5–6 knots at the surface along the northeastern shore. This was apparently consequent to the high banks along the northeastern shore and the presence of a marked deviation of those banks to the west a half mile upriver. At the location of the start the wind deflected from the high northeastern shore was strong along the southwestern shore where another high shore deflected it back onto the river's surface.

We started at the southwestern end of the line, jibed to port, sailed up under the southwestern shore, jibed back in front of the fleet, jibed back to the better wind again and on the next starboard jibe crossed in front of the fleet by fifty yards. Thereafter we stayed close to the outside southwestern shore in stronger breeze as the river gradually turned to the north. As the wind changed direction with changes in the course of the river we sought the most headed jibe. It was possible to hold a progressively higher reaching angle into the stronger wind along an outside bend and then to accept a short jibe back into the channel beyond the bend at a poor angle on the opposite jibe. By so doing we kept to the side of the river where the wind was strongest and spent most of the time on a headed jibe. In this light, stable, patchy airflow it seemed most important to retain position to benefit from velocity advantages and to ignore the possible benefits from continuing a headed jibe into a zone of decreased velocity. At the final bend in the river before it exited into Round Bay, it was possible to hold a headed starboard jibe well into the strong wind on the outside of the bend and to pass the mark at a high angle on port jibe. This course in a final persistent shift permitted the boat to be sailed away from the final shift on the initial jibe (starboard) and to be jibed into a progressively higher sailing angle on the approach to the mark. We had a 300-yard lead as we entered Round Bay and won going away.

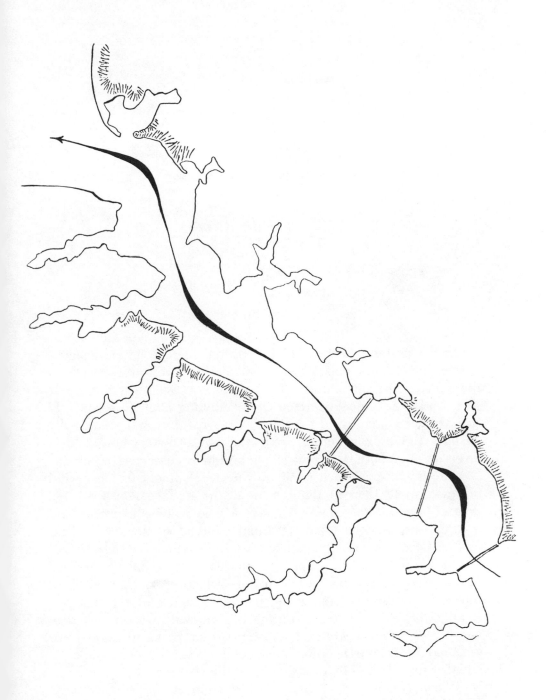

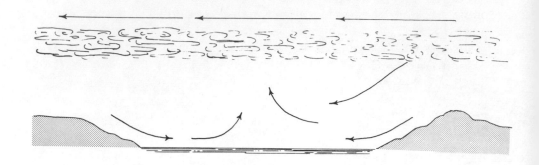

3. Winter on the River—
The Land Breeze

"Pale moon doth rain,
Red moon doth blow;
White moon doth neither rain nor snow."

In the northern sections of the United States winter racing is held on small lakes, ponds, rivers, and harbors well protected from the dangers and discomforts of the open sea. Sailing is done near shore and near the cold surface of surrounding land. Consequently the weather system wind available to the frostbite sailor is usually offshore and usually derives from a stable airflow, whose coldest layer lies at its bottom. Such a stable airflow is characterized by one or more inversions which facilitate the development of local wind in response to thermal differences at the surface. Onshore "sea breeze" flow due to the co-existence of cold water and warm land may appear, but the typical thermal wind of winter is the land breeze. Local offshore flow is likely to occur whenever the weather system wind is excluded from the surface and whenever the surface of the water is warmer than the surface of the land. A land breeze is possible whenever the land is frozen and the water is suitable for racing. Thus frostbiting is almost always conducted in an offshore wind, whether of weather system or local thermal origin, and the major decision demanded of the frostbite sailor is whether to sail close to, or away from, the shore.

Winter sailing is subject to marked contrasts of wind velocity. Either the wind is unstable and very strong or stable and very light.

As the land surface is progressively chilled with the progress of winter and additionally chilled by radiation loss each night, the only wind likely to be colder than the land over which it flows is the northwester. This outflow from a continental polar air mass is likely to be exceedingly strong in winter (the strongest airflow of the year in most parts of the United States) because the cP air mass shifts south in winter and the pressure gradients are steeper. Because the land is chilled further by the advection of this frigid air, the water is likely to be warmer than the land in its presence. The resultant airflow over the water is likely to be more unstable and therefore stronger than the airflow over the land. In many instances the northwesterly is too strong to sail in and, because of the factors enumerated, may persist at high velocity for two or three days, blowing out an entire weekend. It may be possible to sail on a small lake or cove in a strong northwesterly but impossible to sail in it on more open water or on a river whose axis is approximately parallel to the flow and receives it in a channeled and strengthened condition. The instability of this flow—very cold air flowing over warmer land or water—not only brings it to the surface but produces the downdraft gusts that cause it to be so treacherous. If the land is warmer than the water the strongest surface wind will be near the shore, but here the risk of capsize in a sudden bolt of 30-knot air is greater. It may be safer and faster to sail away from the shore in a lighter but steadier surface flow.

If the weather system wind is other than the northwesterly, it is likely to be warmer than the surface over which it flows and therefore stable. Southerly flow on the back of high pressure or easterly flow to the north of low pressure is common along the east coast in winter and characterized by an advection inversion. Little, if any, of the weather system flow is likely to reach the surface unless the land is heated under clear skies and the inversion is broken by thermal lift-off. If cloud cover prevents the dissipation of the inversion, as it will in the presence of the moist airflow about low pressure, the weather system wind may never reach the surface. The result is the bane of the frostbiter—glassy calm, cold rain trickling through the foul weather gear, and chattering teeth which shake the faint indications of shape from the sails. Under these circumstances the land breeze is likely and the dilemma is whether to rely upon it or upon the penetration of the weather system wind to the surface. Should the boat be drifted toward the shore and the land breeze, or offshore away from the blanketing effects that further limit the already slight chance that the weather system wind will appear?

STABLE AIRFLOW

The Ice Bowl of '67 was sailed in a light southwesterly which provided a beam or broad reach up river. No new weather system wind nor any thermal variation was to be expected on this cold, cloudy day in the midst of a slowly moving low-pressure system. With the wind perpendicular to the main course of the river and highly variable in velocity at the start, we felt that success would depend upon vertical influences affecting the surface wind. Choosing the right shore along which to sail would determine the first half of the race, and the choice depended upon whether the wind would be brought to the surface more strongly along the weather shore or the leeward.

We decided that the leeward shore would be preferable, so we started to leeward and slightly ahead of the fleet with a 3-knot wind abeam. We gradually luffed to the weather edge of the fleet, but too late, as *Glastrocity* picked up a puff and swept past under spinnaker. We set ours as the entire fleet took turns blanketing and passing us, and tried to break clear again to leeward. We were a long last when we succeeded. I congratulated myself on now being several hundred feet to leeward and for having lured the fleet close under the weather shore. (A significant asset in racing is the ability to find advantage in disaster and even to believe that it was all intentional!) For a moment it *did* seem advantageous as the fleet stopped beneath the Route 50 bridge and we pulled even again. Moments later we were dead in the water, the wind picked up along the weather shore, and the fleet swept away. A half mile later we were a quarter mile behind. Nothing daunted (perhaps a little?) we worked our way farther to leeward and were at last rewarded. About two miles farther up the river the sickly wind approached death. All that remained was along the leeward shore. We drove relentlessly past boat after boat and entering Round Bay, where the river opened in broad expanse, were second, scant feet astern of *Fantasy*.

The course to the western entrance of the St. Helena Island channel was along the southwestern shore of Round Bay and we once again lured(?) the fleet close up under the weather shore in a series of protective (?) luffs. *Altair, Shdu,* and *Bacalao* holding off to leeward, however, demonstrated the wisdom of my original conviction as they sailed around the rest of us in an easy circle. We were third at the island and a half hour later when we rounded the most upriver mark were still 200 yards astern of *Bacalao.* She (fortunately) held on port toward the weather shore across the two-mile diameter of Round Bay and we recovered most of the distance by taking starboard tack to the east where the wind was close to 8 knots. As we entered the narrow river for the final three-mile beat home, we were but a few feet astern and after two miles of dog fighting at last broke into the lead. While we fought with *Bacalao,* however, *Glastrocity* was returning to the wars and with but a few hundred yards to go was threatening our weather quarter. She tacked to port, we held on toward the leeward shore, watched her die with heartfelt thanks, and broke out from under the bridge in a little air. In the last few yards, recognizing that there would be wind on the weather side of the river at the finish line, which was situated at the mouth of Weem's Creek, we tacked to cross *Glastrocity* and finished a few yards in the lead. Virtue had triumphed, but through such trials!

It is often difficult, as my two glaring errors demonstrate, to hold to the courage of one's convictions, particularly when in the lead and the mob astern is threatening one's weather quarter. And although there were some obvious times when the surface wind was not true to its proper form, every leg of the race ultimately demonstrated the advantage of being to leeward and well away from the weather shore. In a shorter race the result might have been less predictable; in a twelve-mile race, in a narrow river, it was certain. We were sailing in a vertically stable southwesterly, a wind developed in the warm sector of a low which had come up from the south. The airflow was warm (for January 1) moving across snow-covered and frozen land which had no sun to warm it. No mixing of the layer of cold air over the land with the warm air flowing aloft could be expected. Only where the air had moved well beyond (10–20h) the weather shore did the thermostable water, warmer than the land, dissipate that cold, dense surface layer and permit the warm flow aloft to reach the surface. On the lee shore of Round Bay, there was 8 knots of breeze; under the weather shore, throughout most of the lower river, along the southern shore of Round Bay and behind the island, there was almost none.

THE LAND BREEZE

My disastrous showing in the Ice Bowl of '68 prompted my competitors to remark that I wouldn't write this one up for publication. However, disaster to me is a challenge which demands the salvage of some small profit. I barely fought my way out of last in the last few yards of the race—but I learned something (and I can write a chapter about it!). We had sailed up the river in a fitful northerly, coming obliquely off the starboard shore, but as we entered the open waters of Round Bay, near its western margin, it gave what seemed to be a last gasp and died away. This northerly was derived from the back of a low and was bringing in moist, cool air which formed a dense cloud cover at about 5000 feet. Although this cool, moderately unstable wind flow was brought down to the surface along the windward, partially snow-covered shore in intermittent gusts, the high banks screened large areas of the surface. Consequently the best wind in the river had been found well off the starboard shore or along the leeward shore.

The leading boats upon entering Round Bay detected an airflow backed about 75° to the original and on starboard, approaching the port (southwestern) shore, picked up more and more of this new wind. The heat of the day was waning; this new airflow was obviously a land breeze initiated by the local temperature difference between the colder, snow-covered western shore and the warmer, thermostable water. I set off after the two leaders and had soon moved up to third (from seventh) as I gained the advantage of the stronger land breeze nearer shore. A few minutes later, however, two disconcerting changes appeared: slight rifts revealed small patches of blue sky in the cloud cover and the wind commenced a series of brief 75° shifts. Then the entire fleet to the north began to move again in the northerly. Heating of the land had once again brought the northerly to the surface near the weather shore. The old wind was back and by the time it had filled in against the land breeze along the western shore we were far down to leeward and a long last. As the entire fleet disappeared behind St. Helena's Island, we pondered why at 3:30 P.M. on a winter's day heating of the land should have been sufficient to break through the cloud cover, why associated downdrafts should have melted the cloud and brought the cold northerly to the surface, and why our private land breeze was obliterated when it should have been strengthening. The les-

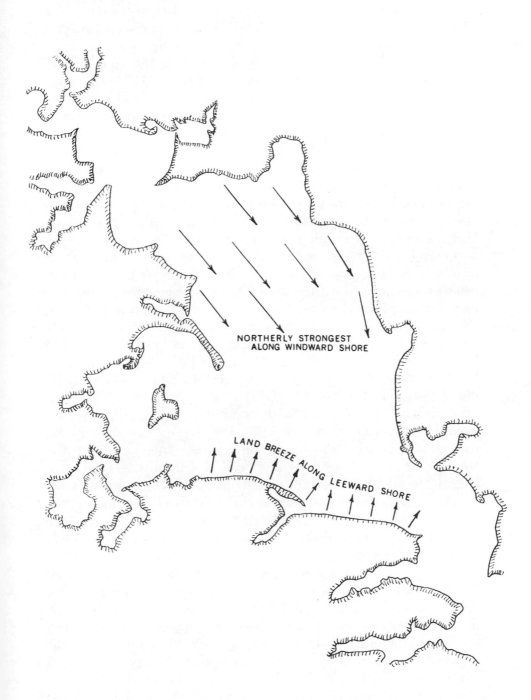

NORTHERLY STRONGEST
ALONG WINDWARD SHORE

LAND BREEZE ALONG LEEWARD SHORE

son: land breezes are always weak and one should be constantly alert to the reappearance at the surface (even late in the day) of a weather system wind—especially when cloud cover changes suggest its reappearance.

If the weather system wind is cooler than the land surface during the period of racing, the strongest wind is likely to be present near the weather shore where the warm land will create the greatest instability. If cloud cover and a conduction inversion over the water surface limit the surface flow, seek the weather shore where downdrafts of upper airflow are most likely to be present. Approach to the weather shore need only be limited by the barrier effect which, depending upon the density of the shore and its coverings, will limit the surface flow up to 20 or 30 altitudes to leeward. (See the chapter on Tom's River for a more complete discussion). If the sky is clear or clearing and the weather system wind from the north (as it was for the Ice Bowl of '68) or west, the weather shore is clearly advantageous. If the sky is clear or clearing and the weather system wind is from the south or east, however, it may remain warmer than the cold land surface over which it is flowing and the weather shore may be disadvantageous. If the sky is cloudy and the weather system wind is south (as it was for the Ice Bowl of '67) or east, it will certainly remain warmer than the cold land surface over which it is flowing and the weather shore will clearly be disadvantageous.

If the weather system wind is completely or partially screened from the surface either by the advection inversion associated with its own stability or by a conduction inversion due to low surface temperature, a land breeze may appear. It will only develop, however, if, in addition, a significant temperature disparity exists between the land and the water. No thermal lift-off can be expected from the "warm" water surface as its temperature will change little during the day (particularly in the presence of an inversion). Only a gradual flow of rising air from above its surface can move shoreward to replace a cold surface outflow from the shore. Thus land breezes are always weak and rarely extend more than a few hundred yards offshore. If the land is frozen or snow-covered, however, a low-level outflow, rarely more than a few hundred feet deep, may move from the dome of dense, cold air above the shore toward the water. An unstable weather system flow will obliterate the upper circulation of the land breeze along the weather shore and prevent its development even though the surface is calm. Under these circumstances (the Ice Bowl of '68) the land breeze can only develop along the leeward shore. A stable weather system wind will support the upper land breeze circulation along the leeward shore and limit it but minimally along the weather shore. When the land is colder than the water, as it must be for the land breeze to develop, the inversion of the stable airflow is particularly strong over the weather shore and protects the land breeze circulation. Thus a land breeze is unlikely to appear at all in an unstable airflow and only then along the leeward shore. In a stable airflow it may appear along either shore but is more likely to appear along the weather shore.

OFFSHORE WEATHER SYSTEM FLOW	LAND BREEZE	CALM
Unstable flow	Stable flow	Stable flow
Flow parallel to the long axis of the water body	Flow perpendicular to the long axis of the water body	Minimal weather system flow
Very cold water	Warm water	Cold water
Land heating with clear sky	Snow-covered or frozen land	Cold land (temperature similar to the water)
Breakthrough of advection inversion	Persistent advection inversion	Conduction inversion

The land breeze may develop along one shore, while the weather system wind appears or persists offshore, away from the influence of the land. The long-shore sailor must decide which wind will ultimately predominate, or, if both are to persist, which will predominate in the area and during the time he wishes to sail? In other words should he elect to utilize the wind along the shore or the wind offshore? Except for short periods after the appearance of a new wind source, two winds will not persist in a single locale unless (1) they are both weak and/or (2) they develop from airflows moving in directions at greater than 90° to each other. Strong thermal flows obliterate weak weather system flows; strong weather system flows prevent the generation of weak thermal flows. Intermittent shifts in direction and strength may occur as one source or the other is stimulated or depressed by thermal influences. Winds whose directions are greater than 90° to each other will depress one another so as to produce either complete calm, a single, overpowering wind flow or two separate winds separated by an intervening zone of calm. The latter result is typical of conditions along the shore when a weak surface flow from a weather system gradient opposes a weak land breeze. Thus the land breeze depends upon weather system airflow approximately perpendicular to the shore. Its circulation will be destroyed if the weather system wind is parallel to the long axis of a river (unless the inversion is unusually strong).

The surface wind that will be present along the shore on a winter's day will depend upon the temperature and direction of the weather system airflow, the temperature of the land, and the temperature of the water.

When faced with the appearance of two winds one must choose between one or the other—inshore or offshore. The choice will depend upon the probable ability of each to reach the surface. Is the weather system wind basically strong or weak, is it cold or warm, is the surface, shore or water, warmer or colder than the airflow above? Will thermal updrafts rising from the land be sufficient to bring the flow aloft to the surface? Is the local thermal wind generated by a strong disparity in land/water temperature, is the time of day conducive to its generation or to its deterioration, is the race course so located relative to the shore that the local thermal will be influential, is the cloud cover dissipating, which suggests the dissolution of an inversion, or accumulating, which suggests the reinforcement of an inversion? The wrong choice will lose the race.

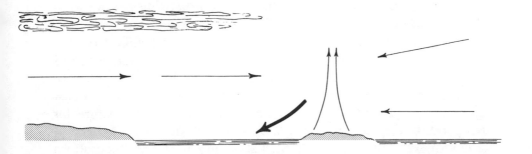

E. The Coastal Winds

High pressure and the sea breeze.
Transmountain winds.
Low pressure and the sea breeze.

1. St. Petersburg and Miami—
The Polar Front in the Subtropics

"Sea gull, sea gull, sitting in the sand,
Always foul weather when you're on land."

At St. Petersburg the big regattas are held in early spring. At this time the polar front ranges across the southern United States and polar air is meeting tropical air over Florida. During the summer the area is drenched in barely moving maritime tropical Gulf (mTg) air and the warm Gulf provides little support to sea breeze generation. Without the late-afternoon thunderstorms, induced in part by the convergence over mid-Florida of low-velocity onshore airflow from both coasts, there would be little summer sailing in Tampa Bay. In March, however, continental polar (cP) air from Canada periodically surges as far south as Florida, bringing with it major variation in the general pressure gradients, and the cold Gulf supports significant sea breeze generation. Tampa Bay, midway down Florida's west coast, lies just above the southern limit of cP air penetration and thus is intermittently beneath this high-pressure outflow. Subsequently as the high-pressure center moves east maritime tropical air enters the circulation as a strong southerly flow. A sea breeze regularly develops within this southerly flow to provide the fine sailing characteristic of the St. Petersburg March regattas. As racing is held in Tampa Bay the sea breeze is offshore from the St. Petersburg peninsula and the oscillating shifts characteristic of this wind are evident. St. Petersburg represents the archetype of the mixed weather system and sea breeze pattern, characteristic of east coast summer conditions but at a higher velocity due to the greater temperature disparity between land, sea, and air.

Whenever I have raced in St. Petersburg in March the pattern has been the same. A cold front passes and behind it cold Canadian air pours in from the northwest or north at 20 to 30 knots. On the following day the outflow velocity subsides as the cold front is halted by the high-pressure maritime tropical Gulf (mTg) air mass in the Caribbean. A stationary front may develop across southern Florida or the cold front may dissipate over the Bahamas to the east. At St. Petersburg a moderate northeasterly persists for half a day before the cP high moves off the Carolinas or Georgia. During the latter part of the second day the wind swings into the east and by the third day after a cold frontal passage the wind is southeast. Stratocumulus forms at low levels as this moist air flows over Florida en route to Tampa Bay and the surface air is hazy. On the fourth day the cP high is well offshore and the airflow at St. Petersburg is southerly, warm and moist. A new frontal system has formed across the mid-continent by this time and on the fifth day the wind is westerly as mTg air funnels through the warm sector between the low-pressure center to the north and the cP high in the Atlantic. By the sixth day a new cold front and another strong northwesterly reach the area as a new mass of cP air roars down from frozen Canada in the wake of the low. This cycle was repeated five times in March 1971 with little variation. Northerly winds from cP outflow were present on eleven days, easterly and southeasterly flow related to the cP high on seven days, southerly flow, drawing in mTg air on five days and westerly mTg flow on seven days.

A typical diurnal variation was evident and was dependent upon this weather system pattern. The first day of cP outflow was typical of this wind anywhere on the east coast; a strong, gusty oscillating

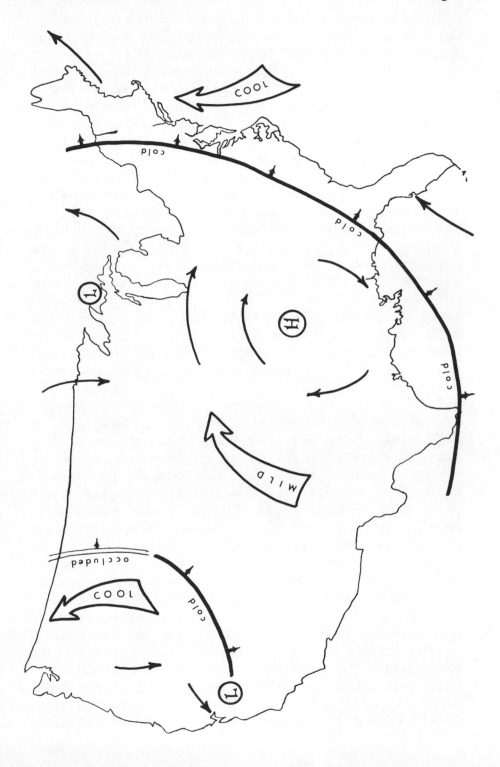

flow increasing in velocity with the heating of the land and subsiding to minimal levels with the evening. The easterly, southeasterly, and southerly wind flows showed the same increase with
the sun in the early morning but, as the stratocumulus cover began
to clear in late morning, fell to half or less their earlier velocity.
During the first SPORT Regatta in 1971 this reduction in velocity
was noted regularly during the latter legs of the morning races and
on two occasions a near calm developed at about noon and persisted until 2:00 or 3:00 P.M. On one occasion the afternoon race
was cancelled but a good breeze appeared before 4:00 P.M. as the
boats were being packed away. If the wind was east or southeast
in the early morning it increased in velocity and veered until about
10:00 A.M. then backed and oscillated for an hour or two before disappearing at about noon. If the wind was southerly in the early
morning it increased in velocity (12–18 knots) and veered until
about 10:30, dropped and backed and oscillated until about noon
and then steadily increased in velocity and veered to southwest
during the afternoon. If the wind was southwesterly or westerly to
begin with there was little decrease in velocity in late morning. Instead, after a morning of increasing strength but frequent oscillating shifts, the wind veered and steadied to a strong westerly by
noon. Once the afternoon breeze, usually south to southwesterly,
had filled in it steadied, strengthened, and persisted until about
6:00 P.M. after which it gradually faded to calm by dusk.

The reason for all this variation in velocity and direction is, of
course, the appearance of the sea breeze. Its arrival each day in late
morning is heralded by the deterioration of the stratocumulus
which at dawn stretches in banks from horizon to horizon beneath
the nocturnal inversion. As heated surface air lifts above the St.
Petersburg peninsula the cloud cover begins to clear. By noon there
is a clear zone above the racing area and the peninsula, sharply
demarcated from the banks of stratocumulus to the east. As each
successive cloud born over the Florida mainland reaches the
heated upper levels of the sea breeze circulation it disintegrates.
Although this upper-level outflow in part flows eastward to burn
away cloud over Tampa Bay the majority flows westward out over
the Gulf. Beneath it the Gulf sea breeze is moving onshore at the
surface early in the morning. After traversing the five miles of the
peninsula the Gulf sea breeze attempts to flow offshore onto Tampa
Bay. If the weather system wind is northeast, east, or southeast the
westerly Gulf sea breeze opposes it. A zone of calm and erratic

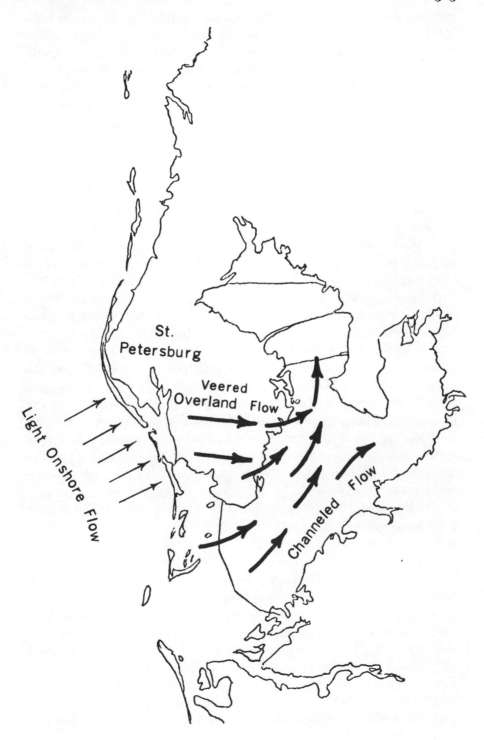

shifting develops at the interface between the two winds. In mid-morning the weather system wind begins to oscillate. The resultant wind veers 20° toward the sea breeze and then backs 10° as it subsides. In general the veer is associated with an increase in velocity; as the velocity drops the wind can be expected to back. If the original wind is in the easterly quadrants a period of complete calm may appear and persist between noon and 2:00 P.M. as the sea breeze forces its way beneath the weather system flow. By mid-afternoon the sea breeze has filled in from the southwest and steadily increases in velocity with an associated moderate veer. When the wind is from the west initially, alignment is complete and the sea breeze fills in imperceptibly as a steady increase in the basic wind flow.

The sea breeze, which is present throughout two-thirds of the majority of racing days in St. Petersburg, is an erratic mixture of buoyant, vertically unstable sea air and heated air lifted from the surface of the peninsula. As it flows offshore onto Tampa Bay it is oscillating irregularly. It is strongest near the weather shore where downdrafts counter to the thermal lift-off bring strong, upper airflow to the surface. It is more veered near that weather shore and progressively backed with increasing distance offshore. On several occasions during SPORT 1971 the boat that took the offshore starboard tack experienced a significant back. Joe Ellis won two races by obtaining such a persistent shift on the second or third beat following a veer. Earlier in these races there had been a persistent veer which favored the port-tack boats and this veer was increasingly evident the closer that they approached the weather (peninsula) shore.

As the westerly sea breeze flows into the mouth of Tampa Bay (the lowest level inflow site along Florida's west coast) it is channeled by the land masses. As the onshore flow turns to flow up the long axis of the Bay it arrives off St. Petersburg as a southwesterly. A major mass of low-level sea breeze flow moves from the southwest toward the headwaters of Tampa Bay and tends to drag the general air mass with it. The westerly Gulf sea breeze which has traversed the St. Petersburg peninsula is refracted as it comes offshore, which adds to the veering effect of the high proportion of upper-level flow near shore. When the sea breeze is westerly offshore, and the weather mark close under that weather shore, the first tack should be to port. When the sea breeze is more southerly and the weather mark well offshore, the veer will be less pronounced for the port-tack boat and the starboard-tack boat may experience a back as she proceeds offshore (the fan effect). Toward the middle of the Bay the wind is lighter, steadier, and more backed due to channeling of the main flow up its long axis. If the layline approach can be timed appropriately in a semipersistent oscillation which reinforces the persistent shift, a major gain is possible. The major risk is overstanding as the expected shift becomes progressively more evident as the layline is approached.

The oscillations characteristic of most offshore wind flows are easily managed at St. Petersburg; it is the major semipersistent shifts that are most significant and most difficult to predict. Early in the day as the sea breeze is beginning to affect the easterly or southerly weather system flow one can expect a veer favoring the early port tack. As the wind increases thereafter one expects additional veering and as it decreases, backing. As the wind drops significantly in late morning a back can be expected. There are large as well as small oscillations and therefore during the morning and early afternoon a marked veer can be expected to be followed by a back and vice versa. Later in the day the wind will veer progressively and ultimately stabilize in the southwest or west with little further shifting. The lighter it is the more evident is the residual influence of the weather system wind and the more persistent are both the large and small oscillations.

The other strategic determinants at St. Petersburg are the steep chop and the current. The shallow depth of Tampa Bay (average 10–12 feet) results in the rapid development of a short, steep chop after a short period of exposure to moderate winds. The choppiness is, of course, directly proportional to the fetch and it is possible to escape into relatively smooth water within a mile of the weather shore. This advantage is significant in strong offshore winds such as the northwesterly and requires that the initial tack be inshore. Tidal current may reach a velocity of over a knot at peak flow and thus significantly alters reaching angles, laylines, and tacking downwind angles. The dredged channel lies within the usual racing area and therefore a major variation in current velocity occurs within the course. One should be alert to the position of the channel so as to sail within it when the current is favorable and avoid it when the current is unfavorable.

MIAMI

The polar front is markedly weakened by the time it reaches Miami and usually approaches as a cold front along a north-south line. The initial wind behind the cold front is usually north and rapidly becomes northeast. Thereafter the wind veers progressively, lingering in the east because of sea breeze reinforcement and rarely swinging past south before a new cold front arrives. The sea breeze at Biscayne Bay (160°–180° in late afternoon) is a modest air flow as the warm Gulf Stream prevents the development of a major land/water temperature differential. It reinforces weather system winds in the easterly and southeasterly quadrants (between 45° and 180°) and interferes with winds in the westerly and northerly quadrants. As is typical at St. Petersburg, in late morning the weather system wind is usually reduced or obliterated by the sea breeze and a series of protracted oscillating shifts between the two winds often occurs. It is essential at both sites to recognize that the usual early morning wind (before 9:00 A.M.) is the weather system wind. (Inversions are weak and dissipate rapidly along the coast because of the proximity of the warm Gulf Stream). The subsequent development of the sea breeze in late morning or early afternoon disrupts the low-level circulation of the weather system wind and reduces its surface velocity. A persistent shift must be expected at this time. As at St. Petersburg, a brief back, as the upper levels of the weather-system wind become excluded from the surface, is followed by oscillating eddies of weather-system wind ahead of the burrowing advance of the sea breeze cold front. After a period of several hours the sea breeze finally fills in, the persistent shifts disappear and only short period oscillations in the sea breeze flow remain.

A unique combination of weather-system wind and sea breeze sometimes occurs on Biscayne Bay with a northwesterly wind flow. One of the races of the 1972 Soling Midwinter Regatta was started at 11:00 A.M. in a weather system wind at 300°. This was cP air immediately behind a cold front but its temperature was in the midseventies and its strength was reduced to a mere 4–6 knots. Large frequent oscillations between 320°, 340°, and 0° were evident during the first beat with huge holes in the wind flow. The best wind was on the mainland side of the course to the west and three boats (Bob Mosbacher, Dave Curtis, and Sam Merrick) escaped from the

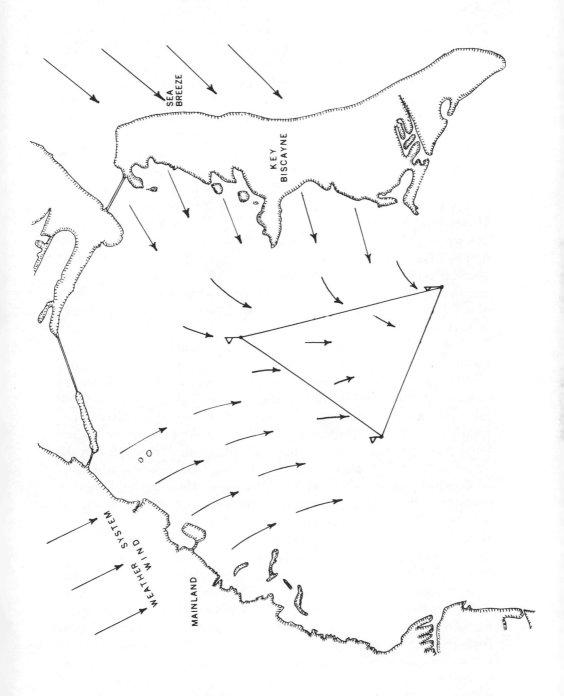

remainder of the fleet into this better air. Large swings, gaps and
gusts continued during the reaches while the median wind gradually veered to about 15°. We worked up to about fourth on the
second beat, while working gradually to the east of the rhumb line,
by playing the large oscillations as they came. We expected that the
sea breeze would eventually solidify and veer the wind to 45° or
more, but weren't sufficiently confident that the shift would be realized during the second beat to forego our middle course. Bruce
Goldsmith had the courage of our convictions, however. He came
from about 12th at the leeward mark straight out to the east along
the Key Biscayne shore, sailing through header after header, to
emerge at the mark ahead of us. He had had more air near the Key
Biscayne shore and an average wind considerably veered to ours.
Meanwhile, however, John Dane and Joachim Schulz-Heik, far to
the west, who we had thought would be left far astern as the sea
breeze filled in to the east, were roaring up in a 6–8 knot northwesterly airflow off the main land shore! We were passed by boats
with stronger and more favorably directed wind flows *on both sides*
of us. On the run and during the subsequent beat the wind finally
settled at about 45°.

It is not unique to have a weather-system wind and a sea breeze
flowing at the surface simultaneously nor to have an area of calm
and oscillating shifts intervening between the two. What was
unique was that the condition persisted and that it was possible to
take advantage of *either* wind to make significant gains toward the
weather mark. On Biscayne Bay both a northerly weather system
wind and a sea breeze are unstable offshore wind flows. The northerly brings cold cP air over heated Florida; the sea breeze brings
cool marine air over heated Key Biscayne. Unstable airflows are
brought to the surface by thermal turbulence over heated land and
are therefore strongest near the weather shore. The weather-
system wind persisted longest and remained strongest along the
mainland shore. The sea breeze appeared first and became strongest
along the Key Biscayne shore. As the race committee selected the
median wind between the 70° different extremes, either wind along
either shore provided a beneficial persistent shift which shortened
the course to the weather mark. In the middle there was only confusion.

A percentage player might have solved the strategic situation
by adhering to one of several basic principles and ignored the
meteorological confusion. "In unstable wind flows seek the shore,"

where the old wind persists longest and the new wind appears first. (On confined waters most winds are unstable and offshore. On lakes "when in doubt, head for the shore.") Or "seek the new wind," take the tack toward the expected persistent shift and keep going 'til between the fleet and the shift. Or "persistent shifts are far more significant than oscillating shifts" and the latter must be ignored while sailing toward a persistent shift. Or finally and most simply (particularly in light air) "avoid the middle!"

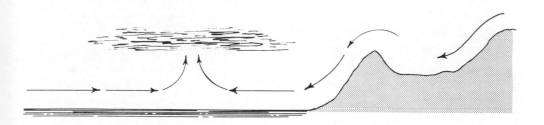

2. The Santa Ana and the Bora—
Transmountain and Drainage Winds

"Circle around the moon,
All hands go aloft full soon."

At Newport the infamous Santa Ana (a classical transmountain wind) is evident to the sailor as a hot, dry, dirty wind and as a surprising (for this coast) offshore flow. The Santa Ana flows strongly from the mountains to the shoreline and dissipates rapidly as it moves out over the water. The hot, stable wind then lifts above the cool surface air and is dissipated aloft in the general high pressure over the eastern Pacific. A mile or so offshore the Santa Ana disappears to be replaced by a band of calm, a calm confused by occasional downdrafts of Santa Ana and surface thrusts of sea breeze. Farther offshore the sea breeze is in full sway, cool marine air flowing directly toward the superheated shore, disintegrating in the Santa Ana before it can reach the beach. In one cruising class race off Newport the big yachts started under spinnaker in a 35-knot

Santa Ana toward an offshore mark only to run into a zone of complete calm a few hundred yards from the line. Those who were alert had their spinnakers down and their light genoas up for the subsequent beat to the now weather mark in the 5- to 8-knot southerly sea breeze. Spinnakers went up as the fleet rounded and headed back to the beach. Again the knowledgeable had genoas ready (this time their heavy ones) as they sailed back into that zone of calm and beyond it met the gale force Santa Ana once again.

In addition to the development of katabatic and anabatic slope winds consequent to thermal differences between the surface air and the air aloft, mountains produce other varieties of wind—drainage winds which are cold and dense and foehn winds, like the Santa Ana, which are hot and dry. These transmountain winds differ from thermal slope winds chiefly because they are initiated by weather system gradients. When a mountain range is interposed in certain weather system flows, downslope winds result which are increased in velocity and markedly modified in temperature and moisture content relative to their origin. Drainage winds result when cold air accumulates over high plateaus or in upland valleys and subsequently drains to lakes or seas far below. Foehn winds result when weather system gradients cause airflow to rise above a mountain range and subsequently sink to lower levels beyond. Cold drainage winds flow downhill in streams and rivulets until they merge in valleys to form rivers of cold air. These winds are so cold at their origin that they remain colder than the air at all levels in their descent despite the heating associated with descent. Their velocity is consequent to gravity and negative buoyancy and therefore related to the rate of change in altitude of the valleys down which they flow. Foehn winds, on the other hand, heated by compression as they descend, become drier and hotter the farther they flow. Their velocity is due to the weather system gradient and to channeling and compression.

Both the drainage wind and the foehn wind are induced by weather system gradients, high pressure on one side of a mountain range, low pressure on the opposite side. They are particularly likely to develop across coastal ranges as low pressure readily develops over warm seas and high pressure readily accumulates behind a mountain range over the center of a land mass. Both winds flow from upland areas, rise a moderate distance to surmount a mountain range, and finally sink a much greater distance downslope, often to sea level. Their rise is associated with cooling, contraction, and loss in velocity. The pressure gradient must be large to induce the airflow to surmount a mountain range despite both gravity and the increasing density of the cooling air. The sinking of both winds down the far slopes of a mountain range is associated with heating, expansion, and increase in velocity. As the circumstances which generate these two winds are so similar why are they so different? Why is the drainage wind so cold and the foehn so hot?

The difference is in the buoyancy, the lapse rate of the airflow. The foehn is a stable airflow. It is composed of warm air because it is derived from a sinking high-pressure system and it flows over cold land (often over mountain snow fields). It is also initially a moist airflow which leaves its moisture condensed in a vast cloud bank about the mountain peaks, the "foehn wall." It is cooled at the adiabatic rate and would sink back as it attempts to surmount the mountain range if it were not for the strong pressure gradient to which it is responding and the heat of condensation released in the formation of the "foehn wall." The foehn starts its descent already heated and gains heat thereafter at the adiabatic rate which is greater than the lapse rate of the surrounding stable, nonbuoyant air. Gaining 1°C. for every 100 meters it sinks toward the distant low pressure, the foehn becomes hotter and hotter. Its highest temperature is reached at sea level.

The drainage wind is an unstable airflow. It is composed of cold air because it is derived from an air mass cooled by long residence over cold surfaces at high altitudes and it flows over surfaces warmer than itself in its transmountain course. It is also a dry airflow usually because it has left its moisture behind in previous transit of another mountain range. It rises readily up the mountain slopes as its adiabatic rate of cooling and contraction is less than that of the surrounding air. It crosses the passes of the mountain range without forming cloud as it contains so little moisture and therefore gains no heat from condensation. Its negative buoyancy causes it to rush downslope on the far side of the mountains with the velocity of a thermal downdraft. It gains heat and expands at the adiabatic rate (less rapidly than the surrounding air) as it descends, and therefore becomes progressively denser and colder than its surroundings as it descends. It finally rushes out over the sea at a combined velocity—due to gravity, the pressure gradient, and negative buoyancy, often in excess of 100 knots.

The bora is the classical drainage wind. It sweeps across the mountainous coast of Yugoslavia bringing ice and snow to the Dalmatian coast and gales to the Adriatic. The pressure gradient which induces the bora is created by the formation of a strong low-pressure system over the eastern Mediterranean. The northeasterly flow around the low-pressure center draws continental polar air from Russia into its circulation. This polar air, dry and cold to begin with, is further dried by lifting over the Carpathians and further cooled by advection over their cold surfaces, en route to the Mediterranean. Outflow from a polar high over Russia is usually deflected to the east by the Carpathians and the mountains of Yugoslavia and thus rarely reaches the Adriatic. Drawn by the low pressure to the south, however, the cold polar air rushes through the mountain passes. Its velocity is increased by gravity as it falls through a major drop in altitude in its last few miles to the coast and by funneling between the coastal mountains. Violent gusts, riding their negative buoyancy, roar down the valleys which penetrate the coast and explode out over the Adriatic. The temperature of this airflow is little different from its surroundings high in the mountain passes, but having gained at the adiabatic rate through descent considerably less heat than the surrounding air it seems an icy blast when it reaches sea level and crosses the Adriatic.

The bora is a particularly dramatic drainage wind but similar winds are found wherever mountain ranges are interposed between high-pressure polar air and low pressure to the south. The mistral is a similar wind which drains across the cold plateau of central France, down the Rhone valley, and out onto the Mediterranean. The Texas norther is in many respects a drainage wind. It is the outflow of cold cP air drawn across the high plains of the central United States by low pressure in the Gulf of Mexico, is unstable (polar air flowing over warm Texas land and warm Gulf water), and rushes across coastal Texas at velocities not much less than those produced by the bora. The Texas norther, like all drainage winds, is a surface airflow, cold, dense air burrowing beneath the warm, displacing all competition. When a norther comes through eastern Texas most craft keep to their moorings; if they race, they race in a cold, violent, gusty airflow, filled with oscillating shifts as varying segments of the turbulent, unstable airflow are brought to the surface.

The classic foehn is a wind which recurrently flows over the Alps in Switzerland when low pressure over the North Sea induces

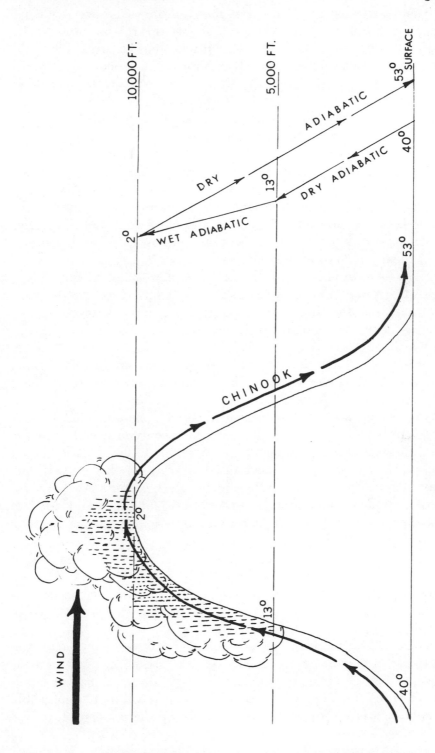

transmountain passage of a warm, moist airflow. The hot, dry wind which rushes down the north slopes of the Alps ripens grapes, splits walls, unglues furniture, and promotes headaches, irritability, and violence in valley inhabitants. It is sometimes called the *"schnee-fresser"* (or snow-eater). In the United States the foehn that flows down the eastern slopes of the Rockies is known as the chinook, and the one that flows down the western slopes of the coastal ranges as the Santa Ana. In March 1900, a chinook which suddenly appeared in Havre, Montana, in response to low pressure developing over the plains, raised the temperature 31°F. in three minutes! The Santa Ana is a mixed blessing in southern California. It sweeps away the marine layer, its overlying inversion and the smog trapped within it, bringing crystal clear skies to Los Angeles but it promotes the disastrous fires characteristic of the region and fans them in clouds of dust at speeds of 60–70 knots.

The Santa Ana is due to the unusual presence of a strong high-pressure system in the Great Basin to the west of the Rockies. Northerly outflow from this high pressure, already dried out by passage over the mountains which surround the Basin, streams down the Central Valley of California and over the coastal range. The hot, dry stable flow sweeps the desert air around the coastal mountains and funnels it at high velocity through the intervening passes. In the Los Angeles basin the Santa Ana appears as gale force blasts around each end of the San Gabriel Mountains and 75-knot downdraft gusts in their lee. In a ten- to twenty-mile wide corridor in the lee of the San Gabriels the sea breeze still flows ashore, aided by anabatic flow up the mountain slopes. Although on Santa Ana days the obvious wind, the big gusts, are the Santa Ana, the sea breeze appears intermittently under the Santa Ana and adds to the general turbulence. It is composed largely of Santa Ana air which has had a brief sojourn off the coast and provides no relief from the desert heat. The hottest air in the Santa Ana flow is that which descends the farthest, that which reaches the coast. Usually cool Newport is not only the hottest spot in the Los Angeles area on Santa Ana days but it has all the smog, swept southward by the hot northerly.

The sea breeze is always present over the ocean on Santa Ana days and it may be found close to shore as the hot Santa Ana air is unable to keep to the ocean surface. The turbulent zone of wind-shear and calm interposed between the two winds is remarkably stationary throughout the day. This is in sharp contrast to the progressive movement of the sea breeze front shoreward against a northwesterly offshore flow along the east coast. Off southern California the Santa Ana and its zone of windshear will often be rediscovered upon return in the afternoon exactly where they were at the time of departure in the morning. Nothing stops the Santa Ana until the high pressure is displaced from the Great Basin and nothing can bring the hot, dry air to the ocean's surface in the face of the sea breeze. On Santa Ana days the surface sea breeze flow is discovered to be a remarkably steady and moderate wind. The upper-level flow characteristic of the usual southern California sea breeze is dissipated by the Santa Ana so that no veered gusts and no gradual veer with the sun are evident. Instead the sea breeze is composed of low-level, directly onshore, southerly (or south-southwesterly) flow similar to that usually found well offshore, and it hardly shifts at all.

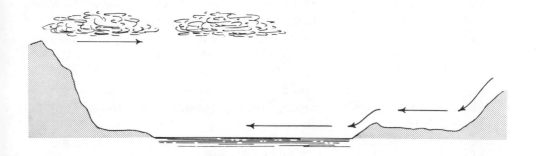

3. Puget Sound—Low Pressure
and the Sea Breeze

"Long foretold, long past,
Short warning, soon past."

The large open Pacific has developed a simple pattern of current flow. On either side of the equator surface flow spreading poleward is deviated to the west by Coriolis force and the easterly trades. This results in the great North and South Equatorial Currents which span the Pacific from Central America to the East Indies. Under thermal and rotational influences the North Equatorial Current turns northward at the Philippines to produce the Japan Cur-

rent, a strong warm flow up the east coast of the Japanese archi-
pelago. Off Hokkaido the Japan Current, composed of dark blue,
low-salinity, tropical water, meets the Oyoshio Current composed
of cold, green, high-salinity polar water flowing southward from the
Bering Sea. Convergence resulting from the meeting of these currents contributes to the temperature extremes characteristic of
northern Japan. The portion of the Oyoshio which does not sink
below the Japan Current joins it in swinging eastward to form the
North Pacific Current, cold along its northern border, warm along
its southern. This current splits offshore of Vancouver Island to
form the northerly flowing Aleutian Current and the southerly flowing California Current. The Aleutian Current acts as a warm current in the Gulf of Alaska bringing fog, mist, and rain to maritime
Alaska and the Pacific Northwest. The California Current acts as a
warm current along the Washington and Oregon coasts ameliorat-
ing the winter temperatures and bringing fog, mist, and rain to the
land. Farther south where the land temperatures are warmer, the
California acts as a cold current. As it diverges from the coast under
the influence of Coriolis force, upwelling of cold, deep water stimulates sea breeze production along the coast. The California Current deviates progressively from shore until off Mexico it joins the
westward-flowing North Equatorial Current to complete the cycle.
Upwelling and sea breeze production is maximal in early summer
along the Washington, Oregon, and California coasts as the subtropical high is then at peak strength and in its farthest north position. When its northerly wind flow is diminished in winter the
California Current flow is diminished and a warm countercurrent,
the Davidson Current forms along its inner edge. This warming
current is sometimes recognized as far north as the Strait of Juan de
Fuca and produces a northerly set for the midwinter racing off
southern California.

Tropical energy is transported to the Washington and British
Columbia coasts in the warm waters of the North Pacific Current
and in the latent heat of the water vapor which is carried in the
warm air overlying it. In winter the advection of cold air—continental polar from Siberia and maritime polar from the Gulf of
Alaska—over the warm water produces marked convection. In
winter a strong continuous depression, the Aleutian Low, analogous
to the low-pressure systems over the North Atlantic, constantly
spawns cyclones in the North Pacific. In summer the constant in-
flux of "warm" water has a moderating influence upon the climate

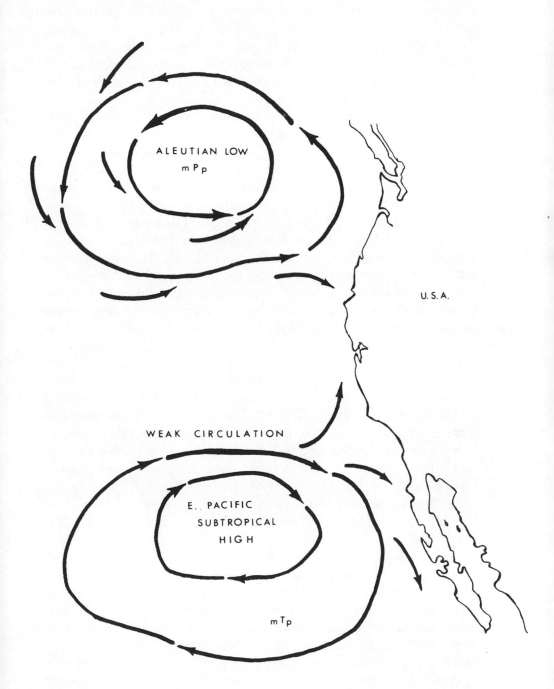

ALEUTIAN LOW
m P p

U. S. A.

WEAK CIRCULATION

E. PACIFIC
SUBTROPICAL
HIGH

m T p

of the coast. The East Pacific High moves northward and the subsiding northwesterly flow along its eastern margins brings warm, dry air toward the coast. As this heated air subsides above the relatively cool waters of the North Pacific Current, an inversion is formed. Beneath the inversion in the marine layer, cool, moist ocean air constantly recirculates.

Although the climate of the Pacific Northwest is determined chiefly by the North Pacific Current, its weather is modified by two additional factors. Its coast is a western continental coast in the mid-latitudes which means that the prevailing westerlies bring ocean air onshore. The coast receives whatever the ocean creates— a marine layer beneath an inversion in summer, a series of low-pressure systems in winter. The Olympic Peninsula and British Columbia, like England, are known for their mild winters, heavy rainfalls, and small seasonal variations in climate. In addition, high mountains rise close to the ocean, the Olympics and the smaller mountains of Vancouver Island nearest the water and farther inland the Cascades. Between the two ranges lies Puget Sound. The marine air and the depressions are deviated by the Olympics, blocked by the Cascades, and trapped between them over Puget Sound.

The frequency of appearance of depressions and of high pressure derived from the East Pacific High, the persistence of such systems and their subsequent course after leaving Puget Sound varies with the seasons. In winter low pressure is more frequent, more persistent and tends to migrate farther north before departing than in summer. A "wet season" extends from mid-October to mid-April. During seven weeks (forty-nine days) of this period in 1971, sixteen separate low-pressure systems traversed the area. Cold fronts trailing these systems crossed the area fifteen times. Warm fronts only developed in three instances. At this time of the year strong high pressure derives from the north, cold air pushing south and eastward over warm. Rarely does the East Pacific High contribute a strong enough flow of warm air to create a warm front ahead of the low. Many depressions move so rapidly that they cross Puget Sound within a single day. The majority linger for two days while a few recede and return for a total of three or more days. In winter depressions usually move up the Frazer River valley eastward at the latitude of the Canadian border. A few recede northward up the coast, reintensify, and then return. A few move inland up the Columbia and then south along either side of the Rockies. The majority of the cyclones which traverse the United States either originate in or are formed from remnants of North Pacific Depressions, reintensified by passage over the Great Lakes or the Gulf. Although depressions seem ever present in the northwest in winter, high pressure is present on almost half the days.

In winter the temperature disparity between the North Pacific Current and the air overlying the Gulf of Alaska is maximal. Frigid continental polar air flows off the Siberian coast producing marked instability over the warm water. Convection induced in the lower levels is strongly reinforced by precipitation as lifting brings the cold, moist air to its dew point at low altitudes. As the moist Pacific air attempts to surmount the coastal mountains low pressure is intensified by the release of energy in orographic precipitation. Isolated depressions originating in the Aleutian Low are swept shoreward by the prevailing westerlies and intensify as they begin to lift over the coastal mountains. As they tend to follow their fuel source, the waters of the Strait of Juan de Fuca lead them around the Olympics into Puget Sound. As a depression approaches the coast from the Gulf of Alaska the wind in Puget Sound is southerly. Because a southerly flow is channeled between the coastal mountains and the Cascades it is strengthened. When the low begins its usual inland passage across British Columbia, the wind shifts to the west and decreases in velocity. The surface wind on Puget Sound is significantly reduced by the blanketing of the Olympics and the lifting associated with the traverse of the Cascades.

During the seven-week winter period referred to above the wind was in the south to west quadrant on thirty-two of the days. On fifteen of these days the wind was southerly ahead of an advancing depression. On eight days, it was southwesterly in the warm sector below a depression. On the remaining nine days the wind was westerly above the farthest northerly invasion of high pressure. On only fourteen days was the wind from a quadrant other than the southwesterly—it was instead between east and northwest—and on these occasions high pressure had moved far enough north to result in northerly or easterly flow over Puget Sound. This high pressure was a northeastern offshoot of the East Pacific High reinforced by continental or maritime polar air. Polar air drawn southward into the circulation behind a low often pushed a cold front ahead, south, and eastward. As the cold front passed, the wind shifted to the west or northwest and high pressure with wind flow from the northerly quadrants persisted for a day or two.

From late spring to early fall the air over the continents is as

warm or warmer than the water brought to the Gulf of Alaska by
the North Pacific Current. The East Pacific High shifts northward
and occupies the ocean to the west of Puget Sound. Depressions
are therefore infrequent and summer is considered a dry season.
The airflow from the northeastern extremity of the East Pacific
High is westerly or northwesterly in the upper atmosphere. A subsidence inversion beneath this airflow is common and moist marine
air recirculates below it along the coast. The cold marine air beneath the inversion is funneled through the Strait of Juan de Fuca
and channeled by the islands of the Sound. The northwesterly flow
of the East Pacific High has little direct effect upon the marine
layer beneath it but, as at San Francisco's Golden Gate, provides
a reservoir of high pressure offshore to assist onshore thermal flow.
The major surface flow in Puget Sound in the summer is the sea
breeze flowing in from the relatively cold ocean through the gaps in
the coastal mountains toward the heated valleys.

As the major gap in the coastline is the Strait, the majority of
flow reaches the Sound through this entrance. A sea breeze cold
front advances down the Strait each morning displacing the stagnant air over the Sound ahead of it. As is true of all sea breezes, its
velocity is directly proportional to heating ashore and is dependent
upon the clear sky provided by the East Pacific High. Friction
reduces the velocity of flow as the cold, dense sea breeze rushes
past the headlands and islands toward the warm valleys between
the shore and the Cascades. The 25- to 30-knot flow in the Strait is
reduced to 10–15 knots in the open Sound. The assistance of
anabatic (upslope) flow enhances the sea breeze flow near the two
major mountains of the Puget Sound basin, Mt. Rainier and Mt.
Baker. Bellingham Bay is known for its strong afternoon sea breeze
flow which, deviated by the islands between the Strait and the Bay
and enhanced by anabatic flow up the slopes of Mt. Baker, is a
southerly. The sea breeze flows inland from all parts of the Sound,
as a southwesterly in the San Juan Islands and as a northerly in
Shilshole Bay off Seattle.

At Shilshole the sea breeze arrives in mid or late afternoon. Protected by the subsidence inversion the sea breeze may flow westerly
through the Strait all night. Its reinforced morning sea breeze front
usually arrives in the inner Strait at about noon and off Seattle by
3:00 P.M. In late summer or early fall the sea breeze may not reach
Shilshole until evening, providing a mere hour of decent sailing between 6:00 and 7:00 P.M. Near the large mountains and even at

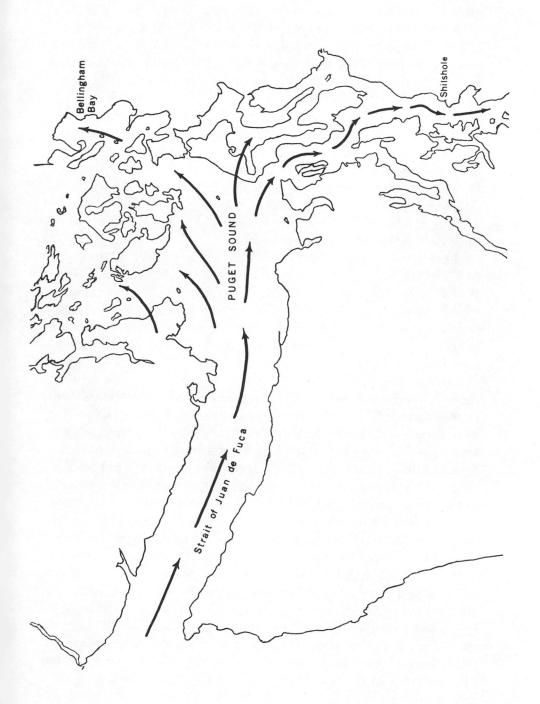

Shilshole a land breeze aided by katabatic flow may develop soon after the disappearance of the evening sea breeze. This may contribute to the late-evening veer of the sea breeze at Shilshole, shifting the flow from north to offshore, northeast. There is little evidence of a progressive veer during the active sea breeze period at Shilshole although the wind does steadily increase in velocity after its appearance. Its direction is far more affected by channeling. Significant deviation is evident at the headland just north of the Shilshole marina. The sea breeze is veered—converging toward the mid-channel—beyond the headland and backed—diverging from the mid-channel—to leeward of the headland. If the weather mark is close to this headland, as it often is, port tack into shore will be lifted progressively in the divergent shift and, if positioned appropriately, starboard tack on the way out to the mark will be lifted progressively in the convergent shift.

Low pressure appears frequently in summer (as it does in winter) and lingers over Puget Sound despite the East Pacific High. When it does appear the sea breeze is less likely to develop, is weaker when it does develop, and often produces a convergence zone between the sea breeze and the pressure-gradient wind. Frequently a low-pressure system lingers off the Oregon coast or inland over northern California and a southerly wind flow is produced in Puget Sound which opposes the northerly sea breeze flow at Shilshole. If there are breaks in the cloud cover and particularly if surface heating results in thunderstorm formation, the sea breeze will be induced and fights its way down the Strait pushing a calm zone of convergence ahead of it. If the sea breeze is but weakly induced, it may merely disrupt the southerly gradient wind at Shilshole without eliminating it. Deprived of the usual protective subsidence inversion, the sea breeze may mix with the low-pressure-gradient flow aloft. The result is calm and/or a series of erratic oscillations between northerly sea breeze and southerly gradient wind. Late in the day the southerly is likely to reappear. It is essential to decide which wind will prevail at the mark ahead and to seek positional advantage in it. Sometimes the sea breeze comes in abruptly and dramatically replaces the southerly. Such a change is associated with the development of a large, dark cloud shield over the Olympics several hours in advance of the shift. A period of erratic shifting from southerly to westerly may then precede the dramatic shift to the northwest as the sea breeze arrives.

Occasionally in summer a portion of the East Pacific High moves inland and a high-pressure center develops over northern British Columbia. The airflow over Puget Sound is then northeasterly from the mountains toward the coast. This means that the air descends from the inland plateaus through the Cascades to reach sea level, heating adiabatically as it descends. Such a foehn wind, already heated by condensation in its ascent of the east face of the Cascades, continues to heat at a rate greater than its surroundings as it descends the western slopes. It is urged onward despite its heating by the pressure gradient. This northeasterly flow from inland high pressure is the Pacific northwest's equivalent of the Santa Ana. At the coast the wind is hot and dry and comes offshore at 20–30 knots. Over the Sound it frequently meets the sea breeze attempting to burrow beneath it. The result is a zone of calm and erratic shifts between the two winds. Near shore the hot easterly usually prevails, offshore the sea breeze should be expected. At Shilshole, the cold weather produces a conduction inversion over which the hot, offshore wind flows. The easterly reaches the surface erratically, strong gusts alternating with abrupt lulls as the hot wind displaces the cold surface air.

We raced a 14 at Shilshole one March in conditions which the local sailors said were most unusual (a standard response). On one of the days the typical sea breeze was present. It arrived early and blew hard. Channeling around the point to the north of marina was evident and the first boat to the weather mark was the one that used the shifts most effectively. On another day that week, although the initial wind was southerly (the residue of low pressure moving down the coast), an offshore easterly appeared in midafternoon. This was the warm transmountain wind from high pressure moving ashore to the north. It gusted out from the shoreline hitting the surface in dark patches near the marina breakwater but lifted above the cold water surface farther offshore. We were leading the fleet toward a windward mark in the southerly when Jeff Ingman picked up a gust of the easterly along the breakwater. I tacked to starboard toward the shore, to cover him and met him on port a few hundred yards from the rocks. He tacked on my lee bow and I foolishly tacked away. He was heading into the strong easterly near shore and I was heading back into the light southerly offshore. Moments later half the fleet, on my weather quarter, lifted in the easterly and roared by before I could get back. As the warm stable easterly

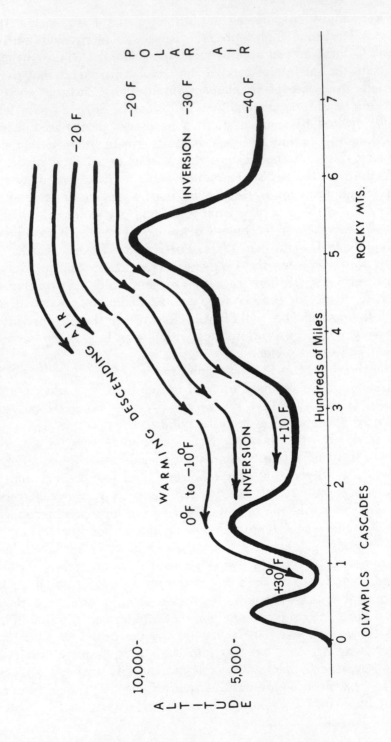

could only be brought to the surface by the convective activity of the warmer underlying shore, I had headed away from the best source of surface flow. Jeff won the race with ease.

In winter and early spring a ridge of high pressure may extend into central British Columbia to produce the same type of north-easterly flow over the Puget Sound Basin. This high pressure is derived from a continental polar air mass, however, and is intensely cold to begin with. When the pool of dense, cold air overflows the Cascade passes, a bora-like outflow rushes down the valleys to the sea. The continental polar air is drawn over the mountains from the Canadian interior by strong low pressure off the coast and is drawn into the northeasterly flow on the back of the low. The cold air flowing over the warm western slopes gains heat at the adiabatic rate, not nearly as rapidly as the surrounding air, and therefore becomes progressively colder and more dense than its surroundings. Responding both to the pressure gradient and to gravity it rushes down the Fraser, Columbia, and other major valleys as a clear, cold gale. It is an infrequent wind and when it does appear it may be too strong to sail in.

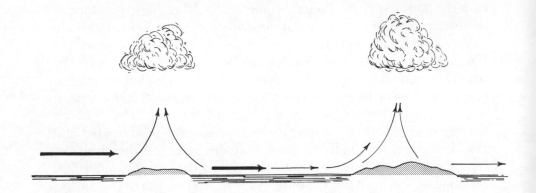

F. The Island Winds

Instability induced by an island.
Convection induced by an island.

1. The Winds of Bermuda

"For I fear a hurricane,
Last night the moon had a golden ring,
And tonight no moon we see."

Bermuda lies in the "horse latitudes." Her surrounding waters were
once strewn with dead horses abandoned by the ships of New
Spain in the notorious calms of the area. International Race Week
participants must be skeptical of this story, however, as in early
May the wind blows in Bermuda. In this apparent paradox lies
much of the explanation for Bermuda's winds—winds which in the
spring are strong, turbulent, and shifty. The island lies 600 miles
off the east coast just beyond the coastal track of the low-pressure
systems spawned over the continent. Lows developed over both the
Gulf and the Great Lakes intermittently (and sometimes simulta-

neously) pass to the north of Bermuda. The island lying in their warm sectors, receives a strong southwesterly airflow on many days in the winter and spring. Periodically the lows and the polar front pass over the island and a northwesterly or westerly outflow appears behind them.

Bermuda Race Week, 1970, commenced in a high-pressure system derived from continental polar (cP) air—dry, cool air which flowed down from Canada like sugar from a scoop. The flow had largely dissipated by the time the high reached Bermuda, but the small pressure gradient that remained provided a 10-knot surface breeze in Bermuda. The flow was gusty as the cool air flowed from the northeast over warmer Gulf Stream waters. During practice sails on Thursday and Friday there were frequent, small shifts as the unstable airflow was further disturbed by the interposition of the island barrier and by convection currents rising from the heated portions of the island to windward.

On the first day of racing a low appeared to the north and a 12- to 15-knot southwesterly flowed under clear skies. As the low moved past, the wind backed into the northeast on the second day. This was cool cP air of lesser velocity (derived from high pressure over New England) but even more shifty. By Monday, the third day of racing, the high had moved on to the east leaving a good southeasterly wind flow on its lower peripheral back. The southeasterly was less gusty but, typical of all Bermuda winds, was composed of many small eddies due to the induction of turbulence by the island mass interposed in the otherwise undisturbed wind stream.

During the night that followed the third day of racing a warm front passed over the island. In the warm sector behind the front the wind flow was south-south-west to southwest for the following two days. This was maritime tropical Gulf air (mTg) derived from the subtropical (Bermuda) high which usually sits over this portion of the Atlantic. This high pressure mass is composed of warm, moist air derived from its sojourn over tropical oceans. On Tuesday the sky was filled with statocumulus and stratus and showers appeared intermittently. The wind was 20–25 knots with stronger gusts in the rain showers. The rising currents and stratocumulus characteristic of warm sectors were enhanced by convection lift-off from the warm land and the warm Gulf Stream waters that surround the island. On Wednesday there was more rain and less wind in the same airstream; racing was abandoned.

By Thursday a new mass of continental polar air punched its

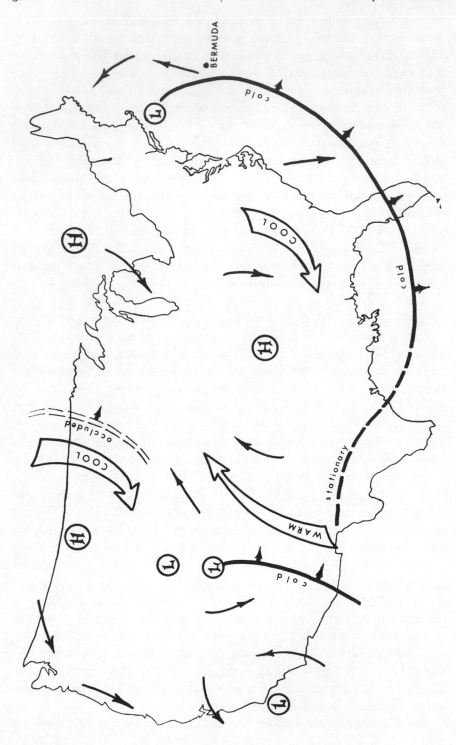

way down to the east of a low-pressure system and brought a cold front all the way to Bermuda. A northerly behind the front roared over the island at 30 knots, gusting to 40. This was cold cP air penetrating beneath the warm, moist air of the subtropical high after picking up moisture en route across the North Atlantic, Stratocumulus, cumulus, and cumulonimbus filled the sky as the warm air lifted and convection and turbulence carried the surface air aloft. On the following day the wind swung around to the northeast as the high moved on to the east, but the moisture-laden air continued to spew stratocumulus about the island.

The winds experienced in this Race Week reveal the factors that determine Bermuda weather, some characteristic of weather everywhere, some typical of island weather, and some unique to this island. They include (1) the season and the associated position of the polar front, (2) the presence of the island in the sea, (3) the presence of the Gulf Stream, and (4) the barrier effects of the island's contours.

SEASON

In the spring Canadian (cP) air periodically extends as far south as Bermuda. Cold air flowing over the warm Gulf Stream and the warm island (where the air temperature almost never falls below 40°) results in the vertical instability that brings gusts of upper airflow to the surface. In the winter and spring the polar front, straddling Bermuda, brings steep gradients, recurrent low pressure, and high-velocity upper airflow to the island. In the summer when Bermuda lies immersed in its own subtropical high, warm airflow over the warm surrounding waters and the warm island produces vertical stability, separates the surface air from the already weak flow aloft, and results in light air or calms at the surface—the "horse latitudes." International Race Week is scheduled in the spring.

THE ISLAND IN THE SEA

Whatever weather system wind is generated comes down to the surface over the sea and over Bermuda about twice as well as it does over the mainland. The lessened friction of the relatively smooth surrounding sea surface results in relatively little speed-robbing turbulence in the lower layers of the wind flow. The island, however, constitutes an abrupt barrier in this otherwise smooth flow. Immediately over, upwind, as well as downwind of the island, significant turbulence is created as the wind flow is deviated from its straight-line trajectory. Recent photographs of the earth from orbiting satellites have revealed turbulent cloud formations above obstacles and for the first time have shown the presence of huge Von Karman vortices, ten times the diameter of an island, swirling off its leeward quarter.

All airflow must approach Bermuda from the sea, picking up moisture en route. Upon arrival in Bermuda this air is often heavily laden with moisture and when subject to rising and cooling (due to frictional turbulence or convection or frontal lifting) will likely condense this moisture and form clouds. The island is often located by Bermuda Race navigators well in advance of sighting because of the cloud concentration overlying it. Even cP air which comes down the mid-continent passes over the North Atlantic en route and contains sufficient moisture to form clouds. Cloud formation is usually in the form of streets of stratocumulus with occasional stratus accompanied by showers. Only the cold, dry northwesterly immediately behind a cold front brings totally clear skies (or minimal scattered cumulus) as it rushes over the warm Gulf Stream and the island.

THE GULF STREAM

The warm waters of the Gulf Stream protect Bermuda, warm its surrounding waters, and insulate it from the chill northerlies and westerlies. As the water temperature of the Gulf Stream is minimally altered at different seasons and as water is extremely thermostable, the temperature of the island and the air immediately overlying it rarely falls below 40°F and rarely rises above 80° day or night. The temperature of all air flowing toward Bermuda is modified toward that of the Gulf Stream as it approaches (advection warming or cooling). Air derived from the American continent and air derived from the eastern and, to some extent, the southeastern Atlantic as well as the North Atlantic is cooler than the Gulf Stream and therefore flows over a layer of warmer air as it approaches and passes over the island. Only air derived from the southwest, from over the Gulf Stream itself, is certain to be warmer than the air over the island. Therefore, most winds produce an unstable airflow, cold air over warm air, resulting in convection turbulence. Thermal development associated with cold airflow over a warm sea is random and continuous, unaffected by cloud cover and unchanged at night. Warm air from over the water and the island rise up through the cold air until cooled to a similar temperature and cold air from aloft rushes to the surface. The result, added to the frictional turbulence due to the island itself, is the characteristic gusty, shifty airflow of Bermuda. Northerlies and easterlies are the most unstable as they derive from over the cold North Atlantic, and southwesterlies the most stable as they derive from over the Gulf Stream. If one is sailing in the Great Sound, the greatest amount of thermolabile land is to the east and therefore the easterlies are even more turbulent than one would predict from their inherent instability.

The sea breeze is rarely evident in Bermuda. The surrounding sea is relatively warm, often warmer than the land. The temperature of the air over the land is controlled chiefly by the water rather than the sun and is therefore also thermostable. The land mass is too small to initiate major movements of air between sea and land. There is very little diurnal variation in the temperature of the land, little obvious heating during the course of the day. The nocturnal inversion is scarcely evident, partly because there is so little land and so much thermostable water and partly because the usual cloud cover impedes nocturnal radiation loss from the island. The infantile sea breeze flowing perpendicular to the shore opposes its counterpart from the opposite shore before it moves very far inland. For all these reasons the sea breeze is limited to light, localized activity in the summer when there is very little other wind generated in the "horse latitudes." In calm conditions during the winter a local land breeze may be generated between the cooling land and the warm Gulf Stream.

THE BARRIER EFFECTS

The unstable, gusty winds that blow over Bermuda are deviated by the land masses they encounter. Lifting of the airflow because of a barrier to windward (blanketing) or because of a barrier to leeward (the 9h effect) is scarcely evident. Unstable air (cold airflow over warm) flows over rather than around objects and therefore is but minimally refracted or subject to windward or leeward lifting. Unstable air is channeled, however, and this is the major topographical effect in the Great Sound. Unstable air is brought to the surface by heating of the land and therefore Bermuda's winds are usually strongest near the windward shore. This may be particularly evident in light air and has been prominent along the Somerset shore in light northwesterlies.

As the upper airflow is brought to the surface by turbulence due to friction and convection, cool downdrafts burst along the surface. Once brought to the surface this turbulent flow seems to hug the water, channeling between the islands and along the shorelines. Where the shorelines converge the airflow converges; where the

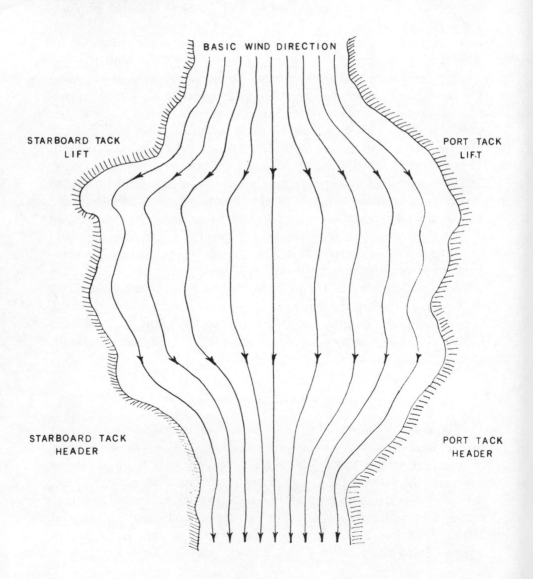

BASIC WIND DIRECTION

STARBOARD TACK
LIFT

PORT TACK
LIFT

STARBOARD TACK
HEADER

PORT TACK
HEADER

shorelines diverge, the airflow diverges. In the center of the Great Sound the wind follows its intended path, veered in the gusts, backed in the lulls. Along each shore the airflow tends to follow the shore, deviating away from its original trajectory as the Sound widens, and back toward its original trajectory as the Sound narrows. In most conditions, therefore, it is evident that the center of the Sound is to be avoided and that one shore or the other will be comparatively favored. When sailing upwind a diverging (from the wind flow) shoreline provides a beneficial lift which should be sailed well into, while a converging (toward the wind flow) shoreline provides a header which should be tacked away from as soon as it is received. The optimal management of any channeled shoreline shift is to approach the shore to windward of its deepest indentation, which provides a lift on the tack in, and to leave the shore just short of a point or headland, which provides a lift on the tack out.

In Bermuda the usual question is not whether the center or the shoreline but which shoreline? The standard Bermuda advice is "when the wind is in the south keep west and when the wind is in the north keep east." Some say "when the wind is in the west go south." Few are sufficiently confident in the thesis to add "when the wind is in the east go north"—but this is because there is no shore nearby to the north (at least not near the course set by the race committee). The point is that the shore is favored, not the middle, and that usually one shore is particularly favored. The additional advantage of the two basic rules, according to the Bermudans, is that one always comes back to the fleet on starboard.

TACTICS

Hartley Watlington once told me that the wind blows true in Bermuda. If he meant by this that its behavior is predictable, I agree with him: he obviously didn't mean that it doesn't shift. I know of no racing area where the wind shifts more. One can take the simple solution for dealing with turbulent wind flows in which vertical currents bring down gusts of veered upper airflow to mix alternately with backed surface air—tack on every header. When the wind is oscillating through a range of ten degrees or more, as it does in most easterlies and northeasterlies in Bermuda, this technique is essential. It may be the only technique necessary if the mark is in mid-Sound and no shore is closely approachable. Experience in many Bermuda Race Weeks indicates to me that westerly winds are also best treated in this fashion. Often a channeled persistent shift is present in addition to the oscillating shifts, however, and there is a sufficient advantage to one side of the course that "tacking on headers" will be insufficient. Hartley's favorite tactic is to ignore the little shifts, to continue out almost to the layline, and then to tack back in persistent shift combined with an appropriate oscillation. As the greatest advantage from a heading oscillating shift is gained by the boat farthest to the side of the course, Hartley wins many races by this technique.

The time of the race is as significant in Bermuda as elsewhere. Heating of the land is accompanied by increased convection, increased upper airflow at the surface, and veering. As most races are started before maximum heating has occurred, progressive veering is to be expected during the race. This is, of course, another reason for taking the early port tack ("go west when the wind is in the south," etc.). If the wind is obviously increasing in velocity keep to the starboard side of the course, expect it to veer, regardless of the time of the day. If the wind is obviously varying in velocity through long intervals and over large areas (as it often does in Bermuda) consider the likelihood of a shift with the change in velocity ahead, particularly for the all-important last tack to the mark. And if the wind is dying late in the day expect it to back. Obviously all such velocity-determined shifts are proportionate in degree to the amount of change in velocity that occurs.

Tack on the headers, look for the velocity shifts, but most of all pick the right shore and tack toward it. On the first day of racing in Race Week, 1970, the wind was in the southwest, and the mark was well up under the Somerset Shore. There were few oscillations in this warm airflow (born over the Gulf Stream) but there was a 5° channeled shift to the west along the Somerset Shore. It paid to go west ("when the wind is in the south") up under the Somerset Shore early in the leg so as to be "inside at the bend," Long Point. However, it was essential to break away as the shoreline started to deviate to the south beyond Long Point and the wind backed about two-thirds the way up the leg. Ding Schoonmaker passed us at this point as he went out on starboard before we did. Subsequently, when the wind was due south and the mark off the U.S. Naval Base (N.O.B.), there was less channeling evident but still an advantage to the early port tack.

When the wind was in the north, as it was when it blew 35–40 knots for the fourth and fifth races of the series, there was a sig-- nificant advantage in an early port tack toward the islands to the east. (In these strong winds another advantage of a tack toward the windward shore was evident—less sea in the protected lee.) The wind was shifted to the east near these islands. It is unlikely that the shift was due to channeling as it persisted where the islands were obviously diverging from the main wind stream. Probably in- creased convection off the islands and a greater mixture of upper airflow veered the wind at the surface. Along the western shore of the sound in a northerly or northwesterly the wind is progres- sively veered (more northeasterly) as the wind channels along the main axis of the Somerset Shore. Thus, although there may be no major advantage to the starboard (eastern) side of the course along the islands, there is usually a major defect on the port (western) side of the course, a persistent veer. When the wind is in the north, play the shifts but avoid the western shore.

On the second beat of the morning race Ding Schoonmaker passed us, to our surprise, by holding off to the west and finding a westerly shift along the Somerset Shore. As the shoreline was di- verging from the basic wind direction in this area, I had expected an easterly shift off Boaz Island. Instead the wind apparently fun- neled through the gap between Boaz and Ireland Islands to provide a net deviation to the west. The duration of the shift was too long to have been a mere oscillation.

We didn't race in a westerly during Race Week, 1970, but this is a common wind in Bermuda. The committee boat is positioned along the eastern edge of the Sound between Spanish Point and Two Rock Passage in a westerly and the usually recommended strategy is to hold starboard tack into the islands to the south. In a strong wind the water is smoother here but there is frequently a beneficial shift as well. This shift is apparently due to channeling along the island chain. If the islands can be approached in the di- verging area, it usually pays to hold starboard into the beach. If, however, the wind is a bit north of west and the initial starboard tack hits the islands farther west, the gambit is less regularly suc- cessful. Where the islands diverge from the westerly wind flow, the wind to their north (in the racing area) is channeled to the north (veered) while the wind to the south of the islands holds to its basic westerly direction. A southwesterly wind will be more southerly in the portion of the Great Sound to the south of these islands, as the long axis of the Sound is north–south in this area; and more west-

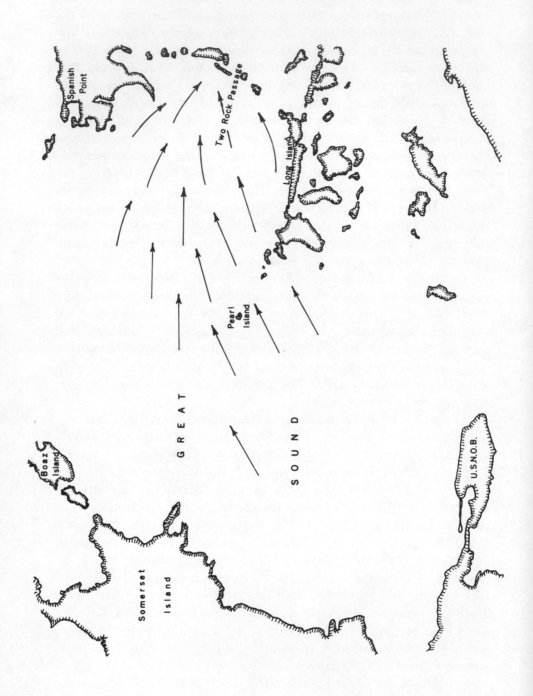

erly to the north of the islands, as the long axis of the Sound is east–west in this area. It may pay to hold out on port early in the leg to take advantage of the veered deviation midway in the leg and then to tack into the islands on starboard where the first large gap appears to the west of Elizabeth Island. Thereafter the backed wind that blows through the gaps between the islands and will be present at the mark requires a position to the south of the fleet. In the old days when the passage to the east of Pearl Island was forbidden this meant hugging Pearl Island and tacking immediately upon passing it. Nowadays the first boat through the passage may be the first to the mark—'inside at the bend" in a channeled wind.

The winds of Bermuda are unstable, turbulent winds which produce frequent oscillating shifts. They are in addition subject to marked channeling along the shores of the Great Sound and through the gaps between the small islands which compose its periphery. Oscillating shifts must be utilized but persistent shifts are always more important. In Bermuda the persistent shifts are predictable and they cannot be ignored.

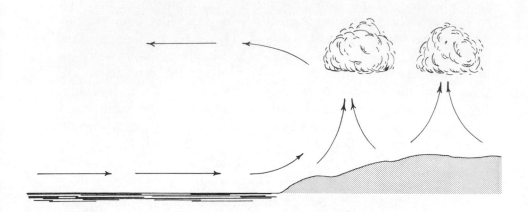

2. The Coasts of England

"Never a circle to the moon,
Should send your topsails down;
But when it is around the sun,
With all masts it must be done."

England, like the Pacific Northwest, lies on the eastern margin of a great ocean in the latitude of the westerlies. Though it lies between 50° and 60° north its climate, like that of Washington and British Columbia, is mild. It is warmed by the North Atlantic Current, the residue of the Gulf Stream, as the Northwest is warmed by the North Pacific Current. It receives the winds of the North Atlantic as the Northwest receives the winds of the North Pacific. In the winter the North Atlantic is relatively warm. Depressions are formed as cold continental air outflows from the North American coast over the warm water. Gales initiated off Cape Hatteras eventually reach England and northern Europe. In summer the North Atlantic is relatively cool, far cooler than the daily heated land. The resultant stability does little to interfere with the development of a sea breeze along all the coasts of England. The air masses that affect England are maritime polar Atlantic, centered near Iceland (and sometimes dry returning polar maritime), and maritime tropical Atlantic, derived from the Azores (subtropical) High. These two masses meet to form the polar front of the North Atlantic.

Surges of air from either mass periodically invade England, polar maritime with its attendant depressions dominating the winter and tropical maritime with its sea breezes dominating the summer.

England has acquired a reputation for high winds, cold, clammy air, and rain. These are the typical conditions of winter and to a lesser degree of spring and fall, but not of summer, when the air is often light, the skies clear, and the temperature warm. Tidal currents are strong. Small-boat racing is conducted in estuaries where current flow varies markedly over the course, or on small rivers, lakes, and ponds ("gravel pits"). Conditions vary markedly in different parts of the country from the cold misery of the Clyde to the warm sunshine of Cornwall and from the great waves off Whitstable to the smooth waters of the Upper Thames. The difficult geographic conditions require a number of variations from typical American racing practices. The great rise and fall of tide prevents the use of a hoist. Most launching is done from launching ramps which are usually fixed, extending steeply between bulkhead walls or for long distances out over mudflats. "Trolleys," simple, light-weight trailers with tires suited to the launching surfaces, are used to move boats about on stages and down launching ramps or across a quarter mile of beach. Starting times in many locations must be scheduled in accordance with the tide; in some areas there is insufficient water for a triangular course, for a weather leg, or even for a starting line when the tide is out. As the weather conditions tend to the extremes and are difficult to predict, boats are conservatively rigged to be prepared for all conditions. There is little evidence of the specialized light air rig, though some boats may be considered to be rigged especially for heavy weather. The variable wind and tidal conditions combined with the limited availability of open water prevent racing conditions from being reproducible. Lack of reproducibility hampers the development of boat speed; it is difficult to test a rigging modification if few opportunities for comparative performance occur.

WINTER WINDS

The seasonal changes in the weather over the North Atlantic determine the seasonal changes in England. In January the Icelandic Low reaches its largest size, its lowest pressure, and its greatest gradient with the Azores High. Low-pressure systems are constantly spawned from above the warm waters of the Gulf Stream in the

Gulf of Mexico or off Hatteras to migrate along the polar front to Europe. The North Atlantic Current carrying the residue of the Gulf Stream keeps the North Atlantic and England warm in winter and provides energy for the frequent winter storms. The air temperature at the entrance to the channel averages 50°F. in January. The heat of the water and the moisture available in the air create frequent gales, occasionally of hurricane force. Depressions passing up the Denmark Strait cause the winter winds of England to be chiefly westerly. In February the North Atlantic temperature is at its lowest as the maritime polar air moves to its farthest south position. Depressions on their farthest south track at this time of the year often produce easterly winds over England. In March gales are decreasing in strength and frequency and the winds are returning to the westerly quadrants.

By April the weather is more settled. Though the winds are westerly, averaging 25 knots in the North Atlantic, they infrequently exceed this strength in the Channel. A dramatic decrease in the frequency of low-pressure systems and gale-force winds occurs in May. In the Channel winds of less than 3 knots are more common than winds above 13 knots. In half the years of record no winds stronger than 25 knots have appeared in the Channel in June or July. Pleasant weather with winds averaging 10 to 15 knots from the south, southwest, and west are characteristic of summer. The Azores High reaches its farthest north position and its greatest pressure in July. The few lows which appear cross Scotland and the North Sea en route to the Baltic where they frequently linger or are succeeded by depression after depression for days on end. In England and particularly along the Channel coast, however, the sea breeze reigns and the sun shines. By August the winds in the Channel are increasing in strength due in part to the marked heating of the land and the resultant strengthening of the afternoon sea breeze. In September the Azores High begins to deteriorate and to move south as the Icelandic Low in the Davis Strait begins to deepen. Maritime polar air begins to penetrate farther south and average winds in the North Atlantic increase to 15 to 20 knots. By October westerly gales are frequent in the Channel. The Icelandic Low deepens progressively into December, which is the stormiest month in the North Atlantic. Winds are westerly or southwesterly to the south of the low-pressure systems which move rapidly at 25 to 30 knots along a northeasterly track. Air temperature is infrequently below 50°F. at the entrance to the Channel but is far colder along the coast and inland where the gales may seem equally strong.

THE SEA BREEZES

The development of the summer sea breeze is dependent upon the reduction in the general pressure gradient and the clear skies associated with the northern movement of the Azores High. Cloud cover is usually present over an island and along a coast dominated by onshore winds as moisture is brought inland and lifted by convection over the land. Sinking air about the Azores High melts England's usual cloud cover and facilitates heating of the land surface. As dry air from the continent is often incorporated into the east and south coast sea breezes, they tend to be associated with less cloud cover and therefore to be stronger than west coast sea breezes. The most significant factor determining sea breeze strength on an island coast is the amount of land inland of the site. The greatest mass of land lies about the counties north of London. The "heat low," the area of reduced pressure due to surface heating, reaches its maximum reduction in pressure in this area. The nearby East Anglia coast receives the maximum benefit from this marked depression inland. The thunderstorms which form over Hertfordshire and demonstrate the strength of this heat low are fueled by the moisture brought ashore by the sea breeze. Outflow from these convection cells, under the influence of the upper-level westerlies, flows aloft over the North Sea and melts the offshore cloud (if any) as it descends to the surface. Less convection over the southern counties provides less upper-level outflow to melt cloud over the Channel. Thus the south coast sea breeze is weaker than the east coast sea breeze chiefly because the trans-shore pressure gradient is more limited by cloud cover over the Channel coast.

In the west country (Cornwall and Devon) sea breezes are particularly weak because the land mass available is small and because outflow from this limited heat source must be divided to spread out from both coasts. A 10- to 15-knot offshore wind may be sufficient to keep the sea breeze out. We spent an entire July week at Falmouth for the 1966 Prince of Wales Cup and experienced but one day of sea breeze. Northerly winds persisted (chiefly from the back of low-pressure systems) throughout the week. On the second day of racing the northerly was a mere 6–8 knots at the start. By 1:00 P.M. as we started the third leg, theoretically a broad reach away from the shore, the wind died, calm reigned for fifteen to twenty minutes, and finally the sea breeze appeared. We worked our way into the lead in the zone of calm which separated the cool offshore flow from the cool onshore sea breeze. As we sailed toward shore again on the second round, we left the sea breeze and returned to the intervening calm which had moved but a half mile farther inshore. The second boat was close astern and acquired an inside overlap as we rounded the (now) leeward mark. She was able to tack to the more offshore port tack before we could and so sailed into the progressively freshening sea breeze ahead of us. We never overcame the deficit.

Although the sea breeze is weak and often neutralized by even a mild offshore wind in Cornwall, it usually succeeds farther east. There its success depends upon the stability of the weather system airflow. If convection is weak, under cloud cover or under a subsidence inversion, the sea breeze will be weak and its front will progress inland very slowly. When the weather system wind is offshore and cool, the sea breeze front advances inland at about 3 knots. If convection is strong inland and the upper layers of the airflow are cold, the sea breeze will progress inland rapidly. It may continue inland far into the evening and be evident over inland waters as late as 10:00 P.M. When convection is strong the south coast sea breeze front may progress all the way across Kent and emerge as an offshore sea breeze in the Thames estuary. The offshore southerly flow, heated by its passage over Kent, lifts over the local northerly sea breeze as it moves offshore. Whitstable, noted for its enormous seas and gale-force winds, is also characterized by protracted calm in part due to the convergence between the two sea breezes. On the north shore of the Thames estuary the two winds occasionally reinforce each other so that in late afternoon the onshore flow is unusually strong.

The effects of a subsidence inversion upon seabreeze development are often clearly evident in the Channel coast estuaries. The sea breeze develops readily beneath such an inversion but as convection is limited by the inversion lid it is unable to generate any great strength or extent. Thermal lift-off rises to but 1500–2000 feet, meets warmer air above and sinks back to be channeled out over the water. A sea breeze derived from such limited sustenance is only able to maintain a short surface flow. It begins close to shore and progresses but a mile or two inland. Its total area of flow after full generation may be but a mile offshore and two miles inland.

As the inversion breaks the initial sea breeze backs and dies, a period of calm and erratic shifting supervenes, and finally, sometimes not until late afternoon, the sea breeze reorganizes and comes in strong. Sometimes the offshore wind is sufficiently strong and/or cold to keep the sea breeze in check all day so that only when the inversion reforms in early evening is it able to invade the estuary and the land. Sometimes a weak sea breeze may be halted by a modest offshore weather system flow and the intervening zone of calm may persist in an estuary such as Chichester Harbor for several hours. These conditions are typical of United States East Coast sailing and often require recognition of the presence of two distinct winds either side of the calm zone, determination of which wind is present at the next mark, and acquisition of advantageous position in *that* wind as soon as possible.

Marked variations in sea breeze velocity and direction due to channeling are characteristic of the Channel coast. Wherever bluffs rise abruptly the lower levels of the dense sea breeze are deviated parallel to the coast, spreading laterally to seek an entrance. Wherever a river mouth or a break in the high shoreline appears, the sea breeze turns and rushes inland. The best sea breezes appear where a break in the shoreline is interposed between long stretches of high bluffs. The Isle of Wight obstructs the lower several hundred feet of the sea breeze flow forcing it to deviate to each side. Thus off Cowes a westerly sea breeze flowing up the West Solent meets an easterly sea breeze flowing up Spithead. This, together with the multiple tidal flows (double flood tides in each cycle) and current convergence behind the island, make the Solent one of the world's worst (or at least, most frustrating) places to sail.

The Prince of Wales Cup was sailed in the Solent in 1967 and we experienced much of its notorious behavior. The POW Cup itself was sailed for in a 20- to 25-knot westerly under clear skies. The weather system gradient was minimal and the wind fitful an hour before the start. By noon, however, the westerly sea breeze appeared advancing up the West Solent and strengthened steadily thereafter. As the basic Channel sea breeze veers with increasing velocity it becomes more and more aligned with the flow up the West Solent. Therefore unless an easterly weather system flow supports the sea breeze flow up Spithead, the West Solent flow can be expected to dominate off Cowes, particularly late in the day. Sometimes a morning easterly abruptly dies and is replaced by the westerly in early afternoon. The strongest sea breeze flow (easterly

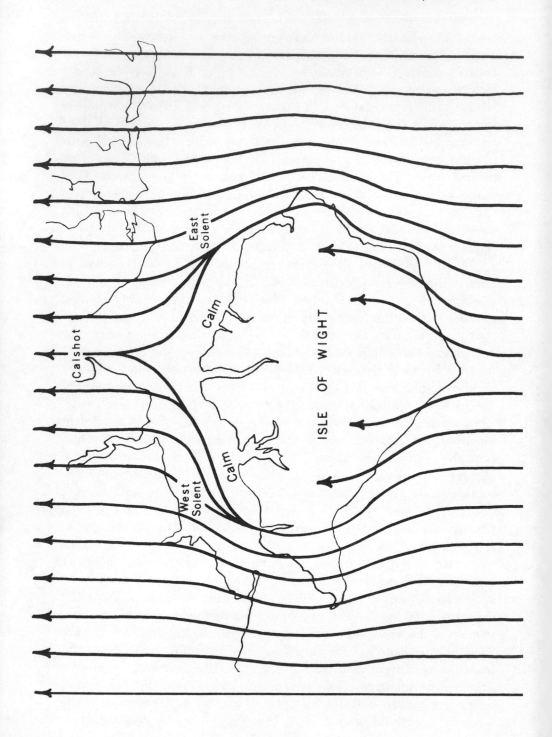

or westerly) channels along the north shore of the Solent. The south shore of the Solent lies in the blanket zone of the hills of the Isle of Wight and in the direct convergence zone between the two sea breezes. In general the further one can keep off the Isle of Wight shore the better the breeze will be. The wind is usually westerly and strong just south of Calshot on the outside of the stream of deviated flow up the West Solent. The southeasterly flow up Spithead channels directly into Southampton Water so that the wind north of Calshot is usually from this direction and a dramatic shift often occurs at the point. This, of course, means that in the Ryde Channel, where much of the round-the-buoys racing is done, the wind may vacillate between easterly or westerly, be simultaneously from both directions on different parts of the course or be absent in the convergence zone between the two winds.

The sea breeze of East Anglia is the best in England. Some of the locally channeled sea breezes of the south coast are comparable in strength at peak generation but the east coast sea breezes are more dependable and more persistent. Early in the day they characteristically begin from north of east, from the North Sea over the flats and broads of Norfolk and Suffolk into the huge inland heat low. Here the prevailing westerlies are directly offshore and although the sea breeze has to bury beneath them its upper-level circulation is reinforced by them. Off Lowestoft the bluffs delay the onset of the sea breeze and prevent onshore movement of the sailing layer until midday. As the sea breeze strengthens here it veers progressively, northeast to east and finally to southeast, probably a greater veer than is found in sea breezes elsewhere in the world.

Uffa Fox first recorded the characteristic behavior of the sea breeze off Lowestoft in describing an early Prince of Wales Cup race there. On a clear day with the current running south along the north-south shore, boats that selected a course over the offshore shoals were the first to the weather mark. By tacking up these shoals they experienced a reduction in the adverse current and were at the same time sailing to starboard of the fleet in the direction of the expected persistent shift, a veer from northeast to east. In the race that he described, a significant veer occurred during the first beat (shortly after noon). The boats that attempted to avoid the current by an inshore course to port of the rhumb line were left on the outside of this shift and "down the drain" after it appeared. This experience emphasizes the greater advantages usually attendant upon proper manipulation of a persistent shift as compared to utilization of current differences.

When I sailed at Lowestoft for the Prince of Wales Cup in 1964 the same conditions existed. I had acquired all the available information concerning the wind and the current, had charted the tidal stream, its direction and strength in the racing area at hourly intervals, and had encased this data plus the necessary portion of the large-scale chart in plastic. We were the first afloat, an hour and a half before the start, which gave us time to check the wind, the line, and the tacks with the compass, the depth of water at crucial points along the shore and to chart the course with a marking pencil across the plastic-covered chart. The morning wind was northeasterly, a combined flow from the high pressure to the north and the typical low-level East Anglia sea breeze. Subsidence in this portion of the maritime tropical air derived from the Azores High could be expected to have produced a significant inversion. The determinant of the race would be the time of breakthrough of this inversion. As breakthrough occurred the northeasterly could be expected to fade, to back and then to veer progressively as the sea breeze reorganized with the inclusion of upper-level flow. Consultation with local sailors, "old-timers," and fishermen indicated that the northeasterly would be unlikely to back more than a few degrees as it died and that it could be expected to veer rapidly as it strengthened. The timing of the well-known veer was apparently anybody's guess, but many races had been won by sticking to the shore on the first beat.

During the hour and a half before the start we noted no significant change in the direction or velocity of the northeasterly. As we started the race the inversion breakthrough did not appear imminent although heating ashore was already marked. We concluded, with some trepidation, that the veer would be delayed until after the completion of the first leg. The wind along the shore, channeled by the bluffs, was slightly stronger and slightly more veered than it was offshore. In the absence of a veer or a significant increase in wind strength offshore, the adverse tide became the dominant consideration. A course up the beach might even have the advantage of a slight back as the low-level sea breeze died and would certainly have the advantage of the "fan effect" as the veer began. We should be able to get around the weather mark about a mile offshore before the veer developed that far out.

We elected to start at the inshore end of the line (although the

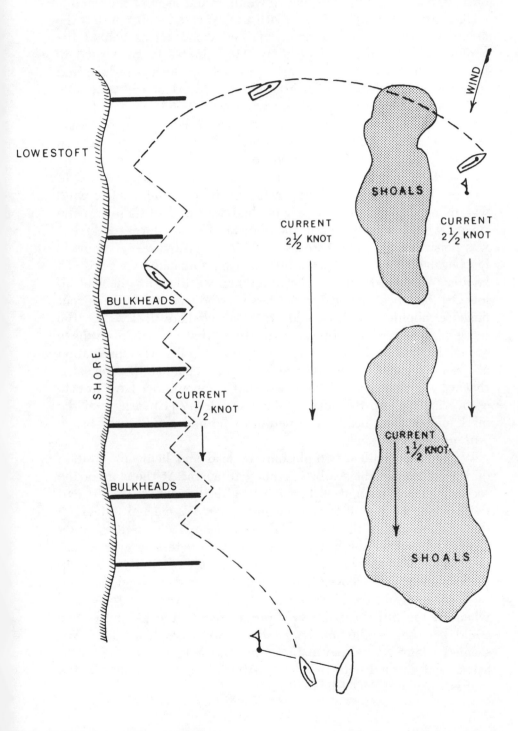

offshore end was slightly farther to weather and most of the pundits were starting there to be inside with the expected shift), tested the layline for the leeward distance marker, came across behind the committee boat on port with about 1½ minutes to go, tacked in front and to leeward of the fleet approaching down the line, and with the gun were off with clear air to leeward of everyone. We had a satisfactory lead worked out when we hit the beach and commenced tacking up between the "groynes" (short-piling breakwaters). Except for Andy Green in *Sabre;* who clung enough to keep us pushing on every tack, we were leaving the major portion of the fleet tacking up the shore with us, and those who had elected to stay out in the tide were disappearing in the jib window. The wind was dying offshore and those who had ventured offshore, up the shoals, were barely stemming the current. The low-level sea breeze was persisting longer inshore (see "Chicago, Milwaukee, Toronto") but began to die and to back a little as we approached the port-tack layline. We tacked out into the tide when we thought sufficient allowance had been made for the lesser wind and stronger current offshore, hoping that we could cross the offshore fleet before the reorganized, veered sea breeze arrived and that we would not have to tack back to starboard in the strong current offshore. Observation of a range created by the mark with a distant channel buoy revealed that we were going to lay the mark, that we would not have to take a covering tack up the offshore shoal which lay just inshore of the mark and that our nearest competitors who had gone up the beach with us had overstood.

We rounded with a two-plusminute–lead and held our position on the reaches as the sea breeze filled in again. At the start of the second beat we recognized that it had already veered 10°–15° and that we could expect it to veer much farther. We elected to tack up the offshore shoals this time while our nearest competitor, Andy Green, headed for the beach again. In the progressive veer we increased our lead to four minutes as Mike Souter who followed us up the offshore course moved into second. We had escaped the veer by the skin of our teeth! Thereafter we were never threatened and when on the fifth beat the veer progressed to the point that we could lay the weather mark, we knew we were home free. We seemed a long way ahead as the followers came around the marks astern and finished with that lead to the hoots and screams of the biggest spectator fleet I had ever seen.

V. *Strategic Implications*

Pre-race plans, interpretations, and investigations.
In-race navigation and organization.
Risks and compromises.

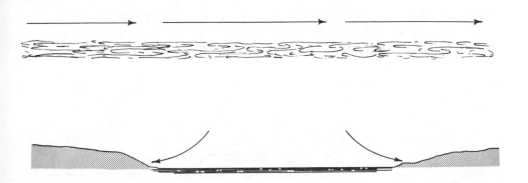

A. Planning the Race

"If the sun goes pale to bed,
'Twill rain tomorrow, it is said."

Stewart Morris has said that most races are won ashore, by preparation, and he is undoubtedly right. Many are won by an appropriate prediction of a change in wind strength or direction or an appropriate analysis of current variation. Such a prediction permits the boat to be appropriately positioned referrable to the change in wind or current. Strategic success is, of course, not necessarily intentional. Although strategy determines the outcome, the winner may have no idea why he assumed an advantageous course. (He may have been forced to it by a competitor!) Luck cannot be prearranged, however, and as it should be equally distributed between good and bad, it can be disregarded. Fewer races are won by boat speed than by strategy, but boat speed is largely achieved prior to the race.

The helmsman needs to determine what the race means to him and to discover realistically what he intends and expects its outcome to be. If there is any indication that victory is not intended or expected, loss can be guaranteed. Consequent to diverse psychological needs, many sailors enter races intending to lose or intending to avoid victory. A useful test to distinguish one's true intention is to consider what preparation has been made for victory. When I remember that I have left my stopwatch in my bureau drawer, I realize that I haven't intended to win. The best-prepared sailor will usually win and the best-prepared sailor is the one who is willing to make the effort to prepare himself—who feels that the time, effort, and energy expended is justified by the satisfaction to be gained in victory.

It's no good complaining that the winner spends more effort preparing, more money equipping, or more time evaluating his boat and his racing. No matter how high or low the general standard of racing in a fleet one of its members will exert a sufficiently greater effort than his competitors to insure victory. Races *are* won ashore and each sailor determines his own likelihood of success. (Not every race is intended to be won, of course; series victory may be more certain if one seeks a conservative high-placing rather than a risky win in a given race).

Each sailor will modify the completeness with which he fulfills the following recommendations in planning a particular race but he can expect his success to be directly proportional to his effort.

DURING THE WEEK BEFORE THE RACE

1. *Chart:* A chart of the racing area should be obtained so as to evaluate its geography. The shorelines and the underwater contours determine the direction and velocity of current in the area. The shorelines and the above-water contours determine the direction and velocity of airflow in the area. Local persistent winds are determined by the local landforms and periodic weather system winds are channeled, resisted, and refracted by them.

2. *Local knowledge of the airflow:* The characteristic wind patterns of the racing area should be determined (if possible). The modifications produced by the local geography can be deduced. The likelihood of significant variations in velocity or direction in the racing area will depend upon the weather system airflow at the time but probable effects can be predicted in advance and can be useful. Local sailors, published literature, summaries of previous wind experience for the particular season should all be sought.

3. *Local knowledge of water flow:* The characteristic current patterns of the racing area should be determined (if possible) and the modifications produced by the local geography deduced.

4. *Weather maps:* The daily weather maps should be evaluated each day for several days in advance of the racing. The weather maps published on the racing day evaluated in conjunction with the weather maps for the previous days will indicate the temperature, moisture, and source of the airflow to be expected. These factors determine the likelihood and nature of the surface airflow.

5. *Current tables:* The timing, velocity, and direction of the tidal current flow can be estimated from the published tables (and from published charts available for certain areas). The greatest value of the current tables is their indication of the velocity of the expected current. Direction is best estimated from the underwater contours indicated on the chart. Timing of tidal changes in most racing areas can only be determined on the water.

THE MORNING OF THE RACE

1. *Weather forecast:* The latest possible telephone, radio, or newspaper forecast should be obtained and considered in the light of the weather map's indications of expected weather system airflow. Forecasts are not designed for sailors and therefore can be misleading unless interpreted in the light of an understanding of the relationship between weather system, local persistent wind, and surface airflow.

2. *The wind at the dock:* The discovery of the determinants of the wind observed should permit a better understanding of the wind expected.

3. *The tide at the dock:* The height and direction of change of the water level indicates the approximate timing of the current change and can be used to confirm the current tables.

4. *Expected wind conditions:* Prior to launching the following estimates should be made:
   a. The origin and nature of the wind expected to be present during the race.

b. The velocity and distribution at the surface of the resultant wind.

c. The possible appearance of a persistent shift due to:
   1. Weather system movement
   2. Local persistent wind development
   3. Geographic influences (horizontal flow distribution)
   4. Temperature and moisture influences (vertical flow distribution)

d. The time and location of such a persistent shift.

e. The possible presence of a vertically unstable wind with its associated oscillating shifts.

5. *Expected current conditions:* Prior to launching the following estimates should be made:
   a. The velocity of the current and its direction during the period of the race.
   b. The time of any change in velocity or direction during the period of the race.
   c. The distribution of the current in the area of the race.

THE HOUR BEFORE THE RACE

1. *The wind on the way to the start:* Compass readings of wind direction and tack headings should be obtained as soon as possible after launching, checked repeatedly thereafter, and as late as possible before the start.

2. *The distribution of the wind in the racing area:* A sail around the course with particular attention to areas near shorelines should be undertaken to determine the presence of variations in wind velocity or direction within the racing area.

3. *The distribution of the current in the racing area:* The current should be checked at various locations around the course particularly at its extremities and wherever dramatic changes in the underwater contours occur. A floating marker should be carried in the boat for this purpose. Its drift must be timed from whatever anchored marks are available.

IMMEDIATELY PRIOR TO THE RACE—THE COURSE PLAN

1. The preferred side of the course for each leg should be determined in the light of the general information acquired

during the week before the race, the morning of the race, the survey of the racing area, and the minutes before the start. The following factors must be considered in their order of significance:

a. *Persistent wind shifts:* If a movement of the weather system, the development of a local persistent wind, a modification of the existing wind by geographic factors, or a modification of the vertical distribution of airflow is expected to produce a persistent wind shift at the surface, this will probably be the major determinant of the outcome of the race

b. *Oscillating wind shifts:* If the wind is expected to be vertically unstable, racing success will depend upon utilization of each shift to gain distance toward the median wind while beating and to obtain the fastest course on the downwind legs

c. *Current:* If the current is expected to vary in direction or velocity within the racing area during the period of the race, the planned course should be modified to incur the least harm and gain the greatest advantage from the variations.

d. *Waves:* If large waves exist but vary in size within the racing area, the planned course should be modified to avoid areas of large waves to windward and to take advantage of such areas while broad reaching and running.

2. The sail trim (with particular attention to sail selection and use) for each reach or run should be determined and will depend upon the factors considered above.

3. The starting plan should be determined with particular attention to a means of reaching the preferred side of the windward leg.

It is desirable to record the information acquired step by step on a form prepared for this purpose. If information is not recorded, that which is most recently acquired will usually receive the greatest consideration without regard to its significance. It is also easy to forget specific numbers for compass headings and to fail to determine the true range of the wind directions experienced unless they are recorded. The record will be available for reference during the heat of battle when differing memories confuse the issue. Finally, mistakes are discovered and understanding gained to future advantage when the results can be analyzed along with a record of experience.

The plan is essential. Its conduct must be modified by tactical considerations as the race develops, but if no plan exists or if it is disregarded the chances of success are severely limited. A successful plan, of course, is not achieved by the acquisition of information, but by the application of an understanding of the determinants and consequences of wind and current to the data acquired. It is necessary first to understand why the wind blows as it does and the current flows as it does and under what circumstances these flows will be modified. Local knowledge must be the first step toward local understanding. Ultimately, an understanding of local conditions should be sufficient to permit an understanding of the determinants of air and water flow in general; then an analysis of the winds and currents of an unknown racing area can become as accurate as the analysis of one's home conditions. When applied to the organized acquisition of information just described, a correct prediction of the wind and current to be experienced during a particular race should be possible. And strategy will win races—if you want to win races.

RACE PLAN

RACE . . . .
DATE . . . .
START TIME . . . .

1. Preliminary
      Navigational chart   Landform Effects . . . .
                     Underwater Form Effects . . . .
      Weather map   Air Mass . . . . Weather System . . . . Position . . . .
         Gradient Flow: Velocity . . . . Direction . . . . Stable? . . . . Unstable? . . . . .
      Current Table   Time of Change . . . . . . Velocity . . . . . . Direction . . . .
      Local Knowledge   . . . .
                          . . . .
                          . . . .

2. Morning of Race
      Forecast   Wind Velocity . . . . Direction . . . . Temp . . . . . Cloud Cover . . . .
      Conditions ashore   Wind Velocity . . . . Direction . . . . Tidal Level . . . .

3. Hour Before the Race   Survey of the Course
      Expected Wind Conditions: Direction . . . .   Expected Current Conditions
         Source . . . . Velocity . . . . Stability . . . . .   Source . . . . Velocity . . . . .
         Distribution Variation   Distribution Variation
            Predicted . . . .   Predicted . . . .
            Discovered . . . .   Discovered . . . .

Persistent Shift: Veer?.... Back?...... Direction Shifts ....
    Weather System?... Geographic?... Time... Location.....
    Inversion Break?... Thunderstorm?.. Weather Mark ....
    Local Sea Breeze?... Fan Effect?... Jibing Mark ....
    Ocean Sea Breeze?... Other?...... Leeward Mark ....
    Time...... Location............

4. The Course Plan
    Advantageous Side of Course for Each Leg (Predicted and Discovered)

	COMPASS BEARINGS	WIND VELOCITY CHANGE?	PERSISTENT SHIFT?	CURRENT	WAVES
First Beat					
First Reach					
Second Reach					
Second Beat					
Run					
Third Beat					

5. Headings   Time...St'b'd...Port...   Time...St'b'd...Port...
   (Determined)   ...   .
    Before start......   ... ... 2nd Beat......   ... ...
    1st Beat   ...   . 3rd Beat......   ... ...
        ...   .
        ...   .

6. Median Wind Start.... 1st Beat.... 2nd Beat....Run... 3rd Beat....

7. Comments ....
....
....
....
....

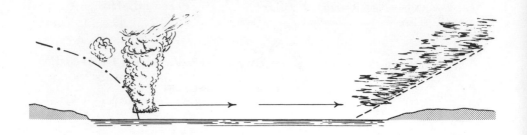

B. Interpreting a Weather Map

"When the wind backs and weatherglass falls
Then be on your guard against gales and squalls."

Preparation for a race includes an attempt to predict the strength, direction, and variation in the surface wind. The assistance of a trained meteorologist would be most useful and the forecasts provided by experts should be considered. However, the sailor must make his own predictions, using all the information he can obtain but relying on none. Although he starts with the weather map, he must apply the principles which govern local surface airflow to determine how the weather system shown will influence the winds to be encountered. Local knowledge is most useful if it is based upon understanding. Ultimately the racing sailor must evaluate the wind that actually blows on the morning of the race. If he understands *why* it is present or absent in the light of all the information available then he can usually predict what modifications will follow as the race develops.

Most people who read weather maps in the newspaper want to know what the temperature will be or whether it will rain. And the people who publish newspapers want to please most people. Fortunately what most people want to know about temperature and moisture is also of importance to the sailor. The determinants of temperature and moisture revealed by the published weather map are the determinants of surface wind flow and therefore the weather map is an essential resource of the racing sailor.

Published weather maps represent a summary of surface conditions—temperature, moisture, and wind—at a particular moment, usually 1:00 P.M. of the day prior to publication. The meteorologist uses a series of such instant synopses together with charts of upper air level conditions (and a computer) to forecast future conditions. The information presented in a single map is sufficient to permit the prediction of the essential elements of the day to come, however, and the sailor must learn to make such interpretations. He must interpret the language as well as the symbols of the published map or of the forecast, if included, knowing they were not intended for him. The better he understands the implications of the weather described by the previous day's weather map, the better he can interpret the forecasts given. Ideally a series of daily weather maps should be utilized to indicate the flow of weather as it moves toward the location of interest. Although a chart showing the height of the 500-millibar pressure level above the surface is the best indicator of the direction of subsequent weather system movement, much can be predicted without it.

A single weather map can be used to determine whether the weather system (pressure-gradient) wind is likely to reach the surface during the racing period, what its approximate strength and

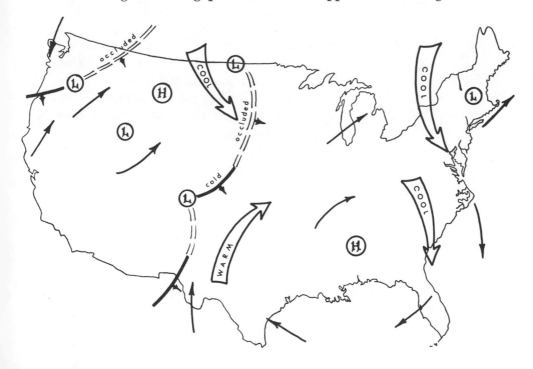

direction will be, and whether, if the weather system wind will not
reach the surface, a local thermal wind will appear. The published
weather map will show the position of fronts, centers of high and
low pressure, arrows indicating wind directions, and numbers indicating temperatures at various locations, all superimposed upon
an outline map of the region. This simple information can be used
to indicate (1) the probable direction of movement of the weather
systems shown, (2) the weather system (high, low, or frontal) expected in the area, (3) the air mass from which the weather system
is derived, (4) where the air carried by the wind has been, and
(5) what it will meet when it reaches the area of interest. Each of
these items must be considered in predicting the temperature, the
moisture content, the upper wind and the surface wind to be encountered. Each weather map must be evaluated systematically,
considering each of those items in turn, so as to arrive at an appropriate prediction of the temperature, moisture content, upper wind,
and surface wind to be encountered subsequently.

Elements
    1. The expected movement of the weather system:
        Generally in the direction of prevailing wind flow (in the
        north temperate zone [United States] a westerly flow)
        a. High Pressure—two major air masses
            Continental polar (cP) air moves south, east of the
            Rockies, and then east across the mid-continent (far-
            thest south penetration occurs in winter)
            Maritime tropical Gulf (mTg) air moves north across
            the Gulf Coast and then east (farthest north penetra-
            tion occurs in summer)
            Small highs move faster than large ones
            Highs that separate a series of lows tend to move
            southward
            Warm highs tend to move slowly or remain stationary
            for several days (mTg air in the summertime)
        b. Low pressure—two major tracks over the United States:
            Beginning over the Great Lakes and moving down
            the St. Lawrence
             Beginning over the Gulf of Mexico and moving up
            the Atlantic Coast
            Warm fronts move more slowly than cold fronts, thus
            cold fronts "catch up" to produce an occlusion and

thereafter the entire low-pressure system moves more slowly

A young low moves parallel to the isobars in its warm sector

Lows tend to move around large, well-established highs in the direction of the airflow around the high

2. The source of the air mass expected:

Continental polar (cP)—cold, dry air from central Canada

Maritime tropical Gulf (mTg)—warm, moist air from the Gulf

Maritime polar (Atlantic or Pacific) (mPa, mPp)—cold, moist air from the North Atlantic or North Pacific

3. The source of the wind expected, advection effects:

From north, cold; from south, warm; from east or west, temperature unchanged

From continent, dry, with extremes of temperature

From ocean or Great Lakes, moist with moderated temperature

Effects

1. The temperature will be determined by:

Weather system movement

Temperature in approaching weather system

Pressure

High pressure—contracting air warms with time

Low pressure—expanding air cools with time

Air mass

cP air—clear—marked diurnal changes in temperature with radiation

mTg air—moist, cloudy—temperature variation limited by "greenhouse effect"

Wind source

Temperature of surfaces over which wind has passed

Site of observer

Temperature of surfaces at site

2. The moisture content will be determined by:

Weather system movement

Rain, snow, cloud cover in approaching weather system

Breadth of the zone of precipitation about a cold front is inversely proportional to its rate of movement

Breadth of the zone of precipitation about a warm front or an occlusion is usually greater than about a cold front

Pressure

High pressure—contracting air warms and accepts more moisture, clouds dissipate

Low pressure—expanding air cools and precipitates moisture, clouds appear

Frontal system—precipitation is proportional to the acuteness of the angle of convergence of the isobars at a front

Air mass

Dry from continental source or moist from maritime

Wind source

Passage over land or water resulting in loss or acquisition of moisture

3. The upper wind flow will be determined by:

Weather system movement

Flow strength and direction in approaching weather system

Pressure

The greater the pressure gradient (the closer the isobars), the stronger the wind flow

Stronger wind flow near periphery of high pressure, center of low pressure

Wind strength deteriorates with age of high and distance traveled

Wind strength of low increases with passage over warm surface and decreases with passage over cold surface

Warm front—abrupt veer (usually change from southerly to westerly flow)

Cold front—abrupt veer (usually change from westerly or southwesterly to northwesterly flow)

Warm sector—westerly or southwesterly flow

Air mass

Moisture in air mass provides fuel for formation of low-pressure systems

Wind source

Geographical barriers deviate wind flow

Rocky Mountains restrict continental polar air flow

Barriers decrease wind velocity, open water preserves velocity

4. The surface wind will be determined by:

Weather system movement

Strong weather system flow creates sufficient turbulence to reach surface

Pressure

Marked gradient differences result in strong surface flow

Vertical instability at frontal surfaces increases turbulence and surface flow

Air mass

Clear cP air associated with thermal formation due to radiation heating induces turbulence and increases surface flow

Moist mTg air associated with enhanced heating, consequent to condensation, results in thunderstorm formation

Wind source and site

Cold air flowing over warm surface causes vertical instability and increases surface flow

Warm air flowing over cold surface causes vertical stability and decreases surface flow

Surface irregularity increases turbulence and surface airflow

Local thermal wind

Will appear at surface in absence of factors indicated above which bring upper airflow to surface

Requires temperature disparity of adjacent surfaces, absence of windshear due to malalignment of upper wind flow, and the induction of thermals due to surface heating

It is sensible to check the published weather maps during the several-day period prior to the race and to study with particular care the one published on the race day. The general principles of weather system movement applied to these maps will indicate the weather system that will be present during the race, the pressure gradients which will determine the upper wind flow, the air mass from which the weather system is derived, and the areas over which the wind flow has passed prior to reaching the racing area. This information can be used to determine the temperature and moisture of the airflow and the strength and direction of the upper wind flow. If the temperature disparity between air and surface results in vertical instability, or the pressure gradient is large, the upper wind flow indicated by the weather map can be expected to reach the surface. If vertical stability is present, particularly if moisture and cloud formation inhibit surface heating, and the pressure gradient is small, the upper wind may never reach the surface. The only remaining hope is then the development of a local thermal wind.

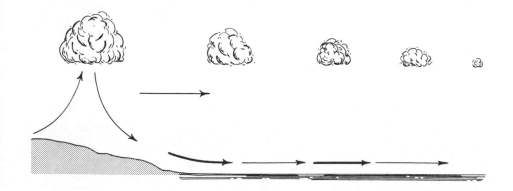

C. Clouds and Other Clues

"When the wheel is far, the storm is n'ar
When the wheel is n'ar, the storm is far."

The weather map provides sufficient information to predict the general variations in the surface winds for a day of racing. However, the usual published map is a day old when it becomes available; the forecast map, if published, is only a forecast from a vantage point twenty-four hours before the fact. It is essential to be able to interpret weather signs on the spot, on the morning of the race, just before its start, and during its course. Frequently even the weather system condition itself is in doubt: a frontal system stalls or reverses direction, a new mass of high pressure moves more rapidly than expected, a low-pressure system occludes and the sailor awakens to unexpected conditions. If he misreads the present weather conditions or blithely accepts the published forecast, his entire analysis of the local surface winds may be awry. But signs are available, clouds and other clues that indicate the weather that is operative now and will be present in the next few hours, signs that indicate (1) the weather system that is present and/or approaching, (2) the likelihood of calm, or (3) strong surface winds, and (4) the development of a new local wind. The lore of the old salt is often only pertinent to deep-sea conditions, but his techniques and his understanding are as essential to the racing sailor as they were to the officers of a China clipper.

WEATHER SYSTEM CONDITIONS

WARM FRONT APPROACHING

Cirrus (*Ci*): The first indication of the approaching warm front is the appearance of cirrus clouds, feathery streaks of ice crystals in the upper troposphere, usually above 30,000 feet. There is so little water vapor at these high altitudes that the clouds that form are thin and delicate and have no shading. They stream

with the upper-level westerlies while ice showers trail astern to fall into the uppermost levels of the weather system circulation below. These "fallstreaks" stream in line with the counterclockwise flow about the advancing low pressure and thus point to the warm sector. Cirrus clouds are formed at the upper and outermost limits of the lifting and spreading warm air which flows up and over the receding cold air at the surface. They may also be seen to the north of a low-pressure system in the absence of frontal lift and behind the cold front where they demonstrate the receding remnants of the warm air. Ahead of the warm front they appear in an otherwise clear sky moving from the west or southwest toward the east or northeast long before the first drop in pressure.

The stronger the wind aloft, the more violent will be the depression that follows. The velocity of the upper airflow is revealed by the cirrus. "Mare's tails" stream out behind the advancing cirrus as it is shredded by upper-level flow of jet stream velocity. Sharp angulation of the fallstreaks indicates that the upper-level flow is much more rapid than the mid-level flow. Jet airplane contrails are often clearly visible in the same blue sky that precipitates cirrus. Their rapid dissipation or shredding is another indication of strong upper-level flow.

Cirrostratus (*Cs*): As the warm front or low-pressure system approaches more closely the cirrus becomes a homogeneous sheet, a thin veil covering all or a major portion of the sky, known as cirrostratus. These clouds are responsible for the halos (due to refraction) about the sun or moon which so concerned the ancient mariners: "Circle around the moon, all hands go aloft full soon." They indicate that the front or the low-pressure system is close and approaching: "The bigger the ring, the nearer the wet."

Cirrocumulus (*Cc*): Small, white, flaky globular masses appear as the cirrus aggregates. This cirrocumulus cloud is distinguished from the cumulus of lower levels because it is too thin to develop shading. They often group together in a rippled or banded appearance which accounts for the designation "mackerel sky." "Mackerel sky and mare's tails make tall ships set low sails." Cirrocumulus is an unusual cloud but it tells the same story as the other cirrus—low pressure or a warm front is approaching—with just a little more urgency.

Altostratus (As): Behind the cirrus and at a slightly lower level comes the altostratus, a uniform grayish-white sheet covering all or a large portion of the sky in uniform broad bands. The sun is either obscured or shines through in a weak, watery fashion. "If the sun goes pale to bed, 'twill rain tomorrow, it is said." There may be almost a complete absence of surface shadows as the sunlight is diffused by altostratus. The lower it forms, the heavier and denser it becomes until it merges with the low-level stratus and nimbostratus.

Stratus (St): Stratus has the uniform grayish-white sheet appearance of altostratus but because it appears at a lower level is denser and darker. Ahead of an approaching warm front stratus may appear as broken, elongated patches. When it reaches the surface it is fog and on mountain slopes is indistinguishable from fog. When broken and wind-blown, stratus is called fractostratus or scud and indicates the immediate presence of the low pressure storm.

Nimbostratus (Ns): The prefix nimbus means rain and indicates that nimbostratus is stratus associated with precipitation. It is a thick, dark shapeless cloud associated with scud, an irregular undersurface, and steady precipitation, rain or snow. In its presence the barometer is falling rapidly and the front or depression has arrived. If the wind veers a warm front is passing

and improved warm sector weather is close behind. If the wind backs a depression unassociated with fronts (a tropical storm) is present or low pressure and its associated fronts are passing to the south. Then the nimbostratus may be expected to persist and the precipitation to be prolonged. "A verring wind brings clear skies: a backing wind to be despised."

WARM SECTOR

Altocumulus (*Ac*): Elliptical, globular cloud occurring at mid-levels (6500–25,000 feet) is altocumulus. The prefix "alto" is applied when a cloud form appears at a level higher than its usual position and distinguishes this cloud from the low-level cumulus. It appears in bands or groups of "sheep" or "wool-pack" clouds with moderate shading on their undersurfaces

associated with patches of clear sky. Altocumulus indicates
mid-level instability, large segments of rising warm air, characteristic of the warm sector, but is also seen to the north of
frontal systems. It is usually seen in the morning in hot weather
or in mountainous regions associated with orographic lift (lift
caused by mountains intruding upon the airstream).

Stratocumulus (*Sc*): Altocumulus may be associated with stratocumulus formation in the warm sector. The latter is arranged
in long, gray parallel bands or large, dark rolls covering all or
most of the sky. Sometimes it forms continuous sheets, vaguely
broken into irregular bands. It is darker, denser, and lower than
the associated altocumulus. It forms characteristically in stable
conditions and is particularly associated with inversions as the
warm air of the warm sector or of an mTg air mass flows over
cooler surfaces. It may form as warm, moist air aloft sinks into
the colder air below the inversion in late afternoon and evening and is added to by cumulus cloud formation consequent to
convection lift-off the following morning. When dark (indicating a large proportion of large-diameter water droplets), stratocumulus is often associated with precipitation. This cloud
usually means a light sea breeze or dead calm as it demonstrates the separation of weather system airflow from the surface.

Cumulonimbus (*Cb*): As the cold front at the western margin
of the warm sector approaches, widespread lifting occurs and
convection is stimulated. Cumulus cloud readily propagates to
form huge cumulus congestus and cumulonimbus towers. The
sky darkens, rain and thundersqualls appear intermittently.
Cumulonimbus is the largest visible structure on earth having
a vertical height in excess of eight to ten miles and a far larger
base. Its top billows into the stratosphere and is blown downwind into the shape of an anvil. Its upper portion is white, its
lower portion black and glowering. The appearance of cumulonimbus, with or without severe squalls or tornadoes, signals
the imminence of the cold front. Within a few hours after its
appearance, a bright line appears beneath the black stratus on
the western horizon, the wind strengthens and begins to veer,
and the cold front arrives.

COLD FRONT PASSAGE

Cumulus (*Cu*): The most beautiful clouds are the fair-weather cumulus which ride down the clear, blue outflow of cP air behind the cold front. These majestic white heap clouds are the consequence of convection between 2000 and 6500 feet and are dependent upon the instability of the lower air levels. They may occur in any season but are particularly prominent in the summertime when surface heating is at its maximum. These

clouds appear, survive for brief periods, and then disappear as
the air in which they are contained flows over water or under
higher cloud cover. They may form in streets aligned across
the direction of wind flow. They are indicators of turbulent
surface airflow and strong, gusty surface winds. In the presence
of cold water they are associated with the development of onshore thermal flow.

INTERPRETATIONS

Cirrus clouds streaming with the upper-level westerlies indicate
the relatively consistent direction of the wind flow at altitudes
above 20,000 feet. Altocumulus and stratocumulus form at middle
levels across (perpendicular to) the everchanging weather system wind flow. Observation of the orientation of these clouds and
the direction of their movement will reveal the direction of the
weather system airflow. Typically the surface wind is backed between 10° and 30° to the isobaric wind at mid-level due to surface friction. If the surface wind and the mid-level weather system wind are parallel or nearly so, no frontal system or depression is near.

The ten major cloud formations discussed are the signposts that indicate the nature of the weather system and the stability of the air mass involved. Many variations of these basic formations occur but recognition of the ten major types is usually sufficient to the purposes of the racing sailor. In addition to recognition of the weather system movements the clouds foretell, the sailor needs to detect the development of local winds and to determine whether the weather system wind or the local wind (or both) will reach the surface. (In other words he needs to be able to answer the six questions posed in the first chapter.)

SURFACE CALM

Surface calm can be expected when one or a combination of the following exists:

1. The pressure gradient is slight. This is characteristic of the center of a region of high pressure and is indicated by a gradual reduction in wind velocity, little temperature variation over a period of hours or days, and clear skies or stratocumulus which burns off early. More evanescent calms are present in the centers of depressions. If these are slow-moving and associated with rain, calm may persist for an entire sailing day.

2. Convergence is occurring. This may be consequent to the meeting of two simultaneous opposing wind flows, usually a local wind (sea breeze, thunderstorm, etc.) and a weather system wind. It may also be consequent to the meeting of channeled flows around an intervening obstacle. Such convergence is usually present for only a brief period at a given site, or if it persists at a given site, the affected area is small. A local zone of convergence will exist immediately to leeward of an island, peninsula, or mountain as the diverged airflow converges beyond the obstacle.

3. Stability is marked. When the air mass that occupies the area is unusually warm for the season (spring or fall, characteristically), a conduction inversion may prevent the surface air from mixing with the upper air. A layer of cold, unmoving air persists at the water surface while the warm weather system wind flows by above. Temperature disparity between water, surface air, and upper air provides the clue. If the wind offshore or onshore is composed of air warmer than the water and

thus warmer than the surface air overlying the water, no wind
will reach the surface. A stagnant pool of cold air often remains between the shores of the Chesapeake, Long Island
Sound, and the Great Lakes as warm air flows above and
neither an offshore weather system wind nor a sea breeze
reaches the surface.

4. An inversion is present. A radiation inversion isolates the
weather system airflow from the surface on most summer
nights and during the early morning and evening of most
summer days. Radiation inversions are to be expected when the
sky is clear and are present when early morning fog, dew, or
frost is evident. (Indicating that the surface air has been
cooled below its dew point.) A subsidence inversion will persist until late morning and in some areas throughout the day.
The weather system wind is then excluded from the surface
during typical racing hours and the racing sailor must rely on
sea breeze development as his only source of wind. Subsidence
is characterized by clear skies (sinking air heats by compression to dissipate cloud) or by stratus or stratocumulus
formation just beneath the inversion level.

5. Absence of surface heating. If cloud cover is total, and particularly if rain is falling, surface heating is minimal. The result is an absence of the thermal turbulence necessary to bring
upper-level, high-velocity airflow to the surface. The exclusion
of upper-level airflow by cloud cover is associated with the
absence of the surface heating that generates sea breeze development. The worst combination of all is cloud cover or rain
in the winter when (relatively) warm air overflows cold water
and a conduction inversion combines with an absence of thermal turbulence.

STRONG SURFACE WIND

Strong surface airflow can be expected when one or a combination of the following exists (conditions opposite to the circumstances which produce surface calm):

1. The pressure gradient is great. This is characteristic of the
outflow periphery of a region of high pressure and is indicated
by an abrupt change in wind velocity, an abrupt alteration in
temperature, and a dramatic change in cloud cover.

2. Channeling is occurring. This may be consequent to the simultaneous presence of two winds which are aligned or to the presence of an obstacle which deviates the wind flow into a narrowed channel. When a weather system wind is aligned with the known direction of a local wind an enhancement of surface flow should be expected. A broad flow of air parallel to the shore which passes a point protruding at right angles to the flow, or an airflow passing through a narrow channel, will be accelerated due to the compression of deviation.

3. Instability is marked. When the surface air is warm and the weather system is bringing in cold air at the upper levels and/ or when the surface is heated under clear skies in the presence of a cold airflow, thermal turbulence is enhanced and strong upper airflow is brought to the surface. Unstable conditions also aid in sea breeze generation so that either a strong weather system wind or a strong sea breeze (or both) may be expected at the surface depending chiefly upon the temperature of the offshore airflow. Instability is to be expected when the sky is clear and the air temperature cool. It is characterized by the appearance of cumulus cloud.

4. Surface heating is marked. Surface heating is associated with instability, thermal turbulence, and sea breeze formation —all stimulators of strong surface airflow. Sea breeze formation is indicated by a marked disparity between water temperature and peak daytime air temperature and by cumulus formation in a generally clear sky. The sea breeze front can be detected when the weather system flow is offshore by a line of disintegrating cumulus in the mid-level offshore-flowing portion of the seabreeze circulation. Near a large city the lower levels of the sea breeze contain the moisture and the smog of the local pollution. Then the sea breeze moves in from the sea against an offshore wind as a wall of dirty, brown fog extending a few hundred feet above the surface.

ABRUPT SURFACE WIND CHANGES

1. Thunderstorm formation is present. The appearance of a cumulus congestus, a cumulus whose base-to-top distance is greater than its base-to-surface distance is the forerunner of cumulonimbus formation. Observation of its movement will

indicate whether the mature storm cell will pass over the course. A cumulus congestus is most likely to mature late in the afternoon in the presence of marked surface heating and a moist weather system (mTg) airflow.

2. Sea breeze generation is occurring. Marked temperature disparity between water and inland surfaces (as indicated by peak daytime temperature predictions), clear skies, and a minimal weather system gradient are the antecedents of sea breeze formation. Cumulus cloud formation inland is strongly suggestive of sea breeze development. If the weather system wind is offshore, the sea breeze front is indicated by a sharp line of cumulus disintegration receding shoreward. If the weather system wind is minimal and conditions are otherwise appropriate, the sea breeze will be delayed only by a conduction inversion at the surface. If the water is very cold and the air warm, the conduction inversion may not break until late in the day. When it does break, the sea breeze comes to the surface in patches which gradually amalgamate. It is as likely to appear initially to leeward of the fleet as to windward. If a light weather system flow at a marked angle to the expected sea breeze flow is present at the surface, the sea breeze may develop at the surface to seaward, appearing as a dark line on the water, and advance slowly toward the shore displacing the weather system flow ahead of it.

3. A subsidence inversion is breaking. If the preceding evening has been clear and stratocumulus fills the sky in the morning, a subsidence inversion may be presumed to be present. Such an inversion can be expected to break between 11:00 A.M. and 12:00 noon. At this time if a sea breeze has been present, the surface wind will drop and back and then fill in again from the backed direction. As the stratocumulus burns off, patches of clear sky are associated with an increase in surface wind and a veer while a return of cloud cover is associated with a decrease in surface wind and a back. If a strong weather system wind has been present above the inversion (which is unlikely in summertime), it will appear at the surface as the inversion breaks. Then a preceding low-level sea breeze will drop and back and then alternate with the first evidences of the weather system wind.

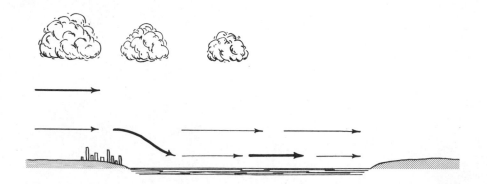

D. Navigation on the Triangle

*"First rise after a low
Squalls expect and more blow."*

The race plan provides a background for the management of the race. Once initiated, however, the plan requires constant re-evaluation. Navigation on the triangle is intended to test the appropriateness of the plan, to determine whether changes in wind or current are occurring as predicted. A plan is dangerous unless it is constantly tested. The most disastrous defeats occur when a plan is pursued in the presence of obvious evidence that its premises are in error.

The most important support for a plan is provided by previous experience in the particular racing water. Each locale has its own patterns of diurnal variation, geographic influence, and local wind generation. Only experience in the local waters can indicate the direction and timing of persistent shifts associated with onset, development, and offset of a sea breeze, for instance. The compass indicates the direction of the present wind. Whether it is backed or veered to the expected wind, whether the shift to follow will be a back or a veer, whether a shift will follow at all can only be known if the present wind can be identified. Identification depends upon the prior determination of compass headings in the same conditions. Sea breezes and other local winds always appear from the same direction and deviate thereafter in a predictable fashion. Once the range of directions characteristic of the local wind are known, a compass heading can be interpreted as a back or a veer relative to the expected wind for the particular time of day and the probable subsequent shift can be predicted. A good race plan depends upon the identification of the wind at hand. Is an onshore wind at 210° at midday backed to the expected sea breeze or fully veered? The first leg and the race depend upon the distinction.

Prior reconnaissance is essential. And the only successful prior reconnaissance is on the water in a sailboat, determining compass headings for each tack during racing hours. Evaluation during racing hours the day before is far more useful than evaluation during the hour before the race. Perhaps more useful is evaluation during an entire week before the race or during a week at the same season the previous year. The data must be recorded in a fashion that will permit it to be available later. I keep a loose-leaf notebook which includes the race plans from all previous races filed under racing area. These race plan forms indicate the wind shifts experienced in previous races (or on testing occasions) and identify them for future reference. I take them with me when I travel and study them before racing.

PAPERS TO BE TAKEN ABOARD BOAT

Carried on clipboard available for consultation during race:

1. *Duty lists*—(if crew inexperienced) for each crew member listing responsibilities and specific duties during major maneuvers, i.e. spinnaker hoist, reach to reach jibe, etc.

2. *Race plan*—partially completed prior to embarkation and added to while sailing to starting line.

3. *Race instructions*—critical items checked in advance. Carried in plastic covers taped to deck for continuous observation during race:

4. *Trim schedule*—sail trim changes and adjustments required for optimal performance in varying wind strengths

5. *Chart 1.*—marked with expected course, wind and current directions.

6. *Chart 2.*—marked with persistent shift patterns. Charts, if not provided in the Race Instructions, must be cut from a standard navigational chart to a usable size. Two charts may be needed, each inserted in a plastic cover and carried on a clipboard or taped to the deck. The first chart should be used to diagram the course, the expected wind direction and variations in current velocity and direction in the racing area. Moderate variations in wind velocity and direction in the area may be included on a plastic overlay of the same chart. The recording of excessive data on one chart may interfere with its usefulness, however; if major persistent shifts are expected, a second chart and overlay should be used to record them. Geographic shifts may be indicated on the overlay (or directly on the chart) in vector form in their expected location. New wind flows affecting the entire racing area should be indicated by a vector alongside the original wind vector. If a persistent shift is expected to occur at a particular time, the time should be recorded alongside the vector.

FACTORS TO BE RECORDED BEFORE THE START

(Headings on embossed tape permanently fixed to the deck are excellent reminders of the need to record this data. A wax pencil may be used to record erasable data on a fiberglass deck or on a white-painted segment of the centerboard trunk, or adhesive tape may be used and later removed in toto. Observations should be made during the hour before the race in the racing area.)

1. *Compass headings for each tack*—maximum back and maximum veer as well as the median heading for each tack should be recorded.

2. *The compass course for each leg*—as provided by the race committee or interpreted from the chart. (It is wise to attempt a short sail at each of the reaching angles to determine the optimal sail combinations and trim.)

3. *Jibing angles for the run*—the compass course for the run, the dead downwind direction and the optimum jibing directions (20°, or such other angle as considered optimum, from the rhumb line).

4. *Time of current change*—if in tidal waters—with current direction and velocity.

5. *Alerts*—indications of persistent shifts, new winds, thunderstorms, etc. (from Chart 2).

RANGE OF HEADINGS, EACH TACK	
Starboard	*Port*
110°–125°–140°	200°–215°–230°

BEARINGS FROM MARK TO MARK		
Beat	*Reach*	*Reach*
150°	15°	285°

EXPECTED JIBE HEADINGS		
Port Jibe	*Run*	*Starboard Jibe*
310°	330°	350°

Alerts

Starboard Tack	145°-Veer
Velocity Drop	11:00 a.m.

The recording of data not only permits its instant recovery during the race but serves to remind the helmsman to consider the major determinants of racing success in his race plan. It is usually better to record these data in large letters on a portion of the deck clearly visible to the helmsman (or navigator or both) rather than on the race plan form. At the conclusion of the race the significant data should be transferred to the race plan form for future reference. *"Alerts"* are the most significant recordings and serve as warning signals when a major strategic factor is changing. If a veer from a sea breeze is expected but a back is possible, as the onshore wind reorganizes beneath an inversion breakthrough, the compass headings which suggest such changes should be recorded under *"Alert."* Starboard tack may have varied between 110° and 130° during the hour prior to the start. A back to 105° or a veer to 135° may then be *"Alerts"* that indicate the development of a persistent back or a persistent veer and should be recorded as such. The factor (or factors) which is considered to be the major determinant of the outcome of the race should be indicated under *"Alert"* by the signal which is expected to reveal it. Negative signals are equally important. If headings or other factors actually observed during the race are outside expected limits, an unexpected phenomenon may be occurring.

Its recognition when an expected *"Alert"* signal fails to develop will permit avoidance of disaster and early acquisition of a new advantage.

DECISIONS TO BE MADE BEFORE THE START

1. Sail trim for beat—all adjustments (compatible with starting maneuvers) made in advance

2. Spinnaker gear for first reach—sheets, halyard, pole, sail, etc. arranged appropriately

3. Spinnaker (or other special sail) selection for each downwind leg—sails stowed appropriately

4. Starting plan—approach, timing, line position, tack, means of reaching preferred side of beat

5. Upwind plan—preferred side of beat, major tack, distance from rhumb line before tacking back, time expected to be spent before reaching layline

NAVIGATION ON THE COURSE

Data collection should be relegated to members of the crew, each of whom should be assigned specific responsibilities. If the helmsman is preoccupied with data collection, he will be unable to maintain optimal boat speed and be handicapped in making strategic decisions. Appropriate information should be fed to him continuously without his having to ask for it and without his having to respond to it. No other conversation should be occurring during a significant race. The crew should be sufficiently knowledgeable that they are not surprised by the decisions which result from data collection; they should not expect explanations. Good crews collect data, furnish it to the skipper, and respond to orders. Skippers, unused to such behavior, make poor crews.

1. *Boat speed to windward:* One crew member (if more than one is available) should be primarily responsible for data collection, reporting, and trim adjustments connected with boat speed.

   a. *Observation of neighboring boats*—"460 to leeward is pointing slightly higher, moving slightly slower. 310 to windward is lifting—appears to be in a different wind," etc., etc.

b. *Wind velocity calls*—"12 knots steady, 12 knots, dropping 10 knots, light spot 6 to 8 knots," etc., etc.

c. *Sail trim*—"Easing jib sheet for motor boat wake, dropping to 6 to 8 knots, easing Cunningham and jib tack downhaul, easing jib traveler for gust," etc., etc.

The final determinant of boat speed must be made by observation of comparative performance with other boats. In many situations it is useful deliberately to stay with other boats and to give them clear air so as to obtain a guide to optimal sail trim. It is easy to fail to recognize changes in wind velocity and as a result to fail to alter sail trim when a change occurs. Continuous calling of wind velocity changes by one responsible crew member is the only means of avoiding this problem. If the crew member is talented he may be able to make velocity judgments without an instrument. On a small boat a hand-held anemometer is extremely useful, probably the second most important instrument on a racing sailboat (after the compass). Major decisions referable to sail trim should be made by the skipper, based upon the data (re other boats and wind velocity) received. Some adjustments which require almost constant modification (such as luff tension) may be assigned to a crew member. The skipper should be able to make traveler adjustments easily himself. He should order (or accomplish) backstay, mast bend, outhaul, mainsheet, jib sheet, and jib lead adjustments in the light of data collected and tactical and strategic requirements.

2. *Strategic considerations to windward:* One crew member (if more than one is available) should be primarily responsible for data collection and reporting connected with strategic decisions.

a. *Compass calls*—"120, 122, 120, 120, 124, 128, 130," etc., etc.

b. *Competitors*—"312 to leeward has tacked to starboard. We can cross her by a boat's length," etc., etc.

c. *Mark*—"The weather mark is at 2 o'clock between the white house and the blue powerboat. We've been on starboard for 12 minutes. We are within a few hundred yards of the layline," etc., etc.

d. *Alert's*—"We're up to 135. This is an alert for a persistent veer.—The velocity has dropped to 6 knots. This is an alert for the development of the sea breeze," etc., etc.

To be useful the compass must be read continuously. The skipper can only make meaningful decisions if he knows the full pattern of direction variations. He should not have to wait until a major shift becomes obvious but should recognize its continuous development. The common major tactical disasters are fouling out, port-starboard, and overstanding. Continuous information regarding other boats and early finding of the weather mark are the best insurance against these disasters. On long courses, in fog, or when a variety of marks are confusing, calculation of time spent per tack relative to the expected length of the beat may prevent overstanding. Someone must be assigned the responsibility. "*Alerts*" are valuable and good reminders, but they are of limited value written on the deck; someone must call attention to the previously determined signals which indicate major strategic changes.

3. *Strategic considerations on reaches:* The crew member responsible for strategic considerations should continue this responsibility on the reaches.
   a. *Compass calls* (prior to reaching the weather mark)— "The course will be 340°. The wind has backed 10°. We want to go high initially. The reach will be tight," etc., etc.
   b. *Competitors*—"510 is attempting to pass to windward. 360 and 410 are bearing away to leeward. 410 is gaining," etc., etc.
   c. *Mark*—"We're on the mark. We're above the rhumb line. I have a range—we're being set to weather of the rhumb line," etc., etc.
   d. *Course*—"The wind is backing. The next reach will be broader than we expected. This is an alert for a persistent back. The channeling we expected is present. We should take starboard tack initially on the second beat," etc., etc.

On the second and third beats the same assignments for boat speed and strategic responsibilities should be continued. At the end of the second reach an estimate should be made of the relationship of the wind to the median wind expected. Is there an oscillation or a persistent veer or back? Which tack will be favored initially? Which tack will be the major tack? Will the layline be significantly shifted? The compass should be called immediately and regularly at the start of

the second beat. If the wind has shifted a new median wind
may exist and should be recorded for future reference.

4. *Strategic considerations on the run:* The crew member responsible for strategic considerations should continue this
responsibility on the run. Prior to arriving at the weather
mark the major jibe should be determined and the boat prepared to assume this jibe shortly after rounding the mark. The
spinnaker pole is set for an optimal sailing angle and the spinnaker trimmed appropriately. The boat is then sailed on a
varied course which keeps the spinnaker trim appropriate to
the changing apparent wind.
   a. *Compass calls*—"The course is 240°. We are sailing 260°–
   262°–265°. We are lifting. 270°—This may be the persistent veer we were expecting," etc., etc.
   b. *Competitors*—"All competitors have jibed toward the shift.
   If we jibe now we will be outside and to leeward of them
   all. 430 is crossing astern attempting to get on our wind,"
   etc., etc.
   c. *Mark*—"We are sailing 240°. The mark bears 205°. We are
   approaching the port jibe layline. The current will sweep
   us toward the mark," etc., etc.

The skipper must arrange in advance for the collection of the
data he wants and for its reporting in the manner he wants. He
must be able to refer to the previously recorded data—recorded
headings on deck, plastic-covered chart—to ascertain the significance of the data. He must update the data as persistent shifts appear and reorganize his interpretation of compass headings. Data
collection prevents the disaster of fouls, overstanding, failure to
recognize persistent shifts. Strategic gains, however, are made by
synthesis of the data into a plan. The skipper must reserve the au-
thority to make final decisions based upon *his* interpretation of the
data. He (presumably) is the best qualified to decide if a set of circumstances indicates an oscillating or a persistent shift. He coor-
dinates data collection with a knowledge of the significance of time,
cloud formations, distance from shore, velocity changes, and a prior
knowledge of local wind patterns—and he decides the course.

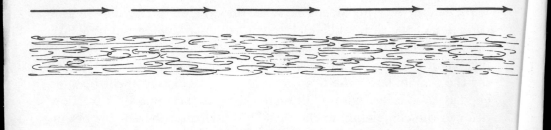

E. Formula for Success

"No one surely pays his debt
As wet to dry and dry to wet."

The management of wind shifts to windward and to leeward is the major strategic determinant of success in sailboat racing. The purpose of this book has been to provide the insight that will permit the reader to manage wind shifts in an appropriate manner on the majority of occasions. No amount of understanding will permit the correct prediction of a wind shift on every occasion, however. Therefore it is essential to establish certain rules which, if followed *when there is doubt,* will result in the greatest frequency of success referable to the majority of competitors. Consistent and reproducible success in each race relative to the majority, not occasional victory in a single race, is the determinant of series success.

Risks are inherent in sailboat racing and therein lies the excitement. If the outcome were predictable and dependent entirely upon boat speed, few would participate. Two major circumstances exist which, dependent upon the nature of the wind shift, require totally opposite solutions. If the shift is an oscillating one, the immediately

desirable tack is the one away from the direction of shift; if the shift is a persistent one the immediately desirable tack is the one toward the direction of shift. If the shift is an oscillating one and a series of shifts is expected to follow, the ideal course is close to the rhumb line avoiding the laylines to the last possible moment. If the shift is a persistent one the ideal course is directly to the layline in the direction of the shift and a tack toward the mark along the new layline. Risk is inherent in the inability of the helmsman to recognize in a given instance whether a given shift is persistent (will persist for the remainder of the beat or run) or is oscillating (will be succeeded by one or more additional shifts in the opposite direction prior to the completion of the beat). And risk is inherent in the inability of the skipper to recognize whether a series of oscillating shifts may not have some persistent tendency to deviate from the previously determined median (i.e., whether a persistent shift is superimposed upon the oscillations). Oscillating shifts may be ignored with little loss; persistent shifts cannot be.

CONSERVATISM—TACKING HALFWAY

Often a single persistent shift is evident during a given beat which, with or without associated oscillating shifts, is clearly decisive. The less experienced the fleet, the more likely becomes the possibility of a big win by a boat which alone takes the ideal course toward such a persistent shift. In large fleets of competent helmsmen success is more likely to derive from a conservative course on each beat, one which minimizes the possibility of loss rather than maximizes the possibility of gain. In some racing areas the only shifts are oscillating ones, or there is a clearly predictable persistent shift which most boats can be expected to handle correctly. Strategy in these areas is predetermined. In other areas, such as Long Island Sound and the Chesapeake, persistent shifts are frequent and difficult to predict. In these circumstances it is essential that beats be sailed conservatively in a manner consistent with an accurate assessment of the inherent possible gains or losses.

The principles governing the risks are as follows:

1. The least gain or loss by one boat relative to another resulting from a given shift occurs when each is on the rhumb line and the greatest gain or loss from a given shift occurs when each is farthest from the rhumb line (closest to the opposite laylines).

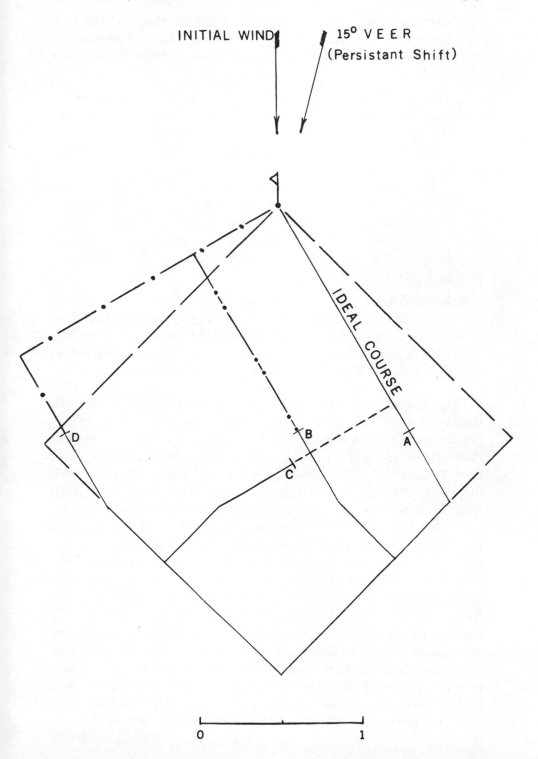

INITIAL WIND   15° VEER
(Persistant Shift)

IDEAL COURSE

D   B   A
C

0   1

2. The maximum gain or loss occurs when one boat on the tack toward the shift reaches the new layline (the layline after the shift) at the time of the shift and the other is on the opposite old layline.

3. The greater the shift the lesser the distance that must be sailed toward it to achieve the maximum gain, i.e., the sooner the new layline is reached. In a 30° shift the new layline is reached by a boat continuing halfway to the original layline. In such a shift a boat proceeding beyond halfway loses progressively. A 45° shift means that boats are on the layline at the start or at the leeward mark and all boats proceeding toward the shift are overstanding. In such a shift or even a slightly lesser shift the preferred initial tack is *away* from the shift as boats on this tack will be ahead and to leeward on the major tack just below the layline.

4. A smaller shift results in a lesser gain or loss and justifies a closer approach to the layline. It is never justifiable to sail all the way to the layline without tacking, however, as on the final approach tack the advantageous position for any subsequent shift is ahead and to leeward, below the layline.

The diagram indicates the relative gains or losses of boats assuming four different courses which subsequently experience a 15° persistent shift. Boat A sails the ideal course: she proceeds toward the shift and receives it precisely when she reaches the new layline. Boat D sails the worst possible course proceeding from the start directly toward the port-tack layline away from the shift. Boat B sails a compromise course—toward the shift initially but back toward the rhumb line (and away from the shift) when halfway to the layline. Boat C also sails a compromise course but in the opposite direction: away from the shift initially and back toward the rhumb line when halfway to the layline. If we presume the weather leg to be 1.5 miles in length, the maximum gain possible from a 15° persistent shift—the difference between the lengths of the courses sailed by boats A and D—is .37 miles. If the boat sailing away from the shift initially (boat C) takes a conservative tack back when halfway to the layline, she reduces her loss by 33 percent to .25 miles. Relative to another conservative boat which tacks back halfway after initially sailing toward the shift (boat B), boat C's loss is reduced to .17 miles. The loss incurred by the boat which proceeds toward the shift initially but tacks back (boat B) relative to boat A which continues to the new layline is but .11 miles.

The boat that tacks back from her initial tack halfway to the layline reduces her chance of loss to almost all other boats. If she has selected the appropriate tack toward the shift, she gains less than she would have had she continued to the new layline and less than boats who continue beyond her toward that new layline. But she gains on all other boats, all those who sail away from the shift and all those who tack back from the advantageous tack sooner than she. She will also gain or lose relatively little to any boats which continue the initial tack beyond the new layline and thus. overstand. As only a few boats will continue beyond her to the new layline (and not beyond) she will gain on the vast majority of the fleet. If she has selected the tack away from the shift she will lose progressively the farther she continues that tack. She will reduce her loss dramatically as soon as she tacks back (if the shift has yet to arrive). If she tacks back when halfway to the layline she will have reduced her loss relative to the few boats which continue toward the shift and reach the new layline by 33 percent. She will gain relative to all boats continuing on the tack away from the shift and reduce her loss relative to boats which tack back early from the tack away and those which tack back early from the tack toward the shift. A boat which continues all the way to the new layline on the preferred tack can only gain approximately one-tenth of a mile on a boat on the same initial tack which tacks back halfway, but she can lose three-eighths of a mile to a boat which has sailed to the new layline on the opposite tack if the shift goes the other way.

Even when a helmsman is quite confident that he is sailing in the right direction toward a persistent shift, there is so little to be gained and so much to be lost by continuing beyond halfway to the layline that it is rarely justified. When he is anything less than confident that he is sailing toward a shift (and shifts are likely) he is assuming an intolerable risk to continue beyond halfway. Most persistent shifts are less than 30° and therefore halfway is unlikely to result in overstanding. If greater shifts are probable, proceeding even halfway to the layline before tacking is unwarranted. In series racing one is bound to be on the wrong side of the course occasionally. More is sometimes lost by continuing too far in the wrong direction on one beat in one race than is gained by continuing beyond halfway in all the others.

FOLLOW THE LEADER

If a persistent shift occurs, or some boats receive an oscillating or geographic shift which others do not, alertness to the position and headings of one's competitors is essential. Some competitors, advertently or otherwise, will obtain an advantage from such shifts. The difference between recovery and disaster may then depend upon how soon the advantage is detected and how soon those who gain are followed (or proceeded). Any continuance of a tack away from a progressive persistent shift increases the loss, so that an immediate response is essential.

Alertness is thus the secret of success. Just after the start one must get his head out of the bilge and his eyes off the compass to watch the boats going off on the opposite tack. It is easy to see a shift developing once out on the course after the fleet spreads out but difficult to detect it in the melee of the start and the confusion of involvement with neighboring boats. A good solution is to tack toward the middle of the course after the start, on port from the port end, or on starboard from the starboard end, of the line. This avoids excessive movement away from a shift in either direction. Port tack provides the real advantage, a break away from the pack and a good view of boats moving in either direction. Once on port a move to follow a shift on either side of the course can readily be accomplished. The theme of the first part of the initial weather leg must be: Get out where you can see and cover.

Successful racing to windward in persistent shifts or in oscillating shifts on short legs depends upon observing the progress of one's competitors early in the leg. If boats on the same tack are pointing higher, tack; if boats on the opposite tack are pointing lower, i.e., greater than 90° to one's own course, tack. This technique results in sailing a lifted tack compared to the opposition early in the leg and covers the opponents who are most likely to gain subsequently. If course alterations by competitors are detected immediately, first leg disasters can be avoided.

AHEAD AND TO LEEWARD NEAR THE LAYLINE

Two of the most important tactical principles of windward sailing are in direct conflict when a major persistent shift appears. If the theoretically ideal "inside, to windward of the fleet" position is

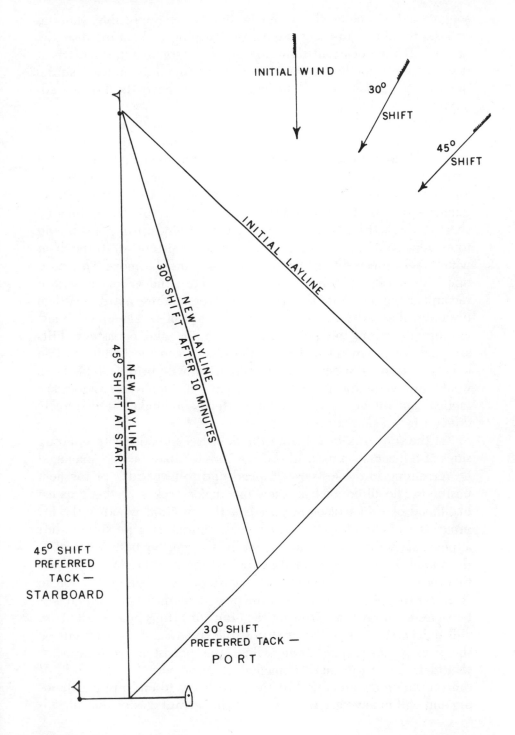

INITIAL WIND

30°
SHIFT

45°
SHIFT

INITIAL LAYLINE

30° SHIFT NEW LAYLINE AFTER 10 MINUTES

45° SHIFT AT START NEW LAYLINE

45° SHIFT
PREFERRED
TACK —
STARBOARD

30° SHIFT
PREFERRED TACK —
PORT

sought and is achieved on the layline, it is impossible simultaneously to adhere to the principle of "keeping to leeward near the layline." If the persistent shift is large or progressive, particularly if it occurs early in the leg, or if any oscillating shift appears subsequently, boats "ahead and to leeward" may have the greater advantage.

Strategic advantage is determined by the position of the boat relative to the "new" layline, the layline at the termination of the leg. If the tack toward the persistent shift results in overstanding then the attempt to sail toward the shift has been carried to excess and boats on the layline to leeward ("ahead and to leeward") have gained more. If the tack toward the persistent shift is terminated short of the layline, boats on the layline to windward ("inside and to windward") have gained more. In a persistent shift the boat which tacks precisely on the new layline gains the most. This position is difficult to gauge from afar and there is never any means of recouping the loss from the windward-overstanding position. When in doubt, therefore, an early tack to leeward of the layline, is most appropriate. From this position a further lift (and persistent shifts are likely to progress) will bring the boat up to the layline (while a header from a superimposed oscillation will bring all boats to weather down in line astern). The leeward position also provides the tactical advantage of the lee-bow effect and makes it extremely difficult for a competitor to get past.

At the start of a beat before the fleet has spread out to opposite sides of the course, a marked shift of 30°–45° may be best managed by remaining in the lee bow ("ahead and to leeward") of the fleet position. The lifted tack is then the major tack and the greatest likelihood of gain will be acquired in this position whether the lift progresses or the old wind (a header) returns. If a persistent shift appears after the fleet is farther out on the leg, boats to leeward of the rhumb line are positioned far below the new layline. They are then best advised to comply with the standard recommendation to "tack for the new wind" toward the persistent shift before their loss becomes even greater. Crossing the "fan" of lifting boats at its base will reduce the loss to the least possible. Boats already well out on the side of the course from which the persistent shift appears should tack for the mark immediately they perceive the shift. If they continue toward the shift they are likely to end up overstanding and will in any case relinquish all the advantages of the "ahead-

and-to-leeward" position (which they could have had) as they sail down the major tack near the layline.

The immediate, reflexive response of any sailor who perceives a new wind that will cause a signficant persistent shift should be to tack immediately toward that wind. Such a tack achieved ahead of the competition may provide victory if it positions the boat inside and to windward of the fleet but to leeward of the layline—the ideal position from which to manage the sea breeze "fan," or the bend in the river, or the refracted wind near the shore. But if such a tack positions the boat on the layline (or beyond it), or if the shift progresses so that at the termination of the leg the boat is above the layline, then all boats to leeward will gain and those ahead and to leeward will win. Go for the new wind: but don't go too far!

One condition modifies this general rule. If the layline lies along the edge of a zone of persistent geographic shift (near a shore, for instance) or a zone of new wind development (the sea breeze progressing under an offshore weather system wind), it is essential to sail well into the shifted wind before tacking even at the risk of overstanding. Tacking early to insure an "ahead-and-to-leeward" position may in these circumstances result in the leeward boat's sailing out of the shift, unable to lay the mark which the windward boat lifts up to lay easily. The fundamental rule when two winds are present simultaneously, of course, is to seek advantageous position in whichever wind is operative at the next mark.

SUMMARY

If an understanding of wind conditions permits an accurate prediction of a persistent shift, an immediate tack should be taken in the direction from which it is expected. The race should be sailed in accordance with the principles governing the management of persistent shifts presented in the chapter "The Utilization of Wind Shifts." The strategy of the beat will be to sail toward the expected shift and a race-winning advantage may be obtained. If the airflow is unstable and oscillating shifts are to be expected, the race should be sailed in accordance with the principles governing the management of oscillating shifts and the strategy of the beat will be to keep to the lifted tack. Persistent shifts due to the development of ocean sea breezes, channeling, or refraction are often accurately predictable as to both location and time. Unfortunately in many areas and in many races persistent shifts (which may or may not be associated with oscillating shifts) cannot be accurately predicted. In many racing areas a persistent shift in either direction is possible but unpredictable. In most racing areas the timing of a persistent shift is uncertain and the likelihood of its appearance during a particular beat is undeterminable. In *these* circumstances a "formula for success" is needed which will provide the least possibility of major loss and the maximum possibility of gain regardless of the direction, time, or location of a persistent shift.

A FORMULA FOR SUCCESS
(particularly applicable to large fleets)

STARTING

In light air:

(1) Start at the end of the line and/or away from other boats—on starboard from the port end, tacking to port from the starboard end—moving away from the fleet and away from the rhumb line.

(2) Continue the tack until a return tack toward the rhumb line to cover will provide clear air across the mass of the fleet.

In moderate air:

(1) Start at one end of the line but close to other boats—on starboard from the starboard end, on port or tacking to port (as soon as possible) from the port end—moving toward the rhumb line.

(2) Continue the starboard tack from the starboard end or the port tack from the port end until upwind of the opposite end of the line. From this vantage point evaluate the distribution and heading of the competitors to determine the tack on which to continue.

In heavy air:

(1) Start away from other boats, usually at a moderate distance from the upwind end of the line or in the middle of the line when the favored side of

the course is in doubt (to avoid the necessity of an early tack)—moving at maximum speed—to obtain clear air away from the rhumb line.

(2) Continue the initial tack until the majority of the fleet is on the opposite tack or until halfway to the layline.

EARLY IN THE
WINDWARD LEG
In all winds:

(1) Watch other boats (and other wind indicators) at the extremities of the course to detect the appearance of a persistent shift.

(2) Watch the compass to determine whether a shift beyond the range of previous oscillations is occurring.

(3) Tack immediately toward any persistent shift revealed by (1) or (2).

LATER IN THE
WINDWARD LEG
If no persistent
shift has appeared:

(1) Tack back toward the rhumb line at or prior to the halfway position to the layline.

(2) Assume such a tack back toward the rhumb line so as to be ahead and to leeward of the majority of competitors who were previously on the same tack (between them and the rhumb line).

(3) Tack back toward the same layline or continue across the rhumb line so as to be astern and to windward or dead to windward of the majority of competitors.

(4) Continue to cross from side to side of the rhumb line, keeping nearer to the rhumb line than the majority of the competitors (or significant competitors).

(5) Keep alert to the possibility of a persistent shift (watch other boats and compass) and tack toward it immediately after its detection.

LATE IN THE   (1) Tack so as to be ahead and to lee-
WINDWARD LEG   ward of the majority of competitors
Near the layline: on or near the layline.
                       (2) Keep alert to the possibility of a per-
                            sistent shift occurring in a zone at or
                            just beyond the layline and assume
                            or continue the tack toward it (if the
                            windward mark lies within it) over-
                            standing slightly if necessary to reach
                            it.

The possibility of strategic gain is directly proportional to the possibility of strategic loss. The farther one sails from the rhumb line or the farther one separates from the remainder of the fleet, the greater is the possibility of gain and the greater is the possibility of loss. Ultimately the risks taken should be equated to the need. What placing in the race is sufficient to series victory? How many places must be gained to achieve that placing? Can the single place to be gained by a particular course of action justify the possible loss of several places which may result? Separation from the rhumb line and the fleet should be sufficient to accomplish the task at hand. When in the lead no separation is justified; when far back in the fleet a single tack to the layline is appropriate. Don't be greedy; take what you've got when you've got it. Tack back whenever the fleet to weather falls in line astern *and* whenever the fleet to weather starts to lift. On the first beat set your sights on fifth or sixth so as to avoid first leg disasters—the major determinant of race disasters. On subsequent beats and runs pick the advantageous side of the course and sail slightly, but only slightly farther, to the preferred side of the course than the competition. Once in good position, let your opponents make the mistakes. Sail fast and conservatively. The risk of loss may outweigh the chance of gain if the strategic decision is in doubt.

Glossary

Adiabatic lapse rate—the rate of change in temperature of a mass of lifted or sinking air associated with its expansion or compression with change in altitude (1°C./100M.).

Advection—the horizontal movement of air, the wind.

Air mass—a large segment of the atmosphere with the same weather properties, temperature, humidity, and stability, throughout.

Altocumulus—a fleecy, mid-level heap cloud larger than those that comprise cirrocumulus.

Altostratus—a mid-level layer cloud, grayish or bluish in color and usually covering the whole sky.

Anabatic wind—a wind that flows upslope because the surface air along the slope becomes warmer and less dense than the air at a distance from the slope surface.

Apparent wind—the wind observed from a boat underway. Apparent wind can be represented by a vector resultant from the vectors of the true wind, the wind due to the boat's motion, and the current wind, if any.

Approach tack—the tack that is headed toward and will terminate at the mark, the shore, or other specified object.

Arctic air mass—a mass of air that originated in the Arctic.

Atmospheric envelope—the body of air that envelopes the earth. The atmosphere is thicker (less dense) at the equator than it is at the poles.

Axial flow—surface airflow channeled parallel to the long axis of an enclosed body of water.

Back—a counter-clockwise shift in wind direction.

Barrier—an obstruction to wind flow (usually referring to a surface protrusion along the shoreline).

Bermuda high—the semipermanent high situated in the middle of the North Atlantic Ocean from late spring until early fall. A subtropical high is caused by downward flowing air from convergence in the upper atmosphere.

Blanketing—the reduction and disturbance in wind flow to leeward of a barrier.

Buoyancy—the tendency of a given mass of air to perpetuate the lifting or sinking of a vertically moving segment of air, associated with a lapse rate higher than the adiabatic.

Calm—the absence of wind flow at the surface.

Channeling—the deviation of a surface wind parallel to a shoreline.

Circulation—the vertical or horizontal circle of air or water movement which permits the maintenance of a pressure gradient and continuance of flow.

Cirrostratus—a high-altitude, whitish veil of ice cloud associated with a halo about the sun.

Cirrus—a high-altitude delicate, fibrous ice cloud, white and silky in appearance.

Col—a ridge between two high-pressure centers.

Cold front—the boundary line between cold and warm air when cold air is invading warmer territory and lifting the warm air ahead.

Compression—the increase in density of a mass of air consequent to its sinking, associated with an increase in temperature.

Condensation (cloud formation)—the process by which water vapor is converted to its liquid form (water droplets) associated with the release of heat (the latent heat of condensation) and the heating of the surrounding air.

Condensation nuclei—small particles of chemicals, dust, or salt, that attract and cause the condensation of water vapor. As more and more of these microscopic droplets join together they form raindrops. Atmospheric ice crystals are especially effective as condensation nuclei.

Continental polar (cP) air—dry, cold sinking air derived from the high-pressure air mass that accumulates over the plains of Northern Canada and produces the clear, cold northwesterly outflow.

Convection—vertical air movement (usually considered in meteorology to imply updraft).

Convergence—the "coming together" of air in a horizontal plane. Surface calm and vertical airflow result.

Converging shoreline—a shoreline which with distance downwind deviates toward and deviates the surface wind toward the median wind direction. A converging wind flows parallel to a converging shoreline.

Cool (current, airflow)—an air or water mass cooler than its surroundings.

Coriolis force—an apparent force caused by the rotation of the earth from west to east. Winds and currents that would normally flow in a straight line are deflected to the right in the Northern Hemisphere (veered) and to the left in the Southern Hemisphere (backed).

Crest—the forward-moving portion of orbiting water at the top of the wave.

Cumulonimbus—a low- to high-altitude, black heap cloud caused by strong thermal uplift and associated with thunderstorms or squalls.

Cumulus—a low-altitude, white billowy heap cloud associated with high pressure, otherwise clear skies and thermal turbulence.

Cyclone—convergent airflow associated with low pressure.

Dew point—the temperature to which air must be cooled to cause saturation and condensation.

Divergence—the horizontal outward movement of air that results at the surface beneath a descending column.

Diverging shoreline—a shoreline that with distance downwind deviates away and deviates the surface wind away from the median wind direction. A diverging wind flows parallel to a diverging shoreline.

Doldrums—a belt of calm or light winds in the Equatorial Convergence Zone.

Downdraft—a descending current associated with convection which brings high-velocity, veered upper airflow to the surface.

Drainage wind—a cold surface flow which drains down from an upland plateau through surrounding air which has a high lapse rate.

Expansion—the decrease in density of a mass of air consequent to its lifting, associated with a decrease in temperature.

Equatorial Convergence Zone—a broad band near the equator where the trade winds of the Northern and Southern Hemisphere meet.

Evaporation (cloud dissolution)—the process by which liquid water is converted to its gaseous form (water vapor) associated with the acquisition of heat by the water and cooling of the surrounding air.

Fog—minute water droplets suspended in the surface air that reduce visibility—stratus cloud at the surface. Classified by cause as radiation, conduction, orographic, or advection fog.

Front—the boundary line between two air masses of different density.

Gradient wind (weather system wind)—the wind which flows in response to the pressure gradient induced by weather system (high or low) development.

Gust—the horizontal outflow resulting from a convection downdraft. A gust cell travels with the speed of the mean wind and is composed of both a downdraft and an updraft.

Gyral—the circular circulation characteristic of the global currents in each major ocean.

Header (heading shift)—a shift in wind direction toward the direction the boat is heading.

Headed jibe—the jibe that is affected by a header, which may, while keeping the same sailing angle, permit the boat to deviate more in line with the median wind.

Headed tack—the tack that is affected by a header, which forces the boat to point away from the median wind.

High, or high-pressure area—a large mass of sinking air that is denser and has a higher barometric pressure than the surrounding air. A high is normally circular or oval-shaped, and its vertical cross-section is shaped like a dome. Air diverges outward at the surface beneath a high.

Humidity—the amount of water vapor in the air.

Instability—temperature distribution of the atmosphere in which cold air overlies warm. The lapse rate is high (greater than the adiabatic) and buoyancy is present.

Inversion—an abrupt reversal of the usual vertical temperature gradient (lapse rate) so that warm air lies above cold. A conduction inversion is consequent to contact of the surface air with a cold underlying water surface. A radiation inversion is consequent to contact of the surface air with a cold underlying land surface which has cooled due to nocturnal radiation. An advection inversion is consequent to the horizontal flow (advection) of warm air over cold surface air. A subsidence inversion is consequent to the heating (by compression) of subsiding air above a cold layer of surface air (particularly marine air).

Isobar—a line on a weather map connecting points of equal pressure.

Isotherm—a line connecting points of equal temperature (usually referable to a body of water).

Jet stream—a narrow band of strong winds in the upper air above 30,000 feet. Usually stronger than 50 knots and sometimes stronger than 200 knots.

Katabatic—a wind that flows downslope because the surface air along the slope is colder and denser than the air at a distance from the slope surface.

Lake breeze—a local onshore wind due to the temperature disparity between the heated, surrounding land and the cool surface of a lake.

Land breeze—an offshore flow of cold surface air from cold land toward warmer water.

Lapse rate—the change in temperature with altitude. The normal lapse rate is a regular reduction in temperature with height (.66°C./ 100M.).

Latent heat of condensation—the heat emitted when water vapor is condensed into liquid droplets.

Layline—the course which permits a close-hauled boat to clear the weather mark in the existing wind. The "new layline" is the course which permits a close-hauled boat to clear the weather mark after a wind shift.

Lift (lifting shift)—a shift in wind direction away from the direction the boat is heading.

Lifting—the elevation of a mass of air caused by its impinging upon cold air (frontal lift), a mountain (orographic lift), or another surface airflow moving in the opposite direction (convergence) or by heating of the underlying surface (thermal lift).

Lifted jibe—the jibe that is affected by a lift which requires the boat in order to keep the same sailing angle, to deviate away from the median wind.

Lifted tack—the tack that is affected by a lift, which permits the boat to point closer to the median wind.

Low-level—the segment of the troposphere, its winds and clouds (stratus and cumulus) which are typically present below an altitude of 6500 ft. When referable to the sea breeze, the backed, low-velocity lower portion of the onshore flow.

Low pressure (cyclone, depression)—a weather system characterized by rising air, counterclockwise circulation (in the Northern Hemisphere) and precipitation about a center of reduced pressure.

Lull—a transient reduction in surface wind velocity, typically present at the base of an updraft.

Marine layer—the lowest level of the troposphere overlying the ocean surface, usually the lowest 1000–2000 feet that moves ashore beneath a subsidence inversion.

Maritime polar Atlantic (mPa) air—moist, cold sinking air derived from the high-pressure mass that accumulates over the North Atlantic and occasionally is drawn into continental circulation ahead of a cP high.

Maritime polar Pacific (mPp) air—moist, cool, sinking air derived from the high-pressure mass that accumulates over the North Pacific, periodically comes ashore in the Pacific Northwest and occasionally migrates across the continent.

Maritime tropical Gulf (mTg) air—moist, warm sinking air derived from the high-pressure mass that accumulates over the Gulf of Mexico and produces the warm southerly (or southwesterly) outflow typical of the east coast summer.

Median wind—the wind that flows at the median direction between the extreme range of its shifts.

Mid-level—the segment of the troposphere, its winds and clouds (alto), that are typically present between 6500 and 20,000 feet.

Moisture content—the amount of water vapor contained in a mass of air that determines its dew point and its latent heat of condensation.

New wind—a wind from a new source that appears during or following the presence of an existing wind.

Nimbo-stratus—a low altitude sheetlike layer cloud from which rain is falling.

Norther—a cold winter wind from the northerly quadrants that appears along the northern Gulf Coast when the outflow from a continental polar air mass appears.

Occlusion, or occluded front—the end result of a cold front overtaking a warm front.

Optimal sailing angle—the sailing angle (usually referring to a running angle) that permits the greatest speed.

Orographic—induced by mountains, as orographic fog, orographic lifting, orographic cloud.

Oscillating shift—a shift in wind direction which is followed by a return shift to the original direction prior to completion of the weather leg.

Outflow—the peripheral surface divergence of airflow away from a dome of high pressure, most pronounced at the first appearance of the high pressure.

Overstanding—an approach tack that clears the weather mark by a greater distance than necessary consequent to sailing beyond the layline on the previous tack.

Persistent shift—a shift in wind direction that is not followed by a return shift to the original wind direction prior to completion of the weather leg.

Polar front—the line of meeting between polar and tropical air masses in the temperate zones associated with frontal disturbances and cyclone formation.

Polar highs—anticyclones formed when air of the general upper circulation cools and descends near the poles.

Pressure—the weight of the column of air above a given surface or level in the atmosphere.

Pressure gradient—the difference in pressure between two sites at the same altitude which results in horizontal air movement.

Pressure trough—an elongated area of low pressure. A trough differs from a cyclone in that there are no closed isobars associated with it.

Progressive shift—a persistent shift that continues progressively in the same direction.

Radiational cooling—cooling of the earth and the layer of air in immediate contact with it by loss of heat during the night.

Refraction—a shift of wind direction in a zone near the shore more perpendicular to the shoreline (due to differences in surface friction).

Rhumb line—the straight-line course between one mark and the next.

Roll cloud—the low, black cigarlike cloud at the leading edge of a thunderstorm.

Rounding tack—the tack (following an approach tack) which takes the boat around the mark or obstruction.

Santa Ana wind—a strong, dry wind that blows downslope in response to a pressure gradient and is heated by descent.

Saturation—the state of the atmosphere in which the air is holding the maximum amount of water vapor—100 percent humidity.

Sea breeze—a small-scale wind circulation caused by the heating of the land in the presence of cold water. The cold surface flow is onshore from the water toward the land.

Shear—Turbulence in the atmosphere where two wind flows are in conflict horizontally.

Squall—a brief, violent windstorm, usually, but not necessarily, accompanied by rain or snow and cumulonimbus cloud.

Squall cloud—a large cumulus congestus or cumulonimbus cloud that contains strong downdrafts.

Squall line—a line of thunderstorms, or other heavy weather, running parallel to, and ahead of, an accelerating cold front.

Stability—temperature distribution of the atmosphere in which warm air overlies cold. The lapse rate is low (less than the adiabatic) and buoyancy is lacking.

Stratocumulus—a low-altitude layer cloud with some vertical heap development often appearing just beneath an inversion.

Stratosphere—the portion of the atmosphere above the troposphere, between 15 and 31 miles above the surface.

Stratus—a low-altitude sheetlike, layer cloud, sometimes called "high fog."

Subsidence—large-scale sinking within an air mass associated with divergence, heating, and inversion formation (often above a marine layer).

Subtropical high—subsiding air over the ocean at approximately 30° latitude from which divergent air produces the trade winds to the south and the westerlies to the north.

Swell—ocean waves with a long wavelength that have traveled for many miles over the open ocean.

Thermal lift-off—the separation from the surface and vertical movement of segments of heated air associated with buoyancy and vertical instability.

Thunderstorm—a major convection cell whose energy derives from a heated surface and the release of heat from massive condensation.

Trade winds—relatively constant easterly winds of tropical and subtropical latitudes produced by the outward flow of air from the semipermanent subtropical highs toward the equatorial lows.

Transmountain wind—an airflow that has risen above a mountain range and subsequently descends on its far side.

Troposphere—the lower 60,000–70,000 feet of the atmosphere which contains almost all water vapor, weather systems, and cloud formations.

Turbulence—eddy formation induced by surface friction, atmospheric instability and windshear, proportionate to the general wind velocity.

Updraft—a rising current (continuous or intermittent) associated with convection which carries heated, backed, low-velocity surface air aloft.

Upper level—the segment of the troposphere, its winds and clouds (cirrus), which are typically present between 20,000 and 60,000 feet. When referable to the sea breeze, the veered, high-velocity upper portion of the onshore flow.

Upwelling—elevation of cold bottom water to the surface in response to the divergence of surface water away from a coast.

Valley wind—anabatic (upslope) or katabatic (downslope) flow in a valley which may be perpendicular to the lateral slopes, axial or both.

Veer—a clockwise change in wind direction.

Velocity gradient—the change in wind velocity with height (usually a gradual increase).

Warm (current, airflow)—an air or water mass warmer than its surroundings.

Warm front—the boundary line between warm and cold air when warm air is invading colder territory and is rising above the cold air ahead.

Warm sector—that portion of a low-pressure area (or cyclone) composed of warm air that lies behind the warm front and ahead of the cold front.

Water vapor—water in the form of a gas subject to condensation with cooling.

Weather systems (pressure systems)—high- or low-pressure systems affecting chiefly the mid-level of the troposphere, characterized by circular flow about the center, divergent under high pressure, convergent under low, associated with gradient winds.

Westerlies—the prevailing flow of upper-level air over the entire globe and mid-level air in the mid-latitudes induced by Coriolis force.

Bibliography

Donn, William L. *Meteorology*. New York: McGraw Hill, 1965.

Gloyne, R. W. "Some Effects of Shelter Belts and Wind Breaks." *Meteorological Magazine*, No. 99, Vol. 84.

Hall, Clifford D. "Forecasting the Lake Breeze and its Effects on Visibility at Chicago Midway Airport." *Bulletin of the American Meteorological Society*, March 1954.

Marchaz, C. A. *Sailing Theory and Practice*. New York: Dodd, Mead, 1964.

Weather Ways. Canada: Meteorological Branch, Department of Transport, 1961.

Miller, Robert C. *The Sea*. New York: Random House, 1966.

Proctor, Ian. *Sailing Wind and Current*. London, England: Adlard Coles, 1964.

Trewartha, Glenn T. *An Introduction to Climate*. New York: McGraw Hill, 1968.

Walker, Stuart II. *The Techniques of Small Boat Racing*. New York: W. W. Norton, 1960.

Wallington, C. E. "The Structure of the Sea Breeze as Revealed by Gliding Flights." Weather, August 1959.

Watts, A. J. "The Sea Breeze at Thorney Island." *Meteorological Magazine*, January 1955.

Watts, A. J. "The Wind Goes Down with the Tide." *Yachting World*, December 1961.

Watts, Alan. *Wind and Sailing Boats*. Chicago: Quadrangle Books, 1967.

Watts, Alan. *Instant Weather Forecasting*. New York: Dodd, Mead, 1968.

Whelfley, Donald A. *Weather, Water, and Boating*. Cambridge, Maryland: Cornell Maritime Press, 1961.

Index